Shaping America

Shaping America

The Supreme Court and American Society

Edward F. Mannino

The University of South Carolina Press

Published by the University of South Carolina Press
Columbia, South Carolina 29208

www.sc.edu/uscpress

Manufactured in the United States of America

18 17 16 15 14 13 12 11 10 09 10 9 8 7 6 5 4 3 2 1

Library of Congress Cataloging-in-Publication Data

Mannino, Edward F.
Shaping America : the Supreme Court and American society / Edward F. Mannino.
p. cm.
Includes bibliographical references and index.
ISBN 978-1-57003-857-0 (cloth : alk. paper)
1. United States. Supreme Court—History. 2. Sociological jurisprudence—United States. 3. Constitutional history—United States. I. Title.
KF8742.M265 2009
347.73'26—dc22

2009021890

This book was printed on Glatfelter Natures, a recycled paper with 30 percent postconsumer waste content.

For Toni, the damsel with the dulcimer

Contents

Acknowledgments

I am heavily indebted to Bruce Kuklick and Toni O'Connell, both of whom were kind enough to review an earlier draft of this manuscript. Their thoughtful suggestions, as well as those of two anonymous outside readers, have improved the final product. Any errors are mine.

I would also like to express my gratitude to the University of South Carolina Press for its support for this book. Alexander Moore and Linda Fogle in particular were of great help and were extremely supportive in finalizing the manuscript for publication.

Thanks are also due to my students at the University of Pennsylvania from 2001 through 2006 in my classes U.S. Legal History, America since the Civil War, and the American Catholic Experience. I have benefited from several student papers prepared for these courses, particularly those cited in the notes. This book originated with my experience in teaching U.S. Legal History in 2002.

Many good friends also supported this effort not only with their friendship but also by discussions and by sending me relevant articles and books. Chief among these were Bruce Kuklick, David Toole, and Donna Dorn. My wife, Toni, to whom this book is dedicated, was a continuing source of encouragement and assistance.

Finally I extend my thanks to the many justices who wrote the opinions reviewed in this book for their public service, past and present. The Supreme Court, often divided on matters of great public moment, remains a band of brothers and more recently sisters as well.

Cases Discussed

Abington School District v. Schempp, 374 U.S. 203 (1963)
Ableman v. Booth, 21 How. (62 U.S.) 506 (1859)
Abrams v. United States, 250 U.S. 616 (1919)
Adkins v. Children's Hospital, 261 U.S. 525 (1923)
Agostini v. Felton, 521 U.S. 203 (1997)
Aguilar v. Felton, 473 U.S. 402 (1985)
Alexander v. Holmes County Board of Education, 396 U.S. 19 (1969)
Allegheny County v. ACLU, 492 U.S. 573 (1989)
Allgeyer v. Louisiana, 165 U.S. 578 (1897)
The Antelope, 10 Wheaton (23 U.S.) 66 (1825)
Bank of Augusta v. Earle, 13 Pet. (38 U.S.) 519 (1839)
Board of Education v. Allen, 392 U.S. 236 (1968)
Bolling v. Sharpe, 347 U.S. 497 (1954)
Boumediene v. Bush, 553 U.S. — (2008)
Boynton v. Virginia, 364 U.S. 454 (1960)
Brandenburg v. Ohio, 395 U.S. 444 (1969)
Briscoe v. Bank of Kentucky, 11 Pet. (36 U.S.) 257 (1837)
Brown v. Board of Education, 347 U.S. 483 (1954)
Brown v. Board of Education II, 349 U.S. 294 (1955)
Buck v. Bell, 274 U.S. 200 (1927)
Bunting v. Oregon, 243 U.S. 426 (1917)
Bush v. Gore, 531 U.S. 98 (2000)
Cantwell v. Connecticut, 310 U.S. 296 (1940)
Carter v. Carter Coal Co., 298 U.S. 238 (1936)
[Proprietors of] Charles River Bridge v. [Proprietors of] Warren Bridge, 11 Pet. (36 U.S.) 420 (1837)
Cherokee Nation v. Georgia, 5 Pet. (30 U.S.) 1 (1831)
Chicago, Milwaukee & St. Paul Ry. Co. v. Minnesota, 134 U.S. 418 (1890)
Chisholm v. Georgia, 2 Dall. (2 U.S.) 419 (1793)
City of Boerne v. Flores, 521 U.S. 507 (1997)
Civil Rights Cases, 109 U.S. 3 (1883)
Clyatt v. United States, 197 U.S. 207 (1905)
Cohens v. Virginia, 6 Wheat. (19 U.S.) 264 (1821)
Continental T.V. Inc. v. GTE Sylvania, Inc., 433 U.S. 36 (1977)
Cooley v. Board of Wardens, 12 How. (53 U.S.) 299 (1852)
Cooper v. Aaron, 358 U.S. 1 (1958)
County of Santa Clara v. Southern Pacific RR Co., 118 U.S. 394 (1886)
[Trustees of] Dartmouth College v. Woodward, 4 Wheat. (17 U.S.) 518 (1819)
Debs v. United States, 249 U.S. 211 (1919)
Dennis v. United States, 341 U.S. 494 (1951)
District of Columbia v. Heller, 554 U.S. — (2008)
Doe v. Bolton, 410 U.S. 179 (1973)
Edwards v. Aguillard, 482 U.S. 578 (1987)
Employment Division v. Smith, 494 U.S. 872 (1990)
Engel v. Vitale, 370 U.S. 421 (1962)
Epperson v. Arkansas, 393 U.S. 97 (1968)
Erie R.R. Co. v. Tompkins, 304 U.S. 64 (1938)

Everson v. Board of Education, 330 U.S. 1 (1947)
Ex Parte Bollman, 4 Cranch (8 U.S.) 75 (1807)
Ex Parte Endo, 323 U.S. 283 (1944)
Ex Parte McCardle, 74 U.S. 506 (1869)
Ex Parte Merryman, 17 Fed. Cases 144 (Cir. Ct. Md. 1861) (No. 9,487)
Ex Parte Milligan, 71 U.S. (4 Wallace) 2 (1866)
Ex Parte Quirin, 317 U.S. 1 (1942)
Ex Parte Vallandigham, 68 U.S. (1 Wallace) 243 (1864)
Fletcher v. Peck, 6 Cranch (10 U.S.) 87 (1810)
Gibbons v. Ogden, 9 Wheat. (22 U.S.) 1 (1824)
Gonzales v. Carhart, 550 U.S. 124 (2007)
Gonzales v. O Centro Espirita Beneficente Uniao Do Vegetal, 546 U.S. 418 (2006)
Gonzales v. Raich, 545 U.S. 1 (2005)
Gratz v. Bollinger, 539 U.S. 244 (2003)
Green v. County School Board, 391 U.S. 430 (1968)
Griffin v. County School Board, 377 U.S. 218 (1964)
Griswold v. Connecticut, 381 U.S. 479 (1965)
Grutter v. Bollinger, 539 U.S. 306 (2003)
Hamdan v. Rumsfeld, 548 U.S. 557 (2006)
Hamdi v. Rumsfeld, 542 U.S. 507 (2004)
Hammer v. Dagenhart, 247 U.S. 251 (1918)
Harman v. Forssenius, 380 U.S. 528 (1965)
Harris v. McRae, 448 U.S. 297 (1980)
Heart of Atlanta Motel, Inc. v. United States, 379 U.S. 241 (1964)
Helvering v. Davis, 301 U.S. 619 (1937)
Henderson v. United States, 339 U.S. 816 (1950)
Hill v. Colorado, 530 U.S. 703 (2000)
Hirabayashi v. United States, 320 U.S. 81 (1943)
In re Debs, 158 U.S. 564 (1895)
Jones v. Alfred H. Mayer Co., 392 U.S. 409 (1968)
Jones v. Van Zandt, 5 How. (46 U.S.) 215 (1847)
Katzenbach v. McClung, 379 U.S. 294 (1964)
Knight Co. v. United States, 156 U.S. 1 (1895)
Korematsu v. United States, 323 U.S. 214 (1944)
Laidlaw v. Organ, 2 Wheat. (15 U.S.) 178 (1817)
Lawrence v. Texas, 539 U.S. 558 (2003)
Lee v. Weisman, 505 U.S. 577 (1992)
Lemon v. Kurtzman, 403 U.S. 602 (1971)
Lochner v. New York, 198 U.S. 45 (1905)
Locke v. Davey, 540 U.S. 712 (2004)
Louisville Joint Stock Land Bank v. Radford, 295 U.S. 555 (1935)
Lynch v. Donnelly, 465 U.S. 668 (1984)
Marbury v. Madison, 1 Cranch (5 U.S.) 137 (1803)
Martin v. Hunter's Lessee, 1 Wheat. (14 U.S.) 304 (1816)
McCollum v. Board of Education, 333 U.S. 203 (1948)
McCreary County v. ACLU, 545 U.S. 844 (2005)
McCulloch v. Maryland, 4 Wheat. (17 U.S.) 316 (1819)
McLaurin v. Oklahoma State Regents, 339 U.S. 637 (1950)
Meyer v. Nebraska, 262 U.S. 390 (1923)
Milliken v. Bradley, 418 U.S. 717 (1974)
Minersville School District v. Gobitis, 310 U.S. 586 (1940)
Missouri ex rel Gaines v. Canada, 305 U.S. 337 (1938)
Mitchell v. Helms, 530 U.S. 793 (2000)
Mulford v. Smith, 307 U.S. 38 (1939)
Muller v. Oregon, 208 U.S. 412 (1908)
Munn v. Illinois, 94 U.S. 113 (1877)
New State Ice Co. v. Liebmann, 285 U.S. 262 (1932)
NLRB v. Jones & Laughlin Steel Corp., 301 U.S. 1 (1937)
Northern Securities Co. v. United States, 193 U.S. 197 (1904)

Parents Involved in Community Schools v. Seattle School District No. 1, 551 U.S. — (2007)
Pierce v. Society of Sisters, 268 U.S. 510 (1925)
Planned Parenthood v. Casey, 505 U.S. 833 (1992)
Plessy v. Ferguson, 163 U.S. 537 (1896)
Pollock v. Farmers' Loan & Trust Co., 157 U.S. 429 (1895)
Powell v. McCormack, 395 U.S. 486 (1969)
Prigg v. Pennsylvania, 16 Pet. (41 U.S.) 539 (1842)
Regents of the University of California v. Bakke, 438 U.S. 265 (1978)
Reynolds v. United States, 98 U.S. 145 (1879)
Roe v. Wade, 410 U.S. 113 (1973)
Roper v. Simmons, 543 U.S. 551 (2005)
Saenz v. Roe, 526 U.S. 489 (1999)
Santa Fe Independent School District v. Doe, 530 U.S. 290 (2000)
Schechter Poultry Corp. v. United States, 295 U.S. 495 (1935)
Schenck v. Pro-Choice Network, 519 U.S. 357 (1997)
Schenck v. United States, 249 U.S. 47 (1919)
Scott v. Sandford, 19 How. (16 U.S.) 393 (1857)
Selective Draft Law Cases [Arver v. United States], 245 U.S. 366 (1918)
Shelley v. Kramer, 334 U.S. 1 (1948)
Sherbert v. Verner, 374 U.S. 398 (1963)
Slaughterhouse Cases, 16 Wall. (83 U.S.) 36 (1873)
Smyth v. Ames, 169 U.S. 466 (1898)
South Carolina v. Katzenbach, 383 U.S. 301 (1966)
Standard Oil Co. v. United States, 221 U.S. 1 (1911)
Stenberg v. Carhart, 530 U.S. 914 (2000)
Steward Machine Co. v. Davis, 301 U.S. 548 (1937)
Swann v. Charlotte-Mecklenburg County Board, 402 U.S. 1 (1971)
Sweatt v. Painter, 339 U.S. 629 (1950)
Swift v. Tyson, 16 Pet. (41 U.S.) 1 (1842)
United States v. Butler, 297 U.S. 1 (1936)
United States v. Carolene Products Co., 304 U.S. 144 (1938)
United States v. Cruikshank, 92 U.S. 542 (1876)
United States v. Darby, 312 U.S. 100 (1941)
United States v. Fries, 9 Fed. Cas. 826 (Cir. Ct. D. Pa. 1800)
United States v. Lopez, 514 U.S. 549 (1995)
United States v. Mitchell, 26 Fed. Cas. 1277 (Cir. Ct. D. Pa. 1795)
United States v. Morrison, 529 U.S. 598 (2000)
United States v. Reese, 92 U.S. 214 (1876)
United States v. Trans-Missouri Freight Ass'n, 166 U.S. 290 (1897)
United States v. Vigol, 28 Fed. Cas. 376 (Cir. Ct. D. Pa. 1795)
Van Orden v. Perry, 545 U.S. 677 (2005)
Wabash, St. Louis & Pacific Ry. Co. v. Illinois, 118 U.S. 557 (1886)
Wallace v. Jaffree, 472 U.S. 38 (1985)
Ware v. Hylton, 3 Dall. (3 U.S.) 199 (1796)
Webster v. Reproductive Health Services, 492 U.S. 490 (1989)
West Coast Hotel Co. v. Parrish, 300 U.S. 379 (1937)
West Virginia State Board of Education v. Barnette, 319 U.S. 624 (1943)
Whitney v. California, 274 U.S. 357 (1927)
Wickard v. Filburn, 317 U.S. 111 (1942)
Williams v. Mississippi, 170 U.S. 213 (1898)
Wisconsin v. Yoder, 406 U.S. 205 (1972)
Worcester v. Georgia, 6 Pet. (31 U.S.) 515 (1832)
Yates v. United States, 354 U.S. 298 (1957)
Yick Wo v. Hopkins, 118 U.S. 356 (1886)
Zelman v. Simmons-Harris, 536 U.S. 639 (2002)
Zorach v. Clauson, 343 U.S. 306 (1952)

Chronology

1787 The Northwest Ordinance
Constitution approved at the Philadelphia convention.

1789 George Washington is inaugurated as first president.
Judiciary Act
John Jay is appointed as first chief justice.
The first federal judges are appointed.

1790 First federal census
Petitions to Congress to abolish African slave trade and slavery

1791 Hamilton's *Report on the Subject of Manufactures*
The First Bank of the United States is chartered (to 1811).
Vermont is admitted as the fourteenth state.
The Bill of Rights is ratified.

1792 Kentucky is admitted as the fifteenth state.

1793 Washington is inaugurated for his second term.
Chisholm v. Georgia
First federal Fugitive Slave Act

1794 Whiskey Rebellion

1795 John Rutledge is appointed chief justice.
United States v. Vigol
United States v. Mitchell

1796 Oliver Ellsworth is appointed chief justice.
Ware v. Hylton
Tennessee is admitted as the sixteenth state.

1797 John Adams is inaugurated as second president.

1798 The Eleventh Amendment is ratified.

1799 Fries Rebellion

1800 *United States v. Fries*

1801 Judiciary Act
John Marshall is appointed chief justice.
Thomas Jefferson is inaugurated as third president.
The Judiciary Act is repealed.

1803 *Marbury v. Madison*
Ohio is admitted as the seventeenth state.

1804 *Seixas & Seixas v. Woods*
The Twelfth Amendment is ratified.

1805 Jefferson is inaugurated for his second term.
Impeachment trial of Justice Samuel Chase

1807 *Ex Parte Bollman*

1808 African slave trade is abolished under Article I, Section 9.

1809 James Madison is inaugurated as fourth president.

1810 *Fletcher v. Peck*

1811 Joseph Story is appointed to the Supreme Court.

1812 War of 1812 (to 1814)
Louisiana is admitted as the eighteenth state.

1813 Madison is inaugurated for his second term.

1816 *Martin v. Hunter's Lessee*

The Second Bank of the United States is chartered (to 1836).
Indiana is admitted as the nineteenth state.

1817 James Monroe is inaugurated as fifth president.
Laidlaw v. Organ
Mississippi is admitted as the twentieth state.

1818 Illinois is admitted as the twenty-first state.

1819 *McCulloch v. Maryland*
Dartmouth College v. Woodward
Panic of 1819
Alabama is admitted as the twenty-second state.

1820 Missouri Compromise
Maine is admitted as the twenty-third state.

1821 Monroe is inaugurated for his second term.
Cohens v. Virginia
Missouri is admitted as the twenty-fourth state.

1824 *Gibbons v. Ogden*

1825 John Quincy Adams is inaugurated as sixth president.
The Antelope

1826 The Pennsylvania Fugitive Slave Act is enacted.
Second Great Awakening: Charles Grandison Finney's Utica revival

1828 "Tariff of Abominations"
John C. Calhoun's *South Carolina Exposition and Protest*

1829 Andrew Jackson is inaugurated as seventh president.

1830 Indian Removal Act

1831 First issue of the *Liberator*
Nat Turner's rebellion in Virginia
Corn Tassel is executed by the State of Georgia.
Cherokee Nation v. Georgia
John C. Calhoun's Fort Hill address
One hundred thousand people join a church.

1832 *Worcester v. Georgia*
President Jackson vetoes recharter of Second Bank of the United States.
South Carolina Ordinance of Nullification
John C. Calhoun resigns as vice president and is elected a senator from South Carolina.

1833 Jackson is inaugurated for his second term.
Jackson orders removal of federal deposits from the Second Bank of the United States.

1835 John Marshall dies.
Treaty of New Echota
Petitions to abolish slavery in District of Columbia

1836 Roger B. Taney is appointed chief justice.
Slavery "Gag Rule" is passed in the House of Representatives.
Deposit Act
"Specie Circular" is issued by President Jackson.
Arkansas is admitted as the twenty-fifth state.

1837 Martin Van Buren is inaugurated as eighth president.
Panic of 1837
Briscoe v. Bank of Kentucky
Charles River Bridge v. Warren Bridge
Michigan is admitted as the twenty-sixth state.

1838 "Trail of Tears"
"Specie Circular" is suspended.

1839 *Bank of Augusta v. Earle*
McFarland v. Newman

1841 William Henry Harrison is inaugurated as ninth president.
John Tyler is inaugurated as tenth president.

1842 *Swift v. Tyson*
Prigg v. Pennsylvania
Massachusetts enacts the "Latimer Law."
Farwell v. The Boston & Worcester RR Co.

1845 James K. Polk is inaugurated as eleventh president.
Justice Joseph Story dies.
Florida is admitted as the twenty-seventh state.
Texas is admitted as the twenty-eighth state.

1846 Walker Tariff
Iowa is admitted as the twenty-ninth state.

1847 *Jones v. Van Zandt*

1848 Wisconsin is admitted as the thirtieth state.

1849 Zachary Taylor is inaugurated as twelfth president.

1850 Millard Fillmore is inaugurated as thirteenth president.
Compromise of 1850
Fugitive Slave Act of 1850
California is admitted as the thirty-first state.

1851 Christiana, Pennsylvania, riot and *United States v. Hanway*
Fugitive slave Thomas Sims is returned to Georgia from Boston.

1852 *Cooley v. Board of Wardens*
Harriet Beecher Stowe's *Uncle Tom's Cabin*

1853 Franklin Pierce is inaugurated as fourteenth president.

1854 Kansas-Nebraska Act
Fugitive slave Anthony Burns is returned to Virginia from Boston.
Fugitive slave Joshua Glover is jailed in Wisconsin, broken out, and sent to Canada.
The Republican Party begins.

1856 Fugitive slave Margaret Garner kills her daughter to prevent her return to slavery.
John Brown's Kansas terrorism
Senator Charles Sumner is caned on the Senate floor by Representative Preston Brooks.
The Republican Party nominates John C. Fremont for president.
Grey v. Ohio & Pennsylvania RR Co.

1857 James Buchanan is inaugurated as fifteenth president.
Scott v. Sandford
The American Medical Association attempts to outlaw abortion.

1858 Abraham Lincoln's "House Divided" speech
Minnesota is admitted as the thirty-second state.

1859 John Brown's raid on Harper's Ferry federal arsenal
Abelman v. Booth
Oregon is admitted as the thirty-third state.

1860 Abraham Lincoln is elected sixteenth president.
South Carolina secedes from the Union.

1861 *Ex Parte Merryman*
Kansas is admitted as the thirty-fourth state.
Mississippi, Florida, Alabama, Georgia, Louisiana, and Texas secede from the Union.
Abraham Lincoln is inaugurated as sixteenth president.
South Carolina fires on Fort Sumter; the Civil War begins.
Virginia, North Carolina, Arkansas, and Tennessee secede from the Union.

1863 West Virginia is admitted as the thirty-fifth state.

1864 *Ex Parte Vallandigham*
Roger B. Taney dies.
Nevada is admitted as the thirty-sixth state.
1865 Lincoln is inaugurated for his second term.
Lincoln is assassinated.
Andrew Johnson is inaugurated as seventeenth president.
The Thirteenth Amendment is ratified.
Black Codes are enacted.
1866 *Ex Parte Milligan*
Ryan v. New York Central RR Co.
Civil Rights Act
1867 Reconstruction Act
Peonage Act
Nebraska is admitted as the thirty-seventh state.
The Patrons of Husbandry (Grange) organization is founded.
1868 The Fourteenth Amendment is ratified.
Impeachment of President Andrew Johnson
1869 *Ex Parte McCardle*
Ulysses S. Grant is inaugurated as eighteenth president.
The Knights of Labor organization is founded.
1870 The Fifteenth Amendment is ratified.
1873 *Slaughterhouse Cases*
President Ulysses S. Grant is inaugurated for his second term.
Panic of 1873
The Greenback Party is founded.
The Illinois Railroad Commission begins.
1875 Civil Rights Act
William Graham Sumner's *What Social Classes Owe to One Another*
1876 *United States v. Reese*
United States v. Cruikshank
Hayes-Tilden presidential election
Colorado is admitted as the thirty-eighth state.
1877 *Munn v. Illinois*
National railroad strike
Reconstruction ends with the Compromise of 1877.
Rutherford B. Hayes is inaugurated as nineteenth president.
1878 California Constitutional Convention and Chinese Exclusion Referendum
1879 *Reynolds v. United States*
1881 James A. Garfield is inaugurated as twentieth president.
Garfield is assassinated.
Chester A. Arthur is inaugurated as twenty-first president.
1882 First Chinese Exclusion Act
1883 *Civil Rights Cases*
"Jim Crow" laws begin.
1885 Grover Cleveland is inaugurated as twenty-second president.
1886 *Yick Wo v. Hopkins*
County of Santa Clara v. Southern Pacific RR Co.
Wabash, St. Louis & Pacific Ry. Co. v. Illinois
McCormick Harvester Strike and Haymarket Riot
1887 Interstate Commerce Act
1889 Benjamin Harrison is inaugurated as twenty-third president.
North Dakota, South Dakota, Montana, and Washington are admitted as the thirty-ninth through forty-second states.
1890 *Chicago, Milwaukee & St. Paul Ry. Co. v. Minnesota*
Idaho and Wyoming are admitted as forty-third and forty-fourth states.
1892 Homestead Strike
Second Chinese Exclusion Act

Populist Party Omaha Convention
1893 Grover Cleveland is inaugurated as twenty-fourth president for his second, nonconsecutive term.
Panic of 1893
1894 Pullman Strike and jailing of Eugene Debs
1895 *In re Debs*
Knight Co. v. United States
Pollock v. Farmers' Loan & Trust Co.
Medical groups campaign to cut down on abortions.
1896 *Plessy v. Ferguson*
Utah is admitted as the forty-fifth state.
1897 *Allgeyer v. Louisiana*
William McKinley is inaugurated as the twenty-fifth president.
1898 *Williams v. Mississippi*
Smyth v. Ames
1901 President McKinley is assassinated.
Theodore Roosevelt is inaugurated as twenty-sixth president.
1902 The Chinese Exclusion Act is made permanent.
1904 *Northern Securities Co. v. United States*
1905 President Theodore Roosevelt is inaugurated for his first full term.
Lochner v. New York
Clyatt v. United States
1907 Oklahoma is admitted as the forty-sixth state.
1908 *Muller v. Oregon* ("Brandeis Brief" case)
1909 William Howard Taft is inaugurated as twenty-seventh president.
1911 *Standard Oil Co. v. United States*
1912 New Mexico and Arizona are admitted as the forty-seventh and forty-eighth states.
1913 Woodrow Wilson is inaugurated as twenty-eighth president.
1917 President Woodrow Wilson is inaugurated for second term.
Bunting v. Oregon
The Espionage Act is passed.
1918 *Hammer v. Dagenhart*
Selective Draft Law Cases
1919 Package bombs are delivered to Holmes, Palmer, and other notables.
The Sedition Act is passed.
Schenck v. United States
Debs v. United States
Abrams v. United States
1920 Palmer Raids
Sacco and Vanzetti are indicted.
1921 Warren G. Harding is inaugurated as twenty-ninth president.
1923 Calvin Coolidge is inaugurated as thirtieth president.
Adkins v. Children's Hospital
Meyer v. Nebraska
1925 President Calvin Coolidge is inaugurated for his first full term.
Pierce v. Society of Sisters
1927 *Buck v. Bell*
Whitney v. California
Sacco and Vanzetti are executed.
1929 Herbert Hoover is inaugurated as thirty-first president.
1932 *New State Ice Co. v. Liebmann*
1933 Franklin Delano Roosevelt is inaugurated as thirty-second president.
1935 *Schechter Poultry Corp. v. United States*
Louisville Joint Stock Land Bank v. Radford
1936 *United States v. Butler*
Carter v. Carter Coal Co.
1937 President Franklin Delano Roosevelt is inaugurated for his second term.

The Roosevelt "court-packing" plan is proposed.
West Coast Hotel Co. v. Parrish
NLRB v. Jones & Laughlin Steel Corp.
Steward Machine Co. v. Davis
Helvering v. Davis

1938 *Erie R.R. Co. v. Tompkins*
United States v. Carolene Products Co.
Missouri ex rel Gaines v. Canada

1939 *Mulford v. Smith*

1940 *Cantwell v. Connecticut*
Minersville School District v. Gobitis

1941 President Franklin Delano Roosevelt is inaugurated for his third term.
United States v. Darby

1942 *Ex Parte Quirin*
Wickard v. Filburn

1943 *Hirabayashi v. United States*
West Virginia State Board of Education v. Barnette

1944 *Korematsu v. United States*
Ex Parte Endo

1945 President Franklin Delano Roosevelt is inaugurated for his fourth term.
Harry Truman is inaugurated as thirty-third president.
Winston Churchill's "Iron Curtain" speech in Fulton, Missouri

1947 The Truman Doctrine is announced.
George Kennan ("Mister X")'s "The Sources of Soviet Conduct" containment article appears in *Foreign Affairs.*
Everson v. Board of Education

1948 Alger Hiss–Whittaker Chambers HUAC hearings
McCollum v. Board of Education
Shelley v. Kramer

1949 President Harry Truman is inaugurated for his second term.
Communists take over the government of mainland China.
NATO is formed.

1950 Outbreak of Korean War
Senator Joseph McCarthy's Wheeling, West Virginia, list of Communists speech
Alger Hiss is convicted of perjury and jailed 1951–54.
Sweatt v. Painter
McLaurin v. Oklahoma State Regents
Henderson v. United States

1951 Indictments of Julius and Ethel Rosenberg
Dennis v. United States

1952 *Zorach v. Clauson*

1953 President Dwight D. Eisenhower is inaugurated as thirty-fourth president.
Death of Joseph Stalin
Julius and Ethel Rosenberg are both executed.

1954 Army–McCarthy Hearings
Senate censure of Senator Joseph McCarthy
Brown v. Board of Education
Bolling v. Sharpe

1955 *Brown v. Board of Education II*
Planned Parenthood Conference on Abortion, with statement calling for liberalization of abortion laws

1957 President Dwight D. Eisenhower is inaugurated for his second term.
Death of Senator Joseph McCarthy
Yates v. United States

1958 *Cooper v. Aaron*

1959 Alaska and Hawaii are admitted as the forty-ninth and fiftieth states.

American Law Institute's Model Penal Code proposal on abortion regulation

1960 Sit-ins at restaurants and other public accommodations in nine states

Arrest and imprisonment of Martin Luther King for sit-in at segregated lunch counter

Boynton v. Virginia

1961 John F. Kennedy is inaugurated as thirty-fifth president.

1962 *Engel v. Vitale*

Sherri Finkbine Thalidomide abortion controversy

1963 President John F. Kennedy is assassinated.

Civil rights demonstrations in Birmingham, Alabama

March on Washington for Jobs and Freedom

Lyndon B. Johnson is inaugurated as thirty-sixth president.

Abington School District v. Schempp

Sherbert v. Verner

1964 *Griffin v. County School Board*

Civil Rights Act

Heart of Atlanta Motel, Inc. v. United States

Katzenbach v. McClung

The Twenty-fourth Amendment is ratified.

1965 President Lyndon B. Johnson is inaugurated for his first full term.

Griswold v. Connecticut

Voting Rights Act

Harman v. Forssenius

1966 *South Carolina v. Katzenbach*

1968 *Board of Education v. Allen*

Epperson v. Arkansas

Green v. County School Board

Jones v. Alfred H. Mayer Co.

Governor George Wallace of Alabama polls 13.5 percent of presidential votes and receives forty-six electoral votes in five southern states.

1969 Richard M. Nixon is inaugurated as thirty-seventh president.

Brandenburg v. Ohio

Alexander v. Holmes County Board of Education

Powell v. McCormick

NARAL is founded.

1970 Repeal of abortion laws in New York, Alaska, and Hawaii

1971 *Lemon v. Kurtzman*

Swann v. Charlotte-Mecklenburg County Board

1972 *Wisconsin v. Yoder*

The Equal Rights Amendment is passed by Congress.

1973 President Richard M. Nixon is inaugurated for his second term.

Roe v. Wade

Doe v. Bolton

1974 President Richard M. Nixon is impeached and resigns from the presidency.

Gerald Ford is inaugurated as thirty-eighth president.

Milliken v. Bradley

1977 Jimmy Carter is inaugurated as thirty-ninth president.

Continental T.V. Inc. v. GTE Sylvania, Inc.

1978 *Regents of the University of California v. Bakke*

1979 Founding of the Moral Majority

1980 *Harris v. McRae*

1981 Ronald Reagan is inaugurated as fortieth president.

Sandra Day O'Connor becomes the first woman appointed to the Supreme Court.

1982 The Equal Rights Amendment fails to gain necessary approvals by thirty-four states.
1983 *Akron v. Akron Center for Reproductive Health, Inc.*
1984 *Lynch v. Donnelly*
1985 President Ronald Reagan is inaugurated for his second term.
Wallace v. Jaffree
Aguilar v. Felton
1986 Justice William H. Rehnquist is elevated to chief justice.
Antonin Scalia is appointed to the Supreme Court.
Thornburgh v. American College of Obstetricians & Gynecologists
Bowers v. Hardwick
1987 Robert Bork's nomination to the Supreme Court is rejected by the United States Senate.
Anthony Kennedy is appointed to the Supreme Court.
Founding of Operation Rescue
Edwards v. Aguillard
1989 George H. W. Bush is inaugurated as forty-first president.
Allegheny County v. ACLU
Webster v. Reproductive Health Services
Stanford v. Kentucky
1990 *Employment Division v. Smith*
David Souter is appointed to the Supreme Court.
1991 Clarence Thomas is appointed to the Supreme Court.
1992 *Lee v. Weisman*
Planned Parenthood v. Casey
1993 William J. Clinton is inaugurated as forty-second president.
Ruth Bader Ginsburg is appointed to the Supreme Court.
1994 Stephen Breyer is appointed to the Supreme Court.
Freedom of Access to Clinic Entrances (FACE) Act
1995 *United States v. Lopez*
1997 President William J. Clinton is inaugurated for his second term.
Agostini v. Felton
City of Boerne v. Flores
Schenck v. Pro-Choice Network
1999 *Saenz v. Roe*
2000 *Santa Fe Independent School District v. Doe*
Mitchell v. Helms
Stenberg v. Carhart
Hill v. Colorado
Bush v. Gore
United States v. Morrison
2001 George W. Bush is inaugurated as forty-third president.
Islamic terrorists attack the World Trade Center towers in New York and the Pentagon; three thousand people die.
2002 *Zelman v. Simmons-Harris*
2003 *Grutter v. Bollinger*
Gratz v. Bollinger
Lawrence v. Texas
2004 *Locke v. Davey*
Hamdi v. Rumsfeld
2005 President George W. Bush is inaugurated for his second term.
McCreary County v. ACLU
Van Orden v. Perry
Roper v. Simmons
Gonzales v. Raich
John Roberts is appointed chief justice.
2006 Samuel Alito is appointed to the Supreme Court.
Gonzales v. O Centro Espirita Beneficente Uniao Do Vegetal
Hamdan v. Rumsfeld
2007 *Gonzales v. Carhart*
Parents Involved in Community Schools v. Seattle School District No. 1
2008 *Boumediene v. Bush*
District of Columbia v. Heller

Shaping America

Introduction

The "Least Dangerous" Branch

The rational study of law is still to
a large extent the study of history.

Oliver Wendell Holmes

Why study the history of the Supreme Court of the United States? Has the Court gone through different stages in its development over time? What influences have shaped it? This book explores each of these issues through a detailed study of important decisions, examining both what the justices who decided them said in the texts of their opinions, as well as the underlying contexts in which they were decided by specific justices who were products of their times and political cultures.

Why the History of the Supreme Court Is Important

Why study the Supreme Court's history? The influence of the Supreme Court of the United States on our daily life is pervasive. Today, the Court determines such important issues as

- when and where we can pray or give visible expression to our religious beliefs (chapter 8)
- who can go to public schools with our children and what can be taught there (chapters 4, 8, and 9)
- when a woman can have an abortion (chapter 10)
- what individuals can say about the government (chapter 7)
- how much your business can be regulated, and by whom (chapters 3, 5, 6, and 11)
- when foreign nationals or suspected terrorists can be detained (chapter 7)
- to whom local diners and inns must open their doors and serve (chapters 4 and 9)
- what a farmer may grow on his land, and what drugs a patient may take (chapters 6 and 11).

The Stages of Supreme Court Development

That all this power could be exercised by the Supreme Court would have shocked most of the founders. In Federalist 78 Alexander Hamilton famously declared that the judicial branch would be the "least dangerous" of the three, reasoning that it "has no influence over either the sword or the purse; no direction either of the strength or of the wealth of the society; and can take no active resolution whatever. It may truly be said to have neither FORCE nor WILL, but merely judgment; and must ultimately depend upon the aid of the executive arm even for the efficacy of its judgments."

This restricted view of the judicial power limited early presidents in recruiting justices for the Supreme Court. John Jay, appointed by President Washington as the first chief justice of the Supreme Court in 1789, spent part of his time negotiating the Jay Treaty with England in 1794 and resigned as chief justice in 1795, when he was elected governor of New York. When President Adams offered Jay his former judicial post in 1800, he turned it down, informing the president that the Court lacked "energy, weight, and dignity."

Other famous founders and legal scholars also turned down appointments to the Court. President Washington, for example, could not convince either Patrick Henry or George Wythe to assume positions on the Court. This reluctance to serve stemmed not only from the perception that the Court was a weak reed, but also from the facts that justices had a limited appellate docket in the beginning and were assigned the arduous duty of "riding circuit." This required them not only to sit for duty on the Supreme Court, hearing mainly appeals from lower courts, but also to ride hundreds of miles a year from one federal district to another in their assigned federal circuits to dispose of cases in lower courts, often sitting as trial judges in important cases. No separate circuit judges were appointed until 1869, and the practice of riding circuit was not fully abolished until 1891.

The following chapters trace how the Supreme Court overcame this slow beginning to assume its current powers. We can divide the history of the Court into three phases of development. In the first, lasting roughly from 1789 to the outbreak of civil war in 1860, the Supreme Court sought to build federal power and encourage the growth of American commerce under Chief Justices John Marshall and Roger Taney. It crippled itself institutionally toward the end of the period by embracing a national "solution" for the problem of slavery. During this initial period of its history, the size of the Court changed several times. The initial complement of six justices was reduced to five in 1801, but restored to six the next year. As the size of the country, and the corresponding number of federal circuit courts expanded, the number of justices also increased. A seventh justice was added in 1807, and two more were added in 1837. The Court reached its maximum size of ten in 1863, partially to assist the Lincoln administration's war policies.

The second period, from approximately 1865 to 1960, began as a period of relative passivity, in which the Court regularly limited federal and state regulation of all forms of commercial activity. This reflected the influence of a steady stream of Republican presidents, interrupted only by the two-term presidencies of

Democrats Grover Cleveland and Woodrow Wilson, until the election of Franklin D. Roosevelt in 1932. As the New Deal took hold politically and new justices were appointed, the pendulum swung toward upholding expansive federal regulation across the entire economy, coupled with a mixed record for protecting civil liberties. During this time the Court's membership declined from ten justices in 1863 to seven in 1866. In 1869 the number of justices was increased to nine, where it has remained since then, with only the Franklin Roosevelt "court-packing" plan of 1937 seriously questioning that number.

The third period, from about 1960 to today, is one that began with Court-endorsed and Court-enforced federal regulation, during which the powers of all branches of the federal government became paramount across a broad spectrum of daily activities, threatening the dual sovereignty concept underlying earlier visions of American society. During this time the Supreme Court also recognized new constitutional rights, protected minority rights, and limited the presence of organized religion both in public schools and in the public square as well. Finally reaching critical mass in the 1990s, the Supreme Court began a partial retreat from federal supremacy in favor of a new, but limited, federalism, with cases often decided in fractured five-to-four decisions, with multiple separate opinions, despite the best efforts of a new chief justice, John Roberts, to strive for more uniform rulings. That the coverage in this book of Supreme Court decisions in these last 60 years is longer than that of the preceding 150 is testimony to the increasing and pervasive influence of the Court on American life in the period following World War II.

The Influences That Shaped the Supreme Court's Role in American Society

The decisions of the Supreme Court in each of the periods we have identified generally reflected a confluence of three factors, which interacted in different ways throughout these time frames. Those factors were first the appointments made to the Court, at times, of dominating justices, both at the chief and associate justice levels; second the influence of the dominant political cultures of the respective times, rather than of abstract theories of constitutional adjudication; and third the attitudes of the general public on specific issues that captured its attention at various times. Viewing these catalyzing factors, we are reminded of Abraham Lincoln's view that "we cannot escape history." Some examples may help to orient the reader in following the discussions of individual cases.

The critical influence of specific justices on the Court's development is shown from its beginnings. After two of his three ineffective predecessors resigned and a third was denied confirmation, John Marshall became chief justice in 1801 and served until 1835. Marshall became the dominant influence on the Court. Making changes to prior practice, he undermined the custom of each justice's delivering a separate opinion in favor of crafting an opinion that spoke for the majority. Over the next thirty years, Marshall himself wrote many of those opinions, often in sweeping and clear language accessible to nonlawyers, including those in such historic cases as *Marbury v. Madison* in 1803 and *McCulloch v. Maryland* in 1819. Having served in the Revolutionary War under General George Washington—including suffering through the harsh winter of 1777–78 in Valley Forge—Marshall personally experienced the need for a strong national government. His opinions established the constitutional existence of a broad power in the federal government to legislate in areas many founders thought were reserved to the states. Without Marshall that jurisprudence may not have emerged or might have done so in a more muted fashion.

Marshall's successor as chief justice was Roger Taney, who served from 1836 to 1864. Together they presided over the Court in its evolutionary stages, from the election of Thomas Jefferson as president to nearly the end of the Civil War. Taney brought the lens of Jacksonian democracy to the Court. While he did preserve Marshall's concept of a strong federal government, he also developed a sophisticated model of dual sovereignty, preserving the rights of the states also to legislate in specific areas, often concurrently with the federal government.

What transpired at the beginnings of the Supreme Court remains true today, where the appointment of specific new justices to the Court can be a significant catalyst to changes or refinements in doctrine. Two examples are found in the appointments of Antonin Scalia and Clarence Thomas as associate justices in 1986 and 1991. As we shall see in the later chapters of this book, Thomas's appointment was particularly significant because his strong conservative views on such issues as federalism, the powers of states to legislate, and the First Amendment religion clauses, replaced the opposing liberal views of Thurgood Marshall, whose seat Thomas assumed on the Court. When Thomas's opinions combined with the direct and forceful language of Justice Scalia's, which were quoted widely in the press, their conservative views reached a wide audience and directly affected the development of constitutional law toward more conservative outcomes.

The impact of the prevailing political cultures of the times may be illustrated by two examples, one in the nineteenth century and the other in the twentieth century. First, as we shall see in chapter 3, the Taney Court incorporated the antimonopoly focus of the Jacksonian Democrats in several of its decisions, most notably in Taney's 1837 opinion in the *Charles River Bridge* case. There the protections of mercantile and commercial interests to which the Marshall Court gave primacy were balanced against the needs of the Jacksonian constituency—"the humble members of society—the farmers, mechanics, and laborers"—whom Andrew Jackson invoked in his veto message on the renewal of the charter of the Bank of the United States. Second, as will be examined in chapter 4, the Supreme

Court's evisceration of the Fourteenth Amendment by restrictive interpretations of its various clauses, which foreclosed the enactment of affirmative civil rights legislation and limited its use to bar state action but not that taken by individuals, can be traced to widespread views held in the predominating political culture. Thus the free labor philosophy of Abraham Lincoln and the dominant nineteenth-century Republican Party held that equality was guaranteed only in *legal* treatment of the different races but did not extend to the *social* sphere because social equality had be "earned." This focus explains the outcomes in such cases as the *Civil Rights Cases* of 1883 and the reviled 1896 decision in *Plessy v. Ferguson.*

Finally the impact of strong public attitudes on specific issues as an influence on Court decisions is exemplified by current public reaction to recent decisions on the use of race in school assignments and the rights of citizens to keep and bear arms. As we shall see in chapters 9 and 11, the public (but not the legal community) overwhelmingly supported the Court's decisions in the *Seattle School District* and *Heller* cases in 2007 and 2008. By a five-to-four margin, the *Seattle* case limited the use of race as a factor in assigning grade-school children to particular schools. This reflected prevailing public attitudes, as documented by an August 16, 2007, Quinnipiac University poll, which reported some 71 percent of the public approving that outcome. Similarly the *Heller* opinion, again in a five-to-four vote, upheld the right of individuals to own and keep guns, striking down some onerous District of Columbia laws banning or restricting the ownership or use of handguns. Again this outcome received overwhelming public support. Both the issues of school assignment and gun ownership were widely covered in the media for years before these decisions, and strong public attitudes on both were well known.

This is not to suggest, with the fictional "Mr. Dooley," that "the Supreme Court follows the election returns." Indeed, many decisions were and are intensely unpopular. Chapter 8, for example, discusses the very unpopular school-prayer cases, and the violent disagreement they engendered in large parts of the public. What is significant, however, is that some pivotal issues assume and retain intense public attention, and that is ultimately reflected in the outcome of presidential elections and the consequent selection by those newly elected presidents of Supreme Court nominees who they hope will reflect their views while serving on the Court. All this raises a critical public policy and jurisprudential issue—what is the proper balance of popular opinion and judicial decision making? Writing on the issue of whether the Supreme Court should continue to rely on foreign law in deciding cases, a practice widely opposed by the public, Professor Steven Calabresi of Northwestern University Law School has suggested that "where the elite lawyerly culture of the Supreme Court conflicts with the mass culture of most Americans as expressed over four hundred years, it is the mass culture that ought to govern the Court, assuming that the Court should look to anything beyond the text and original history of the Constitution." Does this suggest a rule of decision that the Supreme Court should embrace? That is a question we will revisit in the conclusion, following our review of the Supreme Court's leading decisions over the last 220 years.

Part I

From the Founding to the Civil War

One

Building Federal Power

Until the mid–twentieth century, the principal units of government in the United States were state and local. Indeed, until the Gettysburg Address, "United States" was grammatically a plural phrase, recognizing the plenary power of the various sovereign states to legislate for themselves and their citizens. While the theoretical system was one of dual sovereignty, the states held most of the legislative cards in the early republic. In most towns the only visible federal presence was a post office, and the host of federal agencies and their attendant edifices we know today were unknown before the New Deal.

The early Supreme Court, particularly under the leadership of Chief Justice John Marshall, who served in that position from 1801 to 1835, laid the ground judicially for the stronger federal government that would emerge much later in all three branches. Marshall saw his states' rights opponents as wishing to perpetuate a view of the United States as "a meer [*sic*] league of states" and saw their attacks on his Court as "in fact an attack upon the union." His prime intellectual opponent, Thomas Jefferson, by contrast, embraced the notion that the United States was a "confederated fabric," while Marshall and his colleagues wished to reverse that, turning a "general and special" government into "a general and supreme one alone."

The Supreme Court began to build federal power from the Court's earliest days, in several areas. These included:

- protecting the federal taxing power
- exercising jurisdiction over sovereign states
- declaring state legislation unconstitutional
- declaring the Supreme Court's supremacy over state courts
- expansively interpreting the powers of the federal government
- federalizing the slavery question
- building a national commercial law.

We discuss the first five of these initiatives in this chapter. Separate chapters follow on the slavery and commercial law initiatives.

Treason and the Tax Collector

Opposition to taxation by a distant government was ingrained in the heritage of revolutionary America, where the Boston Tea Party of 1773 was an iconic symbol. Thus, when the new federal government began in the first decade of its existence to impose taxes to fund its needs, some patriots who had earlier fought for independence opposed those taxes as redolent of British oppression. Pennsylvanians were particularly vocal and active in resisting these taxes, leading to two historic confrontations between citizen and federal tax collector.

The first such confrontation, which began in 1794, became known as the Whiskey Rebellion because the tax at issue was a 1791 excise tax levied on distillers of that substance. Prominent among those affected by the tax were western Pennsylvania farmers who used their spare corn to distill whiskey. Many refused to pay the tax in the first three years of its levy, but their peaceful protests went unheeded, leading to more violent tactics in 1794. Those tactics included armed visits to the excise officials, seizure of their papers, threats of violence to their persons, forced oaths that the officials "would never act again in the execution of the excise law," tarring and feathering, and action by the conspirators to "ransack . . . and burn" the house of one official. Calling out the militia from four states, President Washington, along with Treasury Secretary Alexander Hamilton, led an army of some thirteen thousand to put down the revolt.

One hundred fifty men were arrested and charged with treason, but only thirty-one indictments for that offense were returned by a grand jury sitting in Philadelphia, to which the prisoners had been marched hundreds of miles from Pittsburgh in cold winter weather. The treason charges were surprising, for the Constitution—drafted after all by men who were guilty of that offense themselves under English law—narrowly limited the definition of that capital crime. Article III, Section 3, of the Constitution provided that "Treason against the United States, shall consist only in *levying War against them,* or in adhering to their Enemies, giving them Aid and Comfort."

Only two of the treason cases went to trial—*United States v. Vigol* (1795) and *United States v. Mitchell* (1795). Both cases were tried by Supreme Court justices sitting on circuit together with a federal district judge. In his opinion in *Mitchell,* Justice William Patterson, who served on the Court from 1793 to 1806, declared that "if [the] object [of the insurrection] was to suppress the excise offices and to prevent the execution of an act of Congress, by force and intimidation, the offense in legal estimation is high treason; it is an usurpation of the authority of government; it is high treason by levying of war."

Both Vigol and Mitchell were convicted of high treason and sentenced to death by hanging. Having made the point, Washington was politically astute and chose to pardon both, on the grounds of alleged mental incompetence. None of the others indicted for treason was ever tried since Washington pardoned them as well.

The second confrontation with federal taxing power was named after its leader, John Fries, a patriot from Bucks County in eastern Pennsylvania who had fought for the new nation as a soldier in the Revolutionary War. Indeed, in an ironic turn of history, Fries had fought against the Whiskey rebels as a member of Washington's militia force of thirteen thousand a few years before he came to public notoriety for the same offense of high treason.

The tax involved in Fries's Rebellion was the work of President John Adams. Fearing an impending war with France, he obtained the enactment of a federal tax on houses in 1798 to finance projected war costs. In an attempt to impose a progressive tax, the amount levied was calculated by the number of windows in the house. The burden fell heavily on Pennsylvania homeowners, with that state given a quota of more than 10 percent of the total tax across the thirteen states.

Curiously, out of the entire nation, only the eastern part of Pennsylvania made any significant protest against the tax. After initial peaceful protests and a petition drawn by Fries and signed by fifty-two taxpayers were unsuccessful, Fries used force to stop the assessors from collecting the tax and then led a small band to a jail in Bethlehem, Pennsylvania, using threats of force to obtain the release of other tax protesters.

Fries and several of his band were then indicted for treason, with Fries tried first. There were two trials for Fries, and he was convicted in both. The first trial was before Supreme Court justice James Iredell and Pennsylvania district judge Richard Peters. After a nine-day trial, the jury was given substantially the same charge on the elements of treason that had been given in the cases of the Whiskey rebels. It came back with a guilty verdict in three hours, and Fries was then sentenced to death. After the discovery that one juror had prejudged the case, however, the verdict was set aside for jury misconduct, and Fries was retried, this time before Judge Peters and Supreme Court justice Samuel Chase.

In the second trial, Chase made a critical tactical error, which became the basis for one of the charges against him when the Jeffersonian Republicans later impeached him. Chase gave his jury charge, which followed the precedent in *Mitchell* and *Vigol,* in written form to the defense at the start of the trial. This violated the applicable practice at the time because lawyers in their closings argued the law as well as the facts, and Chase's actions prevented this by declaring what the law was at the start of the trial. This was critical to Fries. His only real defense to the treason charge was to argue that the law announced in his first trial and in the trials of Whiskey rebels Mitchell and Vigol was wrong. Given the evisceration of their planned defense, the skilled defense counsel of wily Philadelphia lawyers refused to proceed and convinced Fries to decline any replacement counsel. Chase then remarkably decided to represent Fries himself, while simultaneously serving as co–trial judge. His charge to the jury explained that "the court are of opinion, that if a body of people conspire and mediate an insurrection to resist or oppose the execution of any statute of the United States by force, that they are only guilty of a high misdemeanour; but if they proceed to carry such intention into execution by force, [then] they are guilty of the treason of levying war, and the quantum of force employed neither lessens nor increases the crime."

Fries was again convicted and again sentenced to death. Other trials of Fries's rebels followed. Two others were convicted and sentenced to death; two more were acquitted. Once again all were pardoned, this time by President Adams.

What emerges from the trials of the Whiskey rebels and Fries's rebels is a strong judicial proclamation of federal power, making any use of force against the implementation of any federal statute a capital crime. Although no death sentence was ever carried out, the power to do so was meant to cow tax protesters into submission, and the threat worked; there was no more forcible resistance to federal tax collectors in the early republic. While certainly stretching the treason clause of the Constitution in defining so broadly what constitutes "levying War," the law declared in these cases by Supreme Court justices sitting on circuit was substantially embraced by the full Court in *Ex Parte Bollman* (1807) and is still the law today.

Judging Sovereign States

Less than five years after it was established, the Supreme Court delivered one of its most audacious decisions in favor of an expanded federal judicial power, at the expense of traditional state sovereignty. In *Chisholm v. Georgia* (1793), it decided by a vote of four to one that the State of Georgia could be ordered to pay a judgment to the estate of a South Carolina merchant who had sold clothing during the Revolutionary War to agents of Georgia. At issue was the proper construction of Article III, Section 2, of the Constitution, which provided for federal trial-court jurisdiction over controversies between "a State and Citizens of another State."

While this provision undoubtedly conferred *jurisdiction* over such cases in the federal courts, it did not expressly deal with the more critical issue of whether state sovereign immunity barred the *exercise* of such jurisdiction to render a judgment against a sovereign state where it had not waived sovereign immunity. In Federalist 81 even Hamilton had conceded that sovereign immunity survived the creation of the federal judicial power. In considering the criticism that the proposed judicial power might lead to the prosecution of one state for payment of a public debt in federal court through the assignment of its public securities to a citizen of another state, Hamilton demurred, stating that such a suggestion was "without foundation," because of the "inherent" nature of state sovereignty, which rendered a state "not to be amenable to the suit of an individual *without its consent.*" He therefore considered it "altogether forced and unwarrantable" to suggest the existence of such a power in the federal courts.

At the trial-court level, Justice James Iredell of North Carolina, sitting on circuit with the local federal trial judge, agreed and ordered the suit dismissed. On appeal Georgia refused to appear in the Supreme Court, and the case was argued in its absence. Appearing for the merchant's estate, Edmund Randolph, the sitting attorney general of the United States, acting (as was then permitted) in his private capacity, made a strenuous and successful argument that the text of the Constitution supported exercise of jurisdiction over a state by the federal judiciary. In that era, in which each justice delivered a separate opinion, four of the five (all except Iredell) agreed with Randolph's conclusion, although on different grounds.

Pennsylvania's justice James Wilson, a noted legal scholar who founded the University of Pennsylvania Law School, delivered the most-detailed opinion in favor of this expansive federal judicial power. Wilson, who believed in the concept of "popular sovereignty" that would later find acceptance in the era of the Marshall Court, declared that, for purposes of the United States as a union, Georgia was "not a sovereign state."

The reaction to the *Chisholm* decision was immediate and totally negative, not only from Georgia and Virginia, but from Massachusetts as well. Within two days a constitutional amendment was introduced into Congress, and it passed in the following Congress, being enacted as the Eleventh Amendment in 1798. It provides that "the Judicial power of the United States shall not be construed to extend to any suit in law or equity, commenced or prosecuted against one of the United States by Citizens of another State, or by Citizens or Subjects of any Foreign State."

Georgia's immediate reaction was even more hostile. Its lower house passed a bill that provided the death penalty—by hanging and "without benefit of clergy"—for any federal official who tried to execute on the *Chisholm* judgment. While the Eleventh Amendment prohibition was repeatedly skirted by the Court in later years, the concept of inherent state sovereignty has received significant support on the Court in recent years, particularly from Justice Clarence Thomas.

Invalidating State Legislation

An inherent part of sovereignty is the power to legislate. From the earliest days, however, strongly nationalist founders had announced that the federal courts could invalidate legislation that contravened provisions of the Constitution. In Federalist 78, for example, Hamilton declared that "no legislative act . . . contrary to the Constitution can be valid," and further that "whenever a particular statute contravenes the Constitution, it will be the duty of the judicial tribunals to adhere to the latter and disregard the former." In the Virginia debates considering ratification of the Constitution, John Marshall agreed, stating, "if Congress were to make a law not warranted by any of the powers enumerated, it would be considered by the judges as an infringement of the Constitution which they are to guard. . . . They would declare it void."

Marbury v. Madison

When the Supreme Court authoritatively addressed this issue, it followed the Federalist view in the landmark case of *Marbury v. Madison* (1803). There Chief Justice

Marshall's opinion for a unanimous five-member Court proclaimed the view both he and Hamilton had previously expressed. He announced that "It is emphatically the province and duty of the judicial department to say what the law is. . . . If two laws conflict with each other, the courts must decide on the operation of each." Most significantly he concluded that "a law repugnant to the constitution is void; and . . . courts, as well as other departments, are bound by that instrument."

Marbury arose in the fallout from the defeat of President John Adams and the Federalist Party in the presidential election of 1800. After Thomas Jefferson of the new Republican Party won that election, the Federalists secured passage of the Judiciary Act of 1801 in the lame-duck session that followed the election but preceded Jefferson's inauguration as president. That legislation created new judicial positions that were filled in the waning days of the Adams administration with so-called midnight judges. This court-packing plan aroused immediate and vigorous attacks by the Republicans.

One midnight appointment under the 1801 act was that of Justice of the Peace William Marbury in the District of Columbia. Marbury's commission for that office was signed by the outgoing secretary of state John Marshall but was not delivered to him. When the new secretary of state, James Madison, refused to deliver the commission, Marbury sued to compel Madison to do so.

In his opinion Chief Justice Marshall outlined why Marbury would be entitled to delivery of his commission but declined to grant such relief. He ruled instead that the provision of the Judiciary Act of 1789 conferring original jurisdiction on the Supreme Court to award such relief was itself unconstitutional because it was inconsistent with the Constitution.

Significantly the Judiciary Act of 1801 was repealed before the decision in *Marbury,* and judges appointed under its authorization were dismissed. Republicans continued thereafter to attack the Federalists for attempting to undermine the Republican electoral victory by packing the courts. Indeed two Federalist judges—District Judge John Pickering of New Hampshire and Justice Samuel Chase of the Supreme Court—were impeached in 1803 and 1804 respectively. Pickering, who was senile, was convicted in 1804, but the Senate acquitted Chase in 1805. By his approach in the 1803 *Marbury* opinion, Marshall avoided exacerbating the existing political upheaval in favor of a more important longer-term outcome. He accomplished this by simultaneously announcing the principle of judicial review while denying Marbury the delivery of his midnight commission.

Ware v. Hylton

Marbury invalidated a *federal* law, the first of the two times the Supreme Court did so before the Civil War. (The other was the infamous decision involving Dred Scott, *Scott v. Sanford* [1857], discussed below in chapter 2.) After *Marbury,* however, the question remained as to whether and to what degree this power of the federal judiciary over a coordinate branch of the federal government also extended to declare laws passed by sovereign states unconstitutional. In the early case of *Ware v. Hylton* (1796), the Supreme Court had considered the constitutionality of a 1777 Virginia law that permitted Virginia debtors to British subjects to discharge their debts by making payment to the Virginia state treasury in inflated American currency. The impact of this law in the case before the Court would have been to permit the Virginia debtor to discharge his debt of fifteen hundred pounds sterling incurred in 1774 for an effective payment of fifteen pounds.

The constitutional issue arose when British creditors made a challenge to this law, invoking federal court jurisdiction under the 1783 Treaty of Paris, which permitted foreign creditors to recover on their loans without legal restrictions. In separate opinions all four justices agreed that the Virginia law was contrary to the treaty and must therefore fall under the Supremacy Clause of Article VI of the Constitution. In reaching this decision, the Court rejected the mainly technical arguments based on international law and a strained construction of the Treaty of Paris made by Virginia's counsel, future chief justice John Marshall, who lost the only case he ever argued before the Court he would lead for nearly thirty-five years.

Fletcher v. Peck

Ware v. Hylton was not a frontal challenge on the general power of states to legislate without federal court interference because it involved the construction of a treaty, a subject that clearly fell within the sphere of federal governmental power. The broader issue of state sovereign power to legislate on domestic matters arose in the great case of *Fletcher v. Peck* (1810), which involved the power of the Georgia state legislature to undo a corrupt action of the previous state legislature in the notorious Yazoo land scandal. In 1795 the first legislature sold thirty-five million acres of land to private companies at about 1.5 cents per acre. All but one of the state legislators who voted in favor of this deal were bribed, and the next legislature therefore voted to set the land purchase aside in 1796. In the interim, however, millions of acres were sold to third parties, whose rights in the land they had purchased would be invalidated by the act of the second group of Georgia state legislators. Many prominent northern Federalists were among those who invested in Yazoo lands, including Supreme Court justice James Wilson and Robert Morris, the financier of the American Revolution and the founder of the first great commercial bank in the United States, which later would be known as First Pennsylvania Bank. Both served time in debtors' prison as a result of their failed Yazoo and other investments.

Having confronted Georgia before and lost in the fallout from the *Chisholm* case, the Court was not able to decide the validity of the rescinding legislation in a suit involving the state as a defendant, given the intervening passage of the Eleventh

Amendment, which prohibited suits against a state to be filed in a federal court. To get a case before a federal court, a band of Federalists representing a Massachusetts company that had bought much of the Yazoo land and resold it at great profits created a contrived case. Thus both sides in the case—supposedly adversaries—wanted to invalidate the actions of the rescinding legislature and thereby insulate the purchasers from the original land company from the remedial legislation.

The case that was brought involved a purchaser from New Hampshire (Fletcher) who sued his Massachusetts seller (Peck) in federal court, basing jurisdiction on the fact that this was a "dispute" between citizens of different states. Fletcher sued for breach of warranty of title, claiming that Peck lacked the ability to transfer clear title to him because of the cloud on his title from the rescinding legislation.

The case provided the foundation for building a federal commercial law, a subject to which we will return in chapter 3. For present purposes, however, the significance of *Fletcher v. Peck* is that it settled that the federal courts would exercise the power to invalidate state legislation on domestic matters, where that legislation violated the Constitution.

In *Fletcher*, Chief Justice Marshall's opinion for four of the five members of the Court discussed the provisions of Article I, Section 10, of the Constitution, which prohibited any state from passing "any . . . Law impairing the Obligation of Contracts." The Court ruled that the 1795 law functioned as a contract and that the purchasers whose title depended on the validity of that law had protected contractual rights under which they had received "a title good at law." As such, "when absolute rights have vested under that contract, a repeal of the law cannot [divest] those rights." The novelty of this ruling was its treatment of state legislation as akin to a contract and the consequent application of the Contracts Clause of the Constitution to it. This twist was so unprecedented that the Supreme Court left the precise foundation of its ruling vague, concluding only that "the State of Georgia was restrained, *either* by general principles, which are common to our free institutions, or by particular provisions of the Constitution of the United States." In either event the rescinding state legislation could not stand.

The Cherokee Cases

Georgia and the Supreme Court continued their decades-long adversity after *Chisholm* and *Fletcher*, and squared off for a third time more than twenty years after *Fletcher* in two historic cases involving the rights of Native Americans. Both *Cherokee Nation v. Georgia* (1831) and *Worcester v. Georgia* (1832) arose from Georgia's actions in claiming legislative power over Cherokee Nation lands situated within its borders. Those legislative incursions onto Native American lands were challenged, first by the Cherokee Nation itself and next by a Congregationalist minister who succeeded legally where the Cherokees had failed.

The background of these cases involved attempts by certain southern states to pass laws affecting tribal lands occupied by the so-called Five Civilized Tribes in the South. These were the Cherokee in Georgia and adjoining states, the Creek in Alabama, the Chickasaw and Choctaw in Mississippi and Alabama, and the Seminole in Florida. Georgia led these efforts, passing a law in December 1828 that would place all Native Americans within its territorial boundaries under state jurisdiction in six months. Georgia's action was prompted by the Cherokee Nation's previous declaration of complete sovereignty, its adoption of an American-style constitution, and its installation of a capital at New Echota in northern Georgia. The Cherokee were truly "civilized" according to the mores of the time; they had a written language, a newspaper, and schools for their children. Indeed, in a particularly odious imitation of their white models, some even owned slaves.

The existing frictions between whites and Native Americans in the American South were soon exacerbated by the influx of white prospectors into northern Georgia after gold was discovered there in the summer of 1829. To address the problem, President Andrew Jackson supported relocation of the Five Civilized Tribes to a new Indian territory located in present-day Oklahoma. The Removal Act passed in May 1830 provided for the voluntary exchange of the new land for the southern tribal lands. Jackson's case for the Removal Act included the reasoning that "it will relieve the whole State of Mississippi and the western part of Alabama of Indian occupancy, and *enable those States to advance rapidly in population, wealth, and power.* It will separate the Indians from immediate contact with settlements of whites; free them from the power of the States; enable them to pursue happiness in their own way and under their own rude institutions; will retard the progress of decay, which is lessening their numbers, and perhaps cause them gradually, under the protection of the Government and through the influence of good counsels, to cast off their savage habits and become an interesting, civilized, and Christian community." Jackson concluded with a question that to him was rhetorical: "What good man would prefer a country covered with forests and ranged by a few thousand savages to our extensive Republic, studded with cities, towns, and prosperous farms, embellished with all the improvements which art can devise or industry execute, occupied by more than 12,000,000 happy people, and filled with all the blessings of liberty, civilization, and religion?"

All the Five Civilized Tribes eventually accepted the exchange of lands authorized by the Removal Act but only after pressure and threats and only after litigation by the Cherokee Nation to protect its rights guaranteed by treaties with the federal government came to nothing. The Cherokee were forced into litigation against Georgia when Georgia began to enforce its state law claiming jurisdiction over the Cherokee living within state borders. In January 1831 Georgia executed a Cherokee named Corn Tassel for a murder committed within Cherokee lands, doing so despite a Supreme Court stay of execution granted pending its review of the case. In the same month, the Cherokee Nation filed suit seeking an injunction against Georgia's further exercise of power over Cherokee land and people, having hired former attorney general William Wirt, who later became the 1832 presidential candidate of the Anti-Mason Party, to plead their case. Wirt chose to file an action against the State of Georgia directly in the Supreme Court, under its original jurisdiction, which was authorized despite the Eleventh Amendment, if the Cherokee Nation were found to be a "foreign state." Georgia, following a pattern it began in the *Chisholm* case, simply refused to appear or submit to Supreme Court jurisdiction.

Chief Justice Marshall's short opinion was lyrical in its description of the Cherokee and their plight: "If courts were permitted to indulge their sympathies, a case better calculated to excite them can scarcely be imagined. A people once numerous, powerful, and truly independent, found by our ancestors in the quiet and uncontrolled possession of an ample domain, gradually sinking beneath our superior policy, our arts and our arms, have yielded their lands by successive treaties, each of which contains a solemn guarantee of the residue, until they retain no more of their formerly extensive territory than is deemed necessary to their comfortable subsistence. To preserve this remnant, the present application is made."

Lyricism notwithstanding, the Cherokee lost. Marshall found that the Court lacked jurisdiction even to hear the case because the Cherokee were not a "foreign state" but rather a "domestic dependent nation," a "ward" of their "guardian," the federal government, and a people still "in a state of pupilage." In so ruling, he found support in the wording of Article I, Section 8, of the Constitution, which permitted Congress to "regulate Commerce with foreign Nations, and among the several States, and with the Indian Tribes," thus distinguishing those tribes from "foreign nations."

A second Georgia law, passed in December 1830, came before the Court in the *Worcester* case. Under that state law, no white was permitted to enter Cherokee land in Georgia without a license or permit from the Georgia governor. For violations of this law, eleven men were arrested, nine of whom took pardons, conditioned on their leaving the state. One who did not was Samuel Worcester, a white Congregationalist minister who also served as the federal postmaster of New Echota, a position from which President Jackson promptly fired him to prevent the interposition of a federal-official defense. Worcester was sentenced to four years at hard labor and appealed his conviction to the Supreme Court.

Once again Georgia failed to appear. This time, however, the Supreme Court chose to decide the case, jurisdiction being clear, since Worcester was a citizen of Vermont and could appeal his criminal conviction under the Eleventh Amendment exception recognized in *Cohens v. Virginia* (1821). Speaking for four of the Court's six members, with a fifth concurring in the outcome, Marshall ignored his prior year's opinion in the *Cherokee Nation* case and ruled that the Cherokee were in fact a nation entitled to enter into treaties and that those treaties, which were the supreme law of the land, had been violated by the Georgia law. For good measure Marshall also accepted Wirt's arguments that the Georgia law violated the Contracts and Commerce clauses of the Constitution.

The outcome of *Worcester* did not save the Cherokee people, or even the victorious minister. He served out part of his term before being pardoned and expelled from the state. A small minority of the Cherokee Nation, under the "Treaty Party" led by Major and John Ridge, signed the 1835 Treaty of New Echota, named for their short-lived capital city. Under that treaty they accepted an exchange of lands. Some eight million acres of Cherokee land in Georgia, North Carolina, Tennessee, and Alabama were surrendered for a payment of $4.5 million. The Cherokee were given two years to move to their new lands in the west. When the deadline passed, they were forcibly removed. Some eighteen thousand were taken to relocation camps, put on steamboats and transported down the Tennessee River, loaded thereafter onto railroad boxcars, and then forced to walk what became known as "The Trail of Tears" to their final destination. Of the eighteen thousand who made this long journey, estimates of the number who died range from a low of four thousand to a high of nearly ten thousand. All in all, some one hundred million acres of Native American land were acquired by the United States in the eight years of the Jackson presidency, with more than forty-five thousand Native Americans "relocated."

Declaring Federal Judicial Supremacy

While the Supreme Court established its supremacy over state *legislatures* in its early decisions in *Ware v. Hylton* and *Fletcher v. Peck*, the question of its power over state *courts* was still open in the second decade of the nineteenth century. That question was finally resolved by Justice Joseph Story's decisive opinion for a unanimous Supreme Court in *Martin v. Hunter's Lessee* (1816).

Martin involved a challenge to a Virginia state law by the heirs of the Fairfax family of Virginia. Since those heirs were British subjects, their rights to inherit the land were voided by a Virginia state law, and the land was sold off to third parties, including none other than Chief Justice Marshall and his brother. The Fairfax interests challenged the state law as unconstitutional in light of international treaties that they argued confirmed their title. The case came before the Supreme Court twice, with Chief Justice Marshall not participating in either decision because of his interest in the lands in litigation.

The second decision, in the *Martin* case, posed the question whether the Supreme Court could reverse the decision of the highest court of Virginia on a question of federal constitutional law. The answer was not obvious from the text of the Constitution, which was silent on the question. Congress had, however, in

Section 25 of the original Judiciary Act of 1789 conferred jurisdiction on the Supreme Court to review final judgments of the highest court of a state in several instances, including where a state law was upheld against a federal constitutional challenge, as was true in the *Martin* case. Thus the *Martin* Court needed to determine whether Section 25 was itself constitutional.

Southern legal scholars had argued that the Supreme Court could not displace the rulings of the highest courts of sovereign states even on questions of federal law because the Constitution was the product of a compact among sovereign states, and those states retained any powers not expressly surrendered to the new federal government. Chief among these scholars was Virginia's own Spencer Roane, the son-in-law of Patrick Henry and a judge on the Virginia Court of Appeals, the court from which the *Martin* appeal had been taken. Roane and his colleagues saw their court as entitled to the same deference on questions of constitutional law as the Supreme Court, given the silence of the Constitution on the issue.

Following the same theory of popular sovereignty found in Justice Wilson's earlier opinion in *Chisholm v. Georgia,* Story rejected the retained sovereignty argument, concluding that the Constitution represented a vote of the people of the United States and not that of separate sovereign states. Moreover, Story noted, from a practical standpoint, permitting the highest courts of thirteen separate states each to determine potentially the same issue would only result in "jarring and discordant judgments," which would be destructive of the Constitution and the Union and inconsistent with the Supremacy Clause contained in Article VI of the Constitution. As such Section 25 of the Judiciary Act was constitutional; the judgment of the Virginia court was reversed; and the Fairfax heirs prevailed.

Expanding the Reach of Federal Government

The watershed opinion of the Marshall Court on the powers of the federal government was that delivered for a unanimous Court in *McCulloch v. Maryland* (1819). *McCulloch* involved two questions of vast importance to the future of the country—the power of Congress to incorporate a national bank and the power of a state to impose taxes on such an institution. Marshall's opinion recognized its own significance, stating early on that "the constitution of our country, in its most interesting and vital parts, is to be considered; the conflicting powers of the government of the Union and of its members, as marked in that constitution, are to be discussed; and an opinion given, which may essentially influence the great operations of the government."

The power of Congress to create a national bank was a critical issue debated from the very beginnings of the United States, when Treasury Secretary Alexander Hamilton suggested the concept in 1791 and Secretary of State Thomas Jefferson and his congressional ally from Virginia, James Madison, opposed it. To the

Anti-Federalists, succeeded in turn by the Jeffersonian Republicans and the Jacksonian Democrats, the Bank of the United States was an antidemocratic vehicle of corporate greed and private monopoly, the great white whale to be hunted down and killed, once and for all.

Madison's opposition questioned the constitutional power of Congress to charter a bank, since that power was not explicitly conferred on Congress in Article I of the Constitution. President Washington asked Hamilton and Jefferson to prepare memoranda on the question and accepted the Hamiltonian view that the power to charter a bank was conferred by the "Necessary and Proper" Clause of Article I, Section 8. This led to the creation of the First Bank of the United States under a twenty-year charter that ran from 1791 to 1811. In 1811 the prevailing Republicans under now-president Madison refused to recharter the bank. The impact of the War of 1812 caused Madison to alter his views, however, and the bank was resuscitated in 1816, with a new charter that ran to 1836.

The Second Bank of the United States, the stock of which was held 80 percent by private investors and 20 percent by the United States government, soon began to foster land speculation by granting loans on up to 80 percent of the purported value of the land. This shortly led to a land bubble that burst in the Panic of 1819, causing the failure of many state-chartered banks and large investor losses. This reignited populist antibank sentiment, with many states taxing branches of the Second Bank and two states prohibiting its operations within their borders. One such tax was imposed by Maryland, where two land speculators who lent themselves money on an unsecured basis ran the local Second Bank branch. The constitutionality of this state tax was the subject of the second question decided in *McCulloch.*

Marshall's opinion in *McCulloch* began by upholding the power of Congress to charter a national bank, echoing the arguments of the long-dead Hamilton from nearly thirty years earlier. First the popular sovereignty model was affirmed: "The government of the Union . . . is emphatically, and truly, a government of the people. In form and in substance it emanates from them. Its powers are granted by them, and are to be exercised directly on them, and for their benefit." Second Marshall declared that "the government of the Union, though limited in its powers, is supreme within its sphere of action." Third, relying upon the "Necessary and Proper" Clause, while the power to establish a bank was not expressly granted by the Constitution, "we must never forget, that it is a *constitution* we are expounding." As such "we think the sound construction of the constitution must allow to the national legislature that discretion, with respect to the means by which the powers it confers are to be carried into execution, which will enable that body to perform the high duties assigned to it, in the manner most beneficial to the people. *Let the end be legitimate, let it be within the scope of the constitution, and all means which are appropriate, which are plainly adapted to that end, which are not prohibited, but consist with the letter and spirit of the constitution, are constitutional.*"

On the question of the power of Maryland to tax a creature of the federal legislature, Marshall firmly announced that "the power to tax involves the power to destroy," an apt observation given the actions of many states at that very time either to prohibit outright or to tax the local branches of the Second Bank of the United States in the fallout from what would become the Panic of 1819. The opinion concluded that "the states have no power, by taxation or other-wise, to retard, impede, burden, or in any manner control, the operations of the constitutional laws enacted by Congress to carry into execution the powers vested in the general government. This is, we think, the unavoidable consequence of that supremacy which the constitution has declared."

Opposition to Marshall's broad views of federal power and state subordination soon surfaced in a series of articles by southern judges and theorists, including Spencer Roane. So serious were these attacks that Marshall himself, writing anonymously, answered them with his own series of newspaper essays, defending his view of the federal government's implied powers.

The Hamilton-Marshall view prevailed in both the short and long terms, but was seriously challenged thirteen years after *McCulloch,* when President Andrew Jackson vetoed recharter of the Bank of the United States in 1832. Jackson had a Jeffersonian view of the relationship between the federal and state governments. In 1829, in his first inaugural address, he announced that "in such measures as I may be called on to pursue in regard to the rights of the separate states I hope to be animated by a proper respect for those *sovereign* members of our Union, taking care not to confound the powers they have reserved to themselves with those they have granted to the *confederacy.*"

Jackson's views on the Bank of the United States also reflected a limited view of federal power. Influenced in part by his own financial losses in the Panic of 1819, Jackson saw the bank as a monopoly owned "principally" by "Eastern and foreign stockholders" who were "rich and powerful" and had aligned themselves against "the humble members of society—the farmers, mechanics, and laborers—who have neither the time nor the means of securing like favors to themselves." While the Supreme Court had held in *McCulloch* that Congress possessed the power to establish a national bank, Jackson demurred, reasoning that the view of the Supreme Court was not binding on him but was only entitled "to have . . . such influence as the force of their reasoning may deserve." This was the view Lincoln later adopted with respect to the binding power of the *Scott v. Sandford* decision on slavery. Jackson's attempt to kill the Bank of the United States also failed but only after the Civil War, which arose out of the powder keg of slavery and the political "slave power" of the South.

Two

The Supreme Court and the Slave Power

Slavery was the Achilles heel of American democracy from the beginning of the nation, hidden in, but protected in part by, the Constitution. In 1790 the first federal census recorded five states—South Carolina, Virginia, Georgia, Maryland, and North Carolina—with slave populations from 25 to 43 percent of their total populations. A sixth state—Kentucky—had a slave population of nearly 17 percent, and even a "free" state such as New York still had more than 21,000 slaves living within its borders in 1790. Only Massachusetts (whose state constitution provided that all men were "born free and equal") had no slaves recorded by the 1790 census. That census counted some 694,280 slaves, nearly 18 percent of the recorded population of sixteen existing or future states. The number of slaves rose to approximately 4 million by 1860, representing 13 percent of the nation's population that census year.

Slavery in the late eighteenth century was not a social embarrassment to most slave owners. Washington, Jefferson, and even Justice Samuel Chase of the Supreme Court openly announced the availability of rewards in newspapers or on handbills for the return of their runaway slaves. This would change in the nineteenth century. By the 1840s James Knox Polk, the penultimate president to own slaves during his term of service, pretended to own only "family" slaves bequeathed to him and concealed his purchase of new slaves, many of whom were preteens or teenagers removed from their parents. Polk used straw men to make his slave purchases, taking unrecorded deeds to transfer their ownership to him.

The geography of slavery was also changing between the beginning of the United States and the outbreak of the Civil War. Historians have documented the southern movement of slavery during this time period from the mid-South states of Virginia, Arkansas, Tennessee, and North Carolina to the lower South states of South Carolina, Mississippi, Florida, Alabama, Georgia, Louisiana, and Texas, a trend traceable to the more favorable conditions for growing the key cotton crop in the lower South. During the 1850s at least 308,000 slaves moved from states such as Virginia and Kentucky to states such as Mississippi and Louisiana. These moves included those involved in some 188,000 sales during this period, many of which resulted in breaking up slave families. Polk's slave ownership mirrored this trend, with the future president establishing a second cotton plantation in Mississippi in 1835, to which some of his Tennessee plantation slaves were moved. By the time of secession, the mid-South states averaged a slave population of 32 percent, while the lower South states averaged some 47 percent. Indeed secession followed the percentages of slaves in the various slave states. The lower South states seceded first. By contrast the border slave states of Maryland, Delaware, Missouri, and Kentucky, whose slave population averaged only 13 percent, remained in the union.

Slavery and the Constitution

The words "slave" and "slavery" do not appear in the Constitution. Key provisions nevertheless reflected the felt need to accommodate and protect what later would come to be labeled as the "slave power." While historians have linked many provisions of the Constitution to slavery, sparking many debates as to the validity of some of their claims, it is clear that at least three key provisions related directly to slavery as an institution.

The first such provision was contained in Article I, Section 9, providing that "Migration or Importation of such persons as any of the States now existing shall think proper to admit" (note the many circumlocutions) shall not be prohibited for twenty years, that is, until 1808. This protected the African slave trade for that twenty-year period. Indeed, even after that period had expired and Congress had outlawed the trade at the earliest permissible time, the Supreme Court upheld its validity under international law in Chief Justice Marshall's 1825 opinion in *The Antelope,* which dealt with the proper disposition of slaves first taken by pirates from a slave ship and then seized by an American revenue cutter. The Court found some of the slaves to be American, and they were sent to freedom in Liberia; others were classified as Spanish and sent back to slavery in then Spanish Florida. The Court rendered this adjudication despite Marshall's observation that the slave trade was "contrary to the law of nature."

A second constitutional provision directly linked to slavery appeared in Article I, Section 2, which governed the imposition of "direct taxes" and the computation of the number of seats in the United States House of Representatives. That provision, which was invalidated by Section 2 of the post–Civil War Fourteenth Amendment, awarded House seats based on population, calculated by including first "the whole Number of free persons," and second "three fifths of all other Persons," while excluding "Indians not taxed," a perverse triune calculus of the relative political values of each class to their states. Slaves, although never referred to as such ("all other Persons" meant them), were thus wielded as a political club to increase the slave power's representation in the House of Representatives. The impact of this provision was to increase the representation of the slave states in the House by about 30 percent above what it would have been had slaves not been counted at all. In 1865, for example, the radical Republican House leader,

Thaddeus Stevens of Pennsylvania, quantified the impact of the by-then repealed provision as having given nineteen extra House seats to the slave states of their total seventy.

The provision also gave the South the presidency for most of the pre–Civil War period, since the number of presidential electors in each state was the sum of the state's senators and representatives. This resulted in the election of seven southern presidents, including four of the first five, in the period from 1789 to 1860. Those seven served for a total of forty-seven of the seventy-one years in that period. To take just one early example of the impact of the Three-fifths Clause on presidential elections, Jefferson would not have defeated Adams for the presidency in 1800 without the additional electoral votes awarded the southern states by virtue of the Three-fifths Clause.

The third key provision—and the one that would generate widespread popular discontent beginning with northern abolitionists in the 1830s—was Article IV, Section 2, the so-called Fugitive Slave provision of the Constitution. Added at the last minute, with little commentary on it in the Philadelphia convention, this provision stated that "no Person held to Service or Labour in one State, under the laws thereof, escaping into another, shall, in Consequence of any Law or Regulation therein, be discharged from such Service or Labour, *but shall be delivered up on Claim of the Party to whom such Service or Labour may be due.*" This highlighted language differed from the roughly contemporaneous provisions of the Northwest Ordinance of 1787, which prohibited slavery in those territories, but provided that in the cases of slaves escaping into them, "such fugitive *may be lawfully reclaimed, and conveyed to the person claiming his or her labor or service.*" The key difference of these two organic laws lies between the phrases "may be lawfully reclaimed" and "shall be delivered up," and much debate would ensue over the next seventy years over how Congress would implement the Fugitive Slave Clause of the Constitution by appropriate legislation.

Abolitionism and the Second Great Awakening

Opposition to slavery began early in the new republic. As we have seen, Massachusetts (which then included Maine) had no slaves in 1790, and abolition movements were effective in the last twenty years of the eighteenth century in other states such as Pennsylvania. Indeed the Quakers from Pennsylvania and New York presented petitions to the first Congress early in 1790 to abolish the African slave trade, followed by another petition from the Pennsylvania Abolition Society, bearing the signature of Benjamin Franklin and attacking slavery itself.

After these early efforts failed, the next—and more extreme—abolitionist movement was sparked by the Second Great Awakening, a Protestant revival movement that found great success in the North in the 1820s and 1830s, particularly in industrial towns and cities such as Rochester, New York. By 1850 one in seven

Americans belonged to a church or some organized religious group; in 1800 only one in fifteen had such memberships. In 1831 alone some one hundred thousand people joined a church.

The revival movement stressed personal redemption on an individual level, emphasizing the need to cease sinful ways. Slavery became an exemplar of such sinful ways, with attacks on the "peculiar institution" stoked by preachers such as Congregationalist minister Lyman Beecher. His daughter Harriet Beecher Stowe wrote the antislavery novel *Uncle Tom's Cabin* in 1852, a book that became the nineteenth-century American best seller, with two million copies sold by the eve of the Civil War in 1859. Stowe's brother Henry Ward Beecher, another minister, was more militant against slavery, sending rifles—christened "Beecher's Bibles"—to antislavery settlers in "Bleeding Kansas" during the 1850s.

The black community also used religion to fight slavery. In 1831 in Virginia a black lay preacher, Nat Turner, led a slave rebellion that killed sixty whites. When apprehended and condemned to death, Turner compared himself to Christ, asking, "Was not Christ crucified?"

In Boston, also in 1831, William Lloyd Garrison, a Baptist who later attacked organized religion for the failure of many ministers to condemn slavery, began publication of the *Liberator,* a newspaper that continued in circulation until the adoption of the Thirteenth Amendment, which abolished slavery, in 1865. Garrison was an early proponent of extreme abolitionism, with his paper's motto the unapologetic statement "I am in earnest—I will not equivocate—I will not excuse—I will not retreat a single inch—and I will be heard."

These abolitionist efforts soon reached the federal Congress, with a flurry of antislavery petitions being presented in 1835 and 1836 to abolish slavery in the District of Columbia. Southern opposition to such petitions led in 1836 to enactment in the House of Representatives of a "gag rule" lasting for nine years and barring their presentation. Representative and former president John Quincy Adams of Massachusetts sought to evade and avoid this rule through a series of parliamentary maneuvers, keeping the controversy at a high boil in Congress. Indeed, in one session alone, in 1838–39, Adams presented 693 petitions.

With these increasingly strident attacks on slavery as an institution, and the fervor of the Second Great Awakening, the flashpoint of the slavery debate was the fugitive slave. Abolitionists sought to ensure the continued freedom of such escaped slaves, while slave owners waived the Constitution to demand that they "be delivered up" and returned to them. In 1842 the Supreme Court at last had occasion to interpret the Fugitive Slave Clause of the Constitution, in its first entry into the domestic confrontation over slavery.

The Supreme Court and the Fugitive Slave in the 1840s

If a slave ever could be described as fortunate, Margaret Morgan was such. Her owner, a Mr. Ashmore of Maryland, allowed her to live as if she were free, even though no formal emancipation had been granted to her. Taking full advantage of her existential freedom, she married a free black named Jerry Morgan, moved to Pennsylvania, and had children with her husband. This happy state of affairs ended abruptly in 1837. In that year, after Mr. Ashmore's death, his daughter hired a "slave catcher" to find and return Mrs. Morgan from Pennsylvania to Maryland.

At that time in Pennsylvania two laws prescribed the process to reclaim a fugitive slave. The federal Fugitive Slave Law of 1793 required the governor of the state into which the slave had escaped to cooperate with the demand for return and to set forth a process for the owner to reclaim his "property." That process was for the owner to exercise self-help and seize the slave, take him or her before a state or federal judge, prove ownership, and obtain a certificate of removal, authorizing the owner to remove the slave from the state to which he or she had fled. The historian Don E. Fehrenbacher has aptly termed this process one for obtaining "a kind of vigilante's license to enforce his rights himself with a minimum of formality."

Pennsylvania also had an 1826 law on the subject, one of several northern state laws enacted around that time and referred to as "personal liberty" laws. These laws had two major purposes—first to prescribe a process to comply with the federal law and second to prevent kidnapping of freed blacks. The Pennsylvania law required the permission of a state official for the slave's removal and set forth procedural standards giving additional protections to the alleged slave's rights beyond those afforded by the federal law, including the right to a trial.

Edward Prigg, the slave catcher who pursued Mrs. Morgan into the free state of Pennsylvania, obtained an arrest warrant and arrested Mrs. Morgan, seizing her youngest child as well. But Prigg failed to obtain a certificate of removal, which both state and federal law required. Nevertheless he took Mrs. Morgan and her child forcibly back to Ms. Ashmore in Maryland, for which illegal act a Pennsylvania grand jury indicted him for kidnapping.

Prigg v. Pennsylvania (1842) presented the Supreme Court with the issue of whether Pennsylvania could place burdens on a slave owner in reclaiming a fugitive slave beyond those prescribed by federal law. Justice Joseph Story, from Massachusetts, wrote the principal opinion in *Prigg,* one of seven opinions written in the case by a Court that had been expanded from seven to nine in 1837. Eight of the nine justices concurred in the opinion that the Pennsylvania law was unconstitutional with only Justice John McLean dissenting, as he would fifteen years later in the Dred Scott case.

Story's opinion explained that the federal government had the *exclusive* power to enforce fugitive slave removal, and that state laws therefore could not impose *additional* restrictions on a slave owner's recapture rights. Moreover, Story concluded, a slave owner had the right of self-help "in every state in the Union, to seize and recapture his slave, whenever he can do it without any breach of the peace, or any illegal violence." But Story went on to announce that states also had no *obligation* beyond a moral one to aid in the recapture of fugitive slaves, a conclusion to which Chief Justice Taney vigorously objected in a concurring opinion. Story commented: "The states cannot . . . be compelled to enforce them; and it might well be deemed an *unconstitutional* exercise of the power of interpretation, to insist that the states are bound to provide means to carry into effect the duties of the national government, nowhere delegated or intrusted to them by the Constitution."

Things Fall Apart: From *Prigg* to *Scott*

In ruling that the fugitive slave issue was solely one of federal competence and that slave owners could pursue their rights even in free states, the Supreme Court in *Prigg v. Pennsylvania* took its first steps toward nationalizing the entire issue of slavery. It thus set the stage for its ruling fifteen years later in the *Scott v. Sandford* case.

While the slave interests were victorious in the outcome of *Prigg*, abolitionists took comfort from Justice Story's observation that states had no legal duty to assist in the recapture of slaves. In Story's own Massachusetts, the case of fugitive slave George Latimer built on Story's opinion in *Prigg* to protect the fugitive slave from the police power of Massachusetts. Latimer was a fugitive slave who escaped from Virginia and was arrested on the complaint of his owner by the Boston police. The Massachusetts courts refused to free Latimer on a petition for habeas corpus filed by abolitionists in that state, and he was ordered to be returned to his owner in Virginia. Determined not to accept the legal outcome, abolitionists took two steps. First they raised four hundred dollars and purchased Latimer's freedom from his owner. More important, through the use of a sixty-five-thousand-signature petition, they seized on the Story dictum to persuade the Massachusetts legislature in the same year as the *Prigg* decision to pass what became known as the "Latimer Law." That legislation, variants of which were enacted in other free states, prohibited the use of state police powers and courts to assist in slave recaptures.

Five years after the decision in *Prigg* and the enactment of the Latimer Law, the Supreme Court was presented with another fugitive slave issue in *Jones v. Van Zandt* (1847). There the focus was not on the fugitive slave but on the penalties that constitutionally could be imposed on those who assisted in slave escapes through the vehicle of the so-called underground railroad. An Ohio man was sued under the Fugitive Slave Act of 1793, which imposed penalties for such activities, after he permitted use of his wagon to enable slaves to escape, including driving one slave to safety hidden under a cover in the back of the wagon. An assault on the act was led by Salmon P. Chase and Senator William Seward of New York in the Supreme Court. Chase, who became famous as "the Attorney General for Fugitive Slaves," would serve in several important state and federal positions, including as governor and United States senator from Ohio, as Lincoln's secretary of the treasury, and as Taney's successor as chief justice of the United States. He served in that last position from 1864 to 1873. Chase's arguments resonate today on both legal and moral grounds, but all were unsuccessful, with rejection by a unanimous Supreme Court.

Chase argued that the federal government could not support slavery, and that the Fugitive Slave Clause of the Constitution was merely a kind of interstate compact only the states could enforce. He also contended that slavery violated the principles of the Declaration of Independence, and the Bill of Rights, including particularly the Due Process Clause of the Fifth Amendment. The Supreme Court, however, saw the Fugitive Slave Clause as one of the "sacred compromises" of the Constitution and held that it had "no authority as a judicial body to modify or overrule" it. Slavery, the Court concluded, was a political question, to be settled by each state for itself.

Continued abolitionist opposition to slavery led a few years later to the Compromise of 1850, devised by Henry Clay, a Whig senator from Kentucky. Before 1850 the balance of power between free and slave states was equal, with fifteen in each camp. When Texas was admitted as a slave state in 1845, it was granted the right to divide into five separate states. With the Mexican War then threatening to add even more slave states, the House of Representatives twice passed a bill offered by Pennsylvania representative David Wilmot. Under the "Wilmot Proviso," which failed to pass the Senate, slavery would have been prohibited in any territory taken from Mexico.

To address the many differences on several aspects of slavery, Clay's Compromise admitted California as a free state; provided that no prohibition of slavery would be permitted in the territories of New Mexico and Utah; and enacted a stricter Fugitive Slave Law. That law of 1850 raised the penalties imposed on those assisting slaves to include both a one thousand dollar fine and a one thousand dollar civil-damages award, together with a prison term of up to six months. In addition the procedure to return a fugitive slave was changed to award the commissioner who returned a slave ten dollars, but only five dollars if the slave was freed, a distinction sought to be justified by the relative amount of paperwork required.

There was widespread and vigorous opposition to the Fugitive Slave Act of 1850. Boston abolitionist and lawyer Wendell Phillips denounced the new law, announcing, "We must trample this law under our feet. . . . As moral and religious men, [we] cannot obey an immoral and irreligious statute. . . . I must reverence the laws of God, come of that what will come." Phillips joined with others who increasingly advocated even the use of violence to end slavery once and for all.

Throughout the 1850s there were an increasing number of public spectacles and confrontations over particular fugitive slave escapes. Presidents Fillmore and Pierce sent federal troops into free states on several occasions to seize runaway slaves. One case that sparked particular public protest, again in Massachusetts, involved seventeen-year-old Thomas Sims, who had escaped from Georgia. Tried in a locked courthouse, he was ordered returned to his master. Led to the Boston Navy Yard for return to Virginia, he was guarded by 300 hundred armed men who turned him over to 250 United States forces at the navy yard. Two years later Boston had another case, this time involving a slave known as Anthony Burns. To avoid Burns's return to slavery, abolitionists stormed the courthouse, killing a deputy. Pierce sent federal troops in to quell the uprising, and efforts to purchase Burns's freedom were rejected. When Burns was marched to the Boston wharf for return to his owner, sullen crowds watched, flying the American flag upside down in protest. On the following Fourth of July, William Lloyd Garrison publicly denounced the United States Constitution, which had been interpreted to permit the return of runaway slaves as "a covenant with death and an agreement with hell." The abolitionist press, armed with the new technology of the steam press, printed broadsides with images of chained and whipped slaves to stir up increased opposition to slavery and its discontents. To the Sims and Burns events was added the tragic 1856 spectacle of Margaret Garner, an escaped slave who fled to Ohio. After her recapture she chose to slit the throat of her daughter, killing her rather than permit their return to life as slaves. The Fugitive Slave Law of 1850 led to relatively few court proceedings. Some 343 cases are known; in those 332 of the accused were found to be slaves and ordered returned to their owners.

The 1850s were also marked by the publication of *Uncle Tom's Cabin* in 1852 and continued political conflict over slavery. Southerners—and even Daniel Webster of Massachusetts—began to call for treason trials against abolitionists to end their opposition. The trials soon came. On September 11, 1851, in Christiana, Pennsylvania, a slave owner and his son were killed in a riot resulting from their attempt to recapture a runaway slave. After President Fillmore sent in the marines to put down the riot, thirty-six black and five white men were indicted for treason for their forcible opposition to the enforcement of the Fugitive Slave Law. Despite precedent for this reading of the treason clause of the Constitution as interpreted in the *Vigol*, *Mitchell*, and *Bollman* cases, Justice Robert Grier of the Supreme Court, a Pennsylvanian sitting on circuit as a trial judge, acquitted the first defendants, and the other cases were dropped. Nevertheless, as one abolitionist put it in a private letter, "These treason Trials have been a great windfall."

Things continued to fall apart in 1854, with the infamous Kansas-Nebraska Act. The act permitted slavery to exist in both states if the residents so chose, thereby repudiating the Missouri Compromise of 1820, which had prohibited slavery in the North. Since only Kansas seemed likely to vote in slavery, both sides rushed partisans into "Bloody Kansas" to rig the vote. It was in Kansas that John Brown began his biblical terrorism, butchering five proslavery settlers with broad swords in May of 1856.

When Senator Charles Sumner of Massachusetts took the floor of the United States Senate in 1856 to attack the South for its share of the Kansas violence, South

Carolina representative Preston Brooks caned him nearly to death for verbally attacking Brooks's cousin, Senator Andrew Butler, and for comparing support for slavery to the love of a whore. Censured by the House of Representatives, Brooks resigned, but he was reelected easily to the same seat.

The Kansas-Nebraska Act killed the Whig Party in the United States, sowing the seeds for the emergence of the Republican Party in 1856 as the first-ever sectional party in United States politics. It also brought Abraham Lincoln back into politics. In 1854 he began his personal campaign against the extension of slavery beyond the South, terming the Kansas-Nebraska Act a "moral wrong" and stating, "The spirit of seventy-six and the spirit of Nebraska are utter antagonisms. . . . Our republican robe is soiled, and trailed in the dust. Let us repurify it." But there was no repurification, only continued violence.

Chief Justice Roger Taney and the Dred Scott Case

During nearly the first two-thirds of the nineteenth century, only two men held the position of chief justice of the United States. The first, John Marshall of Virginia, served for thirty-five years, from 1801 to 1835. He was a towering figure who changed the Court dramatically in a series of opinions he wrote for what was largely a unanimous Court fashioning a nationalist jurisprudence.

Marshall's successor, serving the twenty-eight years from 1836 to 1864, was Roger Taney of Maryland. A former Federalist leader in Maryland, Taney became a Jacksonian Democrat in the 1820s, and joined Jackson's Cabinet as attorney general from 1831 to 1833. An author of Jackson's Bank Veto Message in 1832, Taney switched his cabinet portfolio to the U.S. Treasury in an interim appointment when two predecessors in that position refused to remove federal deposits from the Bank of the United States to state banks. Taney did so, and was refused permanent confirmation as treasury secretary in retaliation. He returned to the private practice of law in Maryland where he remained until Jackson nominated him for a Supreme Court vacancy early in 1835. The Senate refused to confirm him then, but Taney was nominated for chief justice at the end of the same year and was confirmed in early 1836.

Taney is generally ranked by legal historians and other professionals as one of a handful of great justices of the Court. His general reputation, however, is dismal because of the lead opinion he wrote on slavery in the infamous Dred Scott case. Taney was not personally partial to slaveholding. He had inherited and then freed his own slaves, and he remained a Union loyalist during the Civil War, resisting Lincoln's suspension of the rights of political dissidents in *Ex Parte Merryman*, an opinion he wrote sitting on circuit in 1861. But his Jacksonian political philosophy was sensitive to the preservation of states' rights, and slavery was seen as a state prerogative. Taney's careful balancing of federal and states' rights was acclaimed in the commercial law area, which we will examine in the next chapter, and in the subtle nuances of his Court's construction of the Contracts and Commerce clauses of the Constitution, providing for concurrent federal and state jurisdiction in some areas. But he lives on in history principally as the discredited author of the first opinion in *Scott v. Sandford.* His twentieth-century successor Chief Justice Charles Evans Hughes rightly saw Taney as wrongly attempting to use the Court to solve a pressing national political problem, which the Court was institutionally ill-equipped to do then or now.

Scott v. Sandford (1857) posed the question whether a slave who had been taken by his owner to live at different times in both a state and a territory free of slavery became free by virtue of either or both residences. Considerable precedent for that outcome existed at the time, contending that "once free, always free," but the Missouri Supreme Court, which originally decided that issue, held that Scott was still a slave. The Supreme Court of the United States could have avoided the larger issues it decided by simply holding that the slavery issue, being one of state law, had conclusively been decided in the Missouri courts. That might well have been the outcome absent a remarkable series of ex parte contacts between members of the Supreme Court and President-elect James Buchanan, a Pennsylvania Democrat elected with strong southern support.

Scott v. Sandford was argued twice, and the opinion was initially assigned to Justice Samuel Nelson, a New York Jacksonian Democrat, whose draft opinion for the Court avoided the larger issues relating to the constitutionality of the Missouri Compromise. This would not have satisfied Buchanan, who had reached out by letter to Justice John Catron of Tennessee, an old friend, to inquire when the decision would come down, so that he might hopefully incorporate it in his inaugural address. Buchanan added that the Court should "destroy the dangerous slavery agitation and thus restore peace to our distracted country."

Catron wrote back, informing Buchanan that the case would be decided before the inauguration, but would "settle nothing." Two weeks later, Catron sent a second letter to Buchanan, announcing that the Court had now decided to attempt to resolve the Missouri Compromise issue and urging the president-elect to "drop [his fellow Pennsylvanian, Justice] Grier a line" to urge him to join the Court majority in order "to settle the agitation by an affirmative decision of the Supreme Court, the one way or the other."

Buchanan contacted Grier, and Grier wrote back that he would support a broader opinion than Nelson's draft. Grier wrote that he would concur in an outcome holding the Missouri Compromise "to be of *non-effect*" because he was "anxious that it should not appear that the line of latitude should mark the line of division in the court." Grier ultimately joined four southern and border slave state justices in broad rulings that the Missouri Compromise was unconstitutional. Nelson's original narrow opinion of the Court became a concurrence deferring to the Missouri ruling on Scott's slave status without reaching the issue of constitutionality. Only Justices John McLean of Ohio and Benjamin Curtis of Massachusetts dissented on the merits.

Buchanan, armed with this inside information about the outcome, included a passage in his inaugural address about the future of slavery, stating that the issue was before the Supreme Court and that it would "be speedily and finally settled." He added, "To their decision, in common with all good citizens, I shall cheerfully submit, *whatever [the decision] may be.*" He, of course, well knew the outcome in advance.

The *Scott v. Sandford* decision came down in its promised form two days after Buchanan was inaugurated. In his famous "House Divided" speech a year later, Lincoln accused Taney, Buchanan, Stephen Douglas, and former president Franklin Pierce of a "preconcert" and a "common plan" culminating in the *Scott* opinions. As he so often was, Lincoln was dead-on here with respect to the first two.

What did the Supreme Court actually *decide* in the Dred Scott case? Generations of historians, most of whom were not lawyers, have scoured through the more than two hundred pages and nine separate opinions and have reached a wide variety of conclusions on this very basic question. While many points, both procedural and substantive, were discussed and even more precedent from Roman, English, and American law analyzed, two basic rulings emerge from a careful reading of the various opinions.

First, on a procedural matter, five justices (Taney, Wayne, Grier, Campbell, and Daniel) ruled on various grounds that African Americans whose ancestors had been slaves were not "citizens" within the meaning of the Constitution and thus were not able to sue as such in the federal courts. This meant that the Supreme Court lacked jurisdiction to decide the case. McLean and Curtis dissented on this issue while Nelson and Catron did not decide it. Thus four southern or border justices plus Pennsylvania's Grier made up the majority on this issue. Having thus held that the Court lacked jurisdiction to hear the case, the decision could have ended there. Indeed the actual judgment remanded the case to the lower court with a direction to dismiss it for lack of jurisdiction.

Second, on the critical issue of congressional power over slavery in the territories, four justices from southern or border states (Taney, Wayne, Catron, and Campbell)—joined again by Grier—expressly stated in their separate opinions that the Missouri Compromise was invalid, employing different reasoning to come to that conclusion. A fifth southern justice, Daniel of Virginia, strongly suggested that Congress lacked power to overturn a master's property right in his slave but rested his actual decision on the jurisdictional point only. Nelson's opinion did not reach the Missouri Compromise or congressional power issues. McLean and Curtis dissented on the citizenship issue and would have set Scott free as well as upholding the power of Congress to legislate on slavery in the territories.

What is remembered most today about the decision is Taney's opinion, especially its incendiary language on the African American citizenship point. In reviewing colonial and post-1787 state legislation in such areas as the prohibition of intermarriage between the races, barring of black travel and service in the militia, and other restrictions on blacks, Taney argued that these laws showed that the Constitution did not intend to award them the rights of citizenship under the Constitution. Going further, he stated that they showed that blacks were "considered [in 1787] as a subordinate and inferior class of beings who had been subjugated by the dominant race, and, whether emancipated or not, yet remained subject to their authority, and had no rights or privileges but such as those who held the power and the Government might choose to grant them." Further, blacks were considered as "beings of an inferior order . . . [with] no rights which the white man was bound to respect," had a "stigma of the deepest degradation . . . fixed upon the whole race," and were "an unhappy . . . race . . . separated from the white by indelible marks." In Taney's view "these historical facts" showed that there were "fixed opinions" about African Americans that were inconsistent with citizenship status under the Constitution. Moreover, Taney argued, these "facts"—on which he spent almost half of his opinion—showed that a ruling that African Americans were citizens entitled to exercise the privileges and immunities of United States citizenship would not have been acceptable to the South when its states all ratified the Constitution and the Bill of Rights because such a ruling would mean that African Americans had the rights, among others, to travel between states, to bear arms, and to engage in free speech, even presumably against slavery.

On the issue of congressional power over slavery in the territories, Taney's opinion held the Missouri Compromise "void" in prohibiting a slaveholding citizen of the United States "from owning and holding property of this kind" in the affected territories. He reasoned that the Constitution "recognizes the right of property of the master in a slave, and makes no distinction between that description of property and other property." As such it would be a violation of the Fifth Amendment guarantee of due process to deprive a master of his property right in a slave while protecting the rights of other citizens in different species of property. Taney also relied on the protection of the slave trade to 1808 in Article I, Section 9, and on the Fugitive Slave provision of Article IV, Section 2, to bolster his conclusion that "the right of property in a slave is distinctly and expressly affirmed in the Constitution."

Wisconsin Defies the Supreme Court: *Ableman v. Booth*

The reaction to the *Scott v. Sandford* decision was mixed. Abolitionist and Republican newspapers in cities such as New York and Chicago were outraged, while other papers across the country (not only in the South) called for the same deference to the decision that Buchanan had solicited in his inaugural address that same week. Republican reaction was politically clever. On the citizenship issue, Republicans largely avoided criticizing the *result,* since most (including Lincoln) did not favor social equality of the black and white races. On the issue of congressional power over slavery in the territories, the story was very different, since that ruling went to a key feature of the new party's philosophical foundations.

Republicans latched onto the citizenship ruling to marginalize the rest of the opinions' discussions of congressional power as nonbinding observations, called "dictum" by lawyers. This interpretation meant that future courts confronted with the issue would not be obliged to honor the views expressed in *Scott* on the scope of congressional power over slavery. As a matter of strict legal construction, this was correct. As we have seen above, five members of the Court ruled that the federal courts lacked jurisdiction over the case. As such there was no need to reach the merits and the issue of congressional power.

However, at least five members of the Court had also stated opinions that Congress lacked the power to ban slavery in the territories. The practical effect of the mixed ruling and nine opinions was thus to afford the Republicans legal grounds on which to question the binding nature of the *Scott* decision on the issue of congressional power and to keep the issue alive politically without seeming to defy the Supreme Court as an institution.

The slavery issue continued to boil after *Scott v. Sandford,* which settled nothing. First the Kansas Territory adopted a proslavery Constitution that required congressional ratification to become effective. That so-called Lecompton Constitution was ratified by the Senate but narrowly defeated in the House in 1858. Thus Kansas remained a territory; it was not admitted as a free state until 1861, after southern secessions. Second the year 1859 brought John Brown's famous raid on the federal arsenal at Harper's Ferry, Virginia, on October 16, leading to his very public trial, execution, and martyrdom, which was immortalized by Julia Ward Howe in her 1862 "Battle Hymn of the Republic." Third, winding its way before the New York courts was the pivotal case of *Lemmon v. The People,* which posed the question that most troubled northern abolitionists and that Republicans constantly raised: did *Scott v. Sandford* require northern states to permit southern slaveholders to bring their slaves into free states and keep them living there without thereby forfeiting their slave status? Ultimately the highest state court in New York ruled in 1860 that slaves became free if their owner voluntarily brought them into a free state, as had been the case with Scott himself.

Even before the *Scott* decision, northern opposition to the expansion of slavery had been hardening. *Ableman v. Booth* (1859) shows just how far that opposition had gone. In 1854 Joshua Glover, a fugitive slave, had been captured and jailed in Wisconsin. A mob led by a Milwaukee newspaper editor named Sherman Booth broke him out of jail and sent him to freedom in Canada. Booth was arrested by federal authorities and charged with aiding and abetting the escape of a fugitive slave in violation of the Fugitive Slave Law of 1850. Although held in *federal* custody, Booth applied for a writ of habeas corpus to Wisconsin *state* supreme court justice Abram Smith, who granted the writ and ordered Booth released, a judgment that was upheld by the entire Wisconsin Supreme Court on the ground that the Fugitive Slave Law was unconstitutional.

Booth was thereupon rearrested by federal authorities, indicted for the same offense, tried, convicted, and sentenced in federal court to one month in jail and a one-thousand-dollar fine in 1855. He thereupon appealed by petition to the Wisconsin Supreme Court, not to the Supreme Court of the United States, to which a proper appeal would have been directed. Undeterred by these legal niceties, the Wisconsin Supreme Court again ordered Booth released in February 1855. And then the defiance really started. The Wisconsin court refused to release the record or enter an appealable order so as to frustrate review by the Supreme Court of the United States, which did not get the case until March 1857, ironically on the same day as its *Scott* decision. Before the Supreme Court, following in the earlier shoes of Georgia in the Cherokee cases, Wisconsin did not even bother to appear to defend its judgment.

The Supreme Court took two years to render its unanimous judgment reversing the Wisconsin Supreme Court's rulings in both the first and second actions against Booth. In an opinion that Chief Justice Hughes later termed "the crown of [Taney's] legal career," Taney wrote that attempts by a state court to discharge a federal prisoner and to set aside a federal judgment based on violations of federal law are "new in the jurisprudence of the United States," and "would subvert the very foundations of this Government." In a decision still read by every law student today in classes on federal court jurisdiction, Taney held that the federal courts had exclusive jurisdiction in such cases, for to permit state court intervention would "make the superior and appellate tribunal the inferior and subordinate one." Finally, in the next to last paragraph of the opinion, Taney noted that while "unnecessary to discuss these questions . . . they have been decided by the state court," and therefore "it is proper to say that, in the judgment of this court . . . the fugitive slave law is, in all of its provisions, fully authorized by the Constitution of the United States." The reaction to *Ableman* in Wisconsin was outrage and further defiance. The Wisconsin legislature termed the decision an "arbitrary act of power" and judicial "despotism," and called for "positive defiance" by the states, into whose ranks Wisconsin itself had only been recently admitted, in 1848.

In both *Scott v. Sandford* and *Abelmán v. Booth,* the Taney Court attempted to use the Supreme Court to settle once and for all critical national issues relating to slavery in the territories and the rights of slaveholders to pursue and capture runaway slaves. The issues, however, were at their core political ones, and the Supreme Court, like the proverbial King Canute, could not resolve them by ordering the tide of abolitionism to stop. Indeed, because of his Court's attempt to impose a national judicial solution to the problem of slavery, Taney's opinion was prophetic—"the very foundations of this Government" were "subvert[ed]."

Three

Making the Nation Safe for Commerce

The Supreme Court and Economic Development

By 1860 slavery had split the United States economically. The free states were the locus of America's manufacturing and mercantile interests. The slave states by contrast were primarily agricultural in their economy. And the economic division of North and South was accelerating year by year.

Two Nations Divisible: The United States in 1860

In 1860 the industrial North, with large urban populations, had only 40 percent of its citizens engaged in agriculture, compared to 68 percent in 1800. In the South the percentage engaged in agriculture actually increased from 82 percent in 1800 to 84 percent in 1860. Those engaged in manufacturing or mercantile interests also varied dramatically in the free and slave states. With 42 percent of the nation's population in 1860, the South had only 16 percent of its manufacturing capacity—down from 20 percent in 1840.

Popular philosophy and political campaigning sharpened these regional economic differences. The "Cotton Kingdom" saw itself as superior morally and culturally to northern merchants and their philosophy of "free labor," summarized by Lincoln, who explained how poor men could progress economically through their own hard work. "The man who labored for another last year, this year labors for himself, and next year he will hire others to labor for him."

Southern planters looked with disdain on nonagricultural labor. They adopted Jefferson's harsh views, expressed in his *Notes on the State of Virginia,* written in the early 1780s. "Those who labor in the earth are the chosen people of God, if ever he had a chosen people, whose breasts he has made his particular deposit for substantial and genuine virtue." City dwellers were dismissed by Jefferson. He opined that "the mobs of great cities add just so much to the support of pure government, as sores do to the strength of the human body." And the "great cities" were in the industrial North, paradoxically the base of the Democratic Party, whose founders were Jefferson and Andrew Jackson. New York had a population of one million by 1860, followed by Philadelphia and Boston and trailed by

Chicago, with a population of one hundred thousand, which would grow to one million by 1890. In the South the largest city in 1860 was New Orleans, with a population a little over one hundred thousand.

Jefferson's conclusion had been that "while we have land to labor then, let us never wish to see our citizens occupied at a work-bench, or twirling a distaff." Closer to the Civil War, a Texas senator would echo this view, remarking, "We are an agricultural people. . . . We have no cities—we don't want them. . . . We want no manufactures: we desire no trading, no mechanical or manufacturing classes."

These regional economic differences led to dramatic and sapping fights over the divisive political issue of the protective tariff, the keystone of the Hamiltonian view of building America's mercantile and manufacturing capacity. In the Hamiltonian view, such tariffs were necessary to build and protect native industry from foreign competition until it became strong enough to survive on its own. But the South opposed protective tariffs; its agricultural economy depended on exports, and England was the great outlet for southern cotton. Protective tariffs led to retaliation, with tariffs imposed by foreign countries on southern exports. Indeed some writers, including such diverse figures as Karl Marx and Charles Dickens, wrote at the time that the Civil War was really about tariffs, not about freeing the slaves.

The tariff issue first flamed into near war in 1828, with the enactment of what became known in the South as "The Tariff of Abominations." The political fallout produced the South's intellectual defense of its states' rights philosophy in John C. Calhoun's *South Carolina Exposition and Protest,* augmented by his Fort Hill Address in 1831. Calhoun, who was Andrew Jackson's vice president, was a nationalist but one who believed that the rights of substantial minority interests needed to be protected by the national government. He evolved the concept of "concurrent majorities" whose assent was necessary for the legitimate rule of an absolute numerical majority.

When Calhoun's logic failed to persuade Congress, and the tariff was amended in 1832 to assist northern industrial interests, Calhoun's home state of South Carolina (which later became the first state to secede from the Union) called a convention. That convention passed the Ordinance of Nullification on November 24, 1832, declaring the 1828 and 1832 tariffs unconstitutional and prohibiting collection of the tariff duties within the state. Calhoun resigned as vice president, and sabers were rattled, only to be resheathed when President Jackson threatened to send in federal troops and hang for treason those who interfered with the collection of tariff duties. Finally the "Great Compromiser," Senator Henry Clay of Kentucky, proposed a compromise tariff that ended the immediate threat of armed conflict.

Only with the one-term presidency of James Knox Polk was the South successful in turning back the protective tariff, from 1846 to the Panic of 1857. One of Polk's self-proclaimed four "great measures" was the Walker Tariff of 1846, which passed the Senate by one vote, cast by Vice President George Dallas of Pennsylvania to break a tie. After the Civil War, the tariff returned with a vengeance, becoming a permanent part of the Republican Party platform into the twentieth century and a litmus test for Republican candidates on the national level. The South's great aversion to protective tariffs is perhaps most aptly captured by a provision in the Constitution of the Confederate States of America explicitly banning imposition of tariff duties to assist any industry.

Law Follows Economics: The Evolution of Tort and Contract Theories in the Nineteenth Century

From the beginning of the nineteenth century through the end of the Civil War, great changes occurred in the law of contract and tort in the United States, particularly in the industrial and mercantile North. Led by the highest courts in the manufacturing states of Massachusetts, New York, and Pennsylvania, contract law evolved from a focus on the fairness of an exchange to an examination of the question of mutual agreement. In the words of *McFarland v. Newman* (1839), the leading Pennsylvania case that rejected it, the former rule had been that "a sound article is warranted by a sound price." This doctrine had protected the consumer by requiring delivery of an article whose quality was commensurate with the price paid for it. In its place emerged a rule that upheld contracts where there was *some* value exchanged in a transaction to which there was mutual agreement. The protection of the courts was transferred from the buyer to the seller, and the doctrine of caveat emptor took a prominent role.

What led to this fundamental change in focus? As Pennsylvania's notable chief justice John Bannister Gibson put it in *McFarland,* the policy of the old rule was "impracticable, because the operations of commerce are such as to require that the rules for its regulation admit of as few occasions for reclamation as possible." Indeed, in his view the old rule "would put a stop to commerce itself in driving everyone out of it by the terror of endless litigation" over the equivalency of the values exchanged. In reversing a jury verdict in favor of the swindled buyer of a sick horse, Gibson extended the principles established in New York in *Seixas & Sexias v. Woods* (1804) to protect innocent middlemen from litigation seeking to upset commercial transactions that the middlemen had entered into or facilitated. In the 1804 case, buyers of what was thought to be a valuable type of wood sold to them as such by an intermediary who had not inspected the wood when he took possession of it from the original seller, were denied recovery from the middleman defendant. Key to this disposition was the finding that "the defendant was equally ignorant with the plaintiffs." Since neither party had inspected the wood, the loss was allocated to the buyer under the principle of caveat emptor.

Tort law experienced even more radical changes during the same period. Previously, where a party was injured at work, his employer was strictly liable for those injuries in many circumstances. To protect nascent industries from the costs of such suits by their injured workers, tort law shifted from strict liability to negligence theories. First, a party became answerable in tort for damages only if it were negligent. Second, a number of defenses became available to the employer even if it were negligent. These included the doctrines of contributory negligence, assumption of the risk, and the fellow-servant rule. Under the first defense, an employee was denied any recovery if he were found responsible in any way, even 1 percent, for contributing to the forces that led to the accident. Assumption of the risk exculpated the employer from any liability for an injury that was a natural and ordinary risk of the employee's job. The fellow-servant rule exonerated an employer from liability if the accident was caused to one employee by the actions of another employee. In such a case the "fellow servant" (the responsible employee) was solely liable to the injured employee despite the fact that both were legally the agents of their common employer.

Chief Justice Lemuel Shaw of Massachusetts, one of the leading judicial crafters of the new tort law of this period, applied the assumption of the risk and the fellow-servant doctrines to deny tort recovery to an injured railroad engineer in the landmark and often-followed case of *Farwell v. The Boston & Worcester RR. Co.* (1842). He explained the policy animating the fellow-servant doctrine as follows:

> Where several persons are employed in the conduct of one common enterprise or undertaking, and the safety of each depends much on the care and skill with which each other shall perform his appropriate duty, each is an observer of the conduct of the others, can give notice of any misconduct, incapacity or neglect of duty, and leave the service, if the common employer will not take such precautions, and employ such agents as the safety of the whole party may require. By these means the safety of each will be much more effectually secured, than could be done by a resort to the common employer for indemnity in case of loss by the negligence of each other. Regarding it in this light, it is the ordinary case of one sustaining an injury in the course of his own employment, in which he must bear the loss himself, or seek his remedy, if he have any, against the actual wrong-doer.

Aptly described by an 1883 legal commentator as "a species of *protective tariff* for the encouragement of infant railroad industries," the fellow-servant rule became the law in many American states and remained the standard until near the end of the nineteenth century.

By 1900 the various tort-law doctrines described here contributed to denying compensation to an estimated two million workers injured every year on the job. Finally, to cap off these restrictions against employees successfully suing their employers, a rule emerged in some states, such as Massachusetts, prohibiting any wrongful death suits at all, leading to the actuarial conclusion that it was better to kill a worker than to injure him. And workers were killed; nationally an estimated thirty-five thousand died on the job each year during this period of industrial expansion.

Yet another judicial insulation of the emerging corporate enterprise came from narrow interpretations of the proximate cause requirement in tort cases for property and other damages, under which a defendant could only be held liable in damages for injuries directly traceable to its negligence, as opposed to those deemed too remote to be its responsibility. An extreme example of application of this doctrine to protect a corporation from paying the bill for its own negligence comes from the New York case of *Ryan v. New York Central RR. Co.* (1866). There, poor Mr. Ryan had the misfortune to live in Syracuse next door to a railroad shed 130 feet from his property. The shed was set on fire accidentally by the railroad's own negligence ("the careless management . . . of one of its engines"), and the fire spread to Ryan's house, completely destroying it. Ryan sued the railroad and lost when New York's highest court ruled that his injury was too remote, although his property was less than half a football field away from the railroad. Indeed, "to sustain such a claim as the present would subject to a liability against which no prudence could guard, and to meet which no private fortune would be adequate." What then ought to have been done to protect Mr. Ryan? He should have bought insurance! "In a commercial country, each man, by insurance against hazards, is enabled to obtain a reasonable security against loss. To neglect such precaution, and to call upon his neighbor, on whose premises a fire originated, to indemnify him instead, would be to award a punishment quite beyond the offense committed."

Courts also prohibited property owners from using common-law doctrines to impede the development of commerce. In 1856 for example, the Pennsylvania Supreme Court in *Grey v. Ohio & Pennsylvania RR. Co.* ruled that a farmer could not employ the common law doctrine of nuisance to stop the construction of a railroad near his property.

While southern states followed some of these legal innovations in contract and tort, they rejected others because of slavery. Two notable examples of how the slave-based agricultural economy of the southern states affected legal developments in those states come from the rejection of the mutual-agreement model of contract in slave sales and the rejection of the fellow-servant rule in many southern slave states.

A slave was a southern farmer's largest "asset." To purchase one was to invest capital in "property" that must be sound for the crops to be picked and the agricultural enterprise to flourish. Some states, such as the civil code state of Louisiana, regulated slave sales by statute, permitting such sales to be set aside if the slave suffered from various disabilities, such as a propensity to run away. Others—particularly in the lower South, where slavery was most prevalent—found by judicial decision implied warranties in slave sales, under which the seller was deemed to have warranted the sold slave's fitness for the purchaser's business.

The fellow-servant rule met similar opposition. Although adopted early in slave-heavy South Carolina, most states in the lower South rejected it. Why? This was traceable to the practice of slave owners often hiring their slaves out to businesses. If someone was injured by the slave's actions, the master/owner would have been liable to the injured party under the fellow-servant doctrine, making it unacceptable.

The Marshall Court and the Protection of Emerging Mercantile and Corporate Interests

From the early days of John Marshall's service as chief justice, the Supreme Court strained to protect America's emerging mercantile interests, playing an important role in making the law of commerce more certain and predictable. As we have already seen, the early case of *Fletcher v. Peck* (1810) established federal legal protections for sellers, insulating their transactions from being set aside on claims of fraud or other wrongdoing that occurred prior to their acquisition of the property they later sold to others.

In reaching the conclusion that the Georgia law rescinding the sale of the Yazoo lands by the prior corrupt legislature was invalid, the Court stretched the law to find that the original Georgia legislation was akin to a contract. Moreover the Supreme Court was unsure as to the *legal* basis for its ruling, concluding only that Georgia was "restrained, either by general principles which are common to our free institutions, or by the particular provisions of the constitution of the United States."

There was no doubt, however, about the *factual* basis for the ruling. It rested on the need to facilitate commerce. In the words of Chief Justice Marshall, "All titles would be insecure, and the intercourse between man and man would be very seriously obstructed, if this principle be overturned."

The "principle" at issue was what we now know as the bona fide purchaser for value doctrine. Peck, the seller of the land whose title was in question in the Supreme Court, had acquired the land from a seller who had purchased it from the State of Georgia under an act of its legislature that Peck allegedly did not know was corrupt. To the Court, Peck was a bona fide purchaser for value entitled to federal legal protection. "He has paid his money for a title good at law, he is innocent, whatever may be the guilt of others, and equity will not subject him to the penalties attached to that guilt." Notably the rule enunciated by Marshall fit nicely into the stream of jurisprudence that was developing at the time to protect contractual sales from being set aside. He announced that "If there be any concealed defect, arising from the conduct of those who had held the property long before he acquired it, of which he had no notice, that concealed defect cannot be set up against him."

Fletcher v. Peck was a contrived case, advanced on both sides by Hamiltonians who wished to establish federal legal protections for land speculators. Peck's counsel were luminaries from New England's mercantile interests, including both future president John Quincy Adams in the original appeal and Joseph Story thereafter. Story was the intellectual father of American commercial law, serving on the Supreme Court from 1811, when he was only thirty-two, until 1845, during which time he wrote 268 majority opinions for the Court. He also wrote twelve commentaries on the law, including the three-volume *Commentaries on the Constitution of the United States,* and was the Dane Professor of Law at Harvard Law School, which he built from 1 student in 1828 to 156 students from twenty-one states in 1844, the year before he died.

Seven years after *Fletcher v. Peck,* the Supreme Court decided *Laidlaw v. Organ* (1817), a case that reinforced the growing legal trend to bring finality to sales even where claims of inequitable conduct were made. There the validity of the sale of "one hundred and eleven hogsheads of tobacco" was at issue because the sale was made at a price the buyer knew to be too low because of his possession of what we would today call inside information. The buyer knew that the War of 1812 had just ended. This was an important fact affecting the price of tobacco because the British had imposed a naval blockade on the ports out of which tobacco was shipped, thereby depressing the price of the commodity, whose markets had thus been limited. The seller did not know the war had ended since that fact was generally unknown in an era bereft of radio, television, telephone, and other instant means of communication.

In an opinion by Chief Justice Marshall, the Supreme Court described the issue before it as "whether the intelligence of extrinsic circumstances, which might influence the price of the commodity, and which was exclusively within the knowledge of the vendee, ought to have been communicated by him to the vendor?" The Court ruled it need not have been. "The court is of the opinion that he was not bound to communicate it." Why? "It would be difficult to circumscribe the contrary doctrine within proper limits, where the means of intelligence are equally accessible to both parties."

Laidlaw thus rested its decision squarely on the difficulty of establishing limits if a rule of disclosure were imposed. This approach benefits mercantile interests since a lack of clarity endangers commerce and the finality of sales. Commerce prefers bright-line rules, and the Supreme Court partially granted the requested relief. It was only partial, however, since the Court required a trial to determine if "any imposition was practiced by the vendee upon the vendor," since "each party must take care not to do or say any thing tending to impose upon the other." This left the vendor free to claim more than simple nondisclosure by the vendee, in an attempt to prove a case of fraud.

Trustees of Dartmouth College v. Woodward (1819) was the Supreme Court's next, and most significant, foray into the Contracts Clause of the Constitution and the protections it accorded to the contracting parties. It also put the Court in the forefront of the law of corporations, particularly in the separate opinion of Justice Story.

The *Dartmouth College* case had its factual roots in a political turf war in New Hampshire between the out-of-power Federalists and the new Jeffersonian Republican Party. Republicans took control of the legislature and won the election for governor in 1816. At that time Federalists controlled the college, but John Wheelock, the son of the founder, had become estranged from the trustee majority both politically and religiously. Dartmouth was founded under a British royal charter granted to Eleazer Wheelock, a preacher of the First Great Awakening, in 1769. Wheelock meant the college to be an instrument of the Lord to train missionaries to attend to the spiritual needs of the Native American population. The charter gave him broad powers, including the right to name his successor, and established a board of trustees of twelve, with the power to fill all vacancies in their ranks.

John took over from his father on Eleazer's death in 1779. By 1811 a religious split had occurred. John remained a Presbyterian while the local affiliated church turned to the Congregationalist faith. John also became a Republican, and that party enacted legislation in 1816 expanding the board of trustees to twenty-five, making four politicians ex officio members of the board in the interim, and permitting all vacancies to be filled by the governor and council of New Hampshire. This was resisted by the "Octagon," eight of the original twelve trustees, of whom five were lawyers.

Suing the treasurer of Dartmouth to regain possession of the college records and seal, the Octagon trustees, with the advice of Justice Story, framed the state court case to obtain eventual Supreme Court review of the federal issue relating to the Contracts Clause. They contended that the original royal charter granted fifty years earlier was a contract that could not be abridged by the Republican legislature. The New Hampshire court disagreed, finding that the charter was a public contract that could be regulated by the state in the public interest, unlike a private contract, which was protected from infringement by the government.

By a vote of five to one, the Supreme Court sided with the Federalists, accepting the impassioned pleas of their advocates, including Daniel Webster. There were two major opinions in the *Dartmouth College* case. Marshall's opinion of the Court held that the royal charter was a contract protected by the Constitution and that the college was a private eleemosynary corporation whose charter could not be changed by legislative action. Ruling that "the consideration for which they [the donors] stipulated, is the perpetual application of the fund to its object, *in the mode prescribed by themselves,*" the Supreme Court held that the state legislation was void because "the whole power of governing the College is transferred from Trustees, appointed according to the will of the founder, expressed in the charter, to the Executive of New Hampshire. . . . The will of the state is substituted for the will of the donors in every essential operation of the College." Such structural changes were void, under the Contracts Clause, which was "introduced to give *stability to contracts,*" because the changes were "subversive of that contract on the faith of which their property was given."

Story's concurring opinion added corporate law explicitly to the mix, beginning with an explanation that the proper resolution of the case required "an inquiry into the nature, rights and duties of aggregate corporations at common law." After a lengthy examination of that subject, he too concluded that Dartmouth was "a private eleemosynary institution" whose charter was protected by the Constitution. Brushing aside a challenge to the adequacy of the consideration under the charter contract, he observed that "it matters not how trifling the consideration may be—a pepper-corn is as good as a thousand dollars." Most significantly Story concluded that legislatures could protect themselves from perpetual powers being exercised by corporations without governmental restraint only by expressly reserving the power to do so in their grant of the original corporate charter.

The *Dartmouth College* case fueled an explosive growth of corporations in the next decade by assuring venture capitalists that their funds would not be diverted from their intended purposes. By 1830, in New England alone, some nineteen hundred business corporations were formed, of which approximately 30 percent were manufacturing or mining ventures. Assuring "stability to contracts" through the protections of the Contracts Clause of the Constitution was one of the factors that permitted the growth of the American industrial corporation in the early nineteenth century.

The Marshall Court also acted to protect commercial interests by announcing an expansive definition of Article I, Section 8, of the Constitution, which conferred power on Congress, among a long list of other subjects, "to regulate Commerce . . . among the several States." The meaning of these words came before the Court in the pivotal case of *Gibbons v. Ogden* (1824), which construed each word broadly, thereby facilitating the promulgation of uniform rules of commerce by the federal government in the years ahead.

Gibbons was recognized by all involved to be an important case. Indeed the Supreme Court allowed the oral arguments to extend over five days. The case involved a challenge to a New York law that granted the Fulton interests a monopoly on steamboat travel in the navigable waters of New York State and the coastal waterways between New York and New Jersey. Gibbons, represented by the ubiquitous Daniel Webster, had a coastal waterways license to operate a service from Elizabethtown, New Jersey, to Manhattan. That license came from Congress under the Coastal Licensing Act of 1793. Gibbons's rights to operate under this license despite the prohibitions of the New York statute against any competition with the Fulton interests raised high stakes, since the New York law was enforced in the mode of modern drug laws by authorizing the seizure of vessels that operated outside its authority.

Marshall's opinion for a unanimous Court began by construing each of the words of the Commerce Clause. "Regulate" meant "to prescribe the rule by which commerce is to be governed." This established Congress as supreme in this commercial sphere, thereby assuring commercial interests that uniform national laws would govern their affairs in interstate trade where Congress chose to exercise its power.

"Commerce" was similarly construed. It was not limited to mere "traffic" or to "buying and selling, or the interchange of commodities"; instead "Commerce" was meant to describe "the commercial intercourse between nations, and parts of nations, in all its branches." As such it clearly embraced navigation, the subject in dispute in the case.

Finally "among the several States" meant "intermingled with," and thus congressional power "cannot stop at the external boundary line of each State, but may be introduced into the interior." Nevertheless "the completely internal commerce of a State . . . may be considered as reserved for the State itself."

Left for decision after these definitions was the great question: was the power of Congress to regulate commerce exclusive or was there some area in which the states could concurrently regulate some aspects of commerce? Marshall found "great force" in Webster's argument for exclusivity, stating in dictum that "the Court is not satisfied that it has been refuted." But Marshall ducked the issue in the end by deciding that the New York law was void insofar as it violated the rights granted by Congress under the coastal license. As such the "collision" between the federal and state laws required that "the acts of New York must yield to the law of Congress, and the decision sustaining the privilege they confer against a right given by a law of the Union must be erroneous."

Gibbons v. Ogden set the stage for future regulation of all spheres of commerce by the federal government. By the time of Franklin Delano Roosevelt's New Deal, that power would be interpreted in *Wickard v. Filburn* (1942) to extend to the regulation of the production of crops grown on and consumed by farmers on their own acreage for their own family's sustenance.

The Taney Court Attacks Monopoly

When John Marshall died in July 1835, President Andrew Jackson was at the end of his second term. His appointment of Roger Taney, one of his former cabinet officials, to succeed Marshall as chief justice brought a fifth Jacksonian Democrat to the Supreme Court, which then had seven members. This was a legal sea change. The Marshall Federalist era was over, and the Jacksonians were in control of the Court.

America in 1837 was a nation eagerly expanding westward. Jackson of Tennessee was the seventh president. He was the first "western" president and the first not to have been from either Virginia or Massachusetts. At the end of his second term, two new states (Arkansas and Michigan) were added to the nation, and five more joined by 1850, from Florida on the east coast to California on the west, with Texas, Iowa, and Wisconsin in between.

Jackson was a self-made man who gained fame as a military hero. He was also a businessman and lawyer who dabbled in speculative land sales and a slaveholder who seemed oblivious to the moral issues raised by the peculiar institution. His supporters were what he called in his Bank Veto Message "the humble members of society—the farmers, mechanics, and laborers." They were not capitalists, industrialists, or large-scale merchants. In business they were small businessmen who ran the local shops in smaller towns and villages. They opposed protective tariffs and generally aligned with the South against the mercantile Northeast. Their great foe, however, was monopoly power, and they cheered Jackson's attack on Nicholas Biddle of Philadelphia and his Bank of the United States from this vantage point, agreeing with Jackson that the bank was owned by "Eastern and foreign stockholders" who were "rich and powerful."

Monopoly power was a bone of contention from early in the republic. Jefferson and Madison debated whether the Bill of Rights should include a prohibition against monopolies, with Madison prevailing on the theory that monopolies were a spur to "ingenious discoveries." But the issue has never died, and the Supreme Court over the years has regularly confronted issues raised by monopoly power. *Gibbons v. Ogden,* for example, was a case in point, since it broke the Fulton steamboat monopoly by voiding the New York law that established it.

The monopoly issue emerged again in 1837 in two cases decided by the new Taney Court. The first case was *Charles River Bridge v. Warren Bridge* (1837), the opinion on which Taney's high ranking by legal historians principally rests. The case posed a fundamental constitutional issue that the Marshall Court seemed already to have decided. That issue was the extent to which a corporate charter was protected by the Contracts Clause. The charter at issue traced back to a 1640 grant to Harvard College to run a ferry service across the Charles River. In 1785 the Massachusetts legislature granted a charter for a bridge to replace the ferry, granting compensation from the bridge profits to compensate Harvard, whose charter still ran. The new 1785 charter granted the right to build and operate a toll bridge for forty years, with the bridge to revert to the state after that time. Given the growth in Boston in the first quarter of the nineteenth century, four more bridges were chartered by 1820, and the Charles River Bridge charter was extended thirty years to run until 1855 as compensation for the charter of one of these bridges.

By the 1820s the franchise of the Charles River Bridge had significant value. Its stock had tripled in value; it was collecting $20,000 in annual income; and its property was valued at $280,000. And then the bottom fell out for the investors. After five years of lobbying on the issue by merchants who wanted to increase traffic to their shops, the Massachusetts legislature granted a new bridge charter in 1828 to build the Warren Bridge close enough to the Charles River Bridge to divert all of its traffic because the new bridge was authorized to collect tolls only until its costs and 5 percent interest were repaid and to be free thereafter, reverting to state ownership. The only compensation to the Charles River Bridge was to make the Warren Bridge pay half of the required annual annuity to Harvard.

Litigation soon broke out, with the Charles River Bridge claiming that its contract rights had been impaired by the 1828 charter, which rendered its charter rights worthless. These issues, pitting monopoly power and contract rights against the needs of an expanding economy and the public interest, split every court that was called to declare a winner among these competing interests. The Massachusetts Supreme Court split evenly on the issues, which were portrayed by the contending counsel as a battle between the workers and tradesmen and the monopolist bridge. The Supreme Court of the United States was so divided when the case was first argued that the case was put off and not reargued for several years, the length of the delay partially attributable to changes in the Court. In that interval President Jackson had appointed three new justices.

Ultimately the Supreme Court ruled, in a four-to-three decision, that the Warren Bridge Charter was valid and did not impair the charter of the Charles River Bridge. The four majority justices, led by Taney, were all Jacksonians. Two of the three dissenters, led by Story, were old-style Republicans or Federalists.

Story's dissent invoked *Fletcher v. Peck* and *Dartmouth College* and argued that public interest and convenience were best served by rewarding those who undertook the difficult task of building new and valuable public conveniences such as the first bridge in an area. Ridiculing the idea that this was a case of monopoly, Story felt that the ruling "would arrest all public improvements, founded on private capital and enterprise." Why? "No man will hazard his capital in any enterprise, in which, if there be a loss, it must be borne exclusively by himself; and if there be a success, he has not the slightest security of enjoying the rewards of that success, for a single moment." Without a firm and enforceable pledge by the government that their profits will be secure, "every stockholder in every public enterprise of this sort, throughout the whole country" will be "alarm[ed]." Story concluded with a long hypothetical question, the essence of which was who would have invested in the Charles River Bridge if this legal outcome had been foreseeable? "Is there a man living, of ordinary discretion or prudence, who would have accepted such a charter, upon such terms? I fearlessly answer, no."

Taney and the Jacksonian majority saw the issue quite differently. While recognizing that "the rights of private property are sacredly guarded, we must not forget, that the community also have rights, and that the happiness and well-being of every citizen depends on their faithful preservation." To balance these rights, the law prescribes certain rules of construction regarding the terms of franchises imbued with a public interest. Under those rules "any ambiguity in the terms of the contract, must operate against the adventurers, and in favor of the public."

Here the charter did not contain a pledge that no other bridge would be built. To imply such a term would violate the rights of the community. How? "If this court should establish the principles now contended for, what is to become of the numerous railroads established on the same line of travel with turnpike companies; and which rendered the franchises of the turnpike corporations of no value? Let it once be understood, that such charters carry with them these implied contracts . . . ; and you will soon find the old turnpike corporations awakening from their sleep, and calling upon this court to *put down* the improvements which have taken their place." All this would result in the nation, which is "free, active, and enterprising, continually advancing in numbers and wealth," being "thrown back to the improvements of the last century, and obliged to stand still."

The image of the slumbering, slothful giant "putting down" new forms of transportation is an archetypical Jacksonian phrase, meant to resonate with the farmers and mechanics whose beloved pets or farm animals too often had to be dispatched against their owners' deepest instincts and with the deepest sense of loss and tragedy.

Charles River Bridge was the Court's break from the Marshall era's polestar interpretation of the Contracts Clause to protect the "adventurers." In its place a more subtle and nuanced view emerged, recognizing other interests worthy of protection, including those of the general public and Jackson's "farmers, mechanics, and laborers." It was an approach best suited for a growing economy and a nation of diverse interests.

The second great commercial law decision in Taney's first year as chief justice came in *Briscoe v. Bank of Kentucky* (1837). *Briscoe* presented the question whether the issuance of negotiable notes by the Bank of Kentucky, whose stock was completely owned by the state, violated the prohibition of Article I, Section 10, of the Constitution: "No State shall . . . coin Money; *emit Bills of Credit;* make any Thing but gold or silver Coin a Tender in Payment of Debts."

This highly technical question tended to mask the critical issues involved in the case. As we have seen in our prior discussion of Jackson's 1832 veto of the recharter of the Bank of the United States, Jacksonians saw the national bank as a symbol of both privilege and monopoly. Since the bank's charter ran to 1836, Jackson took additional steps before then, with the avowed intention to "kill" the bank even before its charter naturally expired. In 1833 he ordered the removal of federal deposits from the bank, placing them into favored or "pet" state banks that supported him. In 1836, as the bank's charter expired, the Deposit Act mandated that federal surplus revenues be lent to states. These actions expanded the currency supply; the bank, favoring creditors, had contracted it, since no creditor (but every debtor) wanted loans repaid in depreciated currency.

Jackson's actions helped fuel speculation in land sales in the West, with state banks using their fresh federal deposits to fund speculative loans for real estate.

The Deposit Act aggravated this, since the states began to use the funds made available by the federal government to finance new internal improvements. To stop this speculation and rampant spending, Jackson invoked his Specie Circular in July 1836, requiring federal land sales to be paid for in gold or silver, and he vetoed congressional attempts to override his actions in March 1837.

To further combat speculation, Congress recalled the federal deposits from state banks. This action, combined with the collapse of the cotton market and an English crisis that led to the calling of American loans, contracted the currency supply and resulted in American banks stopping payments in gold and silver in May 1837. Under Jackson's successor, Martin Van Buren of New York, the Specie Circular was suspended in May 1838 to bring some stability to this troubled economic scene, which became known as the Panic of 1837.

It was against this economic backdrop that the *Briscoe* case was decided in 1837. The Court, in a majority opinion by the Jacksonian justice McLean (who would twenty years later be a dissenter in the Dred Scott case), ruled that the Constitution had not been violated. This was because its reference to "Bills of Credit" only embraced instruments that were "issued by a state, on the faith of the state, and [are] designed to circulate as money." These notes were issued by the bank, on its credit, not that of the state. McLean reasoned that, under any other interpretation of the clause, "all banks incorporated by a state are unconstitutional." Silently invoking the Jacksonian opposition to centralized national banking controlled by a privileged few for the benefit of the mercantile class, McLean observed that such a result would be "startling, as it strikes a fatal blow against state banks; which have a capital of near $400,000,000, and which *supply almost the entire circulating medium of the country.*" Thus ruling against the state bank would deflate the currency, harm debtors, and restore the financial control of the country to the now-dying Bank of the United States, with its limited currency and antidebtor fiscal policy.

Only Justice Story dissented, in a wild opinion that invoked the ghosts of both the founders and the lately departed chief justice Marshall ("a name never to be pronounced without reverence"; "Had he been living, he would have spoken in the joint names of both of us").

Story also saw the vast fiscal policy implications of the decision. He invoked Madison's explanation of the bills of credit clause in Federalist 44, where Madison spoke of "the pestilent effects of paper money." Story also condemned the current practice of what he twice referred to as "floods" of paper money being issued by states to circulate as currency. Story was a hard-money man; he invoked the founders' view that "whatever paper currency is not directly and immediately, at the mere will of the holder, redeemable in gold and silver, is, and for ever must be liable to constant depreciation." Harking back to the experience of the revolutionary state governments invoked by Madison, Story concluded that "the history of such a currency constituted the darkest pages in the American annals, and had been written in the ruin of thousands, who had staked their property upon the public faith; always freely given, and but too often grossly violated."

Briscoe was a fight over currency reform, with the Supreme Court functioning as a sort of judicial Federal Reserve System making monetary policy for the country. It continued a fight between those favoring the established mercantile and creditor classes against those who championed the rights of the entrepreneur, the upwardly mobile, the small businessman, and debtors across the country, but particularly in the expanding West. It was a fight that would continue, not only with the Greenbacks and the Populists of the nineteenth century, but until today and into all our tomorrows as well.

The Triumph of Commerce

While opposed to monopoly power, the Taney Court was sympathetic to commercial interests and increasingly took steps to facilitate interstate trade. In this area the Court's nationalistic focus paralleled its efforts in the other areas we have surveyed, including an unsuccessful and ill-advised effort to impose by judicial mandate a binding national solution on the issue of slavery in the territories.

Bank of Augusta v. Earle (1839) provides a good early example of the Taney Court's efforts to facilitate commerce among the several states, in that case by protecting "foreign" corporations that were conducting business outside their state of incorporation. The opinion actually covered three cases, raising the same issue—whether a bank incorporated in one state could transact business in another without the express permission of the second state. When obligors on bills of exchange refused to pay, claiming that the banks that bought their debts were not authorized to do business in their states, the ability of "foreign" corporations to transact such business was squarely presented to the Supreme Court, after the circuit court ruled that they were not. That decision, in the words of Justice Story in a July 1838 letter to Charles Sumner, had "frightened half of the lawyers and all the corporations of the country out of all of their proprieties."

Taney's opinion reversed the circuit court and held that the bank was authorized to transact out-of-state business under the law of comity of nations, which recognized that foreign entities could contract in other jurisdictions to facilitate international trade. Taney first noted that although the Bank of Augusta, chartered by the State of Georgia, had "no legal existence" outside of Georgia, it was nevertheless permitted under principles of comity to make contracts in other states. Calling upon "usages of commerce and trade" in the United States, he noted that banks were in fact transacting business regularly in other states and that the principles of comity of nations applied even more forcefully to transactions among the several states because they were bound so "closely together" in an "intimate union" by "deep and vital interests."

The only exception to this principle of comity was where the acts of foreign corporations violated some specific state policy expressed in its laws. Reviewing

Alabama law, Taney found no such policy expressed, even though that state had only chartered seven banks, of which it owned all the stock of five, and 40 percent of the stock of the other two.

Taney concluded by stating that where state policy was offended by foreign corporations transacting business within their borders, federal courts were bound to recognize that policy. But, leaving some doubt even as to that situation, he added that the Court was not deciding "whether there may not be some rights under the Constitution of the United States, which a corporation might claim under peculiar circumstances, in a state other than that in which it was chartered."

In the only dissent, Justice McKinley, who had written the opinion of the circuit court, complained that his home state of Alabama had been "invaded" by the Georgia bank, and that the Court's opinion was conferring "national power" on states such as Georgia, permitting them to bind all of the states to recognize the corporate charters they alone had granted.

Following the *Bank of Augusta* decision, Justice Story wrote to Chief Justice Taney, with whom he had disagreed so violently only two years before in the *Charles River Bridge* and *Briscoe* cases, congratulating him on his opinion. In Story's view the opinion did "great honor" both to Taney and to the Court. Why? The decision permitted corporations freely to do business across the nation, binding it together commercially. Absent specific laws prohibiting them from doing so, corporations were now legally free to seek markets in every state, to the benefit of consumers everywhere.

The crowning achievement of the Taney Court's commercial legacy was Story's opinion for a unanimous Court in *Swift v. Tyson* (1842). The case presented the question of what "laws" the federal courts were required to apply in litigation arising out of commercial transactions between citizens of different states. Under the 1789 Judiciary Act, the Court was bound in such cases to apply the laws of the relevant state. *Swift* presented a commercial law question relating to the bona fide purchaser for value doctrine, a doctrine we last confronted in *Fletcher v. Peck.* The judicial decisions of New York courts were muddled on the doctrine and left it unclear whether a purchaser of a negotiable instrument took it free and clear of disputes between the original parties. Thus, if A and B had entered into a transaction, with A paying B for property with a promissory note, and B in turn paid C a preexisting debt by turning over A's note to C, could A refuse to pay C because, for example, B had never delivered the property to A? If he could do so, commerce in negotiable instruments would grind to a halt. As Story's opinion noted, such a result "would strike a fatal blow at all discounts of negotiable securities for preexisting debts" and would affect "probably, more than one-half of all bank transactions in our country."

Story concluded that New York judicial decisions were not binding on federal courts in commercial transactions. "Laws" in the Judiciary Act meant legislative enactments and statutes, as well as settled "usages," but not judicial decisions. This was because the law of commerce transcended state boundaries. Quoting Cicero, Story found that commercial law was "not the law of a single country only, but of the commercial world," and that commercial law to be applied by federal courts derived from "the general principles and doctrines of commercial jurisprudence."

As to the precise question posed in *Swift,* Story had no hesitation. Proclaiming the bona fide purchaser for value doctrine to be "so essential to the security of negotiable paper, that it is laid up among the fundamentals of the law," he made it binding as a rule of decision in federal court litigation.

This approach of federalizing areas of traditional state law became known as "federal common law," a phenomenon that greatly expanded in the nineteenth century to embrace a wide scope of legal issues beyond commercial law. This remained the controlling law in commercial transactions for nearly a century, until the Supreme Court reversed itself in *Erie R.R. Co. v. Tompkins* (1938), declaring in a pivotal opinion by Justice Brandeis that "there is no federal common law."

The Taney Court also had occasion to decide the issue left open under the Commerce Clause in *Gibbons v. Ogden.* That issue was whether the power of Congress to legislate on matters of "Commerce" was exclusive or concurrent with the states. In *Cooley v. Board of Wardens* (1851), by a vote of six to two, the Court drew a solomonic line in the majority opinion written by Justice Curtis of later *Scott v. Sandford* dissent fame.

Justice Curtis reasoned that "the power to regulate commerce embraces a vast field containing not only many but exceedingly various subjects quite unlike in their nature, some imperatively demanding a single uniform rule operating equally on the commerce of the United States . . . and some . . . as imperatively demanding that diversity which alone can meet the local necessities." While limiting its decision to the easy issue of regulation of pilots and pilotage, which Congress had long left to local regulation, the majority's approach left the window open to state regulation in areas that did not require "a single uniform rule," an exception that did not catch many commercial matters. The triumph of commerce was now virtually complete.

Part 2

From the Civil War to the Cold War

Four

From Emancipation to "Separate but Equal"

The Civil War was the decisive turning point in nineteenth-century American history. What Lincoln said in his second inaugural address on March 4, 1865, a month before the war ended, summed it up—"Neither party expected for the war, the magnitude, or the duration, which it has already attained." The "magnitude" in human terms was staggering and unprecedented. More than six hundred thousand were killed in battle, more than all the American dead in all the other wars fought by Americans up to Vietnam one hundred years later. In the South the stark fact of death claimed one in every four who fought for the Confederacy. On one day alone—September 17, 1862—at Antietam Creek near Sharpsburg, Maryland, more than six thousand died or were mortally wounded. This was twice the toll from the terrorist attacks on the World Trade Center in New York on September 11, 2001, from a population one-eighth the size of 2001. And on both sides, far too many who survived lived their remaining days with lost limbs and broken spirits.

The Civil War led to two major reconstructions of American society. First, following the emancipation of those held in slavery in areas controlled by the Confederacy during the war, the postwar Congress passed three constitutional amendments that were ratified by the states. These amendments—the Thirteenth through the Fifteenth—changed the legal status not only of African Americans formerly living in slavery, but also of all citizens of the United States as well as other persons living here. These three amendments were the first that *granted* powers to the federal government, rather than *limited* them. As a result the balance of power between state and federal government was fundamentally changed, although it took the Supreme Court to the twentieth century to implement this change fully.

Second, the devastated South lost not only its economy but also its national political power. From 1860 to 1912, only one southern-born president, Woodrow Wilson (by then transplanted to New Jersey), was elected. Previously southern presidents held office for forty-seven of the first seventy-one years. Where the Speaker of the House was southern born two-thirds of the time before the Civil

War, there was none for the next fifty years. And the balance of power also shifted in the Supreme Court, with only five southern justices being appointed of the twenty-six who took office in those fifty years. The "Slave Power" was dead.

The end of southern political dominance resulted in the ascendancy of the Republican Party. There were only two Democrats elected president from 1860 to 1932 (Grover Cleveland and Woodrow Wilson), and Republicans controlled both the national agenda and appointments to the Supreme Court during that period. This resulted in a probusiness orientation that facilitated the emergence and largely unfettered growth of industrial capitalism over these seventy years.

This chapter traces the Supreme Court's interpretation of the Thirteenth through Fifteenth amendments to the turn of the twentieth century, while the next chapter examines the Supreme Court's approach to business and economic issues from the Civil War to the New Deal.

The Thirteenth Amendment

In 1861 Congress passed and three states ratified a very different Thirteenth Amendment than that which eventually became law. Under the so-called Corwin Amendment, which died after the outbreak of the Civil War, Congress would have been permanently forbidden to "abolish or interfere" with slavery in the various states. That attempt to save the Union by placating the slave states gave way to the abolition of slavery in the postwar Thirteenth Amendment, which proscribed both "slavery" and "involuntary servitude" except as punishment for a criminal conviction. The amendment also expressly granted Congress the power to enforce it "by appropriate legislation," a phrase the Supreme Court was called upon to interpret in several leading decisions.

Congress responded in 1866 by enacting over President Andrew Johnson's veto a civil rights law that conferred the same rights as white citizens possessed upon all citizens to "inherit, purchase, lease, sell, hold, and convey" both real and personal property. In 1867 it went on to prohibit "peonage," a type of involuntary servitude based on indebtedness, which Congress declared to be "abolished and forever prohibited." These laws and others, along with the Fourteenth Amendment, addressed the emergence of so-called Black Codes in the former confederate states, under which the freedmen were economically shackled by laws that permitted or facilitated contracts requiring "perfect obedience" to the employer, prohibited vagrancy, imposed imprisonment for those without employment, prescribed criminal penalties and loss of prior pay for breaching an employment contract, and forbade freedmen from owning or possessing guns.

In 1883 the Supreme Court had occasion to interpret the Thirteenth Amendment in the *Civil Rights Cases.* Those cases held by a vote of eight to one that the Thirteenth Amendment barred both slavery and "badges of slavery," which were defined as restrictions that could be traced back to the "necessary" or "inseparable incidents" of African slavery. These, the Court ruled, were "compulsory service of the slave for the benefit of the master, restraint of his movements except by the master's will, disability to hold property, to make contracts, to have a standing in court, to be a witness against a white person and such like burdens and incapacities." By contrast the Civil Rights Act of 1875, which mandated equality in public accommodations, was not within the ambit of congressional power to enact under the Thirteenth Amendment because "mere discriminations on account of race or color were not regarded as badges of slavery." Indeed, in the majority's view, discrimination in public accommodations was seen as "a means of preventing . . . escapes, and was no part of the servitude itself."

Justice John Marshall Harlan of Kentucky, a former slave owner, dissented. He expressed his opinion that discrimination in public accommodations was "a badge of servitude, the imposition of which congress may prevent" under the Thirteenth Amendment. Harlan' s position lost in a series of cases decided in the nineteenth century and the interpretation of the Thirteenth Amendment set forth by the majority in the *Civil Rights Cases* remained controlling for eighty-five years.

It was not until *Jones v. Alfred H. Mayer Co.* (1968) that a seven-person majority took a more capacious view of congressional power under the Thirteenth Amendment, holding that the refusal of a private party to sell property to a black person could be proscribed in legislation enacted under the authority of the Thirteenth Amendment. There, the Court noted that "surely, Congress has the power under the Thirteenth Amendment rationally to determine what are the badges and the incidents of slavery, and the authority to translate that determination into effective legislation."

In the time between the *Civil Rights Cases* and *Jones,* however, the use of the Thirteenth Amendment to end discrimination or to implement affirmative-action legislation was severely circumscribed. Congress then turned to the powers conferred upon it in the Fourteenth Amendment to pursue its goals for the freedmen.

The Fourteenth Amendment

Considering its practical impact on the lives of those living in the United States, the Fourteenth Amendment has been the most significant of those adopted to date. In its concepts of due process and equal protection, the Fourteenth Amendment has protected the rights and civil liberties of both individuals and groups directly and through laws rooted in its authorization to Congress to "enforce, by appropriate legislation." Moreover, beginning in the middle of the twentieth century, the amendment was interpreted to "incorporate" most provisions of the Bill of Rights, which were originally designed as restraints upon the *federal* government, to be enforceable against the *states* as well.

The Fourteenth Amendment was the work of the so-called radical Republicans in Congress, and their leader in the House of Representatives was Thaddeus

Stevens of Pennsylvania. Demonized later by most pre–World War II historians, Stevens was contemporaneously called "the Robespierre of the second American Revolution," and vilified for his "ruin . . . of the proud, rich, and cultivated aristocracy" in sections of the South. In their widely assigned college textbook, *The Growth of the American Republic,* the reigning mid–twentieth-century American historians Samuel Eliot Morison and Henry Steele Commager identified Stevens as having been "for two years the virtual ruler of the United States." Stevens served as floor leader in the House for the 1866 and 1867 civil rights acts and for the Fourteenth Amendment. His philosophy was clear—"free every slave" and "slay every traitor." As to southern political power, Stevens's plan was that "the foundations of their institutions . . . must be broken up and rebuilt, or all of our *blood and treasure* have been spent in vain." This sentiment inspired the practice of "waving the bloody shirt," a widespread Republican tactic used in political campaigns against Democratic opponents for most of the rest of the nineteenth century. Indeed Stevens straightforwardly proclaimed that the seceded southern states should not be readmitted to the Union "until the Constitution shall have been so amended . . . as to secure *perpetual ascendancy* to the party of the Union"—his Republican Party. Stevens's goals, both social and political, thus required enfranchisement of the freedmen, who represented a numerical majority of adult males in five southern states, with 80 percent of the Republican vote there. Without them, to whose rights he was honestly and totally committed on a moral level, he could not succeed.

The Fourteenth Amendment implemented Stevens's vision in several ways. To guarantee Republican ascendancy, the second section of the amendent reduced representation in Congress proportionately to the extent that any state denied the vote to "any of the male inhabitants of such State," a provision that would have cost the southern states one-third of their House seats if all black males were excluded from voting. The third section barred from federal and state office all former Confederate officials guilty of treason (those who "shall have engaged in insurrection or rebellion . . . , or given aid and comfort to the enemies [of the United States"]), a disability which could only be removed by a two-thirds vote of each House. Finally Section 4 prohibited paying off any Confederate debt or "any claim for the loss or emancipation of any slave." This latter provision wiped out by part of one sentence the largest "asset" held by southerners—slaves valued at approximately two billion dollars—which formed the economic base of the southern planter aristocracy that Stevens wanted politically to "slay."

While these provisions implemented the radical Republicans' political goals, Section 1 of the Fourteenth Amendment was more significant for the future of those living in the United States than any of these. Section 1 first overturned the *Scott* decision by expressly providing that any person born or naturalized in the United States is a citizen of both the United States and of the state in which he or she resides. It goes on to state that "no State shall make or enforce any law which shall abridge the *privileges or immunities of citizens of the United States;* nor shall any State deprive any person of life, liberty, or property, without *due process of law;* nor deny to any person within its jurisdiction the *equal protection of the laws.*"

Congress approved the Fourteenth Amendment in 1866, but it would take two years and intense politics, including the imposition of military rule in the South, to obtain its ratification. After Lincoln's assassination on Good Friday in 1865, President Andrew Johnson followed Lincoln's liberal readmission policy for southern states such that all were readmitted by early 1866. Indeed some twenty-five former Confederate leaders, including four generals and the vice president of the Confederacy, Alexander Stephens of Georgia, were elected to Congress. These leaders were refused their seats by the radical Republicans, acting under Article I, Section 5, of the Constitution, which makes each house "the Judge of the Elections, Returns and Qualifications of its own Members."

Readmission of the seceded states spelled disaster for the ratification of the Fourteenth Amendment. Of the eleven southern states that were readmitted, all but Tennessee voted against it. The new states then generally enacted variations of the "black codes" previously described above, defeating the radical Republican agenda, restoring southern establishment rule, and depriving African Americans of the civil rights three hundred thousand Union soldiers had died to obtain. In response the radical Republicans obtained passage of the Reconstruction Act of 1867. This divided the South into five military districts, with a twenty-thousand-man northern army of occupation, as the South saw it. All previous readmissions of the seceded states were voided by the act, with future readmissions conditioned upon each former state calling a constitutional convention that would require universal male suffrage and ratification of the Fourteenth Amendment. By 1868 seven states were readmitted on this basis, and the Fourteenth Amendment was finally ratified.

But what did the broad phrases of the Fourteenth Amendment mean by "privileges or immunities of citizens of the United States," by "due process of law," and by "equal protection of the laws," and against whom could these guarantees be enforced? In a series of decisions beginning in 1873, the Supreme Court examined these questions and restrictively interpreted them in all but one of its leading cases, one not involving the rights of freedmen, but instead those of Chinese aliens in California.

The *Slaughterhouse Cases*

The first interpretation of the Fourteenth Amendment by the Supreme Court came in 1873, five years after its enactment. The case that served as the vehicle was an unusual one, brought not by freedmen, but rather by butchers from Louisiana who had been forced to close their slaughterhouses under a public health law passed by a biracial Louisiana Reconstruction legislature. That law, which was modeled on ones from New York and other northern and midwestern states, required that all butchering of animals in the New Orleans area take place in one slaughterhouse located outside of central New Orleans. All other slaughterhouses had to be closed, but the butchers who owned them were permitted to use the new slaughterhouse and could not be excluded from it. The law also required state inspection of all livestock in New Orleans and the three surrounding parishes (as counties are called in Louisiana).

The background of the Louisiana law is significant in assessing it and the opposition it engendered. New Orleans was a city long plagued by disease, including the dreaded cholera. John J. Audubon, the noted naturalist, called it the dirtiest city in the United States and some forty thousand in the area had died from cholera in 1853. Many traced the cause to the proliferation of slaughterhouses in New Orleans, and the legislation that was enacted tracked that from other states and municipalities that had their own slaughterhouse problem. Indeed Samuel Freeman Miller, the Supreme Court justice who wrote the majority opinion in the case, had been a medical doctor who had studied and treated cholera before beginning his legal career, and lived in Keokuk, Iowa, which had its own slaughterhouses and system of regulations.

State and local politics in Louisiana were also important in assessing the case. The Louisiana legislature was unpopular with the white establishment and had passed a "social equality" bill opposed by most of the white community and by the leading newspaper in New Orleans. The situation was further exacerbated by the fact that many of the investors in the new slaughterhouse were northerners.

A team of lawyers in several courts handled the case for the butchers, but the Supreme Court case was devised by John A. Campbell, a former justice himself. Campbell had resigned from the Court in 1861 to serve as assistant secretary of war for the Confederate States of America and had briefly been imprisoned after the Civil War. He had been a Jacksonian states' rights Democrat from Alabama before the Civil War and was a distinguished lawyer whose nomination to the Court in 1853 at the age of forty-one was requested by the Supreme Court itself.

Campbell's argument for the butchers was that they had a right to exercise their trade and that right was protected by the Fourteenth Amendment's prohibition against abridgment of "the privileges or immunities of citizens of the United States." He attacked the new slaughterhouse as an engine of private monopoly created by the state that deprived the butchers of their privilege to pursue their lawful trade. While he also relied on the Due Process and Equal Protection clauses, Miller's opinion dismissed these as not "much pressed."

When originally argued in January 1872, the case resulted in a four-four split. Reargument took place in February 1873, after Justice Samuel Nelson, who had been ill, returned to the bench. By a five-to-four vote, the Louisiana law was upheld in an opinion written by Justice Miller, who had been appointed to the Court by President Lincoln in 1862 and who would serve until 1890. The majority opinion held that the privileges and immunities clause only guaranteed rights held by citizens of the United States, and that these differed from those rights held by citizens of particular states. Citizens of the United States possessed rights that were "fundamental, which belong of right to the citizens of all free governments, and which have at all times been enjoyed by citizens of the several States which compose this Union, from the time of their becoming free, independent, and sovereign." Such rights included protection on the high seas, right of peaceable assembly and to petition the government for redress of grievances, and the right to habeas corpus for unlawful confinement. All of these rights were "comprehended under the following general heads: protection by the government, with the right to acquire and possess property of every kind and to pursue and obtain happiness and safety, subject, nevertheless, to such restraints as the government may prescribe for the general good of the whole." .

Other rights were the province of the states to confer upon their citizens, and Miller did not "see in those [Civil War] amendments any purpose to destroy the main features of the general system." Otherwise, the Supreme Court would become "a perpetual censor upon all legislation of the States, on the civil rights of their own citizens, with authority to nullify such as it did not approve as consistent with those rights, as they existed at the time of the adoption of this amendment." Such a result would "radically change . . . the whole theory of the relations of the State and Federal governments to each other and of both these governments to the people." The rights sought to be protected by the butchers under the privileges and immunities clause were not rights of a citizen of the United States, and the Louisiana law was a valid exercise of the police power, which "always [has been] conceded to belong to the States."

In dismissing the claim that the Louisiana law deprived the butchers of equal protection under the Fourteenth Amendment, Miller stated the equal protection clause was aimed at state laws "directed by way of discrimination against the negroes as a class, or on account of their race." As such "it is so clearly a provision for that race and that emergency that a strong case would be necessary for its application to any other."

Miller's opinion provoked three dissenting opinions. The principal opinion was that written by Justice Stephen J. Field, which was joined by three other justices. Field was a California Democrat who served on the Court for thirty-four years, matching the record years of service of Chief Justice Marshall and Justice Story. His judicial philosophy ultimately prevailed in the commercial decisions of the Supreme Court later in the nineteenth century, as we will see in the next chapter. Field believed in natural law and in certain inalienable rights, especially the right to hold and use property. He found in the Fourteenth Amendment guarantees of those rights through a doctrine that came to be known as substantive due process. That theory has, in various iterations, formed the basis for many controversial decisions of the Supreme Court, from the nineteenth- and early-twentieth-century decisions denying laborers wages and hours protections to the abortion cases of the late twentieth and twenty-first centuries recognizing a woman's right to choose to have an abortion.

While Field conceded the existence of state police power, he found that it did not permit any state "to encroach upon any of the just rights of the citizen, which the Constitution intended to secure against abridgement." He characterized the Louisiana law as creating a private monopoly and stated that the Fourteenth Amendment "inhibit[s] any legislation which confers special and exclusive privileges like these under consideration." Field also found that the privileges and immunities clause protected fundamental rights such as "the right to pursue a lawful employment in a lawful manner, without other restraint than such as equally affects all persons." As such the Fourteenth Amendment protects all citizens "against the creation of *any monopoly whatever*" because "all monopolies in any known trade or manufacture are an invasion of these privileges, for they encroach upon the liberty of citizens to acquire property and pursue happiness."

Field closed his opinion by characterizing the Louisiana law as a violation of "the right of *free labor*, one of the most sacred and imprescriptible [*sic*] rights of man," quoting Adam Smith's *Wealth of Nations* in support. In doing so he enlisted the second of the two most powerful political concepts of the nineteenth century on his side. Much of his opinion rests on the antimonopoly strain of his Jacksonian politics that we last saw in the fight over the Second Bank of the United States in chapter 1. To that Democratic strand, he added the Republican free labor philosophy, which ruled the popular mind throughout this period, resonating in the actual words of several of the opinions examined below. In short this philosophy taught that freedom of labor or of contract defined the rights of free men, and that government should not abridge or limit those rights. The philosophy resonated with the public because it was based on the idea of equal opportunity for all. Abraham Lincoln himself had captured this key theme in his statement defending northern labor over southern slavery when he said that "the man who labored for another last year, this year labors for himself, and next year he will hire others to labor for him."

The impact of the *Slaughterhouse Cases* was significant in limiting the reach of the privileges and immunities clause. In seeking to preserve a public health measure, Miller's opinion eviscerated that clause and cabined its future usefulness. Field's dissent, by contrast, began what became a forced march by the Supreme Court to appropriate the Fourteenth Amendment to the interests of industrial America up until the New Deal in the twentieth century.

The *Civil Rights Cases*

Reconstruction ended with the Compromise of 1877, which followed the disputed Hayes-Tilden presidential election of 1876. Under the Compromise, which effectively awarded the presidency to the Republican Hayes, northern troops were withdrawn from the South and protection of the freedmen's rights was left to the southern states. The Civil Rights Act of 1875 was thus the last great Reconstruction legislation. Introduced first in 1873, it was sponsored by Senator Charles Sumner of Massachusetts, Thaddeus Stevens's counterpart in that chamber, and by Benjamin Butler in the House of Representatives, the Republican leader from the time Stevens died in 1868. As passed after Sumner's death, partially as a tribute to his decades-long crusade for African American civil rights, the act was the first federal public accommodations legislation. It proscribed discrimination in "inns, public conveyances on land or water, theaters, and other places of public amusement." Stripped from the original bill were prohibitions extending the ban on discrimination to schools, churches, and cemeteries.

Further protection of African American rights was controversial among the public at the time. To begin with, Reconstruction had been under vigorous attack by the Democrats in the presidential elections of 1868 and 1872. While the Republican Civil War hero General Ulysses S. Grant had prevailed in both elections and had supported rights for the freedmen, his Democratic opponents, including the influential newspaper publisher Horace Greeley in 1872, had characterized Reconstruction as costly and divisive. Indeed some Democrats went on to assail its African American beneficiaries as "lazy" and "vagabondish." To this clamor was added the opposition of public opinion leaders such as E. L. Godkin of the *Nation,* who attacked Reconstruction in South Carolina in 1874 as placing "the rich thief on top and the degraded Anglo-Saxon at the bottom." In 1875 the year the Civil Rights Act was signed by President Grant, Yale professor William Graham Sumner wrote *What Social Classes Owe to One Another,* in which he invented "the Forgotten Man," whose "chief business in life is to pay," particularly for "every extension of the paternal theory of government" to "the less fortunate classes." This feeling tapped by Sumner resonated with the public, who for decades had been exposed to the Republican free labor philosophy mentioned above. Under that philosophy, there was a wall of separation between political and civil rights, on the one hand, and "social rights," on the other hand. Political and civil rights should be secured by the federal government to assure equality of *opportunity;* social rights, by contrast, had to be earned, since equality of *condition* was not within the realm of legislation properly to confer.

It was in this context that the Supreme Court decided the *Civil Rights Cases* in 1883. There five individual cases from across the country involving discrimination against African Americans in hotels, inns, and theaters and on trains were consolidated for Supreme Court disposition. Over only Justice Harlan's dissent, the

Court declared the Civil Rights Act of 1875 unconstitutional. Justice Joseph P. Bradley's majority opinion held that the Fourteenth Amendment was directed only to official state action, and that Congress was empowered only to enact "corrective legislation" to combat such state action. The opinion stated that "positive rights and privileges are undoubtedly secured by the fourteenth amendment; but they are secured by way of prohibition against state laws and state proceedings affecting those rights and privileges, and by power given to congress to legislate for the purpose of carrying such prohibition into effect." Echoing the *Slaughterhouse Cases,* Bradley cautioned that Congress was not invested "with power to legislate upon subjects which are within the domain of state legislation," nor could it enact a "code of municipal law regulative of all *private rights between man and man in society.*" Making the free labor "social rights" orientation of the Court even more striking was Bradley's observation, made in the context of the Thirteenth Amendment claim discussed previously, that Congress in its 1866 civil rights legislation "did not assume . . . to adjust what may be called *the social rights of men and races in the community.*"

Bradley closed his opinion by underlining the political/civil and social rights dichotomy by observing that "when a man has emerged from slavery, and by the aid of beneficent legislation has shaken off the inseparable concomitants of that state, there must be some stage in the progress of his elevation when he takes the rank of *mere citizen,* and ceases to be *the special favorite of the laws,* and when his rights as a citizen, or a man, are to be protected in the ordinary modes by which other men's rights are protected."

In dissent Justice Harlan made three general points. First, invoking Chief Justice Marshall's *McCulloch* opinion, he argued that the Fourteenth Amendment gave Congress broad powers to enact suitable affirmative legislation. Second, he chided the majority for ignoring precedent that supported broad legislation enacted under the Fugitive Slave Clause to protect slavery, stating that "the national legislature may, without transcending the limits of the constitution, do for human liberty and the fundamental rights of American citizenship, what it did, with the sanction of this court, for the protection of slavery and the rights of the masters of fugitive slaves." Third, Harlan contended that state action, if required, was present in the actions of the public accommodations in question, since the entities covered were subject to state regulation and therefore constituted "agents of the state."

In response to Bradley's "mere citizen" commentary, Harlan replied that it was not "just" to "say that the colored race has been the special favorite of the laws" because "the one underlying purpose of congressional legislation has been to enable the black race to take the rank of mere citizens." Harlan closed by warning of the dangers of "class tyranny," cautioning that "to-day it is the colored race which is denied, by corporations and individuals wielding public authority, rights fundamental in their freedom and citizenship. At some future time it may be some other race that will fall under the ban. If the constitutional amendments be enforced, according to the intent with which, as I conceive, they were adopted, there cannot be, in this republic, any class of human beings in practical subjection to another class, with power in the latter to dole out to the former just such privileges as they may choose to grant."

Popular reaction to the decision in the *Civil Rights Cases* was positive. Newspapers in Chicago, Philadelphia, and Hartford made a telling comparison, stating that African Americans were seeking rights such as admission to hotels that were denied to others, including Jews and Irish Americans specifically. While this ignored that the Civil Rights Act of 1875 applied to "all persons," these newspapers well captured the public opposition to "special privileges." Indeed, at times in their lives, both Justice Bradley and Justice Harlan shared similar views. Bradley wrote, in private correspondence, that "[it] never can be endured that the white shall be compelled to lodge and eat and sit with the negro. The latter can have his freedom and *all legal and essential privileges* without that," and "surely it is no deprivation of civil rights to give each race the right to choose their own company." Similarly, in unsuccessfully campaigning for governor of Kentucky in 1875, the year this Civil Rights Act was signed into law, Harlan declared from the stump that "*social equality* can never exist between the two races in Kentucky," and that "the testimony of candid men must be that the white and black races can move along in this free land of ours, each cherishing . . . *the prejudices of race* without at all interfering with the *just rights* of the other."

It was sentiments such as these, which sopped into the very fabric of American society, including the highest judiciary, that limited the reach of the Fourteenth Amendment to support affirmative legislation. Between them, the *Slaughterhouse Cases* and the *Civil Rights Cases* imposed formidable barriers to such legislation, limiting the usefulness of the privileges and immunities clause and restricting the reach of the Fourteenth Amendment to corrective legislation aimed at discriminatory state action. These cases also set the stage for enactment of "Jim Crow" laws in the post-Reconstruction South, and their vindication in *Plessy v. Ferguson,* the *Scott v. Sandford* decision of the turn of the twentieth century.

Plessy v. Ferguson

Prior to the Supreme Court's opinion in the *Civil Rights Cases,* segregation in the former Confederate states was generally limited to schools and hospitals. This contrasted sharply with the situation in the northern and midwestern states, where separation of the white and black races was often implemented on a broader scale. Starting in Florida in 1887, the southern states began a long march to complete a wall of legal separation between the two races in a systematic attempt to build a completely segregated society. The first laws dealt mainly with public transportation and public accommodations—the areas covered by the Civil Rights Act of 1875, which the Supreme Court had struck down as unconstitutional in 1883. A second wave, extending into the 1950s, expanded the coverage of these laws to places of work, bathrooms, waiting rooms, parks, and even water fountains. By 1891 eight southern states had imposed some new legal restrictions on "race-mixing." These, along with a range of measures that excluded African Americans from voting, isolated and marginalized the black citizens of the southern states. So complete was the mandated separation of races that George Fredrickson, the leading historian of racism, compared it to South African *apartheid,* concluding that "white supremacy attained its fullest ideological and institutional development in the southern United States between the 1890s and the 1950s."

In 1890 Louisiana enacted such legislation in the form of a law that required railroads transporting passengers within its borders to provide "equal but separate accommodations for the white, and colored, races." Violation was punishable by a fine of twenty-five dollars or imprisonment for a term up to twenty days. The black establishment of New Orleans, which had possessed significant political power in the years following the Civil War and had secured passage of a "social equality" bill during that time, resolved to bring a test case to challenge the railroad law under the Thirteenth and Fourteenth amendments. They hired Albion Tourgee to argue their case. Tourgee was a New Yorker who had been a leader in North Carolina politics during Reconstruction and who was the leading civil rights attorney of the day. Homer Plessy, who was an "octoroon"—one-eighth black in the parlance of the racist day—was recruited to be the plaintiff, and the East Louisiana Railway apparently cooperated in arresting Plessy to set the stage for a court challenge. It was in the railroad's interest to do so because the Louisiana law cost it money by requiring it to supply extra cars or to construct partitions in certain cars.

The outcome of *Plessy v. Ferguson* (1896) was predictable given the reasoning followed by the Supreme Court in invalidating the Civil Rights Act of 1875 thirteen years earlier. In an opinion for seven members of the Court, Justice Henry Brown upheld the Louisiana law. Brown, who practiced law in Michigan before coming to the Supreme Court in 1890, was an Anglo-Saxon elitist with a low opinion of blacks, as well as of women, immigrants, and Jews.

As in the *Civil Rights Cases,* the opinion distinguished between political and social rights. Brown wrote that the object of the Fourteenth Amendment "was undoubtedly to enforce the absolute equality of the two races before the law, but, in the nature of things, it could not have been intended to abolish distinctions based upon color, or to enforce *social, as distinguished from political, equality,* or a commingling of the two races upon terms unsatisfactory to either." He concluded that "if the civil and political rights of both races be equal, one cannot be inferior to the other civilly or politically. If one race be inferior to the other socially, the constitution of the United States cannot put them upon the same plane." In Justice Brown's view, "social prejudices may [not] be overcome by legislation," and "if the two races are to meet upon terms of social equality, it must be the result of natural affinities, a mutual appreciation of each other's merits, and a voluntary consent of individuals."

Given this approach, the majority saw the issue as whether the Louisiana law was a "reasonable regulation." It concluded that it was because the state legislature had "large discretion" in passing such laws and could rely upon "the established usages, customs, and traditions of the people, and with a view to the promotion of their comfort, and the preservation of the public peace and good order." Brown pointedly identified school segregation mandated by Congress in the District of Columbia and a pre–Civil War Massachusetts Supreme Court opinion by Chief Justice Shaw upholding school segregation as evidence of such "usages, customs, and traditions."

In a lone dissent, Justice Harlan contended that the Civil War amendments "removed the race line from our governmental systems." Paraphrasing a line from Tourgee's argument, Harlan stated that "our constitution is color-blind, and neither knows nor tolerates classes among citizens. In respect of civil rights, all citizens are equal before the law." Comparing the majority opinion to the *Scott* case, he warned that "sixty millions of whites are in no danger from the presence here of eight millions of blacks. The destinies of the two races, in this country, are indissolubly linked together, and the interests of both require that the common government of all shall not permit the seeds of race hate to be planted under the sanction of law."

Harlan saw "the white race" as "the dominant race in this country . . . in prestige, in achievements, in education, in wealth, and in power." This status imposed on it an obligation to "hold . . . fast to the principles of constitutional liberty" for all "if it remains true to its great heritage."

The opinion in *Plessy v. Ferguson* received little attention in the press, but great attention in southern legislatures, which progressively covered every area of public contact with legislation mandating separation of the races into the 1950s. The Supreme Court had given a green light to do so.

Yick Wo v. Hopkins: A Beacon for the Oppressed

The opinions handed down by the Supreme Court from the *Slaughterhouse Cases* to *Plessy v. Ferguson* generally resulted in a narrowing of the potential reach of the Fourteenth Amendment. But between the *Civil Rights Cases* and *Plessy,* the Court decided a case that showed the future promise of the amendment to serve as a guarantor of the civil rights of all persons living in the United States. That case was *Yick Wo v. Hopkins* (1885). In it the Supreme Court considered the constitutionality under the Fourteenth Amendment of the application to Chinese aliens of some

1880 San Francisco ordinances that required any person seeking to operate a laundry in a wooden building to obtain the consent of the local board of supervisors before doing so. Yick Wo had operated such a laundry in San Francisco for twenty-two years, but was nevertheless imprisoned for ten days when he declined to obtain the required consent and failed to pay the fine imposed for his refusal to do so.

The decision reached by the Supreme Court in *Yick Wo v. Hopkins* came in the historical context of rampant discrimination against the Chinese in California. Some two hundred thousand Chinese had come to California between 1853 and 1882. They represented 9 percent of California's population in 1860 and 25 percent of the California work force in the 1870s. Thirty percent of these Chinese aliens lived in San Francisco, where they worked principally in unskilled trades in manufacturing or other industries that required cheap labor. The Chinese were subjected to the Asian equivalent of the southern black codes in California laws that regulated their behavior and employment. By the 1870s a California Workingmen's Party emerged to confine the Chinese presence in the state further. Led by an Irish immigrant businessman named Denis Kearney, the party took as its war cry the slogan "The Chinese must go!" Kearney attacked the alliance of rich railroad owners living on Nob Hill in San Francisco, whom he called "Nob Hill nabobs," with the Chinese laborers, ten thousand of whom had worked on constructing railroads in the late 1860s. Kearney analogized this alliance to that of the pre–Civil War plantation owners with their African American slaves. He saw the Irish immigrants in California, who represented some 15 percent of the California work force at the time, as the victims of this alliance, since they competed directly with the Chinese for unskilled jobs.

By 1878 the California Workingmen's Party was a dominant political force, and it captured the 1878 California Constitutional Convention, out of which came a constitutional prohibition forbidding the employment of any Chinese on public works projects conducted by California corporations. In a separate referendum, 99.4 percent voted in favor of excluding *all* Chinese from the United States. By 1882 this anti-Chinese fever had infected the national legislature, which passed the first Chinese Exclusion Act in that year.

It was in this context of virulent racism directed at the Chinese that the Supreme Court considered the 1880 San Francisco laundry ordinances. In an opinion by Justice Stanley Matthews, the Court unanimously held that the application of the ordinances to Yick Wo violated the equal protection clause of the Fourteenth Amendment. The opinion first noted that "the Fourteenth Amendment to the Constitution is not confined to the protection of citizens," for its provisions "are universal in their application to all persons within the territorial jurisdiction, without regard to any differences of race, of color, or of nationality, and the equal protection of the laws is a pledge of the protection of equal laws." As such the Fourteenth Amendment did protect the rights of the Chinese aliens who had sought consent to operate their laundries.

While the Court conceded that the ordinances appeared fair on the surface, and were rooted in the reasonable protection of the public against the hazard of fire in wooden buildings, it relied heavily on how the ordinances had been *applied.* Two hundred Chinese aliens had petitioned for the supervisors' consent to operate laundries in wooden buildings; all had been denied. By contrast eighty non-Chinese had petitioned for consent, and all had been approved. These facts led the Court to conclude that the ordinances had been applied "with a mind so unequal and oppressive as to amount to a practical denial by the State of . . . equal protection of the laws." The rule that emerged was that "though the law itself be fair on its face and impartial in appearance, yet, if it is applied and administered by public authority with an evil eye and an unequal hand, so as practically to make unjust and illegal discriminations between persons in similar circumstances, material to their rights, the denial of equal justice is still within the prohibition of the Constitution."

Yick Wo v. Hopkins was a solitary opinion beaconing the safe harbor of the protections of the Fourteenth Amendment in a fog of other opinions limiting its scope. One explanation for its liberal application of the amendment to Yick Wo and his fellow countrymen is found in the fact that the case involved *property rights.* Justice Field, who joined the Court's unanimous opinion, could easily see in it the vindication of his dissent for four members of the Court in the *Slaughterhouse Cases.* This was because the *Yick Wo v. Hopkins* opinion protected the rights of the Chinese laundrymen to pursue their lawful occupation. Indeed, as we will see in the next chapter, the paramount use of the Fourteenth Amendment from this point until the midpoint of the New Deal in 1937 was to protect property rights and freedom of contract for corporate America, not to confer "social rights" upon African Americans.

The Fifteenth Amendment

The last of the Civil War amendments was the Fifteenth, ratified in 1870. It provides that the rights of citizens of the United States to vote "shall not be denied or abridged" by the United States or by any state "on account of *race, color, or previous condition of servitude.*" As in the Thirteenth and Fourteenth amendments, Congress was empowered to enact "appropriate legislation" to enforce the amendment.

What the Fifteenth Amendment does *not* provide is significant. It does not protect a woman's right to vote. It took until 1920 for the Nineteenth Amendment to do so. It does not prohibit impediments to voting such as property qualifications, literacy tests, or poll taxes. It took until 1964 for the Twenty-fourth Amendment to ban poll and other taxes as a device to prevent any citizen from voting.

Early versions of the Fifteenth Amendment had provisions addressing some of these devices, but they were dropped to assure that African American males could vote, so as to protect continued Republican political "ascendancy," as Thaddeus Stevens had put it. At that time, blacks were excluded from voting not only in the southern states but also in eleven of the twenty-one northern states. Indeed, only three years before ratification of the Fifteenth Amendment, the right of African Americans to vote was rejected in the midwestern states of Ohio, Minnesota, and Kansas.

By 1871 Congress had enacted three "Enforcement Acts" to protect the African American vote. Five years later, the Supreme Court examined the Fifteenth Amendment and parts of these laws in the two companion cases of *United States v. Reese* and *United States v. Cruikshank* (1876). *Reese* involved the imposition of a $1.50 "capitation tax" as a prerequisite to voting, while *Cruikshank* was a criminal case, involving the Easter Sunday mass murder of over one hundred blacks and three whites in a protracted election dispute during which the victims had occupied the county courthouse, which the defendants then burned down, shooting those who tried to escape from the flames.

Both opinions were written by Chief Justice Morrison R. Waite, an Ohio Republican and moderate who was appointed by President Grant. Waite served as chief justice between 1874 and 1888. In the *Reese* case, he narrowly interpreted the scope of protection afforded by the Fifteenth Amendment, stating that it "does not confer the right of suffrage upon any one. It *prevents* the States, or the United States, however, from giving preference, in this particular, to one citizen of the United States over another on account of race, color, or previous condition of servitude." Once again, as in the *Slaughterhouse Cases* and the *Civil Rights Cases*, the opinion articulated a states' rights philosophy, noting that the Fifteenth Amendment "interferes with" state electoral laws and effects "a radical change." This fundamental reordering of federal and state rights required that any interference with the rights of states to regulate the qualifications of their citizens to vote must be explicitly spelled out by Congress in any legislation passed under it.

In *Reese* parts of the Enforcement Act relied upon to convict a state election official were struck down under this reasoning. The official had refused to permit a black man named William Garner to vote, because Garner did not have a receipt showing that he had paid the capitation tax. Waite's opinion found the provisions of the act unconstitutional in those parts that did not limit its coverage to cases involving denial of the right to vote because of race, color, or previous condition of servitude. Because the indictment did not charge the state election official with denying Garner the right to vote because of his race, it was defective and the conviction could not stand.

Cruikshank similarly reversed convictions under the Enforcement Act because the indictments in that case did not charge that the mass murders were done with the intent to deprive the victims of their right to vote because of their race. In what surely must rank with the understatements of all time in a Supreme Court opinion, Waite observed that "we may suspect that race was the cause of the hostility; but it is not so averred." What is most notable in the opinion is a lengthy discussion at the beginning of the differences between the rights of citizens of the United States and citizens of states, and the importance of states' rights and federalism in the American system of government. Once again, the Civil War amendments are not seen as designed to alter this fundamental structure and the corresponding limitations upon federal power in areas viewed as involving states' rights.

Two years after its decision in *Plessy v. Ferguson,* the Supreme Court had occasion to examine the use of literacy requirements to deny the right to vote. In *Williams v. Mississippi* (1898), a unanimous Court upheld a requirement added in 1890 to the Mississippi Constitution that permitted rejection of any person attempting to vote where he was unable to convince the election official that he was "able to read any section of the constitution of this state; or he shall be able to understand the same when read to him, or give a reasonable interpretation thereof." The case arrived at the Supreme Court in an unusual posture. A black man named Henry Williams had been convicted of murder and sentenced to hang for that offense. He challenged his conviction on the grounds that blacks had been excluded from his jury. At that time, jurors in Mississippi were selected from the lists of registered voters, and Williams argued that blacks were unfairly stricken from the voting lists under the literacy requirement because of their race. Invoking the *Yick Wo v. Hopkins* case, Williams contended that the voting officials had unlimited discretion under the Mississippi Constitution to deny the right to vote and had exercised that discretion to disproportionately strike black voters.

The opinion rejecting Williams's appeal was written by Justice Joseph McKenna, who was born in Philadelphia of Irish immigrant parents, but had moved to California as a preteenager. After deciding not to become a Catholic priest, McKenna embarked on a legal career, serving first as a district attorney and state legislator, then as a California Republican in the House of Representatives for four terms, as a federal circuit judge on the Ninth Circuit, and briefly as attorney general of the United States immediately before his appointment to the Supreme Court in 1898 by President William McKinley. McKenna replaced the long-serving and influential justice Stephen Field, and served on the Supreme Court until 1925, writing over six hundred opinions during his own lengthy tenure. McKenna voted with the economic conservatives who followed Field's substantive due process approach.

McKenna's opinion in *Williams v. Mississippi* found no proof that the Mississippi Constitution had been unfairly applied, and upheld Williams's conviction. McKenna relied upon a failure of proof in Williams's case, reasoning that the state laws "do not on their face discriminate between the races, and it has not been shown that their actual administration was evil; only that evil was possible under them." At a time before the advent of sophisticated statistical analysis using computer models, such proof was hard to come by. *Yick Wo v. Hopkins* had succeeded only because the statistics in that case were admitted to be accurate by the San Francisco officials, a strategic legal mistake southern voting officials were careful not to repeat in *Williams* or thereafter in other cases.

The constricted interpretation of the Fifteenth Amendment in cases such as *Reese, Cruikshank,* and *Williams* led to the massive exclusion of African Americans from voting through imposition of poll taxes, literacy requirements, and property qualifications, accompanied by violence, intimidation, and local dirty tricks such as not publishing polling place locations or changing them at the last minute without notice to black voters. When combined with the torrent of "Jim Crow" laws that followed the Supreme Court decisions in the *Civil Rights Cases* and *Plessy v. Ferguson,* the promise of the Civil War amendments had been eviscerated by the turn of the twentieth century. As the noted black intellectual W. E. B. DuBois put it, "The slave went free, stood a brief moment in the sun, then moved back again toward slavery."

Five

The Supreme Court and Government Regulation of Business before the New Deal

A second great reconstruction of American society after the Civil War was wrought by the emergence and growth of industrial capitalism. This was facilitated by a population explosion, with the United States more than doubling in population, from thirty-one million in 1860 to seventy-five million in 1900. By 1900 the United States had become the world's largest industrial producer. Six million workers were employed by American industry, representing one-quarter of the nation's work force. Many of the jobs created were labor-intensive and unskilled positions, and immigrant workers filled a large portion of these, driving down the wages of native-born American laborers.

This same period between the end of the Civil War and the beginning of the twentieth century also witnessed the rise of the modern industrial corporation, including several large oligopolies and monopolies. These were often headed by well-known industrialists such as Andrew Carnegie in the steel industry and John D. Rockefeller in the oil industry. Some of these industrialists became immensely wealthy, and the disparity between rich and poor became more pronounced than a free labor society could have contemplated before the Civil War. Indeed by 1890, 51 percent of all property was owned by 1 percent of the population. Corporate size and power grew exponentially during this period, with farmers and laborers increasingly pressed to accept less pay for their labors.

The dominant Republican Party's platforms supported measures that assisted business expansion during the remainder of the nineteenth century. Four principles were paramount—a high protective tariff to insulate American business from foreign competition and incidentally raise revenue; a "sound currency" based upon the gold standard; a prohibition on federal borrowing through incurring public debt; and the expansion of "internal improvements," including railroads. Significantly most Democrats supported the same measures, with the notable exception of the tariff.

Republican presidents during this period sounded these themes in their inaugural addresses. In 1873 President Grant called for "construction of cheap routes of transit throughout the land, to the end that the products of all may find a market and leave a living remuneration to the producer." President Harrison, in his 1889 inaugural address, reported that "the merchant, the ship-master, and the manufacturer discovered and disclosed to our statesmen and to the people that *commercial emancipation* must be added to the political freedom which had been so bravely won." He added that "I look hopefully to the continuance of our protective system and to the consequent development of manufacturing and mining enterprises in the states hitherto wholly given to agriculture as a potent influence in the perfect unification of our people."

The Supreme Court was an important agent in advancing these goals. Well into the first third of the twentieth century, it facilitated the continued growth of commerce, as the Marshall and Taney Courts had done before the Civil War. This chapter examines three interrelated ways in which the Supreme Court advanced the interests of a nascent industrial capitalism: through placing brakes on state regulation of railroads and other businesses affected with the public interest; by developing the doctrine of substantive due process; and by narrowing the reach of the new federal antitrust law.

The Granger Movement Reaches the Supreme Court

Between the end of the Civil War in 1865 and 1877, political opposition to the new industrial system arose, principally among disaffected farmers who had borrowed to expand their farms and to buy new patented equipment, pledging their crops to do so. This expansion was devastated by two economic whirlwinds. First, the Republican "sound money" policy resulted in farmers having to pay back their loans in hard or deflated currency where they had borrowed in inflated currency. The economic impact was that they repaid in real terms far more than they had borrowed in principal, without even counting interest. Second, crop prices plummeted during this period, making debt repayment and daily living expenses even more difficult to finance.

Farmers began to organize to confront these obstacles. Founded in 1867, the Patrons of Husbandry, better known as the Grange, quickly grew in membership in the 1870s, reaching a peak of more than 850,000 members in 1875. At the same time, a laborers' guildlike organization of Christian socialists called the Knights of Labor emerged in 1869, offering help to laborers as well as farmers, and cooperating politically with the Granger movement. Indeed the Knights invited all to join, including black and white, and skilled and unskilled laborers. Only bankers, lawyers, gamblers, and alcoholics were excluded. By 1885 the Knights of Labor counted more than 700,000 members.

The Grangers and the Knights were paralleled in the political sphere by the Greenback Party, which advocated the return of a debtor-friendly, inflated paper currency ("greenbacks") that had been used during the Civil War. An economic recession—the Panic of 1873—catalyzed its formation, and by 1878, fourteen of its members were elected to Congress. In the presidential election of 1880, the Greenback-Labor Party candidate, former Union Army officer James B. Weaver, collected more than three hundred thousand votes, more than enough to have made the difference in an election where the Republican James J. Garfield defeated another Union officer, General Winfield S. Hancock, by a margin of fewer than forty thousand votes nationally.

The first target of the Granger movement was the railroads. Railroads were seen by farmers and laborers as monopolies that overcharged farmers through various methods, including different rates for long and short hauls, charging the farmer more for his short hauls than they charged the businessman for his longer distance transportation. Other railroad practices also put farmers at an economic disadvantage. One such practice was outright discrimination in rates and rebating, where shippers of larger quantities received kickbacks from the railroads for their patronage. The railroads were also political corrupters, bribing elected officials across the country at local, state, and federal levels. One notable example, which further tarnished the Grant presidency, was the Credit Mobilier scandal of the 1870s, in which prominent politicians, including Grant's vice president Schuyler Colfax and future president James J. Garfield, received stock in a holding company tied to the Union Pacific Railroad, which was then receiving federal subsidies, to sidetrack a congressional investigation.

The power of the railroads was met by the formation of railroad commissions in various states, starting in the East in Rhode Island in 1839. Massachusetts established in 1869 what was to become the most prominent commission, chaired by Charles Francis Adams. Adams was the son of President John Quincy Adams, and had been the Free-Soil Party vice presidential candidate in 1848. The Massachusetts commission was given the power of "general supervision" of the railroads, but could only make recommendations and could not establish rates.

The Midwest followed with stronger state regulation of railroads and related entities. These commissions, starting with that established in Illinois in 1873, had the power to set maximum rates. By the 1870s similar bodies had been established across the country, including in Nebraska, Georgia, Texas, and California, the last in the Workingmen's Party-dominated California Constitutional Convention of 1878–79.

The constitutionality of what became known as the "Granger Laws" came before the Supreme Court in the Granger cases (1877). The lead opinion among these cases was delivered by Chief Justice Waite in *Munn v. Illinois* (1877), which involved an Illinois law fixing maximum rates for grain storage warehouses in Chicago. By a seven-to-two majority, the Court upheld the constitutionality of the law, finding that rate regulation was justified because the grain warehouses affected the public interest. Waite wrote that "when . . . one devotes his property to a use in which the public has an interest, he, in effect, grants to the public an interest in that use, and must submit to be controlled by the public for the common good, to the extent of the interest he has thus created." As such, "when private property is devoted to a public use, it is subject to public regulation." Waite saw the Illinois statute as "simply extend[ing] the law so as to meet *this new development of commercial progress.*"

Waite conceded that state regulation could be "abused," but concluded "that is no argument against its existence. *For protection against abuses by legislatures, the people must resort to the polls, not to the courts.*"

Waite's opinion for seven members of the Court settled (or so it seemed) several important points. First, states could regulate and fix maximum rates for businesses affecting the public interest. Second, courts could not sit in judgment on whether this power to regulate was being abused. Third, rate regulation was a political question, to be resolved in democratic elections, not by the courts.

In dissent Justice Field would have none of this. He declared that the question presented in the Granger cases "is one of the greatest importance, whether it is within the competency of a State to fix the compensation which an individual may receive for the use of his own property in his private business, and for his services in connection with it." Stating the question in such free labor terms left little doubt of the conclusion, and Field made his opinion clear. He declared that "the principle upon which the opinion of the majority proceeds is, in my judgment, *subversive of the rights of private property.*" Indeed, "if this be sound law, if there be no protection, either in the principles upon which our republican form of government is founded, or in the prohibitions of the Constitution against such invasion of private rights, *all property and all business in the State are held at the mercy of a majority of its legislature.*"

Future events would convince a majority of the Supreme Court that Field's fears were well founded, and the ringing endorsement of state regulation in *Munn v. Illinois* became progressively muted between 1877 and the close of the nineteenth century.

The Grangers Get Derailed

In the quarter century following its decision in *Munn v. Illinois,* the Supreme Court became progressively more skeptical about unfettered state regulation of railroads and other businesses affected with the public interest. This was a time of significant economic and political unrest in the country. Strikes became commonplace, rising from an average of five hundred a year in the early 1880s to thirteen hundred annually in the 1890s. In several notable strikes, multiple deaths of strikers, police and others, massive property damage, and anarchist involvement focused national attention on the specter of "mob rule."

The most notable early instance of this phenomenon happened four months after the *Munn* decision was announced. The Great Railroad Strike of 1877 started in response to a decision by the nation's largest railroads to reduce wages across the board by 10 percent. Beginning with violence in West Virginia, the strike moved to Baltimore, where federal troops were called out to put it down. Next came Pittsburgh, where twenty died and the state militia was summoned after properties of the Pennsylvania Railroad were burned down and more than two thousand railroad cars and 104 locomotives were destroyed. The strike spread across the country, reaching San Francisco. When it was over two weeks after it began, fifty had died and the railroads had sustained lost profits and property damage totaling some thirty million dollars.

Nine years later, in 1886, strikers called for a national general strike in favor of the eight-hour workday, and parades and demonstrations were held across the country to support their cause. In Chicago's demonstration, police fired on a crowd of strikers, killing several of them. On May 4, 1886, a meeting was called by anarchists in Haymarket Square in Chicago to protest the police action. That meeting was disrupted when an unidentified person threw a bomb into the small group of protesters, killing seven policemen, and injuring sixty-seven bystanders. Eight anarchists were arrested and charged with murder. Of these, four were convicted and executed, one committed suicide, and the other three were pardoned eight years later by reform governor John Peter Altgeld of Illinois.

In 1892 the Homestead, Pennsylvania, steel mill of Andrew Carnegie, under the management of Henry Clay Frick, announced pay cuts and a refusal to deal with the steelworkers' union. Implementing a lockout, Frick hired three hundred private police to protect the mill from the expected violence. The private police were blocked from entering the mill by workers who fired on them, even after a white flag was raised on the boat that carried them to the mill. Finally, after the police surrendered, they were forced to run a gauntlet of angry workers who clubbed and beat them. When the day ended on July 6, 1892, over a dozen policemen and workers were dead, and many more injured.

The eight-thousand-man Pennsylvania state militia was summoned to Homestead by Governor Robert Pattison to maintain order, and the *New York Times* denounced the "mob rule" of the workers. Pennsylvania's chief justice Edward Paxson called for treason indictments to be lodged against the union leaders, and twenty-nine of them were indicted on that charge for creating a state of war, although the charges were later dropped. The anarchist element then entered when a young Russian immigrant named Alexander Berkman went to Frick's office two weeks later, shot him twice in the neck, and then stabbed him three times. Frick lived, and he returned to his office the same day after the bullets were removed from his neck without any anesthesia being administered to him.

A final major national strike took place in 1894, involving the Pullman Company, the manufacturer of luxury railroad cars. Pullman had developed a "model community" for his workers. After the Panic of 1893 struck, businesses were devastated. The stock market crashed, and eight thousand business corporations and 360 banks failed. Four hundred seventy-four railroads failed or entered receivership. These accounted for one-third of all the tracks in the country at that time. Twenty percent of all workers were unemployed as a result, and the Panic represented the worst depression in American history prior to the Great Depression, which began in 1929.

Pullman reacted to the Panic of 1893 by cutting his employees' wages by 25–40 percent, without any reduction in the rents he charged them for housing in his model community. Enlisting the aid of Eugene Debs's American Railway Union, the Pullman strikers led a boycott of Pullman railroad cars, disrupting national transportation, and allegedly stopping the United States mails. Although the strikers had offered to ensure mail deliveries, Attorney General Richard Olney nevertheless filed for, and obtained, a federal court injunction against the strike for disrupting interstate commerce and delivery of the mails. Two thousand federal troops were called out by the Democratic president, Grover Cleveland. Twenty-five of these soldiers were killed in a confrontation after the injunction was ignored. Debs was arrested for contempt of the Court's injunction, and sentenced to six months in jail. He became a Socialist in jail, and ran for president on that ticket in each election from 1900 to 1912 and again in 1920. In 1912 he received more than nine hundred thousand votes, representing 6 percent of the total presidential vote that year.

Represented by Clarence Darrow, Debs appealed his contempt conviction to the Supreme Court. In *In re Debs* (1895), a unanimous Court upheld his conviction, using the word "mob" four times in the course of doing so. Justice David Brewer emphasized that "under this government of and by the people the means of redress of all wrongs are through the courts and at the ballot box, and that no wrong, real or fancied, carries with it legal warrant to invite as a means of redress the cooperation of a *mob,* with its accompanying acts of violence."

The economic upheaval that was manifested in the increasing number of violent strikes that permeated the last quarter of the nineteenth century was paralleled in the political arena. There, the former Greenbackers and various farmers' alliances coalesced their dissent in a new Peoples, or Populist, Party, which held its inaugural convention in Omaha, Nebraska, on July 4, 1892. James B. Weaver, the former Greenback candidate, became the Populist presidential candidate, carrying four states with twenty-two electoral votes. He received 8.5 percent of the total popular vote.

By 1896 most of the Populists fused with the Democratic Party. Their common presidential candidate, thirty-six-year-old William Jennings Bryan of Nebraska, carried all of the western states except California and Oregon, but received only 47.7 percent of the popular vote, losing the election to William McKinley of Ohio, the Republican candidate.

For their times the Populists were legitimate radicals. Unlike the Republicans and Democrats, who agreed on most things except the tariff, the Populists called for public ownership of all railroad, telegraph, and telephone companies; a graduated income tax; an increase in the currency supply; unlimited coinage of gold and silver; direct election of senators; term limits for the president and vice president; and the institution of state initiative and referendum reforms for direct votes by the people on critical public issues. One of their leading speakers, Mary Elizabeth Lease, called on farmers to "raise less corn and more Hell," and said that "Wall Street owns the country . . . The great common people of this country are slaves, and monopoly is the master. . . . Money rules." Calling on the government to end "the accursed foreclosure system" and to make loans directly to impoverished farmers, Lease warned that "the people are at bay; let the bloodhounds of money who have dogged us thus far beware."

Populists won office in many states. Weaver carried Nevada, Colorado, Idaho, and Kansas in 1892, and Bryan won twenty-two western, southern, and midwestern states in 1896.

These political successes, combined with the perceived "mob rule" of the most violent labor strikes, concerned the justices of the Supreme Court. In the first decision invalidating a flat 2 percent income tax on incomes more than four thousand dollars, Justice Field wrote a separate opinion in *Pollock v. Farmers' Loan & Trust Co.* (1895), in which he warned that "the present assault upon capital is but the beginning. It will be but the stepping-stone to others, larger and more sweeping, till our political contests will become a war of the poor against the rich, a war constantly growing in intensity and bitterness." Eight years earlier, Justice Miller, in a commencement address at the University of Iowa, agreed that there was a need for "real and genuine reforms in the fabric of social life as shall tend to ameliorate the hardships of want and to prevent all needless suffering" since the "palaces of the rich are surrounded by the hovels of the poor," but warned of the influence of "anarchists, nihilists, socialists, [and] communists" who wanted to overturn and annihilate the system rather than reform it.

As these economic and political events slowly unfolded after the Supreme Court's decision in *Munn v. Illinois,* the Court progressively restricted the freedom of the states to regulate rates charged by railroads. This constriction of state regulatory power happened gradually and in several stages.

The first major ruling came in *County of Santa Clara v. Southern Pacific R.R. Co.* (1886). There, Chief Justice Waite announced at the outset of oral argument that "the court does not wish to hear argument on the question whether the provision in the Fourteenth Amendment . . . , which forbids a state to deny to any person within its jurisdiction the equal protection of the laws, applies to these corporations. We are all of the opinion that it does." This was a mildly surprising ruling, given Justice Miller's opinion for the Court thirteen years earlier in the

Slaughterhouse Cases, where the Equal Protection Clause was seen as focused upon discrimination against African Americans. In that opinion Justice Miller had written that the clause was "so clearly a provision for that race . . . that a strong case would be necessary for its application to any other"—let alone a corporation!

In the same year, the Supreme Court took another step to limit state regulation of railroad traffic in its opinion in *Wabash, St. Louis & Pacific Ry. Co. v. Illinois* (1886). In a six-to-three decision, the Court held that states were barred under the Interstate Commerce Clause from regulating rates charged for the in-state portion of a longer interstate trip, even where Congress had not enacted legislation regulating the rates charged. Justice Samuel Freeman Miller wrote the majority opinion and conceded that the Court in *Munn v. Illinois,* in an opinion he had joined, had ruled that states could regulate rates as a matter of "domestic concern" in the absence of congressional action, even if the rate regulation might "indirectly operate upon commerce outside its immediate jurisdiction." *Munn,* however, did not end the debate. Miller observed that the question of interstate commerce "was evidently not fully considered" in *Munn.* Indeed the opinion failed to appreciate, as Miller put it in terms familiar to those who listened to the Republican presidents of the period, that "the right of continuous transportation, from one end of the country to the other, is essential, in modern times, to that *freedom of commerce,* from the restraints which the states might choose to impose upon it, that the commerce clause was intended to secure." Miller was a realist, and three years after the *Wabash* opinion, he told readers in his *Lectures on the Constitution* that if the Commerce Clause were removed from the Constitution, "this Union would fall to pieces simply by reason of the struggles of each State to make the property owned in other States pay its expenses."

Given the commercial realities in these "modern times," state rate regulation of intrastate railroad rates influenced interstate commerce and could not be allowed to stand. As such "we must therefore hold that it is not, and never has been, the deliberate opinion of a majority of this court that a statute of a state which attempts to regulate the fares and charges by railroad companies within its limits, for a transportation which constitutes a part of commerce among the states, is a valid law."

Justice Bradley filed a dissenting opinion for three justices, including Chief Justice Waite. Bradley had assisted Waite on the *Munn* opinion with a research memorandum, and was committed to its deference to state regulatory authority. Bradley's chief point was that Congress had not chosen to legislate on railroad rates, and the states had not "contracted away" their power to do so. As such the states were free to create railroads and to regulate their rates, even though their regulations "affect commerce; they incidentally regulate it; but they are acts in relation to the subject which the state has a perfect right to do, subject always to the controlling power of congress over the regulation of commerce when congress sees fit to act."

The debate between Miller and Bradley was mooted in the next year, when Congress established the Interstate Commerce Commission. With the question of regulation of interstate railroad commerce thus being practically as well as legally settled, the Supreme Court then turned to what limits, if any, could be imposed on state regulation of railroad rates for traffic taking place exclusively within a single state. On this question, and over a vigorous and impassioned dissent by Justice Bradley, the Court found unconstitutional a state statute that made rates set by a railroad and warehouse commission final and not subject to judicial review. In *Chicago, Milwaukee & St. Paul Ry. Co. v. Minnesota* (1890), the Supreme Court held that the statute "deprives the company of its right to a judicial investigation, *by due process of law,* under the forms and with the machinery provided by the wisdom of successive ages for the investigation judicially of the truth of a matter in controversy, and substitutes therefor, as an absolute finality, the action of a railroad commission which, in view of the powers conceded to it by the state court, cannot be regarded as clothed with judicial functions, or possessing the machinery of a court of justice."

Writing for three members of the Court in dissent, Bradley properly concluded that the decision "practically overrules *Munn v. Illinois* . . . and the several railroad cases that were decided at the same time." Those cases found that "the regulation and settlement of the fares of railroads and other public accommodations is a legislative prerogative, and not a judicial one." Bradley believed this to have been correct then and still—"I hold that it is a legislative question, not a judicial one, unless the legislature or the law (which is the same thing) has made it judicial by prescribing the rule that the charges shall be reasonable, and leaving it there." Echoing the conclusion of the *Munn* opinion, Bradley ended by stating that "it may be that our legislatures are invested with too much power, *open, as they are, to influences so dangerous to the interests of individuals, corporations, and society.* But such is the constitution of our republican form of government, and we are bound to abide by it till it can be corrected in a legitimate way. If our legislatures become too arbitrary in the exercise of their powers, the people always have a remedy in their hands."

With this dissent Justice Bradley takes his leave of our history of the Supreme Court in American society. He died less than two years later, having served twenty-one eventful years on the Supreme Court. His public service also included supplying the deciding vote in favor of the Republican candidate Rutherford B. Hayes against Democrat Samuel J. Tilden on the Electoral Commission of 1877 for the contested presidential election. He wrote the majority opinion in the *Civil Rights Cases* and dissented in the *Slaughterhouse Cases.* A New Jersey Whig/Republican appointed to the Supreme Court by President Grant, he made his own way in the world, and did not shy away from controversy or firmly held beliefs. Paraphrasing what had been said of others, he was sometimes in error, but rarely in doubt.

In 1898, with Justice Bradley now departed, the Supreme Court reached a unanimous decision in the final railroad rate regulation opinion we will discuss. In *Smyth v. Ames,* the Court reviewed the actions of the Nebraska State Board of Transportation in setting railroad rates that were found to have caused the railroads involved in the case to operate at a loss during most of the periods at issue. Justice Harlan's opinion for the Court first held that the railroads were "persons" included within the protections afforded by the Fourteenth Amendment. He then ruled that the actions of the state board taken under an 1893 act to cut local railroad rates by an average of nearly 30 percent did not permit the railroads to earn "just" compensation, including "a fair return" based upon the "fair value" of their properties devoted to public use. Harlan invoked judicial duty in striking down this result, remarking that "the duty rests upon all courts, federal and state, when their jurisdiction is properly invoked, to see to it that no right secured by the supreme law of the land is impaired or destroyed by legislation. This function and duty of the judiciary distinguishes the American system from all other systems of government. The perpetuity of our institutions, and the liberty which is enjoyed under them, depend, in no small degree, upon the power given the judiciary to declare null and void all legislation that is clearly repugnant to the supreme law of the land."

What makes *Smyth v. Ames* especially fascinating in our context is that politics directly entered the courtroom in the person of the Nebraska Board's lawyer, William Jennings Bryan, who argued its case in the Supreme Court. Bryan had just lost the 1896 presidential election to the Republican candidate, William McKinley, and had run on a platform that attacked the Supreme Court for its decision in *Pollock v. Farmers' Loan & Trust Co.* (1895), which struck down the income tax. Bryan—the "Boy Orator of the Platte" River—came from Populist Nebraska and had represented that state in Congress before his presidential run in 1896, and again in 1900 and 1908. He was memorialized by the American poet Vachel Lindsay, who had seen Bryan campaigning, as a "Gigantic troubadour, speaking like a siege gun / Smashing Plymouth Rock with his boulders from the West." Bryan, we may conclude, was the wrong horse for this Supreme Court course, since the Court had no intention to smash Plymouth Rock (or Wall Street, for that matter). The Supreme Court rejected the Populist's appeal, as the voters did by increasing margins in his three presidential bids.

The Emergence of Substantive Due Process

The Fourteenth Amendment provides that no state shall "deprive any person of life, liberty, or property without due process of law." On its face, this provision seems only to require the use of judicially acceptable *procedures* to reach a result.

Thus, in *Chicago, Milwaukee & St. Paul Ry. Co. v. Minnesota* (1890), as we have seen, the Supreme Court held that a Minnesota statute deprived the railroad of due process of law because it stripped it of the procedural right to have the rates set by the railroad and warehouse commission reviewed by a court of law.

But, if the protections afforded by the Due Process Clause were limited only to requiring certain procedures to be followed in enacting regulatory legislation, this would leave beyond judicial review the substantive actions of state legislatures dominated by groups such as the Populists who were viewed as "radical." This was an acceptable result in the view of the majority in *Munn v. Illinois,* as well as in the dissents of Justice Bradley in the railroad rate cases. But this was not the view of a majority of the Supreme Court in the period from the end of the 1890s to 1937. Instead, the prevailing view was that the Fourteenth Amendment also provided *substantive* protections to corporations and other persons against arbitrary legislative action.

The outlines of this viewpoint were revealed in *Smyth v. Ames* (1898), where the Supreme Court found the rates established by state law for railroad traffic to be confiscatory, and thus violative of the requirements of due process. As this concept evolved over the next several decades, it became known as the doctrine of *substantive due process.* Utilizing both the Fifth Amendment for federal legislation and the Fourteenth for state laws, the Supreme Court painstakingly reviewed legislation against its procrustean judicial yardstick for forty years. During that period, some 184 state laws were struck down under the Due Process and Equal Protection clauses of the Fourteenth Amendment.

In the view of the Supreme Court majority, the question in each case came down to a determination as to whether the state or federal law at issue was *reasonable,* after considering the proper scope of the police power, and/or what was required to safeguard public health or morals, and after giving some deference to the legislature in setting public policy. In its view the judiciary served as a needed check and balance on the actions of the legislative branch of government. In opposition a highly vocal Supreme Court minority invoked the doctrine of *judicial restraint,* under which the judiciary was to bow to the elected legislature's determinations. Led by Justices Oliver Wendell Holmes and Louis Brandeis, this group returned to the approach followed in the *Slaughterhouse Cases* and in *Munn v. Illinois,* finding that the legislature was the proper body to formulate public policy in the area of business regulation.

In applying the doctrine of substantive due process before the New Deal of the 1930s, the Supreme Court followed the prevalent free labor philosophy of the nineteenth century, focusing especially upon the right of the laborer to sell his or her services freely to an employer on the basis of a "freedom of contract" protected by the Fourteenth Amendment Due Process Clause. The first case expressly to apply the freedom of contract doctrine was *Allgeyer v. Louisiana* (1897), which was decided the year before *Smyth v. Ames.* At issue was the legality of a Louisiana law that prohibited residents of that state from doing business with out-of-state marine insurance companies. The defendant was sued for violating this law by mailing to New York a notice of certain cotton goods that were to be shipped from New Orleans to Europe and that were to be placed under an insurance contract previously entered into with a New York insurer.

The Supreme Court ruled unanimously that the Louisiana law was unconstitutional as applied in the case, since the contract was being performed outside the state. In an opinion by Justice Rufus Peckham of New York, the Court concluded that "we think the statute is a violation of the fourteenth amendment of the federal constitution, in that it deprives the defendants of their liberty without due process of law.... The 'liberty' mentioned in that amendment means, not only the right of the citizen to be free from the mere physical restraint of his person, as by incarceration, but the term is deemed to embrace the right of the citizen to be free in the enjoyment of all his faculties; to be free to use them in all lawful ways; to live and work where he will; to earn his livelihood by any lawful calling; to pursue any livelihood or avocation; and for that purpose to enter into all contracts which may be proper, necessary, and essential to his carrying out to a successful conclusion the purposes above mentioned."

Peckham's majority opinion echoed the dissenting opinion of Justice Field in the *Slaughterhouse Cases.* Peckham shared Field's fear of radical legislatures. While serving on New York's highest court, he voted to invalidate a law that set maximum rates to be charged by grain elevators, calling it "communistic in its tendency." Appointed to the Supreme Court by President Grover Cleveland, Peckham served from 1896 to 1909. His brother had previously been nominated to the Supreme Court by Cleveland, but that nomination failed.

Allgeyer reached an uncontroversial result, and most today would agree with that result, if not the reasoning of the opinion. That was not the case, however, with Justice Peckham's most significant substantive due process decision, reached in the infamous case of *Lochner v. New York* (1905). Most twentieth century legal commentators have painted *Lochner* as the *Scott* decision of the Supreme Court in the area of government regulation of business.

Lochner reviewed the constitutionality of a New York labor law that mandated that no baker could be "required or permitted" to work more than ten hours in any one day, or more than sixty hours in any one week. Justice Peckham saw this as an "absolute prohibition" on such hours being worked even if the employee wanted to work longer hours. This was wrong, in the view of the five-person majority, because "the general right to make a contract in relation to his business is part of the liberty of the individual protected by the 14th Amendment."

Peckham framed the question as follows: "In every case that comes before this court . . . where legislation of this character is concerned, and where the protection of the Federal Constitution is sought, the question necessarily arises: Is this a fair, reasonable, and appropriate exercise of the police power of the state, or is it an unreasonable, unnecessary, and arbitrary interference with the right of the individual to his personal liberty, or to enter into those contracts in relation to labor which may seem to him appropriate or necessary for the support of himself and his family?" Here, Peckham found, the answer was no to the first question because there was "no reasonable ground" to interfere with the baker's occupation to make "clean and wholesome bread." While health concerns were cited to support the limitations on hours, Peckham saw them as insubstantial. Indeed, he said, taken to an extreme, the same approach could be used to prohibit lawyers and athletes "to fatigue their brains and bodies by prolonged hours of exercise, lest the fighting strength of the state be impaired."

Notably from a free labor viewpoint, Peckham found that the approach of the New York legislature "might seriously cripple the ability of the laborer to support himself and his family." This was an important point, since no baker had complained about hours. Instead, the suit was brought on a complaint by a third party. Moreover the hourly limitations were supported largely by large corporate bakers with union laborers, in order to reduce competition from small bake shops that often were manned by immigrant Italian and Jewish bakers who worked up to fourteen hours a day to make ends meet.

There were two dissenting opinions in *Lochner.* Justice Harlan, along with Justices White and Day, called for deference to the legislative judgment that bakers might be exposed to health dangers from working long hours. Harlan's opinion cites treatises saying just that, and identifying "white lung" and premature death rates among bakers (most of whom died between the ages of forty and fifty) as hazards of the baking trade. Harlan's opinion concludes that these statistics and data demonstrate "that the question is one about which there is room for debate and for an honest difference of opinion." As such, an elected legislature should be able to legislate restrictions in the area.

A separate dissenting opinion was filed by Justice Oliver Wendell Holmes, who was appointed to the Court by President Theodore Roosevelt in 1902 and served for twenty-nine years until the age of ninety in 1932. Generally regarded as one of the leading Supreme Court justices of all time (an opinion we will return to in a later chapter), Holmes was an excellent stylist, noted for pungent aphorisms and clear reasoning. In *Lochner,* Holmes proclaimed that "this case is decided upon an economic theory which a large part of the country does not entertain. . . . The 14th Amendment does not enact Mr. Herbert Spencer's Social Statics." (Holmes was referring to the best-selling book extolling the virtues of free market economics by the author who later coined the phrase "survival of the fittest.") Holmes also called for the exercise of judicial restraint, noting that the Court's decision overrode "the right of a majority to embody their opinions in law." He concluded, in an opinion of less than two pages, that "a Constitution is not intended to embody a particular economic theory, whether of paternalism and the organic relation of the citizen to the state or of laissez faire. It is made for people of fundamentally differing views, and the accident of our finding certain opinions natural and familiar, or novel, and even shocking, ought not to conclude our judgment upon the question whether statutes embodying them conflict with the Constitution of the United States."

While Holmes criticized the majority, his appeal for judicial restraint was not without limits. Even he acknowledged that a statute could be stricken down if the Court found that "a rational and fair man necessarily would admit that the statute proposed would infringe *fundamental principles* as they have been understood by the traditions of our people and our law." Even Holmes, it seems, had his own view of substantive due process.

Lochner in Retreat

The reaction to *Lochner* was both loud and prolonged. The decision came down in 1905, in the early stages of the Progressive Movement, and was contrary to the approach taken by the Progressives. They invoked the twin goals of structure and order in both the economic and social life of the United States. In the economic sphere, Progressives called for new structures of public and private governance. In the public arena, they began municipal reform movements, installing professionally trained city managers, starting in 1900 in Galveston, Texas. In the area of business and the professions, they encouraged voluntary associations to set standards. Some examples of those formed in the Progressive Era include the National Association of Manufacturers (1895), the American Medical Association (1901), and the United States Chamber of Commerce (1912). In universities, departments adopted a faculty framework of dedicated professional scholars who performed detailed research on a full-time basis, disposing of generalists who often performed outside public functions. In politics national regulatory legislation began to be passed on a wider scale, with Progressive political and literary support. For example Upton Sinclair's novel *The Jungle,* which exposed health hazards in the Chicago stockyards, galvanized enactment of 1906 federal legislation mandating meat inspection and pure food and drugs.

Lochner was seen as erecting a judicial obstacle to social reform, as Theodore Roosevelt put it in 1910. At first, in reacting to Progressive criticism, the Supreme Court appeared to retreat from *Lochner* in two cases involving Oregon legislation regulating maximum hours. Initially, in *Muller v. Oregon* (1908), the Court unanimously upheld a law prohibiting more than ten hours of work in any single day in "any mechanical establishment, or factory, or laundry." Significantly the prohibition was limited to female workers in such establishments. Louis Brandeis, then known as "the People's Attorney," filed a brief that generally ignored case precedents, concentrating instead on comparable legislation and legislative and administrative findings supporting the differential treatment of women laborers. The

Court's opinion, by Justice Brewer, cited the "Brandeis Brief" favorably in reaching its result.

Brewer's opinion carefully noted that the result was reached "without questioning in any respect the decision in Lochner v. New York." What Brewer relied upon to justify the result in *Muller* was the importance of "healthy mothers" to "vigorous offspring," noting that "the physical well-being of woman becomes an object of public interest and care in order to preserve the strength and vigor of the race." As such the working woman was "properly placed in a class by herself."

Muller was followed by *Bunting v. Oregon* (1917), which upheld another Oregon law, this time applying to males as well as females. That law mandated a ten-hour day for mills, factories, and manufacturing establishments. It permitted longer hours to be worked, but only if workers were paid time-and-a-half for those extra hours. In an opinion by Justice McKenna, the Court ruled five to three that the statute was not a wage law, but rather a reasonable health regulation based upon average daily working times for such businesses in both the United States and certain foreign countries. While Chief Justice Edward White and Justices Willis Van Devanter and James McReynolds dissented, no dissenting opinion was filed.

The Four Horsemen Save *Lochner*

After *Bunting* the demise of *Lochner* appeared imminent. Its author was dead, its reasoning was contrary to the prevailing Progressive impulses, and recent precedent seemed to doom it. But, as Warren G. Harding assumed the presidency in 1921, he had the opportunity to reshape the Supreme Court. Although Harding died in office after less than two and one-half years (the fourth shortest term of any president in American history), he made four appointments to the Supreme Court in that time. After Chief Justice Edward White died in 1921, Harding appointed former president William Howard Taft to that position. Taft served ably to 1930, and was perhaps the greatest administrative chief justice in history, securing the current Court edifice as well as legislation reducing the Court's docket, and encouraging unanimous opinions and Court harmony. Taft's appointment was followed in succession by the appointments of George Sutherland, a Harding friend and political confidant, in 1922; Pierce Butler in the same year; and Edward Sanford in 1923, the latter two at Taft's suggestion.

Supreme Court appointments often do make a difference in history, as Harding's appointments demonstrate. Two of his appointments—Sutherland and Butler—joined with two justices already serving on the Court—Willis Van Devanter and James McReynolds—to form what pro–New Deal commentators would call "The Four Horsemen" for their apocalyptic opposition to governmental regulation of business. The four, who served together for nearly fifteen years, seemed on the surface to have had little in common. Two were Democrats (McReynolds and Butler), two were Republicans (Van Devanter and Sutherland), and one (McReynolds) had been Woodrow Wilson's attorney general and was appointed to the Court by that Democratic president. Van Devanter had moved to Wyoming, a territory for most of his time there. McReynolds came from Tennessee; Butler from Minnesota; and Sutherland (by way of England, where he was born) from Utah. Sutherland soon became a spokesman for the group's economic conservatism. He had served as the non-Mormon United States senator from conservative Utah for two terms from 1905 through 1917, and was a political ally and friend of Harding. Butler was one of the Court's two Catholics.

Less than a year after his appointment, Sutherland wrote the majority opinion in the five-to-three decision in *Adkins v. Children's Hospital* (1923). At issue in that case was the constitutionality of federal legislation establishing minimum wages for women and children working in the District of Columbia. Wages were to be set for each occupation by an administrative board; women's minimum wages were to be set by considering "what wages are inadequate to supply the necessary cost of living to women workers in such occupation and to maintain them in health and to protect their morals."

One of the plaintiffs in the case was a twenty-one-year-old woman who had lost her position by virtue of the higher wage prescribed by the board for her position as an elevator operator. She presented the strongest scenario against the legislation, alleging that "the work was light and healthful, the hours short, with surroundings clean and moral, and that she was anxious to continue it for the compensation she was receiving, and that she did not earn more'" and "that she could not secure any other position at which she could make a living with as good physical and moral surroundings, and earn as good wages, and that she was desirous of continuing and would continue the employment, but for the order of the board."

Recognizing that "there is, of course, no such thing as absolute freedom of contract," Sutherland went on to state that "freedom of contract is, nevertheless, the general rule and restraint the exception." He then reviewed the prior cases at length, finding four categories in which the Supreme Court had previously sanctioned "interference" with freedom of contract. Those involved rates charged by "businesses impressed with the public interest" (citing *Munn v. Illinois*); public works contracts; "statutes prescribing the character, methods, and time for payment of wages"; and "statutes fixing hours of labor."

Finding that the District of Columbia legislation did not fall into any of these categories, and quoting *Lochner* at length, Sutherland struck the legislation down because it dealt with "the heart of the contract; that is, the amount of wages to be paid and received." What was most objectionable, in Sutherland's view, was that the statute "exacts from the employer an arbitrary payment for a purpose and upon a basis having no causal connection with his business, or the contract or the work the employee engages to do. The declared basis . . . is not the value of the services rendered, but the extraneous circumstance that the employee needs to get a prescribed sum of money to insure her subsistence, health, and morals. . . . The moral requirement implicit in every contract of employment, viz. that the amount to be paid and the service to be rendered shall bear to each other some relation of just equivalence, is completely ignored."

Sutherland concluded by pointing out that if *high* wages could be set by statute, then so too could *low* wages based on a finding, for example, that wages in the building trades were too high to permit "people of ordinary means" to buy homes. "A wrong decision does not end with itself; it is a precedent, and, with the swing of sentiment, its bad influence may run from one extremity of the arc to the other."

Sutherland was joined by the other three "Horsemen," with the fifth vote cast by Justice McKenna. In dissent two opinions were filed. The first was written by Chief Justice Taft, a consensus builder who filed only four dissenting opinions in his eight years on the Court. His opinion was joined by the fourth Harding appointee, Justice Sanford. Taft noted that he had thought that *Lochner* was effectively overruled by *Bunting,* and that there was no meaningful difference between regulating hours and wages. Moreover, echoing Holmes's dissent in *Lochner,* Taft observed that "it is not the function of this court to hold congressional acts invalid simply because they are passed to carry out economic views which the court believes to be unwise or unsound."

Then Holmes piped in with a separate, "forcible" dissenting opinion that Taft conspicuously declined to join because of his "inability to agree with some [of its] general observations." Holmes declared that freedom of contract was not found in the Constitution, but was merely an example of "doing what you want to do," a part of the "liberty" protected by the Fifth and Fourteenth amendments. "But pretty much all law consists in forbidding men to do some things that they want to do, and contract is no more exempt from law than other acts." He agreed with Taft that *Lochner* "would be allowed a deserved repose," and that women could be treated differently than men under *Muller.* Indeed "it will take more than the Nineteenth Amendment to convince me that there are no differences between men and women, or that legislation cannot take those differences into account."

After *Adkins,* the Supreme Court continued to strike down both federal and state legislation attempting to regulate business, often utilizing freedom of contract and substantive due process theories. As noted previously, some 184 state statutes alone were invalidated by the Supreme Court between 1899 and 1937.

The Iceman Cometh: Preaching a New Federalism with Laboratories of Democracy

Nine years after *Adkins,* and in the wake of the Great Depression, which began in 1929, Justice Sutherland wrote the majority opinion for six members of the Court in *New State Ice Company v. Liebmann* (1932). There, an Oklahoma Depression-era statute required that a permit be obtained to engage in the ice business in the state, obliging the applicant to demonstrate "proof of the necessity for a supply of ice" in the market to be served. Defendant Liebmann had not applied for a permit and operated a competing ice business in Oklahoma City to that of the plaintiff, which had invested five hundred thousand dollars in its enterprise. Finding that the ice business was not a natural monopoly, Sutherland's opinion held that the Oklahoma statute denied, or unreasonably curtailed, "the common right to engage in a lawful private business." Moreover it did not "protect against monopoly, but tends to foster it. The aim is not to encourage competition, but to prevent it; not to regulate the business, but to preclude persons from engaging in it."

Only Justices Louis Brandeis and Harlan Stone dissented. Justice Holmes had retired from the Supreme Court only two months earlier at the age of ninety, the oldest justice ever to serve on the Court. Brandeis, the "People's Attorney," was appointed to the Court by President Woodrow Wilson (for whom he had supplied the intellectual basis for the "New Freedom" philosophy) in 1916. His nomination was bitterly opposed by many in the Protestant establishment of the time, including several presidents of the American Bar Association, with a palpable current of anti-Semitism pouring from some opponents' lips and pens. Brandeis, who was confirmed by a Senate vote of forty-seven to twenty-two, had headed the American Zionist Movement and had argued *Muller v. Oregon* in the Supreme Court, inventing what became known as the "Brandeis Brief," a filing relying more heavily on statistical information and legislative and administrative findings than on precedent. Stone was a Columbia Law School professor and former Dean who also rose to chair the Litigation Department of Sullivan & Cromwell, a white-shoe New York law firm.

Brandeis's heavily footnoted dissenting opinion in *New State Ice* began by noting that Oklahoma had classified the ice business as a "public business" given its vital role in a time before widespread refrigeration and had sought to eliminate the waste the state legislature saw as resulting from an "unbridled competition" that "many persons" saw as a substantial contributing cause to the Great Depression. As such the legislation sought to prevent adding production to an industry "already suffering from overcapacity."

Brandeis then held up the Oklahoma statute as an example of "experimentation" at the state level that should be encouraged in a federal system. He stated in what has become famous as the "laboratories of democracy" approach that "it is one of the happy incidents of the federal system that a single courageous state may, if its citizens choose, serve as a *laboratory;* and try novel social and economic experiments without risk to the rest of the country." Brandeis warned that "this Court has the power to prevent an experiment." To do so, however, ran the hazard of "erect[ing] our prejudices into legal principles. If we would guide by the light of reason, we must let our minds be bold."

But Brandeis and Stone lost. There would be no such "experimentation" permitted while the Four Horsemen were in the saddle. Freedom of contract and substantive due process rode on.

The Supreme Court Confronts the Sherman Antitrust Act

From the 1870s on, American industry became increasingly concentrated. Monopolies emerged in a number of important industries, starting with area or regional railroad monopolies and ending with national monopolies in many areas important to the American consumer, including sugar, oil, matches, whiskey, tobacco, jute, salt, envelopes, and packaging and bags of all types. Political opposition to the "trusts," named after the form of entity that controlled the stock holdings in the corporations in a given industry, emerged with the Grangers, Greenbacks, Knights of Labor, and Farmers' Alliance movements discussed above. By 1888, for example, the Union Labor Party platform called for abolition of all monopolies and trusts, and the Republican and Democratic parties both attacked the power of the trusts.

This increasing popular opposition to monopoly power led to enactment of the Sherman Act, which became effective on July 2, 1890, nearly two years to the day before the Populist Party's first convention. The bill was proposed by Senator John Sherman of Ohio. Sherman was a powerful national figure. He served for thirty-two years in the Senate, as well as secretary of treasury, and later would serve as secretary of state. He unsuccessfully sought the Republican nomination for president in 1888.

The Sherman Act passed the Senate by a vote of fifty-two to one, and by voice vote in the House of Representatives. It was biblical in its prohibitions, declaring criminally and civilly illegal "*every* contract, combination in the form of trust or otherwise, or conspiracy, in restraint of trade or commerce among the several states, or with foreign nations." It also prohibited monopolization and attempts and conspiracies or combinations to monopolize interstate or foreign commerce. Despite the breadth of its language, many believed it only proscribed those monopolies or practices that were illegal under the common law. Nevertheless, business leaders feared it, and President Grover Cleveland's attorney general, Richard Olney, thought it "a law I believed to be no good." He used it sparingly, most notably against the Pullman strikers.

The first major test of the Sherman Act came in *Knight Co. v. United States* (1895). There, the Supreme Court considered whether the acquisition of four local sugar companies by the Philadelphia-based American Sugar Refining Company violated the act because it conferred control over 98 percent of the domestic market in refined sugar on the acquiring company.

The sugar interests were represented by John G. Johnson of Philadelphia, then the most prominent business adviser and trial and appellate lawyer in the country. Son of a blacksmith and a seamstress, Johnson numbered among his clients over sixty banks and many national corporations. His most famous client, J. P. Morgan, was obliged to travel to Philadelphia to confer with Johnson, and took his seat in Johnson's waiting room like any other client and waited his turn. Johnson argued 168 cases in the Supreme Court of the United States, including all three of the cases discussed in this section. Twice offered positions on the Supreme Court, he turned down both a Republican offer by President Garfield and a Democratic offer by President Cleveland. A newspaper account of his oral argument in the *Northern Securities* case discussed below marveled at his "remarkable clearness and conciseness—plus the qualities of gentle warmth and a vein of humor which render it a delight to listen to him." Like Morgan, Frick, and other corporate magnates of the time, Johnson was an avid art collector, and his collection formed the basis for the Philadelphia Museum of Art after his death in 1917.

Johnson could not argue the facts in the *Knight* case since 98 percent of the relevant market confers a monopoly under any legal calculus. So he chose instead to argue the law, contending that the act of acquiring stock did not fall within the prohibitions of the Sherman Act. In an opinion by Chief Justice Melville Fuller for eight members of the Court, Johnson prevailed. Returning to the division of power analysis between state and federal authorities that characterized the civil rights decisions surveyed in the previous chapter, the Court decided that "the relief of the citizens of each state from the burden of monopoly and the evils resulting from the restraint of trade among such citizens was left to the states to deal with." It arrived at this conclusion by distinguishing between commerce, which constitutionally could be regulated by the Sherman Act, and manufacture, which could not. "Commerce succeeds to manufacture, and is not part of it. The power to regulate commerce is the power to prescribe the rule by which commerce shall be governed, and is a power independent of the power to suppress monopoly."

Fuller's opinion stressed the importance from a federalist perspective of preserving some power in the states to regulate monopoly, stating that "it is vital that the independence of the commercial power and of the police power, and the delimitation between them, however sometimes perplexing, should always be recognized and observed, for, while the one furnishes the strongest bond of union, the other is essential to the preservation of the autonomy of the states as required by our dual form of government." Indeed "slight reflection will show that, if the national power extends to all contracts and combinations in manufacture, agriculture, mining, and other productive industries, whose ultimate result may affect external commerce, comparatively little of business operations and affairs would be left for state control."

Justice Harlan alone dissented. Following a detailed review of state court decisions involving monopolies, he concluded that stock acquisitions of the type at issue "had been uniformly held by the courts of the states to be against public policy, and illegal, because of [their] necessary tendency to impose improper restraints upon trade." From this launching point, he opined that "whatever a state may do to protect its completely interior traffic or trade against unlawful restraints, the general government is empowered to do for the protection of the people of all the states. . . . While the states retain, because they have never surrendered, full control of their completely internal traffic, it was not intended by the framers of the constitution that any part of interstate commerce should be excluded from the control of congress. Each state can reach and suppress combinations so far as they unlawfully restrain its interior trade, while the national government may reach and suppress them so far as they unlawfully restrain trade among the states."

T. R., Holmes, Morgan, and Hill

After the *Knight* decision, the Supreme Court interpreted the Sherman Act's prohibitions broadly and literally in a number of opinions, most notably in *United States v. Trans-Missouri Freight Association* (1897). In a majority opinion by Justice Peckham for five members of the Court, the Sherman Act was construed in that case to prohibit *all* restraints of interstate trade and commerce in activities to which it applied, not just to those restraints prohibited by the common law. In dissent Justice White, on behalf of the other four members of the Court, called instead for an interpretation that the Sherman Act only prohibited *unreasonable* restraints.

That was the state of the Sherman Act when President Theodore Roosevelt decided to authorize an antitrust suit against the corporate heavyweights J. P. Morgan and James J. Hill and their Northern Securities Company. Roosevelt, an accidental president who succeeded to the post upon President McKinley's assassination, had a moralistic approach to the trusts problem. He distinguished between "good" and "bad" trusts, and the men who ran them often supplied the dividing line. Those of whom he disapproved he assailed as "malefactors of great wealth." For such miscreants, as he put it in 1907, in a letter to the investment banker Jacob Schiff, while he wished to "do everything in my power to aid every honest businessman. . . . The dishonest businessman I wish to punish simply as I would punish the dishonest man of any type."

The Northern Securities Company was the brainchild of J. P. Morgan. It effectively combined the ownership of two competing railroads, the Northern Pacific and the Great Northern. As Justice Harlan noted in his opinion in *Northern Securities Company v. United States* (1904), "All the stock it held or acquired in the constituent companies was acquired and held to be used in suppressing competition between those companies. It came into existence only for that purpose."

Naming Morgan and Hill personally as defendants was not Roosevelt's style; it was the idea of Roosevelt's attorney general, Philander C. Knox, a wealthy corporate lawyer from Pennsylvania, who had represented Andrew Carnegie and helped form United States Steel. Morgan had requested that he not be forced to give testimony, and he sought to settle the suit shortly after it was announced, famously suggesting that Roosevelt should "send your man to my man and they can fix it up." Roosevelt found this offensive, and the suit proceeded all the way to the Supreme Court.

Harlan wrote for four members of the Court in what is known as a plurality opinion. He found the actions of the Northern Securities Company to have violated the Sherman Act, rejecting a number of defenses advanced by a team of lawyers led by John G. Johnson, including two based upon liberty of contract and the exclusive power of the state to regulate monopolies. Harlan saw the Sherman Act as prohibiting all direct restraints of interstate commerce, including the restraints inevitably flowing from the voting power of the Northern Securities Company over the businesses of the two railroads it controlled. Harlan also rejected the view that prohibiting the holding company from voting the stock of the two railroads would lead to "disaster to business and wide-spread financial ruin." As Harlan saw it, "no combination, however powerful, is stronger than the law."

To obtain a majority, Harlan was aided by Justice Brewer, who wrote a concurring opinion that concluded that the Northern Securities Company had *unreasonably* restrained commerce by its activities, and that the Sherman Act only prohibited such unreasonable restraints. This was noteworthy since, as Brewer himself noted, he had joined the Court's prior opinions interpreting the Sherman Act to forbid *all* restraints of interstate trade and commerce. Now he believed that his new view was necessary because of "fear that the broad and sweeping language of the opinion of the Court might tend to unsettle legitimate business enterprises, stifle or retard wholesome business activities, encourage improper disregard of reasonable contracts, and invite unnecessary litigation."

Two dissenting opinions were filed. That by Justice White properly found the conduct at issue to fall squarely under the holding of the *Knight* case that stock acquisitions fell outside the coverage of the Sherman Act. The more famous dissent was written by Justice Holmes, whom Roosevelt had appointed to the Supreme Court only two years before.

Proclaiming that "great cases, like hard cases, make bad law," Holmes cautioned against a literal reading of the Sherman Act prohibitions. He instead interpreted them only to prohibit agreements or combinations that involved an "external restriction" involving a "contract with a stranger" to restrict competition. As he saw the Sherman Act, "It simply requires that a party's freedom in trade between the states shall not be cut down by contract with a stranger." In a characteristic literary flight of hyperbole, Holmes concluded that any other interpretation would "make eternal the *bellum omnium contra omnes* [the war of all against all] and disintegrate society so far as it could into individual atoms. . . . It would be an attempt to reconstruct society."

Holmes, in private correspondence, wrote that "the Sherman Act is a humbug based on economic ignorance and incompetence." His dissent notes that "size, in the case of railroads, is an inevitable incident." These views were those of a believing Social Darwinist. Notably, however, they conflicted with the views of Congress in enacting antitrust legislation. Holmes, the exponent of the will of the majority and of judicial restraint in the dissenting opinions he wrote against freedom of contract, thwarted both the popular and congressional wills in his interpretation of the Sherman Act. He did this by basing his dissent on his own personal views. Ironically this was the same fault for which he would criticize the *Lochner* majority in the following year.

Roosevelt's reaction to the narrow victory in the *Northern Securities* case was noteworthy in two respects. First, he felt that "the most powerful men in the country were held to accountability before the law." Second, as to Holmes, he was dismissive: "I could carve out of a banana a judge with more backbone than that."

The Rule of Reason Finally Prevails

Within seven years, the four-justice plurality of the *Northern Securities* case vanished. President William Howard Taft appointed five new justices to the Supreme Court, as well as a new chief justice, in his one four-year term between 1909 and 1913. These new justices included four appointed by 1910. During the same period, both Justice William Moody, who had joined Justice Harlan's opinion in *Northern Securities,* and Justice David Brewer, who had concurred in that opinion, left the Supreme Court. The new chief justice was Edward White of Louisiana, a former Confederate soldier who had fought in the Civil War and was captured and held as a Union prisoner during that war. He later served in the United State Senate from his home state, where he functioned chiefly as a spokesman for Louisiana sugar interests. Originally appointed to the Supreme Court in 1894 by a Democratic president, Grover Cleveland, White was only the second Catholic to serve on the Court in over one hundred years. He was the first associate justice of the Supreme Court who was later elevated to chief justice. White served on the Supreme Court for twenty-seven years until his death in 1921. Former president Taft, who had appointed him, took his place as chief justice in that year.

White's greatest opinion was that delivered for eight members of the Court in *Standard Oil Company v. United States* (1911), the most important decision to date on the reach of the federal antitrust laws. At issue was whether Standard Oil, which had been a major target of the Progressive Era "muckraking" journalists, had violated the Sherman Act and whether it should be dissolved. Founded by John D. Rockefeller, the richest man in the United States from 1911 to his death in 1937 at the age of ninety-seven, Standard Oil had left a trail of ruined competitors behind it. In a bill that spanned forty years of detailed misconduct, the United States focused on the actions of Standard Oil in three periods. In the first period, up to

1882, Standard Oil acquired more than thirty oil refineries in Ohio and extracted preferential treatment on rates and rebates from the railroads that shipped its products. Next, it formed a trust that controlled forty different corporations up to 1899. Finally, from 1899 to the filing of the bill, Standard Oil acquired stock majorities in these corporations and monopolized interstate commerce in petroleum and petroleum by-products by such acts as obtaining rebates and other preferential treatment from railroads; unfair competition, including local price-cutting to drive area competitors out of business; corporate espionage; division of territories in which its subsidiaries could sell their products; and exaction of "enormous and unreasonable profits."

In his opinion White spent little time on whether Standard Oil had violated the Sherman Act. He found the stock control and acquisitions of multiple companies in the oil industry to have constituted "aggregating so vast a capital" as to raise a presumption of monopolistic intent, a presumption that he found was validated by the "exercise of power" to exclude others from the market Standard Oil monopolized. He also found dissolution to be an appropriate remedy for Standard Oil's misconduct.

White saw the Sherman Act as having been enacted in 1890 because of "the economic condition of the times; that is, the vast accumulation of wealth in the hands of corporations and individuals, the enormous development of corporate organization, the facility for combination which such organizations afforded, the fact that the facility was being used, and that combinations known as trusts were being multiplied, and the widespread impression that their power had been and would be exerted to oppress individuals and injure the public generally." He traced its broadly worded prohibitions to the need to meet "the many new forms of contracts and combinations which were being evolved from existing economic conditions," a development requiring "an all-embracing enumeration" to capture all conceivable wrongdoing. As such the statutory language only marked off the "ulterior boundaries" of potential wrongdoing.

Given this approach, White concluded that while Congress did not specify a standard to judge which restraints within these boundaries were illegal, the statute, "indubitably contemplating and requiring a standard," must have intended to employ the common law "standard of reason." This "rule of reason" was required because "to hold to the contrary would require the conclusion either that every contract, act, or combination of any kind or nature, whether it operated a restraint of trade or not, was within the statute." Such a conclusion, White reasoned, "would be *destructive of all right to contract*" and thus a rule of reason was required.

Justice Harlan dissented in an outraged opinion delivered only a few months before his death in October of the same year. He saw the origin of the Sherman Act differently than the majority did—"All who recall the condition of the country in 1890 will remember that there was everywhere, among the people generally, a deep feeling of unrest. The nation had been rid of human slavery, fortunately,—as all now feel,—but the conviction was universal that the country was in real danger from *another kind of slavery* sought to be fastened on the American people; namely the slavery that would result from aggregations of capital in the hands of a few individuals and corporations controlling, for their own profit and advantage exclusively, the entire business of the country, including the production and sale of the necessaries of life."

Harlan then accused his brethren of ignoring the Supreme Court's own antitrust precedents and of rewriting the Sherman Act in a way that constituted "usurpation by the judicial branch . . . of the functions of the legislative department." He concluded that the antitrust laws had been eviscerated. Indeed, under the "rule of reason," corporate malefactors were simply being told: "'You may now restrain such commerce, provided you are reasonable about it; only take care that the restraint is not undue.'"

White's opinion and Harlan's dissent reflected a national debate that would resonate in the presidential election held the next year. That 1912 election involved four notable candidates seeking the presidency—the incumbent Republican, President William Howard Taft; former president Theodore Roosevelt, running as a third-party "Bull Moose" Progressive; the Democratic challenger, Governor Woodrow Wilson of New Jersey, who had also served as president of Princeton University; and the Socialist candidate, Eugene Debs of Pullman Strike fame.

These four had different views of how to control the "trusts." Debs would turn them over to government control or, like Justice Harlan, break them up. But the other three sought a middle ground. Roosevelt, who as president had distinguished between "good" and "bad" trusts, was closest to the *Standard Oil* rule-of-reason approach. In the 1912 campaign, he had refined his approach, calling for a new National Industrial Commission to regulate all trusts operating in interstate commerce and to "moderate" capitalism. Taft's approach was to pursue litigation enforcing the antitrust laws. In his four years as president, he authorized the filing of some seventy antitrust suits, compared to forty-four (including *Standard Oil*) filed by Roosevelt in his seven years as president. While Taft announced that he supported the Supreme Court's decision in *Standard Oil,* in fact he had opposed a rule-of-reason approach previously, feeling that it conferred too much discretion upon the courts over the economy.

Wilson took yet another approach, calling for a "New Freedom," conceptualized by Louis Brandeis, whom he later named to the Supreme Court. As we saw in Brandeis's *New State Ice* dissent, this approach opposed wasteful competition. Wilson sought to restructure competition by imposing rules of engagement. In the 1912 election, he called for "the destruction of monopoly not by regulation, but by the enactment of specific legislation." These would become the Clayton Act and Federal Trade Commission Act after Wilson's election. The Clayton Act prohibited certain practices thought to be anticompetitive, including price discrimination, mergers that substantially lessened competition, interlocking directorates, and tying arrangements, under which one product was only sold in combination with another, less desired, one. The Federal Trade Commission looked for other, unspecified "unfair methods of competition," and was empowered to issue cease-and-desist orders. These legislative approaches reflected the Progressive Era system of imposing structure and order everywhere, with the government serving as a watchmaker deity over society.

Today the rule-of-reason approach continues generally to be the polestar in antitrust litigation. Initially, after *Standard Oil*, the courts differentiated between restraints that were to be judged under the rule of reason and others that were deemed to be so pernicious as to be labeled as "per se" violations of the Sherman Act. These per se violations included price fixing and division of territories between competitors. In the era after World War II until the mid-1970s, the Supreme Court broadened this per se approach, following a populist consumer impact model that resulted in protecting small competitors and consumer interests rather than competition itself. That model was abandoned starting with the 1977 opinion in *Continental T.V., Inc. v. GTE Sylvania, Inc.*, in favor of an expanded rule-of-reason inquiry using economic analysis in place of a consumer-impact model. This reflected the influence of the Chicago school of economics, supported on the Supreme Court by Justices Lewis Powell, a former president of the American Bar Association, and John Paul Stevens, a former antitrust lawyer from Chicago. Today, most restraints are judged under a rule-of-reason approach that asks whether a restraint promotes or suppresses competition. The Supreme Court has explained that this rule-of-reason approach requires a court to decide "whether the questioned practice imposes an unreasonable restraint on competition, taking into account a variety of factors, including specific information about the relevant business, its condition before and after the restraint was imposed, and the restraint's history, nature, and effect." By permitting businesses thus to justify most types of restraints and by elevating economic analysis over populist ideals of preserving small producers and competitors, this approach continues a history tracing back to the Marshall Court of the Supreme Court's protection of business against overregulation, a history interrupted only briefly from the later New Deal years in the 1930s to 1977.

Six

The Supreme Court and the New Deal

The carefully constructed doctrine of substantive due process created a liberty of contract that could not be abridged or regulated by the government. The Supreme Court applied that doctrine for forty years, often over vigorous dissent, to strike down scores of federal and state regulatory laws. Federal laws were also subjected to inconsistent, but often restrictive, views about the range of the Commerce Clause, as well as to expanded views about the power of the state as compared to that of the federal government. This doctrinal edifice came crashing down abruptly in the brief period from 1937 to 1942. By 1942 federal regulatory power over virtually every aspect of the economy was not only recognized, but appeared limitless.

This reconstruction of legal doctrine was a direct consequence of economic crisis. Starting with the notorious stock market crash on October 29, 1929, the economy spiraled downward for more than a decade, recovering only after the United States entered World War II. The stock market average of 452 in October 1929 decreased to a low of 58 in July 1932, and the 1933 Gross National Product was only 76 percent of that of 1929. There were thirty million individuals unemployed in 1930, with some 25 percent of the labor force in that situation by 1932. Farm income declined 70 percent between 1929 and 1932. Some ten thousand banks failed, merged, or closed between 1930 and 1932, with depositors losing more than $2.5 billion in savings.

President Herbert Hoover was unable to stop this downward economic spiral, and, perhaps more important, could not inspire confidence in the public. By 1932 Hoover was entirely discredited and lost the presidential election in that year by seven million votes to Governor Franklin Delano Roosevelt of New York. Roosevelt's electoral vote total was even more impressive, beating Hoover by a margin of 472 to 59.

Committed to experimentation until he came upon the right solution, Roosevelt started his first "New Deal" with a flurry of legislation in the first hundred days of his administration. Beginning with relief and construction projects to supply money and jobs for the unemployed, he also closed all the banks in the country and initiated wide-ranging banking legislation at the federal level. These reforms included establishing the Federal Deposit Insurance Corporation, with deposit insurance to protect the savings of individual depositors; mandating federal examinations of financial institutions; and separating commercial banking from investment banking. Roosevelt followed with legislation regulating the securities markets in the Securities Act of 1933 and the Securities Exchange Act of 1934. This revolutionary legislation sought to equalize access to information by making the securities markets transparent, with mandated disclosures of material financial information to existing and prospective investors.

But the centerpieces of the first New Deal came in parallel legislation passed in the first one hundred days regulating first the agricultural, and next the industrial, market. In the Agricultural Adjustment Act of May 1933, the producers of seven key commodities, including such staples as wheat, cotton, and tobacco, were permitted to set prices for those commodities. In addition, in a radical departure from free enterprise, farmers were given subsidies *not* to grow crops. Moreover the federal government acted to construct an artificial parity between prices charged for manufactured goods and those charged for farm goods. The costs of the crop subsidies were funded, under the act, by a tax on processors of farm goods.

This same type of cooperative economics, modeled upon the European fascist approach to regulating economic markets as well as on Hoover's previous efforts, was employed in the National Industrial Recovery Act (NIRA). That legislation was passed in June 1933, as part of the one hundred days legislative initiative. Under the act, producers of industrial goods were permitted to enter into "codes of fair competition" which were reviewed and approved by a National Recovery Administration (NRA). More than seven hundred such codes were devised, covering twenty-three million people. They were designed to, and did, set prices, allocate markets, and cut production, all in an effort to end ruinous competition and stabilize markets. As part of the bargain to permit businesses the privilege of self-regulation, the NIRA required them to establish minimum wages and maximum hours as part of the industry codes. Extensive publicity was devoted to encouraging all businesses to join the NRA. Adopting a Blue Eagle modeled on the Native American Thunderbird as its symbol, the NRA provided posters for participating businesses to display in their windows, proclaiming "We Do Our Part." Some two million people participated in a parade in New York City to support the NRA in September 1933. But the celebration would be short-lived. The NRA would be dead within two years.

The Supreme Court Strikes Back

On May 27, 1935, the Supreme Court struck down both the National Industrial Recovery Act and the Frazier-Lemke Act of 1934, which sought to protect farm owners threatened with loss of their farms by mortgage foreclosures. In *Schechter Poultry Corporation v. United States* (1935), the Supreme Court reviewed the criminal convictions of slaughterhouse operators who were indicted and convicted on eighteen counts of violating the Live Poultry Code for the New York metropolitan area. That Code was adopted as a code of fair competition under the NIRA and approved by President Roosevelt. The Schechters were convicted of a host of crimes, including failure to pay the minimum wage, permitting work in excess of maximum hours, selling an unfit chicken to a butcher, and on ten counts of permitting favored butchers to select individual chickens, rather than requiring them to accept the run of the chicken coop, as required under the Live Poultry Code.

In attempting to save the NIRA, Solicitor General Stanley Reed pointed to the "grave national crisis." In an opinion for a unanimous Court, Chief Justice Charles Evans Hughes replied that "extraordinary conditions may call for extraordinary remedies," but such conditions "do not create or enlarge congressional power." In the Court's view, Congress exceeded its power in two ways in enacting the NIRA. First, the statute was found to be an unlawful delegation of legislative power. Second, it was a violation of the Commerce Clause to attempt to regulate intrastate commerce that had only an indirect effect upon interstate commerce.

The codes of fair competition permitted under the NIRA had virtually no limits. Other than prohibitions against monopolies and discrimination against small businesses, the businesses that put the codes together were free to "roam at will, and the President may approve or disapprove their proposals as he may see fit." The Court found this to be unacceptable, because "Congress cannot delegate legislative power to the President to exercise an unfettered discretion to make whatever laws he thinks may be needed or advisable for the rehabilitation and expansion of trade or industry." In a concurring opinion, liberal justice Benjamin Cardozo saw this as "delegation running riot." As such all the justices agreed that permitting the enactment of codes where there were "no standards," constituted "an unconstitutional delegation of legislative power."

In addition attempting to regulate the operations of the Schechters' poultry business violated the Commerce Clause. Once the poultry had been sold to the Schechters, it had come to its final rest, and "the flow in interstate commerce had ceased." Chief Justice Hughes explained that this conclusion flowed from the "necessary and well-established distinction between direct and indirect effects." Under that distinction, "where the effect of intrastate transactions upon interstate commerce is merely indirect, such transactions remain within the *domain of state power.* If the Commerce Clause were construed to reach all enterprises and transactions that could be said to have an indirect effect upon interstate commerce, *the federal authority would embrace practically all the activities of the people,* and the authority of the state over its domestic concerns would exist only by sufferance of the federal government." As the Supreme Court saw it unanimously in May 1935, permitting the regulation of transactions that had an indirect effect upon interstate commerce would mean that "there would be *virtually no limit to the federal power, and for all practical purposes, we should have a completely centralized government.*"

On the same day, in *Louisville Joint Stock Land Bank v. Radford* (1935), the Supreme Court ruled that the 1934 Frazier-Lemke Amendment to the Federal Bankruptcy Act was also unconstitutional. Under the act, a farm owner threatened with loss of his or her property because of a mortgage foreclosure could request the assent of the mortgage lender to purchase the property for its appraised value over a six-year time period. If the lender refused to do so, the farmer could obtain a five-year stay of foreclosure from the bankruptcy court, during which period the farmer would retain possession of the farm and pay a reasonable rental.

In a unanimous opinion written for the Court by Justice Louis Brandeis, the Court found that the Frazier-Lemke Act violated the Fifth Amendment by depriving the mortgage lender of its property rights under state law. These rights included controlling the property during the period of default, determining when a mortgage foreclosure sale should be held, and retaining a mortgage lien until the lender was paid in full. Brandeis rejected the argument that the legislation had a valid public purpose because it sought to promote national welfare by assuring that "our farms be individually owned by those who operate them." Indeed the proponents argued that "to permit widespread foreclosure of farm mortgages would result in transferring ownership, in large measure, to great corporations; would transform farmer owners into tenants or farm laborers; and would tend to *create a peasant class.*"

While emotionally appealing, these arguments were unavailing. A unanimous Court replied that "the Fifth Amendment commands that, however great the nation's need, private property shall not be thus taken even for a wholly public use without just compensation. If the public interest requires, and permits, the taking of property of individual mortgagees in order to relieve the necessities of individual mortgagors, resort must be had to proceedings by eminent domain; so that, through taxation, the burden of the relief afforded in the public interest may be borne by the public."

Seven months after the opinions in *Schechter* and *Radford*, the Supreme Court began the new year by invalidating the Agricultural Adjustment Act. In *United States v. Butler* (1936), decided on January 6, 1936, the Supreme Court considered the constitutionality of the tax imposed on processors of farm goods to fund payments to farm producers to limit their crop production. Once again Solicitor General Stanley Reed argued for the government, but this time he attempted to defend the legislation on the basis of the taxing power conferred on the federal government under Article 1, Section 8. Under that provision, Congress is expressly empowered to "lay and collect Taxes . . . to . . . provide for the . . . general Welfare of the United States."

In a six-to-three decision, the Supreme Court declared the Agricultural Adjustment Act unconstitutional. The majority, in an opinion by Justice Owen J. Roberts, found it unnecessary to determine how far the federal government could go to lay taxes under the General Welfare Clause because the Agricultural Adjustment Act "invades the reserved rights of the states." Justice Roberts explained that the act "was a statutory plan to regulate and control agricultural production, a matter beyond the powers delegated to the federal government." Relying upon a theory of federalism that was enunciated in its post–Civil War civil rights decisions, the majority declared that "ours is a dual form of government; . . . in every state there are two governments; the state and the United States. . . . The federal union is a government of delegated powers. It has only such as are expressly conferred upon it and such as are reasonably to be implied from those granted."

In the majority's view, permitting the use of the taxing power to regulate agricultural production would permit "the regulation of all industry throughout the United States." Indeed Justice Roberts pointed out that the federal government would be able to avoid the ruling of the Supreme Court in *Schechter* by the simple expedient of "appropriating money to be paid to employers from the federal treasury under contracts whereby they agree to comply with certain standards fixed by federal law or by contract."

Unlike *Schechter*, however, the Supreme Court was not unanimous in the *Butler* decision. Writing for himself and Justices Brandeis and Cardozo, Justice Stone dissented, concluding that "the power to tax and spend includes the power to relieve *a nationwide economic maladjustment* by conditional gifts of money." He pointed out what he felt were the "absurd consequences" of the majority's approach: "The government may give seeds to farmers, but may not condition the gift upon their being planted in places where they are most needed or even planted at all. The government may give money to the unemployed, but may not ask that those who get it shall give labor in return, or even use it to support their families. It may give money to sufferers from earthquake, fire, tornado, pestilence, or flood, but may not impose conditions, health precautions, designed to prevent the spread of disease, or induce the movement of population to safer or more sanitary areas. All that, because it is . . . regulation infringing state powers, must be left for the states, who are unable or unwilling to supply the necessary relief."

Schechter and *Butler* endangered the first New Deal's core programs by imposing a combination of three separate constitutional obstacles to federal regulation of business and agriculture. These were limitations on the scope of congressional power under the Commerce Clause, an expanded view of the reserved powers of the states, and unlawful delegation. These formidable obstacles, combined with increased pressure being placed on President Roosevelt by the political left, led him to an ill-advised attempt to "pack" the Supreme Court with new congressional legislation expanding its membership. This situation was exacerbated when the Supreme Court in May 1936—six months before the presidential election—decided *Carter v. Carter Coal Company* (1936). In that case Justice Sutherland wrote a lengthy opinion, over partial dissents by Chief Justice Hughes and by Justices

Cardozo, Brandeis, and Stone. *Carter* reaffirmed *Schechter*'s narrow construction of the power of the federal government under the Commerce Clause, as well as *Butler*'s states' rights philosophy, in striking down the Bituminous Coal Conservation Act of 1935.

From *Schechter* to *Carter*, the Supreme Court divided, starting with a unanimous Court, and ending with a five-to-four split. And then came the election of 1936, reelecting Franklin D. Roosevelt with overwhelming legislative majorities for the Democratic Party in both houses of Congress. This permitted Roosevelt to appoint a new majority of Supreme Court justices.

Pressure from the Left

While he was very popular with a majority of the American people, there was fierce opposition to Roosevelt from both the right and left. On the right, the American Liberty League provided a focal point for conservative opposition. It numbered among its leaders the two Democratic presidential candidates immediately preceding Roosevelt—Al Smith and John W. Davis. Business leaders, including Albert Sloan of General Motors, considered Roosevelt a "class traitor." A famous Peter Arno cartoon from 1936 showed a group of well-dressed people walking down a street. After spotting a friend on the ground floor of a brownstone, they exclaimed, "Come along, we're going to the Trans-Lux to hiss Roosevelt."

While this opposition from the Right was disturbing, the greater political threat came from the Left. Liberals and intellectuals formed the League for Independent Political Action, which called for the destruction of capitalism. Its members included the philosopher John Dewey and future Democratic senator Paul Douglas. The Farmer-Labor Party of Minnesota called for government ownership of key industries to form a "cooperative Commonwealth," and its leader, Governor Floyd Olson, announced, "I am not a liberal. I am a radical." Communists and Socialists also opposed Roosevelt's approach in the first New Deal. They drew into their net noted intellectuals, including the novelist John Dos Passos and the poet Langston Hughes.

Roosevelt's most significant opposition from the Left came from three individuals who joined forces for the election of 1936. These were Dr. Francis Townsend, Father Charles Coughlin, and Senator Huey P. Long. Townsend was a retired California doctor who was disturbed by the widespread poverty all around him. In January 1934 he proposed a plan to pay workers a two-hundred-dollar monthly allowance on the conditions that they retire and spend all the money within thirty days. Mimicking Roosevelt's approach in the Agricultural Adjustment Act, which was designed to retire crops, Townsend's plan would be financed by a 2 percent sales tax. The idea was wildly popular, with more than five thousand Townsend Clubs springing up and claiming two million members by 1936.

Father Charles Coughlin was an even more significant political opponent for Roosevelt. A Roman Catholic priest in the suburbs of Detroit, Michigan, Coughlin began a religious program on a local radio station in 1930 to honor St. Therese, known as "the Little Flower." His radio program—"The Golden Hour of the Little Flower"—was even more popular than the television broadcasts featuring another Catholic clergyman, Bishop Fulton J. Sheen, in the 1950s. Coughlin's radio audience multiplied exponentially, soon numbering forty million listeners. Coughlin needed four secretaries and 106 clerks to open and sort his mail. He received more mail than President Roosevelt.

Originally a supporter of the New Deal, Coughlin soon turned against Roosevelt. His religious program metamorphosized into a political one. Coughlin's approach combined elements of Populism with those of Catholic social teachings, particularly ideas from the labor encyclicals of the popes. He was strongly prolabor, supporting his autoworker parishioners. Coughlin was fiercely against monopoly and believed in monetary solutions to social problems. He viewed finance capitalism as an evil and proposed to redeem it with a program calling for greater use of greenbacks and silver, abolition of the Federal Reserve System, and nationalization of all banks. He also proposed a national welfare system and general control of the economy by the state. To provide a national base for his ideas, Coughlin began the National Union for Social Justice in November 1934. That organization served as the platform for a third-party candidacy against Roosevelt's reelection in 1936.

The candidate both Father Coughlin and Dr. Townsend planned to support was Huey P. Long of Louisiana. An American original, Long combined the best and worst of American politics. Popularly known as "the Kingfish," Long was the model for the protagonist in Robert Penn Warren's novel, *All the King's Men.* He served in turn first as governor, and then as a United States senator, from Louisiana. Long was an unabashed populist and a big spender. He poured millions of dollars into building highways, bridges, hospitals, and schools, and provided free schoolbooks to the children of southern Louisiana, including those attending Catholic schools. In 1928 his slogan in running for governor was "every man a king, but no man wears a crown," a phrase he borrowed from William Jennings Bryan. Often portrayed as a backwoods redneck rube, Long was a sophisticated lawyer and politician. Indeed, after he argued a utility case before the Supreme Court of the United States, Chief Justice William Howard Taft observed that Long was the "most brilliant, competent and intelligent attorney" Taft had seen in his years on the Court.

Long planned a run for the presidency in 1936. To that end, in October 1933 he published a campaign autobiography entitled *Every Man a King,* and in January 1934, he issued a platform popularly known as the "Soak the Rich" plan. Long pointed out that 4 percent of the people (whom he called "Morgan and Rockefeller,

Mellon and Baruch") controlled 85 percent of the nation's wealth. To combat this monetary monopoly, Long called for limitation of incomes, first to five million dollars, and later to one million. His plan also would limit inheritances to five million. For ordinary workers Long would guarantee an annual wage of twenty-five hundred dollars, along with workers' pensions and free college education. Long's political organization catalyzed a proliferation of "Share the Wealth" Clubs, which grew to millions of members before 1936. President Roosevelt's political expert, Postmaster General James Farley, calculated that Long could take 10 percent of the presidential vote in 1936.

That was not to be. Long was shot on September 6, 1935, in Louisiana, dying two days later at the age of forty-two. Feared as a fascist, and labeled "Der Kingfish" by liberal opponents, Long was loved by the common man in Louisiana. Some 250,000 attended his funeral with a procession of cars spanning some eight miles. Three acres of flowers were left in the cemetery.

The triumvirate of Townsend, Coughlin, and Long demonstrably forced President Roosevelt to the left. Pressed by the influence of all three, Roosevelt proposed Social Security in 1935. His approach differed from that of the Townsend plan. Payments would be financed not by a sales tax, but rather by contributions from both employees and the employer. In addition to workers' pensions, Social Security would also provide unemployment compensation and aid to the disabled and to dependent children.

Coughlin's social justice programs for labor induced Roosevelt to support not only unemployment compensation, but also the National Labor Relations Act. Passed in 1935, the "Wagner Act" compelled recognition of unions, banned the antiunion "yellow dog" contract, and barred the use of injunctions in labor disputes. It also established the National Labor Relations Board, which advanced the interests of organized labor, adjudicating "unfair labor practices." The Board grew rapidly, with its original staff of 14 lawyers growing to 226 between 1935 and 1939.

Long's influence was seen in both the unemployment compensation and old-age pension features of Social Security, as well as in Roosevelt's aggressive increase of income, corporate, and inheritance taxes. On incomes exceeding five million dollars, the Democratic Congress assessed the tax rate at 79 percent. That tax rate applied to a single individual—John D. Rockefeller. Roosevelt candidly told a reporter that "it might be necessary to throw to the wolves" individuals making more than one million dollars a year. On the inheritance tax, Roosevelt told Congress that "the transmission of wealth from generation to generation of vast fortunes . . . is not consistent with the ideas and sentiments of the American people." Roosevelt also turned his Justice Department on the visibly rich. One of the most notable prosecutions for tax evasion was that of former treasury secretary Andrew Mellon, a prosecution that ultimately failed. All of these steps led Roosevelt to proclaim that "we have earned the hatred of entrenched greed."

By the time of the 1936 presidential election, Roosevelt had neutralized his opponents, with the assistance of Long's assassin. Franklin D. Roosevelt was reelected president in 1936 by a margin exceeding 11 million popular votes. His electoral vote total was staggering. He defeated the Republican candidate, Governor Alf Landon of Kansas, with 523 electoral votes to Landon's 8, the largest margin in over one hundred years. Landon carried only Maine and Vermont. With Long deceased, the National Union for Social Justice and its Union Party ran William Lemke, the congressman from North Dakota who had written the Frazier-Lemke farm mortgage bill and had argued for its constitutionality before the Supreme Court in the *Radford* case. Lemke received nine hundred thousand votes, less than 2 percent of the popular vote.

Roosevelt Strikes Back: The "Court-Packing" Plan

Roosevelt's landslide victory carried along huge majorities for the Democrats in Congress. After the election of 1936, the Democratic Party controlled some 75 percent of the seats in both the United States Senate and the House of Representatives. With this overwhelming legislative majority, Roosevelt decided to take on the Supreme Court of the United States. Having secretly devised a plan to expand the Court to add members more friendly to the second New Deal of Social Security, the Wagner Act, a revived Agricultural Adjustment Act, and other New Deal social legislation, Roosevelt sprung the idea on congressional leaders the very day the bill was introduced on February 5, 1937. The plan called for the addition of one justice, up to a total of six, for each justice on the Supreme Court who was over seventy years of age. At the time the bill was introduced, the average age of the Supreme Court justices was seventy-one.

Roosevelt took his case directly to the American people on the radio, in a "fireside chat" on March 9, 1937. He denounced the Supreme Court's invalidation of New Deal legislation as having caused a "crisis." He depicted Congress, the Executive, and the Judiciary as a "three-horse team" that was not pulling together. As Roosevelt put it, the Supreme Court had been "acting not as a judicial body, but as a policymaking body" and "a super-legislature." Acting to "save the Constitution from the Court, and the Court from itself," Roosevelt pledged to appoint justices "who will act as Justices and not as legislators." Relying upon an 1803 quote from Justice Bushrod Washington, Roosevelt called for the Court to presume the validity of any law passed by Congress unless it was shown to be unconstitutional beyond a reasonable doubt.

Roosevelt's court-packing plan died in its infancy. There was great opposition in both Congress and the press. Editorial cartoons in most major newspapers opposed the plan, with one having a dejected voter looking downward and saying that he voted for Roosevelt but "Not for That." Roosevelt had little cause for worry, however, since the Supreme Court majority soon shifted to permit the expansion of federal power embodied in the Second New Deal.

The "Switch in Time Saves Nine"

On March 29, 1937, less than three weeks after Roosevelt's radio address, the Supreme Court decided *West Coast Hotel Co. v. Parrish* (1937). That case presented a challenge to a Washington state law regulating wages much along the lines of the law struck down by the Supreme Court in *Adkins v. Children's Hospital* (1923). In an opinion by Chief Justice Hughes for five members of the Court, the law was upheld, and "the case of Adkins v. Children's Hospital . . . is overruled."

In deciding to reconsider its fourteen-year-old decision in *Adkins,* Chief Justice Hughes noted several factors, including the "close division" in that case, "the economic conditions which have supervened," and the "importance of the question." Hughes announced that "the Constitution does not speak about freedom of contract. It speaks of liberty and prohibits the deprivation of liberty without due process of law. . . . Liberty under the Constitution is . . . necessarily subject to the restraints of due process, and regulation which is reasonable in relation to its subject and is adopted in the interests of the community is due process. This essential limitation of liberty in general governs freedom of contract in particular." Moreover the *Adkins* opinion represented a "departure from the true application of the principles governing the regulation by the state of the relation of employer and employed."

Hughes ended his opinion for the majority with a reference to the depressed economy. He stated that "there is an additional and compelling consideration which recent economic experience has brought into a strong light. The *exploitation of a class of workers who are in an unequal position with respect to bargaining power and are thus relatively defenseless against the denial of a living wage* is not only detrimental to their health and well being, but casts a direct burden for their support upon the community. What these workers lose in wages the taxpayers are called upon to pay. . . . We may take judicial notice of the unparalleled demands for relief which arose during the recent period of depression and still continue to an alarming extent despite the degree of economic recovery which has been achieved. . . . *The community is not bound to provide what is in effect a subsidy for unconscionable employers.*"

Not surprisingly the "Four Horsemen" dissented vigorously, in an opinion by Justice Sutherland, the author of the *Adkins* opinion. Perhaps responding to Roosevelt's "fireside chat" call for judicial self-restraint, Sutherland announced that "self-restraint belongs in the domain of will and not of judgment." He rebuffed the idea of the need for "fresh consideration" of the questions presented in *Adkins,* proclaiming that "the meaning of the Constitution does not change with the ebb and flow of economic events." Recapitulating the authorities that supported the result reached in *Adkins,* Sutherland concluded that "if the Constitution, intelligently and reasonably construed in the light of these principles, stands in the way of desirable legislation, the blame must rest upon that instrument, and not upon the court for enforcing it according to its terms. The remedy in that situation—and the only true remedy—is to amend the Constitution."

West Coast Hotel marked the beginning of the end of the doctrine of liberty of contract and other restraints upon federal power. By the end of the term, Justice Van Devanter announced his retirement, on the same day that Congress formally rejected President Roosevelt's "court-packing" plan. The Four Horsemen were all departed, by death or resignation, by 1941. Roosevelt was able to appoint seven new associate justices, and a new chief justice, elevating Harlan Stone to that position in 1941. His appointments were New Deal stalwarts, beginning with Senator Hugo L. Black from Alabama in 1937. His other appointments included Solicitor General Stanley Reed (who argued and lost the previous New Deal cases) in 1938; Harvard professor Felix Frankfurter in 1939; law professor and SEC commissioner William O. Douglas in 1939; attorney general and New Deal governor of Michigan, Frank Murphy, in 1940; New Deal prosecutor Robert H. Jackson in 1941: and law professor Wiley B. Rutledge in 1943. Only two members of the *Schechter* Court remained: Justices Roberts and Stone. A new era had begun, and within a few years it appeared that all restraints on the growth of federal power had been abandoned.

A New Court Reviews the Second New Deal

The Supreme Court's decision in *West Coast Hotel v. Parrish* did nothing to remove the two key obstacles to upholding legislation enacted by the second New Deal. *Parrish* did not address either restrictions on federal power to enact legislation under the Commerce Clause, or the reserved powers of the states under the Tenth Amendment. Applying these doctrines, the Supreme Court had struck down the National Industrial Recovery Act, the Agricultural Adjustment Act, and other major legislation enacted in the first New Deal. Following *Parrish,* however, the Supreme Court shifted course and upheld the Wagner Act, the Social Security Act, the Fair Labor Standards Act, and the second Agricultural Adjustment Act, saving the second New Deal. It did so by abandoning the direct/indirect effects distinction under the Commerce Clause, and by more narrowly construing the exclusive powers of the state governments compared to those of the federal government.

The first case to manifest this shift was *National Labor Relations Board v. Jones & Laughlin Steel Corp.* (1937), which was decided less than one month after *Parrish.* This was one of five cases that reached the Supreme Court at the same time, challenging the constitutionality of the Wagner Act under the Commerce Clause, as well as under the doctrine of liberty of contract which *Parrish* had repudiated. In a five-to-four decision, the Wagner Act was upheld, with the majority opinion written by Chief Justice Hughes, over a dissent by Justice McReynolds on behalf of the Four Horsemen.

Jones & Laughlin operated a large international steel business, with sales offices in twenty cities throughout the United States and operations in Canada. It had ten thousand employees located in the Pennsylvania plant involved in the case, where several union leaders had been fired. The ability of the federal government under the Commerce Clause to reach into employment affairs at the local plant was the critical, unresolved issue presented in the case.

In his opinion for the majority, Chief Justice Hughes interpreted the Wagner Act to apply only to "acts which directly burden or obstruct interstate or foreign commerce, or its free flow." As Hughes saw it, "Although activities may be intrastate in character when separately considered, if they have such a close and substantial relation to interstate commerce that their control is essential or appropriate to protect that commerce from burdens and obstructions, Congress cannot be denied the power to exercise that control. . . . Undoubtedly the scope of this power must be considered in the light of our dual system of government and may not be extended so as to embrace effects upon interstate commerce so indirect and remote that to embrace them, in view of our complex society, would effectually obliterate the distinction between what is national and what is local and create a completely centralized government. . . . The question is necessarily one of degree."

None of this represented a significant departure from the prior Supreme Court decisions on the legislation of the first New Deal. Indeed Hughes cited the unanimous opinion in *Schechter* in support of his reasoning. His limited conclusion was simply that "the stoppage of these operations by industrial strife would have a most serious effect upon interstate commerce."

Hughes's limited approach did not satisfy the Four Horsemen. In his dissenting opinion, McReynolds saw the decision as a departure from "well-established principles" that had been followed in both *Schechter* and *Carter.* In his view any interference with interstate commerce resulting from the firing of the union officials "is far too indirect to justify congressional regulation. Almost anything—marriage, birth, death—may in some fashion affect commerce." Congress, however, has only the power to legislate "to prevent *direct and material* interference with the conduct of interstate commerce."

After *Jones & Laughlin* the Supreme Court turned its focus to the reserved powers of the states in two decisions involving the constitutionality of the Social Security Act. In *Charles C. Steward Machine Co. v. Davis* (1937), the Court upheld the constitutionality of the tax imposed upon employers to fund unemployment compensation under the act, while in *Helvering v. Davis* (1937), it sustained the validity of the old-age pension feature of the act. The Four Horsemen all dissented in the first case, but only McReynolds and Butler found the old-age pension feature to be unconstitutional under the Tenth Amendment.

The majority opinions in both cases were written by Justice Benjamin Cardozo. In the *Steward* case, he examined the mechanics of the unemployment compensation system, under which an employer received a 90 percent credit against the federal tax if it paid a comparable state tax that had been certified by the Social

Security Board as acceptable. This approach was attacked as unconstitutional because it allegedly involved an "unlawful invasion of the reserved powers of the states," a contention accepted by the four dissenters.

In rejecting this argument, Cardozo relied heavily upon recent history. He referred to "unprecedented" levels of unemployment of "16 million or more," noting that "the fact developed quickly that the states were unable to give the requisite relief. *The problem had become national in area and dimensions. There was need of help from the nation if the people were not to starve. It is too late today for the argument to be heard with tolerance that in a crisis so extreme the use of the moneys of the nation to relieve the unemployed and their dependents is a use for any purpose narrower than the promotion of the general welfare.*" The *Butler* states-rights opinion was distinguished by Cardozo on several grounds, including the presence in *Steward* of a lawful end embraced by the legislation, which was "the relief of unemployment."

Cardozo further articulated the majority's view of federal power in the companion *Helvering* case, which upheld the constitutionality of old-age pensions under the Social Security Act. He stated that "Congress may spend money in aid of the 'general welfare.' . . . There have been great statesmen in our history who have stood for other views. We will not resurrect the contest. It is now settled by decision. United States v. Butler, supra. The conception of the spending power advocated by Hamilton and strongly reinforced by [Justice] Story has prevailed over that of Madison, which has not been lacking in adherents." Cardozo conceded, however, that lines still needed to be drawn between permissible and impermissible exercises of the spending power. In a significant departure from prior precedent, Cardozo indicated that, in drawing such lines, "the *discretion belongs to Congress, unless the choice is clearly wrong, a display of arbitrary power, not an exercise of judgment. . . . Needs that were narrow or parochial a century ago may be interwoven in our day with the well-being of the nation. What is critical or urgent changes with the times.*" The Court's concern, as seen by the majority, "is with power, not with wisdom." Thus "whether wisdom or unwisdom resides in the scheme of benefits set forth [in the Social Security Act] is not for us to say. The answer to such inquiries must come from Congress, not the courts."

This expanded view of congressional discretion, and the limited role of the courts in reviewing that discretion, was reinforced the next year in *United States v. Carolene Products Co.* (1938), a case that upheld the federal "Filled Milk Act." That legislation prohibited the shipment in interstate commerce of certain types of skimmed milk. In rejecting the claim that the act invaded the reserved powers of the states under the Tenth Amendment, Justice Stone's opinion observed that "the existence of facts supporting the legislative judgment is to be presumed, for regulatory legislation affecting ordinary commercial transactions is not to be pronounced unconstitutional unless in the light of the facts made known or generally assumed it is of such a character as to preclude the assumption that it rests upon some rational basis within the knowledge and experience of the legislators." In calling for such a presumption, Stone's opinion effectively accepted the call of President Roosevelt thirteen months before in his fireside chat on the "court-packing" bill for the Court to presume that congressional legislation was constitutional.

The Supreme Court next considered the constitutionality of the second Agricultural Adjustment Act, upholding that legislation in *Mulford v. Smith* (1939). In a seven-to-two decision, with McReynolds and Butler dissenting, Justice Roberts's majority opinion upheld the constitutionality of imposing crop quotas. The second Agricultural Adjustment Act imposed these quotas under the authority of the Commerce Clause, rather than under the taxing power relied upon in *United States v. Butler.* Significantly Justice Roberts wrote the majority opinions in both *Mulford* and *Butler,* and he did not even refer to the three-year-old opinion in *Butler* in his opinion in the *Mulford* case.

The act limited the imposition of quotas to those times in which the supply of tobacco was excessive, and the quota was not deemed effective if more than one-third of tobacco producers opposed its imposition. This plan was attacked, in the very words of the *Butler* opinion, as a "statutory plan to control agricultural production" that was beyond the powers delegated to Congress. Roberts's majority opinion found that the quotas were a proper regulation of interstate commerce because of extensive interstate shipments of tobacco, and the impossibility of separating intrastate and interstate tobacco in the warehouses in which they were sold. Because of this impossibility, "regulation to be effective must, and therefore may constitutionally, apply to all sales."

Roberts noted that the motive of Congress in enacting legislation is irrelevant, and that the Court's role is simply to determine the validity of such legislation. Roberts's remarks were addressed to Justice Butler's dissent, which had argued that "whatever may be its declared policy or appearance, the enactment operates to control quantity raised by each farmer," an end that *Butler* had ruled to be beyond the powers conferred upon Congress.

Two years after *Mulford,* at a time when all the Four Horsemen had died or retired, a unanimous Supreme Court upheld the constitutionality of the Fair Labor Standards Act (FLSA) in *United States v. Darby* (1941). Under the FLSA, goods manufactured by laborers who were not paid the minimum wage or who worked more than the maximum hours prescribed by the legislation were prohibited from being shipped in interstate commerce. A similar approach designed to prohibit such shipment of goods manufactured with child labor had been declared unconstitutional in *Hammer v. Dagenhart* (1918). In his opinion Justice Stone rejected the argument that the legislation was beyond the power of Congress under the Commerce Clause and represented a regulation of the hours and wages of laborers, invading the right of the states to regulate those matters.

Stone's opinion held that Congress may regulate intrastate activities "where they have a *substantial effect* on interstate commerce." Finding that *Hammer v. Dagenhart* "was a departure from the principles which have prevailed in the interpretation of the commerce clause both before and since the decision and that [its] vitality, as a precedent, as it then had has long since been exhausted," *Darby* explicitly overruled it.

As the Social Security cases had removed the reserved rights of the states as an obstacle to federal legislation, *Darby* extinguished what a unanimous Supreme Court in *Schechter* had described as the "necessary and well-established" distinction between direct and indirect effects under the Commerce Clause, by which the federal government was limited solely to legislating where the impact of an economic activity on interstate commerce was direct. Six years after *Schechter,* what had been "well-established" went unmentioned, and a new test of "substantial effect" replaced it, removing the last obstacle to the exercise of federal power in the field of economic regulation.

No Limits: *Wickard v. Filburn* and the Triumph of Federal Power

Within a year, the "substantial effect" test was stretched to the ultimate limits of its elasticity in the celebrated case of *Wickard v. Filburn* (1942). Roscoe Filburn was the owner of a "small farm" in Ohio, on which he grew "a small acreage of winter wheat," some of which he sold, and some of which he used on the farm, or for his own "home consumption." In 1941 he violated the wheat quota established for that year by the Agricultural Adjustment Act, growing wheat on 23 acres, rather than on the 11.1 acres permitted under the act. Because "the intended disposition of the crop here involved has not been expressly stated," the Supreme Court assumed that at least a portion of the crop would be used for home consumption in determining Filburn's challenge to the constitutionality of the quota under the Commerce Clause.

The unanimous opinion rejecting Filburn's challenge was written by a new justice, Robert Jackson, who had argued the New Deal's position in the Supreme Court in both the *Mulford* and *Darby* cases. As Jackson saw it, the Commerce Clause question "would merit little consideration" after the *Darby* opinion "except for the fact that this Act extends federal regulation to production not intended in any part for commerce but wholly for consumption on the farm." Filburn claimed that such regulation was "a regulation of production and consumption of wheat," and therefore was "beyond the reach of Congressional power under the Commerce Clause, since [the farming activities] are local in character, and their effects upon interstate commerce are at most 'indirect.'"

In rejecting this argument on behalf of a unanimous Court—eight of whose members had been appointed by President Franklin D. Roosevelt—Jackson stated that "once an economic measure of the reach of the power granted to Congress in the Commerce Clause is accepted, questions of federal power cannot be decided simply by finding the activity in question to be 'production' nor can consideration of its economic effects be foreclosed by calling them 'indirect.' . . . Whether the subject of the regulation in question was 'production,' 'consumption,' or 'marketing' is, therefore, not material for purposes of deciding the question of federal power before us." This was so because "even if [Filburn's] activity be local and though it may not be regarded as commerce, it may still, whatever its nature, be reached by Congress if it exerts *a substantial economic effect* on interstate commerce and this irrespective of whether such effect is what might at some earlier time have been defined as 'direct' or 'indirect.'"

Jackson then explained how Filburn's 11.9 excess acres of wheat used for home consumption could have such a substantial effect. "It can hardly be denied that a factor of such volume and variability as home-consumed wheat would have a substantial influence on price and market conditions. This may arise because being in marketable condition such wheat overhangs the market and if induced by rising prices tends to flow into the market and check price increases. But if we assume that it is never marketed, it supplies a need of the man who grew it which would otherwise be reflected by purchases in the open market. Home-grown wheat in this sense competes with wheat in commerce."

This reasoning and the outcome in *Wickard* would have been incomprehensible to the Supreme Court majority only a few years earlier. The concerns expressed only seven years earlier by a unanimous Supreme Court in the *Schechter* case, warning against empowering the federal government to "embrace practically all the activities of the people" were forgotten. Indeed the facts of *Wickard* had been utilized prophetically by Justice White in his dissenting opinion for four justices, including Oliver Wendell Holmes, in the 1904 *Northern Securities* case. There White set up what he saw as a *reductio ad absurdam* in opposing a broad construction of the Sherman Act. He warned that it would lead to a situation in which "if it were judged by Congress that the farmer in sowing his crops should be limited to a certain production because overproduction would give power to affect commerce, Congress could regulate that subject." This White saw as a result that would "destroy the state and Federal governments," creating in their stead "a government endowed with the arbitrary power to disregard the great guaranty of life, liberty, and property and every other safeguard upon which organized civil society depends."

With *Wickard*'s liberal reading of the *Darby* "substantial effect" test, permissible federal regulation of economic activity appeared to be limitless. And, indeed, that was the case in the Supreme Court for fifty years.

The Roosevelt Revolution: A Postscript

Historians have long debated whether the court-packing plan of February 1937 or the election of 1936 explained the shift in the Supreme Court majority that upheld the Second New Deal. It is often pointed out that Justice Roberts had already cast his vote to overrule *Adkins* prior to the announcement of the plan, and that liberty of contract was a controversial doctrine for years before the *West Coast Hotel* decision, and had been eroded during that time. As such it is fair to see the abandonment of liberty of contract as the result of an evolution of legal doctrine accelerated by changed economic conditions, and not merely a reaction to either the court-packing plan or the 1936 election.

The limits upon Congress under the Commerce Clause also had inconsistent readings by the Court before 1937, and cases such as *Jones & Laughlin* fell within the range of prior decisions, and did not represent a radical departure from them. By contrast the states' rights philosophy of *Butler* was more settled, tracing its heritage back to the Supreme Court's civil rights opinions after the Civil War. The erosion of that concept was more of a dramatic shift, traceable to the perceived inability of the states to handle the problems brought about by a severe economic depression.

Evolution of legal doctrine thus explains some of what happened in the Supreme Court beginning in 1937, but politics catalyzed that evolution. While the impact of the court-packing plan is questionable, the effect of the election of 1936 is not. At a minimum, that election permitted President Roosevelt to appoint, before the next election in 1940, five new justices of the Supreme Court committed to upholding New Deal legislation. Those justices replaced three of the Four Horsemen who had typically imposed limits upon Congress under the Commerce Clause and the Tenth Amendment, which the new justices then abandoned. That much is undeniable. There was a Roosevelt Revolution.

Seven

The Supreme Court and Civil Liberties

Prior to the Civil War, there were no Supreme Court decisions of consequence in the area of what we now call civil liberties. First Amendment law was nonexistent because that amendment's protection of free speech and free exercise of religion was held only to apply against actions of the federal government. Moreover no restrictions on free speech were imposed by federal legislation after the ill-fated Alien and Sedition Acts of 1798, and none of the prosecutions under that legislation ever reached the Supreme Court for review.

The Civil War raised significant civil liberties issues in the area of free speech in wartime. These included the availability of habeas corpus, an extraordinary writ under which one who was imprisoned could challenge the legality of his detention in a court, and the use of military tribunals to adjudicate the guilt of those opposing the federal government's war efforts by speech or action. Subsequent wars, most notably World Wars I and II, raised the free speech issues once again, and World War II brought to the Supreme Court several cases involving the registration and forced relocation of aliens and American citizens of foreign descent and the use of military tribunals to try both. Finally the cold war led to cases questioning what rights Communists might possess to advocate the overthrow of the capitalist system.

In the area of due process under the Fourteenth Amendment, we have previously seen in chapter 4 how the Supreme Court interpreted the Civil War amendments in the context of African American freedmen and Chinese aliens, and in chapter 5, how the Court applied the Fourteenth Amendment to protect corporations from undue regulation in business activity. These business cases gave rise to substantive due process theories that were applied in the first half of the twentieth century to protect the rights of parents and teachers to choose both the manner and substance of educating their children. The rights of the mentally disabled under the Due Process Clause were also explored and rejected in a short, cruel opinion by Justice Holmes. Finally the practice of polygamy in the new state of Utah by members of the Church of Jesus Christ of Latter-day Saints closed the nineteenth century with the first important Supreme Court opinion on the scope of protection afforded practitioners of a religion under the Free Exercise Clause of the First Amendment.

Freedom of Speech in Wartime: The Civil War Experience

The right of a citizen to criticize and oppose the government in wartime was raised, but not resolved, in the case of *Ex Parte Vallandigham* (1864), which was decided during the Civil War. Clement Vallandigham was an Ohio lawyer and politician who opposed the Civil War as a "Peace Democrat." In May 1863 he gave a two-hour speech to a crowd of fifteen thousand to twenty thousand people. He attacked the Civil War and "King Lincoln," and challenged the imposition of martial law in Ohio and neighboring states by General Ambrose Burnside. Vallandigham told the crowd that "the present war was a wicked, cruel, and unnecessary war, one not waged for the preservation of the Union, but for the purpose of crushing out liberty and to erect a despotism; a war for the freedom of the blacks and the enslavement of the whites." He also assailed Burnside's actions as "a base usurpation of arbitrary authority," and allegedly "invite[d] his hearers to resist the same."

Over one hundred of Burnside's soldiers broke into Vallandigham's home at 2:30 the next morning to arrest him for violations of General Order No. 38. That Order prohibited any declaration of "sympathies for the enemy," and prescribed trial by a military commission with a death sentence to be imposed for any violation. Vallandigham was tried by a military commission for the next two days, found guilty of most charges, and sentenced to be imprisoned for the duration of the Civil War at a military facility. That sentence, which was loudly protested by newspapers in both Ohio and in most northern cities, was later changed by President Lincoln to banishment behind Confederate lines. When the South refused to take him, Vallandigham escaped to Canada, and the Peace Democrats nominated him as their (unsuccessful) candidate for governor of Ohio.

Lincoln defended the arrest and conviction of Vallandigham. While admitting that it would have been wrong to arrest him for criticizing the government, Lincoln insisted that Vallandigham's actions went beyond mere criticism and constituted attempts to interfere with the raising of troops and to encourage Union soldiers to desert. As Lincoln put it, "Must I shoot a simple-minded soldier boy who deserts while I must not touch a hair of a wily agitator who induces him to desert?"

Vallandigham requested the Supreme Court to review his sentence and declare it illegal on several grounds. First, he argued that he could not be tried by a military commission since he was not a member of the military forces. Second, he pointed out that none of his actions violated any provision of either the Constitution or of any federal statute and that he was merely uttering "words of criticism upon the policy of the public servants of the people, by which policy it was alleged that the welfare of the country was not promoted." Finally he claimed a due process entitlement to the full panoply of rights granted an accused by the Bill of Rights, including indictment or presentment by a grand jury, and thereafter a speedy trial by a jury of his peers. None of these was provided in a military commission.

The Supreme Court did not decide any of these vital issues. Instead, it refused to review Vallandigham's case. It found that the actions of a military commission were not actions of a "court" within the meaning of the provision of the Judiciary Act of 1789, which authorized the Supreme Court to review actions of lower tribunals. The critical questions raised by Vallandigham would not be resolved until later, after the Civil War ended. When the war ended, Vallandigham returned to Ohio and the practice of law.

The Writ of Habeas Corpus and the Use of Military Tribunals in Wartime: The Civil War Experience

Article I, Section 9 of the Constitution provides that "the Privilege of the Writ of Habeas Corpus shall not be suspended, unless when in Cases of Rebellion or Invasion, the public Safety may require it." This provision appears in the part of the Constitution that deals with the Legislative Branch of the federal government, but it is silent on which branch may act to "suspend" the "Privilege." During the Civil War, President Lincoln suspended the writ some eight times, and the numbers of civilians arrested without resort to habeas corpus remedies are estimated to have been between thirteen thousand and thirty-eight thousand. In March 1863 Congress expressly conferred the power to suspend habeas corpus on the president.

Early in the Civil War, Lincoln permitted General Winfield Scott to suspend the writ in April 1861 to suppress "an insurrection against the laws of the United States" in Maryland after riots in Baltimore, where a mob of twenty thousand people sought to prevent the passage of Union troops through that city, into Washington, D.C. One of those arrested under martial law was John Merryman, a Maryland farmer and legislator who was involved in the destruction of bridges to prevent federal troop movements in Maryland. He was arrested by military troops and held at Fort McHenry.

Merryman filed a writ of habeas corpus in the District of Maryland federal court, where the case was heard by Chief Justice Roger Taney, acting individually. In *Ex Parte Merryman* (1861), Taney held that only Congress could suspend the writ of habeas corpus, and that military tribunals could not try any person not a member of the military. He ordered the transcript of the proceedings in the *Merryman* case to be sent to Lincoln "to take care that the laws be faithfully executed to determine what measures he will take to cause the civil process of the United States to be respected and enforced."

Lincoln ignored Taney, and even briefly considered arresting the chief justice. In a message to Congress on July 4, 1861, Lincoln explained that Taney's opinion would permit "all the laws, *but one,* to go unexecuted, and the government itself go to pieces, lest that one be violated."

Merryman was ultimately indicted for conspiracy to commit treason, but was never tried. Taney would not permit any such treason trials to proceed while martial law was in force in the district.

Taney's opinion in *Merryman* was never reviewed by the full Supreme Court, but the questions it raised needed to be resolved given the numbers of people arrested while the writ of habeas corpus was suspended. The issue finally reached the Supreme Court after the Civil War had ended, in *Ex Parte Milligan* (1866), which is one of the foundational Supreme Court decisions on civil liberties.

Lambdin Milligan was an Indiana lawyer and Democratic politician and gubernatorial candidate who was active in a secret society originally called the American Knights and later renamed the Sons of Liberty. That group, whose leader was Clement Vallandigham, allegedly conspired to overthrow the Union government, seize war munitions from government arsenals, liberate Confederate prisoners of war held in the area, and encourage resistance to the draft. Milligan, a civilian, was arrested and tried by military authorities in Indiana, which was not a venue of war at the time. The charges against him included conspiracy against the United States government, affording aid and comfort to the rebels, inciting insurrection, disloyal practices, and violation of the laws of war. Tried by a military commission, he was found guilty and sentenced to death by hanging. In a review of the evidence, William H. Rehnquist, the late chief justice of the United States, found it weak against Milligan, consisting mainly of his expressing opposition to the war, calling Lincoln a "tyrant" and "usurper," and attending some meetings at which "vague military plans" were discussed. Notably the crimes for which Milligan was tried were similar to ones punishable under federal statutes then in force by prison terms not to exceed ten years. By contrast a military commission, by a two-thirds vote, could impose the death penalty for such offenses.

The *Milligan* case was afforded immense attention by the Supreme Court. There were seven days of oral argument by seven different lawyers—three for the government and four for Milligan. Milligan's lawyers included future president James Garfield (then barely thirty-five); David Dudley Field, a brother of Justice Stephen Field (who sat on the Court at the time) and one of the most prominent lawyers in the country; and Jeremiah Black. Black was the former chief justice of Pennsylvania, and he had been President Buchanan's attorney general and secretary of state. He was a spell-binding orator, with a sarcastic, acerbic style of argument. He had been nominated to the Supreme Court by Buchanan, but no vote was taken on his nomination because of the secession of southern states at the time. Black was very close to Justice David Davis, who wrote the majority opinion in *Milligan.*

All the justices found that Milligan should be freed. The majority joined an opinion by Justice Davis, while four other justices joined a concurring opinion by Chief Justice Salmon P. Chase. An Illinois lawyer, Davis was a close friend and adviser of Abraham Lincoln and had served as his campaign manager in 1860 at the Republican Convention. He was Lincoln's third appointment to the Supreme Court and served for fourteen years until he resigned in 1877 to take a seat in the United States Senate. Chase, known as a great defender of fugitive slaves before the Civil War, opposed Lincoln for the presidential nomination in 1860 and 1864, served as Lincoln's secretary of the treasury, and was appointed chief justice by Lincoln in 1864. He served on the Court for eight years until his death in 1873.

Milligan's challenge to his sentence was instituted by filing a writ of habeas corpus, thereby avoiding the jurisdictional problem of appeals from a military commission that had insulated Vallandigham's conviction from Supreme Court review. Early in his opinion for the majority, Davis announced that the availability of habeas corpus was of utmost importance because "it involves the very framework of the government and the fundamental principles of American liberty." Davis then stated that the Civil War had impeded a proper determination of the issue previously because "during the late wicked Rebellion, the temper of the times did not allow that calmness in deliberation and discussion so necessary to a correct conclusion of a purely judicial question."

Davis characterized habeas corpus as "the birthright of every American citizen." Without the protection of the laws, the accused "are at the mercy of wicked rulers, or the clamor of an excited people." He found that war does not suspend the Constitution, stating that "the Constitution of the United States is a law for rulers and people, equally in war and in peace, and covers with the shield of its protection all classes of men, at all times, and under all circumstances. No doctrine, involving more pernicious consequences, was ever invented by the wit of man than that any of its provisions can be suspended during any of the great exigencies of government. Such a doctrine leads directly to anarchy or despotism, but the theory of necessity on which it is based is false; for the government, within the Constitution, has all the powers granted to it, which are necessary to preserve its existence; as has been happily proved by the result of the great effort to throw off its great authority."

Davis recognized that the Constitution expressly permitted suspension of the writ "in a great crisis, like the one we have just passed through," but held that "martial rule can never exist *where the courts are open,* and in the proper and unobstructed exercise of their jurisdiction." Moreover "it is also confined to the locality of actual war." Since the Indiana courts were open and functioning, and since Indiana was not a site of war at the time, Milligan was entitled to the full protections of the Bill of Rights, including trial by jury. If he was guilty of the "enormous crime" for which he was convicted, he should be tried by a jury and, if convicted properly, he should receive "the heaviest penalties of the law."

Chief Justice Chase and three others agreed that Milligan should be freed, since the statute suspending habeas corpus prescribed certain procedures that were not followed in Milligan's case. They disagreed that Congress could not suspend the writ of habeas corpus under the facts presented and believed that Congress could authorize military commissions even in localities where the courts were open, including Indiana at the time of Milligan's trial. This power was vested in Congress by the Constitution in its grant of "authority to raise and support armies and to declare war, if not from its constitutional authority to provide for governing the national forces." Thus, "in Indiana, for example, at the time of the arrest of Milligan and his co-conspirators, it is established by the papers in the record, that the state was a military district, was the theatre of military operations, had been actually invaded, and was constantly threatened with invasion. It appears, also, that a powerful secret organization, composed of citizens and others, existed within the state, under military organization, conspiring against the draft, and plotting insurrection, the liberation of prisoners of war at various depots, the seizure of the state and national arsenals, armed cooperation with the enemy, and war against the national government."

Milligan was decided in April 1866, but the opinions were not released until December. When they were released, the press reaction to *Milligan* was loud and mostly negative outside of newspapers associated with the Democratic Party. There was fear at the time that the Supreme Court might ally itself with President Andrew Johnson (who was impeached two years later) and impede congressional Reconstruction as devised by the radical Republican majorities in both houses of Congress. Indeed it was felt that the enactment of "Black Codes" and the advent of the Ku Klux Klan in the South would require the use of military rule, which was imposed in the Reconstruction Acts of 1867 and 1868, which divided the South into military districts. As such some commentators questioned why the Supreme Court would go beyond what the concurring justices stated, since their reasoning was sufficient to decide the case on narrow, statutory grounds, making the broader question of when military rule was appropriate unnecessary to decide. In this context some legal and popular commentators compared the majority opinion in *Milligan* to that of Chief Justice Taney in *Scott* for resolving important constitutional questions that were both divisive and unnecessary to resolution of the case before the Court.

Fearing what the Supreme Court might do to Reconstruction legislation, Congress amended the Judiciary Act to strip the Court of appellate jurisdiction under the Habeas Corpus Act of 1867. Remarkably Congress did so after argument, but before decision, in a controversial case involving the arrest and proposed trial by a military commission of a southern newspaper editor in Vicksburg, Mississippi. In *Ex Parte McCardle* (1869), a unanimous Court held that Congress had the power to do so under the Constitution, thereby avoiding a constitutional crisis between the legislative and judicial branches.

Freedom of Speech in Wartime: The World War I Experience

The free speech issues that were presented to the Supreme Court in 1864 by Clement Vallandigham, but left unresolved then, came back to the Court more than fifty years later in the aftermath of World War I. When that war began in August 1914, the United States remained neutral under the lead of President Woodrow Wilson. There was a politically powerful isolationist element in the country at the time, particularly in the western and midwestern states, and a significant portion of the American populace traced their ancestry to Germany, Italy, or Austria-Hungary, which were three of the belligerent nations at war with England, France, and Russia at the beginning of World War I. In addition to the political isolationists and the foreign-born and their children, nativist elements also opposed entry into the war, while also opposing Catholic and Jewish immigration from non-English-speaking countries. These nativist elements sparked the rebirth of the Ku Klux Klan in the South and Midwest and turned the remnants of the Populist Party in the South into an anti-Catholic, anti-Semitic, and anti-immigration force. Tom Watson of Georgia, the Populist presidential candidate in 1904 and 1908, opposed entry into the war, and demonized blacks, Jews, and Catholics into the 1920s. He was elected to the United States Senate with Klan support in 1920. Midwestern isolationism became laced with the same prejudices, and the largest Klan membership at this time was in Indiana. In 1924 Congress passed the National Origins Act, greatly restricting future immigration, and using 1890 immigration as a base so as to exclude immigration from southern and eastern Europe. In the following year, the Klan sponsored a March on Washington, D.C., in which five hundred thousand protested the near nomination of Al Smith, the Roman Catholic governor of New York, as the Democratic presidential candidate in 1924. Smith got the nomination in 1928 and was soundly defeated by Herbert Hoover.

The United States entered the war in 1917, after Germany resumed unrestricted submarine warfare and its foreign minister sent the "Zimmerman telegram" offering aid to Mexico to recapture territory lost to the United States if Mexico entered the war on Germany's side. The congressional vote was far from unanimous. In the Senate six opposed declaring war, and fifty did so in the House. To foster financial and emotional support of the United States war effort, Wilson established a Committee on Public Information under the leadership of George Creel, a skilled media expert. Under Creel, the committee produced seventy-five million pieces of literature and arranged seventy-five thousand four-minute speeches to sell "Liberty Bonds" in movie theaters. Creel also produced short films shown in movie theaters with titles such as *The Kaiser: The Beast of Berlin.* The concept named "100% Americanism" was born, and anti-German actions multiplied. These included lynching of Germans by a mob near St. Louis, Missouri, the firing of the German conductors of both the Boston and Chicago Symphonies, the renaming of German foods (sauerkraut became "Liberty cabbage"), and the banning of German-language instruction in schools (which led to a Supreme Court decision discussed in this chapter).

President Wilson contributed to this anti-German and anti-immigrant paranoia. In his *History of the American People,* he had described Poles and Hungarians as "the *coarse crew* that come crowding in every year at the eastern ports." He also repeatedly denounced some naturalized American citizens, declaring that "the passions and intrigues of certain active groups and combinations of men amongst us *who were born under foreign flags* injected the *poison of disloyalty* into our most critical affairs . . . that small *alien element amongst us* which puts loyalty to any foreign power before loyalty to the United States."

It was in this combustible context that Congress enacted the Espionage Act in 1917 and the Sedition Act in 1918. The first made illegal a wide range of conduct, including willfully attempting to cause insubordination, disloyalty, mutiny, or refusal of duty; making false reports or statements with the intent to interfere with the success of the military effort or to promote the success of the enemy; and "obstruct[ing] the recruiting or enlistment service of the United States." Violations of the Espionage Act were punishable by a prison term up to twenty years. Wilson repeatedly attempted to broaden the scope of the Espionage Act, failing in several ways, including rejection by Congress of his proposal to permit censorship of the press during wartime.

The Sedition Act succeeded in criminalizing additional conduct. Among other things, it proscribed criticism of the United States government, Constitution, flag, military or naval forces, and military uniforms. It also prohibited opposing "the cause of the United States" or supporting the cause of any country at war with the United States.

More than two thousand were prosecuted under the Espionage Act, with more than one thousand convicted, including Eugene Debs. These prosecutions killed nascent socialist parties in Oklahoma and South Dakota and resulted in the deportation of many, including the Haymarket and Homestead anarchists Emma Goldman and Alexander Berkman.

The constitutionality of the Espionage Act under the First Amendment came before the Supreme Court in several cases decided right after the end of World War I. The initial lead case was *Schenck v. United States* (1919), which resulted in a unanimous opinion written by Justice Holmes, who had fought in the Civil War and was wounded three times in that conflict. Schenck was a Socialist Party official in Philadelphia. Under his supervision, leaflets were sent to men who had been drafted. Those leaflets stated that conscription violated the Thirteenth Amendment, that "a conscript is little better than a convict," and that readers of the leaflet should "Assert your rights" and "not submit to intimidation" since even silent consent to the draft laws would help support an "infamous conspiracy." Based on the distribution of this leaflet to draftees, Schenck was indicted for violating the Espionage Act provision prohibiting obstruction of the draft.

Holmes found that the effect of the leaflet could only be expected by Schenck "to influence [draftees] to obstruct the carrying of [the draft] out." While such speech would be protected "in ordinary times . . . the character of every act depends upon the circumstances in which it is done. . . . The most stringent protection of free speech would not protect a man in falsely shouting fire in a theatre and causing a panic." The test of protection for speech under the First Amendment is therefore "whether the words used are used in such circumstances and are of such a nature as to create a *clear and present danger* that they will bring about the substantive evils that Congress has a right to prevent." Here such a danger of obstructing the draft was presented and Schenck's conviction was upheld.

In *Debs v. United States* (1919), decided one week later, the conviction and ten-year sentence of Pullman strike leader Eugene Debs was upheld under the Espionage Act. Debs was found to have obstructed the draft in a speech in which he expressed pride in three men who had been convicted of aiding and abetting another man in failing to register for the draft and in which he also praised two women who were convicted for obstructing the draft. Debs made his case worse in two ways. First, he told his audience that if one of the women was guilty, "so was he, and that he would not be cowardly enough to plead his innocence." Second, he addressed the jury in his own trial, telling the members "I have been accused of obstructing the war. I admit it. Gentlemen, I abhor war. I would oppose the war if I stood alone." Debs's chief defense was the First Amendment, which Holmes, again for a unanimous Court, found had been "disposed of" in *Schenck.*

The *Schenck* cases were the first Supreme Court cases to interpret the First Amendment protection of free speech. In relevant part that amendment provides that "Congress shall make no law . . . abridging the freedom of speech, or of the press." As Holmes pointed out in *Schenck,* the prevailing view at the time was that the First Amendment only prohibited the imposition of prior restraints on speech, not the punishment of speech after the words were published. Holmes's test was more liberal, but the *Schenck* opinion evoked opposition in both radical and liberal circles. In April 1919, the month after the opinion was delivered, thirty-four bombs were discovered in the United States mails, addressed to many notables, including Justice Holmes. In June 1919 bombs went off nearly simultaneously at eight places in eight cities, including at the home of Attorney General A. Mitchell Palmer, who had orchestrated the wartime prosecutions. On January 2, 1920, Mitchell sent J. Edgar Hoover and the predecessor to the Federal Bureau of Investigation on raids that resulted in the arrests of more than four thousand in some thirty-three cities.

Liberals in academia criticized Holmes's *Schenck* and *Debs* opinions in liberal outlets, including the *New Republic.* Professor Zechariah Chafee followed up with a scholarly article in the *Harvard Law Review,* and a young federal judge, Learned Hand, employed another test supported by liberals that required direct incitement to strip speech of protection under the First Amendment. Holmes was accustomed to adulation by fawning admirers, not criticism in the liberal press and academic journals. These articles, together with meeting with Hand and corresponding with his circle of intellectuals, caused him to reevaluate the standard to be used under the First Amendment. While continuing to insist that *Schenck* and *Debs* were correctly decided, he changed his approach to the First Amendment in *Abrams v. United States* (1919), decided eight months after *Schenck.*

Abrams was a prosecution under the Sedition Act, involving the distribution of two leaflets, which were thrown out of a factory window near a war munitions plant. The first, in English, was entitled "The Hypocrisy of the United States and her Allies." It denounced President Wilson as a hypocrite and coward, and called on workers to "Awake! Arise! Put down your enemy and mine!" The second leaflet, written in Yiddish, and translated differently in the course of the Court proceedings, was headed "Workers—Wake Up." It stated that "Workers in the ammunition factories, you are producing bullets, bayonets, cannon, to murder not only the Germans, but also your dearest, best, who are in Russia and are fighting for freedom." It went on, "Workers, up to fight," called for a general strike, and was signed "the Rebels."

Justice John Clarke, an Ohio Progressive appointed to the Supreme Court by President Wilson in 1916, wrote the majority opinion in *Abrams.* Applying the *Schenck* test, he upheld the convictions and twenty-year sentences of the five defendants, all of whom he noted early in his opinion "were born in Russia." He found that the leaflets encouraged resistance to the United States in the war effort and that the call for a general strike was a call to curtail war production, making them guilty on two counts of the indictment charging them with those offenses.

Justices Holmes and Brandeis dissented, in the first of series of dissents that endeared them to the liberal and academic communities. Their position ultimately prevailed, with a variant being adopted by the Supreme Court unanimously in *Brandenburg v. Ohio* (1969). Holmes's dissent in *Abrams* reaffirmed his belief that *Schenck* and *Debs* were "rightly decided," but found that the *Abrams* defendants had no specific intent to hinder war production. They had argued that they were only supporting the revolution in Russia and that Russia was not at war with the United States.

More significantly Holmes announced a new standard he and Brandeis would follow. Instead of a clear-and-present-danger test focusing on the bad tendency of the speech in question, he urged a test of whether the speech posed "the present danger of immediate evil" that later cases turned into a "direct incitement" test. In *Abrams,* Holmes found no such danger in either leaflet, and he dismissed the second publication as "a silly leaflet by an unknown man" that espoused a "creed of ignorance and immaturity." In a famous passage, he closed by noting that "the ultimate good desired is better reached by *free trade in ideas*—that the best test of truth is the power of the thought to get itself accepted in the *competition of the market,* and that truth is the only ground upon which their wishes safely can be carried out. That at any rate is the theory of our Constitution. It is an experiment, as all life is an experiment." Holmes would only stop the experiment when the expression of opinion would "so imminently threaten *immediate interference* with the lawful and pressing purposes of the law that an *immediate check is required to save the country.*"

Freedom of Speech in Wartime: The World War II Experience

In mid-June of 1942, eight German saboteurs were dropped off by submarines, in two separate operations, on Long Island, New York, and Ponte Vedra Beach, Florida. They immediately changed out of their uniforms, buried them, and put on civilian clothing. Their mission was to destroy United States war industries and war facilities. One of the saboteurs traveled to Washington, D.C., and voluntarily revealed the operation to the Federal Bureau of Investigation.

The Trial of Unlawful Combatants

All of the saboteurs were promptly apprehended and tried by a military tribunal established by presidential order under congressional authorization. The tribunal was authorized to try "offenses against the law of war," and defendants subject to its jurisdiction were denied access to the courts.

All eight were convicted by the tribunal, and six were sentenced to death, including a naturalized American citizen named Hans Haupt. Within six weeks of their capture, seven of their cases were reviewed by the Supreme Court, which heard oral argument on July 29 and 30, 1942. The Court announced its decision the next day in a brief order, without an opinion. The six sentenced to death were electrocuted eight days after the decision was announced, and the remaining two, including the informant, were sentenced to thirty years' imprisonment. Those two were later deported to Germany by order of President Harry Truman in 1948.

In a unanimous opinion delivered three months after the decision was announced, Chief Justice Harlan Stone rejected the saboteurs' claims that they were entitled under *Ex Parte Milligan* to trial by jury in civilian courts and that the presidential order establishing the procedures for the military tribunal was unconstitutional.

Stone explained that the power to declare war vested by the Constitution in Congress permitted it to enact the Articles of War legislation under which President

Franklin D. Roosevelt had established the rules and procedures for the military tribunal. In the Articles of War, Congress had permitted offenses against "the law of war" to be tried in military courts. Significantly the Court noted that it was not necessary "to determine to what extent the President as Commander in Chief has constitutional power to create military commissions without the support of Congressional legislation."

The *Milligan* claim was dismissed in Stone's opinion because the Constitution does not require trial by jury of "an offense against the law of war." Here, by removing their uniforms and proceeding in civilian clothes to implement their sabotage, the saboteurs became "unlawful combatants" who were "subject to trial and punishment by military tribunals for acts which render their belligerency unlawful."

Even the American citizen Haupt was subject to trial in a military tribunal because of the charge of "unlawful belligerency." Stone explained: "Petitioners, and especially petitioner Haupt, stress the pronouncement of this Court in the Milligan case . . . that the law of war 'can never be applied to citizens in states which have upheld the authority of the government, and where the courts are open and their process unobstructed.' Elsewhere in its opinion . . . , the Court was at pains to point out that Milligan, a citizen twenty years resident in Indiana, who had never been a resident of any of the states in rebellion, was not an *enemy belligerent* either entitled to the status of prisoner of war or subject to the penalties imposed upon unlawful belligerents." Given the nature of the charges, and given the fact that even troops in the military service of the United States could be tried in military tribunals for offenses against the law of war, the saboteurs' due process claims were unfounded and were not supported by *Milligan.*

Ex Parte Quirin was and is a controversial decision for several reasons. First, there is evidence that Justice Felix Frankfurter was involved in ex parte discussions with the Roosevelt administration about how to structure the tribunal that tried the *Quirin* saboteurs. Second, the justices had been informed that President Roosevelt would not honor any writ of habeas corpus the Court might issue, and would execute the men in any event. Third, the Supreme Court did not issue its opinion until after six of the saboteurs were executed. It took Stone nearly three months to write the opinion, a process he later described to be "a mortification of the flesh." Indeed the opinion itself concedes that the Court was divided upon the "the appropriate grounds for decision." Moreover the opinion notes that "we have no occasion now to define with meticulous care the ultimate boundaries of the jurisdiction of military tribunals to try persons according to the law of war."

The Japanese Internment Cases

Fear of the "alien among us" has pervaded most of American history. Coming to a boil with the pre–Civil War American ("Know-Nothing") Party, and progressing through the Populist rants against foreigners and immigrants, this paranoid tendency manifested itself again in both twentieth-century world wars. In World War I, as we have seen, the Wilson administration focused its legal resources on a crusade against Bolsheviks, anarchists, and disloyal Americans, both real and imagined. In World War II, an entire ethnic group became the target.

At the start of World War II, in the wake of the sneak attack by the Japanese air forces on Pearl Harbor, Hawaii, on December 7, 1941, some 120,000 Japanese lived on the West Coast of the United States. These Japanese Americans were concentrated in California, where they represented about 10 percent of the total population. From two-thirds to three-quarters were United States citizens. There was considerable fear of armed attacks on the West Coast by Japanese forces and concern that Japanese Americans were a fifth column whose loyalty was questionable. Japanese were all seen as "prints off the same negative" and lumped together as a dangerous alien presence. Those fears were exacerbated by a few isolated incidents. In 1942 there were two bombings by a single Japanese plane on forests in Oregon, and two shellings of the California and Oregon coasts by Japanese warships. Public outcry led to a series of measures taken by the Western Defense Command, led by General John L. DeWitt.

In February 1942 DeWitt requested authority to remove all persons of Japanese ancestry from the West Coast. This was approved in Executive Order 9066 issued in the same month under the authority of the Espionage Act of 1917 and later legislation from 1940 and 1941. The Executive Order permitted the *exclusion* of any person from designated military areas, and Dewitt designated whole portions of the West Coast as such. When the Japanese Americans were subjected to curfews imposed under the Executive Order, some fifteen thousand left the area voluntarily. That led, in March 1942, to freeze orders, under which Japanese Americans were not permitted to leave, but were required to report to *assembly centers.* After they reported, they were sent off to ten *relocation centers* located as far away as Arkansas. This relocation began in June 1942, and more than one hundred thousand Japanese Americans were forced from their homes for a period of two years or more. By mid-1944 some twenty-five thousand were released after being found to be loyal citizens.

In late 1943 a final report on the Japanese evacuation was issued by DeWitt, claiming military necessity as the justification for the exclusion, relocation, and internment of the Japanese Americans on the West Coast. The accuracy of that report was questioned by Justice Department lawyers handling the case of *Korematsu v. United States* (1944). They prepared a footnote to the government's brief in that case, asking the Supreme Court *not* to take judicial notice of the "facts" in the report. That footnote was ordered removed from the final draft by the assistant secretary of war, John J. McCloy, who was a prominent Wall Street lawyer in a white-shoe law firm that still bears his name.

The first Supreme Court case to consider the constitutionality of any of these measures was *Hirabayashi v. United States* (1943). That case ruled only on the legality of a *curfew* ordered under the Executive Order. The curfew applied to all designated military areas and required all persons of Japanese, Italian, or German ancestry to remain in their houses from 8 P.M. to 6 A.M. The defendant, known as Gordon (but sued as Kiyoshi) Hirabayashi, was a United States citizen who was born and lived in Seattle, Washington. He was a senior at the University of Washington and had never visited Japan. He violated the curfew and refused to report to the designated assembly center, two separate offenses of which he was found guilty in civilian courts and sentenced to three months in jail, the sentences to run concurrently (three months in total), not consecutively (six months in total).

Hirabayashi argued that the curfew violated his Fifth Amendment right to due process of law. This contention was rejected in a unanimous decision, with several opinions. Speaking for the majority, Chief Justice Harlan Stone addressed only the curfew, reasoning that because of the concurrent sentences imposed, if the conviction for violating the curfew stood, the Court had no need to rule on the constitutionality of the separate requirement of reporting to an assembly center.

Citing the *Quirin* case, Stone ruled that the curfew was justified as "an exercise of the power to wage war," which "extends to every matter and activity so related to war as substantially to affect its conduct and progress." Moreover the conditions of war call for the "exercise of judgment and discretion" and "it is not for any court to sit in review of the wisdom of their action or substitute its judgment for theirs." The application of the curfew to Japanese Americans was found justified based on several factors. First, Stone cited General DeWitt's suspicion of "widespread fifth-column activity among Japanese," dual citizenship, and "propaganda disseminated by Japanese consuls, Buddhist priests, and other leaders, among American-born children of Japanese." Next, he found "support for the view" that the Japanese had not been assimilated "as an integral part of the white population," invoking "Japanese language schools" and the sending to Japan for "all or part of their education" of approximately ten thousand American-born children of Japanese parentage. Stone concluded that there was a "reasonable basis" for classifying Japanese Americans in a different category, stating, "We cannot close our eyes to the fact, demonstrated by experience, that in time of war residents having ethnic affiliations with an invading enemy may be a greater source of danger than those of a different ancestry."

Three justices, William O. Douglas, Frank Murphy, and Wiley Rutledge, wrote concurring opinions. While agreeing that the curfew was a permissible exercise of the war powers, each expressed misgivings. Douglas, who would become known as a great civil libertarian, found that the exigencies of war did not permit time for an individual "sorting process" to distinguish the loyal from the disloyal, but noted that the Japanese American must be given time and a process to prove his or her personal loyalty.

Murphy was less circumspect. A New Deal Democratic politician, Murphy had been mayor of Detroit and governor of Michigan, where he supported labor unions, refusing to evict the United Auto Workers sit-in strikers. When Murphy lost his reelection campaign for governor, President Franklin D. Roosevelt appointed him first as attorney general and then as an associate justice on the Supreme Court, where he sat from 1940 until his death in 1949. A devout Roman Catholic, he assumed the "Catholic seat" vacated by Pierce Butler, one of the conservative "Four Horsemen." Murphy was perhaps the most liberal justice ever to sit on the Court. Often short on legal analysis, his approach became known as "tempering justice with Murphy."

Murphy came off of the bench swinging in *Hirabayashi.* Citing *Milligan,* he reminded the Court that "the mere existence of a state of war" did not suspend the Constitution, and that "while this Court sits, it has the inescapable duty of seeing that the mandates of the Constitution are obeyed." He reluctantly found the curfew justified only because of the "peril of imminent enemy attack" when it was first imposed. Murphy nevertheless attacked the premises of the majority opinion, noting that "to say that any group cannot be assimilated is to admit that the great American experiment has failed, that our way of life has failed when confronted with the normal attachment of certain groups to the lands of their forefathers. As a nation we embrace many groups, some of them among the oldest settlements in our midst, which have isolated themselves for religious and cultural reasons. Today is the first time, so far as I am aware, that we have sustained a substantial restriction of the personal liberty of citizens of the United States based upon the accident of race or ancestry. Under the curfew order here challenged no less than seventy thousand American citizens have been placed under a special ban and deprived of their liberty because of their particular racial inheritance. In this sense it *bears a melancholy resemblance to the treatment accorded to members of the Jewish race in Germany and in other parts of Europe.* The result is the creation in this country of two classes of citizens for the purposes of a critical and perilous hour—to sanction discrimination between groups of United States citizens on the basis of ancestry. *In my opinion this goes to the very brink of constitutional power.*"

The Supreme Court faced this Japanese American discrimination issue again the next year, first in *Korematsu v. United States* (1944). Fred (sued as Toyosaburo) Korematsu was a Japanese American United States citizen who had assimilated. He worked as a welder in a defense plant, lived in northern California, and had an Italian American girlfriend. He had even tried to enlist in the United States military, but was rejected on health grounds. Korematsu did not want to leave Alameda County, where he had lived all his life. To avoid relocation he had facial surgery, changed his name to Clyde Sarah, and claimed to be "Mexican-Hawaiian."

Korematsu was convicted of remaining in a restricted military zone. His conviction was upheld by six members of a bitterly divided Court. The majority opinion was written by Justice Hugo L. Black, who, along with Justice Douglas, would later become lionized for their fidelity to the protections of the First Amendment. Black had previously served in the United States Senate from Alabama. A member of the Ku Klux Klan from 1923 to 1926, Black was Franklin D. Roosevelt's first appointment to the Supreme Court, where he served from 1937 to his retirement (shortly before his death) in 1971. In 1967, commenting to a newspaper reporter on his opinion in *Korematsu,* he proclaimed that "they all look alike to a person not a Jap."

Black's opinion had lasting significance in its holding that laws applying only to a "single racial group" are "immediately suspect" and must be subjected to the "most rigid scrutiny." Nevertheless, he found the exclusion provisions appropriate based upon a reported inability by the military to segregate loyal Japanese Americans from those who were disloyal. He found support for this view in several facts, including "investigations made subsequent to the exclusion" in which "approximately five thousand American citizens of Japanese ancestry refused to swear unqualified allegiance to the United States and to renounce allegiance to the Japanese Emperor, and several thousand evacuees requested repatriation to Japan." Black rejected the constitutional claims, finding that "hardships are part of war, and war is an aggregation of hardships." He concluded by resting on the perceived "military urgency of the situation," presumably unaware that the Justice Department had questioned the reliability of DeWitt's final report, since the government lawyers' cautionary footnote was deleted on McCloy's orders from the government's Supreme Court brief.

Black refused to go further to address the "serious constitutional issues" relating to assembly center and relocation orders, since Korematsu had not been charged with crimes relating to those requirements.

In dissent Justice Owen J. Roberts, a Philadelphia lawyer by training, twice referred to the relocation centers as "concentration camps," a description that sent Black into judicial apoplexy. Roberts noted that *Hirabayashi* only involved "keeping people off the street at night," while *Korematsu* was a case of "convicting a citizen as a punishment for not submitting to imprisonment in a concentration camp." This was not fair, since the conviction, as Black noted, was for failing to obey an exclusion order. Nevertheless, Roberts made a persuasive case for reading all the restrictions as "single and indivisible" and faulted the Court for not reaching the issues relating to the assembly and relocation centers. Roberts saw these requirements as imposing unconstitutional restrictions on Japanese Americans.

Justice Murphy went even further, characterizing the *Korematsu* majority opinion as falling "into the ugly abyss of racism." He saw the exclusion orders as "excommunicating" Japanese Americans based on an "erroneous assumption of racial guilt." He pointed to evidence that "people with racial and economic prejudices," including white farmers who were undersold by their Japanese American neighbors, generated "misinformation, half-truths and insinuations" that the military relied upon to justify the exclusion orders. He also noted how Italian and German citizens had been afforded hearings on an individual basis, finding no reason why the same approach could not have been taken with the Japanese American citizenry.

A final dissent was delivered by Justice Robert Jackson, a close friend and confidant of President Roosevelt. A New York Democrat, Jackson was appointed to the Court in 1941 after a brief stint as attorney general (replacing Frank Murphy). He served until his premature death at the age of sixty-two in 1954. In 1945 and 1946 Jackson took a leave of absence from the Supreme Court to serve as chief counsel for the prosecution at the Nuremberg War Crimes Trials of the Nazi German leaders.

Jackson wrote that no reasonable basis existed for the orders issued by General DeWitt. In a passage ironic for its lack of knowledge of the deleted footnote questioning the credibility of the DeWitt final report, Jackson questioned, "How does the Court know that these orders have a reasonable basis in necessity? No evidence whatsoever on that subject has been taken by this or any other Court. There is sharp controversy as to the credibility of the DeWitt report. So the Court, having no real evidence before it, has no choice but to accept General DeWitt's own unsworn, self-serving statement, untested by any cross-examination, that what he did was reasonable. And thus it will always be when courts try to look into the reasonableness of a military order."

Jackson then observed that justifying the orders "validated the principle of racial discrimination" that then "lies around like a loaded weapon ready for the hand of any authority that can bring forward a plausible claim of an urgent need." What Jackson also may not have known was that General DeWitt had been a friend of Justice Black and his wife.

In the mid-1980s both Gordon Hirabayashi and Fred Korematsu's convictions were overturned. Korematsu then became the unlikely recipient of the Presidential Medal of Freedom, awarded to him by President William Jefferson Clinton in 1998.

The final Japanese internment case was *Ex Parte Endo* (1944), decided on the same day as *Korematsu,* but often ignored. A Japanese American woman who was admitted by the military authorities to be loyal to the United States sued in habeas corpus for her release from a relocation camp. In an opinion by Justice Douglas that carefully reviewed the sequence of executive orders and congressional legislation ratifying them, the Court noted that *detention* was not authorized by any of these. As such, since Endo was admittedly loyal, the war powers of Congress could not justify her further detention and she was entitled to her unconditional release.

The constitutional issues were again left unaddressed, to the expressed consternation of concurring Justices Murphy and Roberts. Both would have ruled detention unconstitutional in the absence of evidence of disloyalty. To Murphy detention "regardless of loyalty" was "another example of the unconstitutional *resort to racism* inherent in the entire evacuation program."

The Cold War and the Crusade against Communism

In the beginning years of the twentieth century, Communists were generally viewed as just another type of anarchist. As such they were deemed to be largely ineffectual, although capable of causing acute episodes of violence such as those manifested in the labor violence at the end of the nineteenth century, and in the assassination of President McKinley in 1901. This view changed dramatically after the Russian Revolution and the overthrow of the czarist regime. As we have seen, Bolshevism became a code word for violence and anarchy, leading to the "Red Scare" after World War I. This fear of Bolshevism accelerated after the first World War, particularly among members of the Catholic Church when Communists supported the antichurch faction in the Spanish Civil War in the 1930s. During World War II, however, Russia was an ally of the United States, and little opposition was voiced to Communism during that fateful period.

When the war ended, it was replaced by the cold war, with Winston Churchill noting in 1945 that an "iron curtain" had descended over Europe. Communists took over the governments in many European countries, including Czechoslovakia and Poland. Additional threats to Greece and Turkey led to the declaration of the Truman Doctrine in 1947, under which the United States pledged itself to support free governments in their resistance to Communism. In 1949 the North Atlantic Treaty Organization was formed to combat further Communist aggression. The geographic threat from Communism spread to Asia in the same year, when China was "lost" to the West. In 1950 the Asian threat of Communism was further manifested by the invasion of South Korea by North Korea.

Carefully assessing the earliest of these developments, a young State Department official, George Kennan, wrote a famous article in *Foreign Affairs* magazine in 1947, concluding that Russia was expansionist by history, ideology, and politics. This article, "The Sources of Soviet Conduct," was written anonymously by Kennan as "Mr. X," and gave birth to the containment doctrine, under which the United States would seek to contain the further expansion of Russian territorial ambitions.

Fear of Communism also led to the activation of the House un-American Activities Committee (HUAC) shortly after the war. Formed as a special committee in 1938, it became a permanent committee in 1945, and began holding extensive hearings in 1947. Between 1947 and 1953, it summoned more than three thousand witnesses, questioning their loyalty and generally searching for Communists in every branch of American life. The most famous hearings it held related to the presence of Communists in Hollywood, leading to the blacklisting of many actors and playwrights for years to come.

Public fear of the Communist menace worsened with the revelation of spies and traitors in American government and society. In 1951 Julius and Ethel Rosenberg were indicted for passing the secrets of the atomic bomb to the Russians. After a widely publicized trial, both were executed in 1953. Earlier, in 1948, the HUAC held incendiary hearings involving Alger Hiss, an establishment figure who had held high positions in the State Department. Hiss was accused by newsman Whittaker Chambers of being a Soviet spy. When Hiss sued Chambers for libel, a young congressman, Richard Nixon, exposed Hiss as a traitor, and Hiss was ultimately convicted, after two trials, of perjury, for lying to the HUAC.

The Hiss case was particularly volatile, since the good character of Hiss was attested to by many famous establishment figures, including Truman's secretary of state, Dean Acheson. Hiss had a stellar resume. He had been a law clerk for Justice Holmes, a delegate of the State Department at the Yalta Conference, and the president of the Carnegie Foundation for International Peace. Hiss was not alone as a traitor at the highest levels of American government. When the Venona Cables of Russian intelligence were released in the 1990s, two other traitors were unmasked—Harry Dexter White, an assistant secretary of the treasury under both Presidents Roosevelt and Truman, and Laughlin Currie, an administrative assistant to President Roosevelt.

This unmasking of treason in the government led to the emergence of Senator Joseph McCarthy of Wisconsin as the self-appointed spokesperson for the common man who felt that he had been stabbed in the back by the establishment. McCarthy was elected to United States Senate in 1946 at the age of thirty-eight, having defeated Robert LaFollette Jr., the son of Wisconsin's noted progressive leader, in the Republican primary. In February 1950, seeking a cause that would gain him further notoriety, McCarthy gave a speech at Wheeling, West Virginia, in which he claimed that he had in his hand a list of 205 Communists in the United States government. McCarthy assailed "twenty years of treason," personally attacking President Truman and Secretary of Defense George Marshall, whom he labeled a traitor. Calling for Truman's impeachment, McCarthy became the most powerful man in American government. Between 1950 and 1954, his popularity rating was at 50 percent, with a negative rating of only 29 percent. His popularity among his fellow Catholics reached 56 percent. McCarthy reigned supreme until 1954, when he took on the United States Army, which had failed to give preferential treatment to one of his aides. In a series of hearings televised over the course of thirty-six days, McCarthy self-destructed, with the assistance of the noted television newsman Edward R. Murrow, who devoted a special broadcast to McCarthy's tactics.

Television carried a popular series between 1953 and 1956 that further stoked fears of a hidden Communist element invading American society. Entitled "I Led Three Lives," the series was based upon the actual experiences of Herbert Philbrick, a Boston advertising executive who had infiltrated the Communist Party USA for the FBI.

It was against this background, and in this context, that the Supreme Court began to consider criminal cases filed against members of the Communist Party of the United States under the Smith Act. Passed in 1940, before the United States entered World War II, that legislation aimed to counter both fascist and Communist propaganda and agitation, making it a criminal offense to advocate the forcible overthrow of the United States government. The Smith Act was first employed against Communists in the United States in the celebrated case of *Dennis v. United States* (1951).

Dennis arose from a 1948 indictment of all twelve members of the Communist Party USA's executive board, including its general secretary, Eugene Dennis. It became the longest criminal trial to that date in the history of United States, lasting for more than nine months, and generating sixteen thousand pages of transcript. All eleven defendants who went to trial were convicted; ten received the maximum permissible sentence of five years. Only a former war hero, Robert Thompson, received a more lenient sentence of three years. The trial, conducted by federal judge Harold Medina, was tumultuous, and Medina sentenced all five of the trial lawyers for the defendants to prison terms for contempt of court. The trial and appeals took place during the height of the fears regarding the Communist menace. Indeed, while the case was on appeal, Communist North Korea invaded South Korea.

There was no opinion joined by a majority of the justices in the *Dennis* case. Four members of the Court joined an opinion by Chief Justice Fred Vinson. Vinson had been appointed chief justice by President Harry Truman in 1946 and served until his death in 1953. Vinson had served in all three branches of government prior to being named chief justice. He was a New Deal liberal in the House of Representatives, was appointed to the District of Columbia Circuit Court of Appeals, and had served as President Truman's secretary of the treasury. Given the dissension on the Court, and the threat of two justices to resign if Justice Jackson was appointed chief justice, Truman turned to his friend Vinson to restore harmony to the Court.

Vinson's opinion quickly reviewed the state of First Amendment law under the clear-and-present-danger test to that point in time. The difficulty with that test was that there was no real imminent danger of any Communist takeover in the United States at that time. Nevertheless, Vinson stated that "we reject any principle of governmental helplessness in the face of preparation for revolution, which principle, carried to its logical conclusion, must lead to anarchy." Moreover he noted that "the mere fact that from the period 1945 to 1948 petitioners' activities did not result in an attempt to overthrow the Government by force and violence is of course no answer to the fact that there was a group that was ready to make the attempt."

Struggling to find a new standard to apply, Vinson adopted that formulated in the appeals court by now chief judge Learned Hand. Hand had suggested that courts must ask "whether the gravity of the 'evil' discounted by its improbability, justifies such invasion of free speech as is necessary to avoid the danger." Vinson found the activities of the Communists in advocating overthrow of the United States government to be criminally punishable under this standard. He observed that, under the clear-and-present-danger standard, "obviously, the words cannot mean that before the Government can act, it must wait until the putsch is about to be executed, the plans have been laid, and the signal is awaited." Vinson concluded that "the formation by petitioners of such a highly organized conspiracy, with rigidly disciplined members subject to call when the leaders, these petitioners, felt that the time had come for action, coupled with *the inflammable nature of world conditions, similar uprisings in other countries, and the touch-and-go nature of our relations with countries with whom petitioners were in the very least ideologically attuned,* convince us that their convictions were justified on this score."

Justice Black, who wrote an impassioned dissent, scribbled a number of comments on Vinson's draft opinion. In one of these, he noted that the new test "permits courts to sustain anything," while in another, he remarked that "the goblin'll get you." Next to the "the putsch is about to be executed" comment, Black wrote "Good semantic emotionalism and ghost conjuring!" Black summed up Vinson's opinion as standing for the proposition that these were "Bad men! To jail with them!"

In his two-page dissent, Black found that the clear-and-present-danger test had been abandoned. He stated that "no matter how it is worded, this is a virulent form of prior censorship of speech and press, which I believe the First Amendment forbids." Black finished by observing that "*public opinion being what it now is,* few will protest the conviction of these Communist petitioners. There is hope, however, that *in calmer times, when present pressures, passions and fears subside,* this or some later Court will restore the First Amendment liberties to the high preferred place where they belong in a free society."

Justice Douglas echoed similar views, stating that free speech could not be abridged by Congress "except in the extreme case of peril from the speech itself."

Justices Frankfurter and Jackson filed separate opinions, both concurring in the result reached by Vinson's opinion. Frankfurter comprehensively reviewed all of the First Amendment cases starting with *Schenck.* Referring to the "*impregnating atmosphere of the times,*" he called for reference to principles established in "*more tranquil periods.*" Reviewing the Court record and the history of the times,

Frankfurter noted the organization, structure, and "intricate chain of command" of the Communist Party, concluding that the convictions were justified.

Justice Jackson traced the approach of the Smith Act to concerns regarding "anarchistic terrorism that plagued this country about the turn of the century, which lags at least two generations behind Communist Party techniques." Jackson cited the Haymarket riots, the attempt on Henry Clay Frick's life, and the assassination of President McKinley as examples of the fears of anarchism. In contrast to anarchy, however, Jackson noted that Communism was "a more sophisticated, dynamic and realistic movement." Jackson went on to observe that the clear-and-present-danger test was "outwit[ted]" by Communism, and was not sufficient to combat its dangers. That test was designed for "a hot-headed speech on a street corner, or circulation of a few incendiary pamphlets, or parading by some zealots behind a red flag."

By contrast Communism required a different approach legally, to contain it. This Jackson found in conspiracy theory, since the crime of conspiracy is rooted in the notion that the conspiracy itself is the evil to be punished. Here, the officials of the Communist Party of the United States were in fact indicted and tried for the crime of conspiracy under the Smith Act. The proof adduced was sufficient in Jackson's view to uphold their convictions on that theory, without need for resort to reinterpretations of the clear-and-present-danger test.

Dennis generated a flood of indictments, with more than 130 individuals being charged with crimes under the Smith Act. More than 100 individuals were tried, with the conviction rate approaching 90 percent. One of the principal prosecutions was the case of *Yates v. United States* (1957), in which the leaders of the Communist Party of the United States in California were indicted. After a trial of more than six months, all the defendants were convicted and each was sentenced to the maximum five-year prison term. The Supreme Court did not review the case until 1957. By that time both the domestic and world scenes had changed. Stalin had died in 1953, the Korean War had ended, and Senator Joseph McCarthy died the month before the Supreme Court announced its decision in *Yates*. As a result of the Smith Act prosecutions, moreover, the leadership of the Communist Party of the United States had been eviscerated. The Supreme Court itself also had changed, with President Eisenhower having appointed four new justices, including Chief Justice Earl Warren.

The lead opinion in *Yates* was joined by only three justices and was written by the recently appointed justice John M. Harlan, the grandson of the nineteenth-century Supreme Court justice of the same name. Harlan served on the Supreme Court between 1955 and 1971. He had been a successful Wall Street antitrust and trial lawyer who counted the DuPont Corporation among his clients. Harlan became noted as a careful, restrained jurist who followed what would now be called a minimalist approach to constitutional questions. His opinion in *Yates* was a good example. That opinion held that the Smith Act did not prohibit "advocacy and teaching of forcible overthrow as an abstract principle, divorced from any effort to instigate action to that end." This was the case even if "such advocacy or teaching is engaged in with evil intent."

This was an interpretation of the statutory language, and Harlan's opinion took this approach to avoid deciding the constitutional questions. The *Dennis* opinion was distinguished on the basis that the advocacy in that case was "advocacy of action, not ideas." Harlan explained: "The essential distinction is that those to whom the advocacy is addressed must be urged to *do* something, now or in the future, rather than merely to *believe* in something."

Applying this standard, Harlan found that five of the fourteen defendants should be acquitted, with the other nine retried.

Only two other justices joined Harlan's opinion, while two others—the recently appointed William Brennan and Charles Whittaker—did not participate in the case. The remaining four justices filed separate opinions. Justices Black and Douglas took an absolutist position. In an opinion written by Black, they stated that they believed "the First Amendment forbids Congress to punish people for talking about public affairs, whether or not such discussion incites to action, legal or illegal." Black explained that "unless there is complete freedom for expression of all ideas, whether we like them or not, concerning the way government should be run and who shall run it, I doubt if any views in the long-run can be secured against the censor. The First Amendment provides the only kind of security system that can preserve a free government—one that leaves the way wide open for people to favor, discuss, advocate, or incite causes and doctrines however obnoxious and antagonistic such views may be to the rest of us."

Justice Tom Clark, who had been President Truman's attorney general, dissented. He found the case indistinguishable from *Dennis,* observing that the defendants "served in the same army and have engaged in the same mission." As such he would uphold the convictions.

Conservative politicians and media roundly criticized the *Yates* opinion. Senator William Jenner of Indiana accused the Supreme Court of "making law—substituting its judgment for the judgment of the legislative branch." As a result of *Yates,* prosecutions under the Smith Act evaporated. There were no new prosecutions for advocacy violations under that act, and the cases then pending against ninety defendants were dropped entirely.

Over the next decade, the Supreme Court struggled to find an acceptable reformulation of the clear-and-present-danger standard for abridging speech. Finally, in *Brandenburg v. Ohio* (1969), the Court determined that the First Amendment "do[es] not permit a State to forbid or proscribe advocacy of the use of force or of law violation except where such advocacy is directed to inciting or producing imminent lawless action and is likely to incite or produce such action."

Brandenburg involved the prosecution of a leader of the Ku Klux Klan in Ohio for giving a speech making derogatory comments about African Americans and Jews. No one was present at the speech except the Klan participants and a newsman. The prosecution was brought under a criminal syndicalism statute of a type that had been enacted in twenty states and two territories between 1917 and 1920, the constitutionality of which had previously been upheld by the Supreme Court in *Whitney v. California* (1927). *Brandenburg* overruled *Whitney*, ending fifty years of confusion over the scope of First Amendment protections of speech, a confusion that began with Holmes's 1919 opinion in *Schenck*.

September 11, 2001, and the War against Terror

On September 11, 2001, Islamic terrorists hijacked four American commercial airliners. Two were crashed by the terrorists into the World Trade Center towers in New York City, killing nearly two thousand and leveling the twin towers, while a third was crashed into the Pentagon in Washington, D.C., killing still more, and causing significant structural damage. The hijackers on the fourth plane, presumed to have been targeted on the United States Capitol Building, met spirited resistance from the American passengers and crashed into the Pennsylvania countryside, killing all aboard.

These terrorist attacks led initially to the U.S. bombing of, and ground war in, Afghanistan, which was home to the Islamic terrorists known as the Taliban. Many of the enemy combatants in the war on terror, some of whom were American citizens, were captured by American forces in Afghanistan and elsewhere and then transported to the American military base at Guantanamo Bay, Cuba, where they were held without trial as enemy combatants. Their detention led to several Supreme Court decisions, three of which are discussed below.

In *Hamdi v. Rumsfeld* (2004), the plurality opinion of Justice Sandra Day O'Connor on behalf of four justices upheld the legality of military detention of a United States citizen captured in Afghanistan, but also ruled that due process required that any such enemy combatant be permitted to challenge the factual basis for his confinement before a neutral decision maker. Two years later, in *Hamdan v. Rumsfeld* (2006), five members of the Court held that enemy combatants could not be tried by a military commission established by President George W. Bush in 2001 because the structures and procedures of the commission violated both the Uniform Code of Military Justice and four Geneva Conventions. Both cases left many fundamental constitutional questions unresolved, including whether any class of enemy combatants possessed the right to habeas corpus.

In 2008 the Supreme Court resolved the habeas corpus issue in *Boumediene v. Bush* (2008). Five members of the Court, in a majority opinion by Justice Anthony Kennedy, held that the right of habeas corpus extended to all enemy combatants, including aliens. Boumediene himself was an alien, born in Algeria.

He was originally detained in Bosnia in October of 2001 for alleged involvement in a terrorist plot to attack the United States Embassy in that European country, and thereafter was transferred by United States forces to Guantanamo Bay and held there as an enemy combatant.

Justice Kennedy's majority opinion is noteworthy for its conclusion, for the first time in American jurisprudence, that an alien held outside United States sovereign territory had a right to the habeas corpus remedy. Kennedy acknowledged the unprecedented nature of this conclusion, but found no contrary authority on point. Dissenting Justice Antonin Scalia, joined by Chief Justice Roberts and Justices Thomas and Alito, strenuously disagreed, arguing that "*all* available historical evidence points to the conclusion that the writ would not have been available at common law for aliens captured and held outside the sovereign territory of the Crown."

The majority opinion focused on the crucial importance of the writ of habeas corpus to protect individual liberty in both English and American law, and reviewed the prior Supreme Court opinions. It concluded that while the writ of habeas corpus may constitutionally be suspended, "at least three factors are relevant in determining the reach of the Suspension Clause: (1) the citizenship and status of the detainee and the adequacy of the process through which that status determination was made; (2) the nature of the sites where apprehension and then detention took place; and (3) the practical obstacles inherent in resolving the prisoner's entitlement to the writ." Finding that these factors supported the availability of the writ for the Guantanamo Bay detainees, the majority held that the constitutional guarantee of habeas corpus in Article I, Section 9, Clause 2, "has full effect at Guantanamo Bay." The majority opinion further noted that an adequate substitute for habeas corpus could be legislated by Congress, and that the Court would not "offer a comprehensive summary of the requisites." It also noted the limited range of its holding, stating that it "should not be read to imply that a habeas court should intervene the moment an enemy combatant steps foot in a territory where the writ runs." Nevertheless, the primacy of the writ must be protected by courts because "the laws and Constitution are designed to survive, and remain in force, in extraordinary times. Liberty and security can be reconciled; and in our system they are reconciled within the framework of the law. The Framers decided that habeas corpus, a right of first importance, must be a part of that framework, a part of that law."

There were two dissenting opinions, both on behalf of four justices, one by Chief Justice Roberts and the second by Justice Scalia. Chief Justice Roberts contended that the majority should not have decided whether habeas corpus was an available remedy because the process accorded to the *alien* detainees by Congress was at least as extensive as that prescribed for *American citizens* by the plurality opinion in *Hamdi.* Justice Scalia's dissenting opinion reviewed historical precedents from English and American law, concluding that habeas corpus was not available to aliens held outside a sovereign's territory. Concluding that "the Nation will live to regret what the Court has done today," he pointed out that some thirty enemy combatants who had been released by the military from Guantanamo Bay had returned to terrorist activities, killing among others Afghan and Iraqi soldiers, an Afghan judge, a United Nations engineer, and some Chinese workers. Based on these activities, he observed that the majority opinion "will almost certainly cause more Americans to be killed."

Given the fact-specific three-part test enunciated by the majority for determining when the availability of the writ could be suspended, as well as the unanswered questions as to what process would have to be accorded these enemy combatants in a habeas corpus proceeding, the ultimate impact of *Boumediene* is unclear. Moreover the more than six-year-long detention of the petitioners, coupled with intense international criticism of the Guantanamo Bay facility and American weariness with the war in Iraq, all colored the outcome, and the force of the five-justice majority opinion for future enemy combatants held for shorter periods in different wars is questionable.

Eugenics in the Supreme Court: "A Different Kind of Men and Women"

After beginning construction of a First Amendment jurisprudence, the Supreme Court turned in the 1920s to other civil liberties issues. One of these related to the rights of the mentally disabled. Throughout the Progressive Era, legislators sought to reform both the economic and social spheres. In city government, for example, the early part of the twentieth century saw the beginnings of a municipal reform movement, including creation of the city manager concept. Businesses were professionalized through trade associations such as the National Association of Manufacturers, the American Medical Association, and the United States Chamber of Commerce. These economic initiatives were paralleled by significant, far-ranging social legislation. Much of this legislation was aimed at what the Social Gospel minister Washington Gladden called the creation of "a different kind of men and women." In seeking to bring the kingdom of God to Earth, progressives enacted legislation that sought to control the conduct of new immigrants and groups thought to be dangerous to the American way of life, as they visualized it. This legislation mandated compulsory attendance at grade and or high schools; special juvenile courts to deal with rebellious youths; Sunday "Blue Laws," which closed taverns and businesses; Prohibition, which denied liquor to African Americans, immigrants, and other elements perceived to be dangerous; Jim Crow laws in the South, which increasingly segregated African Americans from white society; and public morality legislation, including most notably the Mann Act. That federal legislation, which was aimed at what was termed "white slavery," was employed to convict the heavyweight boxing champion, African American Jack Johnson, for having an affair with a white mistress of long-standing.

But, most significantly for the Supreme Court, this progressive attempt to create "a new kind of men and women" led to the enactment of eugenics laws in some thirty states, with the resultant sterilization of some twenty thousand Americans by 1935. Eugenics, which means "wellborn" in Greek, began as a movement in the 1890s. It originated in fears of Catholics and Jews, especially those who were immigrants. Under the leadership of Harry Laughlin, a Eugenics Record Office was established, and a Model Act written for legislators to utilize in their states. The eugenics movement sought to purify the white race by eliminating reproductive rights for the blind, the near-blind, the deaf, the near-deaf, "ne'er-do-wells," the homeless, tramps, and paupers. Its goal was to remove "the most worthless one-tenth of our present population." The Laughlin 1922 Model Act was the basis for Nazi Germany's own later law, which led to the sterilization of some 375,000 individual human beings in Europe.

The first American eugenics law was enacted in Pennsylvania in 1905, but was vetoed by the governor. The first eugenics law that went into force was enacted in Indiana, which (not coincidentally) was the state with the largest membership at the time in the second Ku Klux Klan. The two states that most enforced their sterilization laws were California and Virginia. About ten thousand individuals were sterilized in California by 1935, with approximately four thousand additional humans sterilized in Virginia between 1924 and 1972.

These laws were enthusiastically embraced by many mainline Protestant ministers, as well as by "progressive" legislators. The only opposition of note in the 1920s to compulsory sterilization and the eugenics movement was the Catholic Church. Indeed the popular Catholic controversialist G. K. Chesterton wrote a book in 1922 entitled *Eugenics and Other Evils.*

Against this backdrop, and at the end of the Progressive Era, the Supreme Court decided the infamous case of *Buck v. Bell* (1927). With only Pierce Butler, the sole Catholic justice on the Court at that time, dissenting (without writing an opinion), the Supreme Court upheld the forced sterilization of Carrie Buck, in a short, cruel opinion by Justice Holmes. Buck and her mother had been institutionalized at the State Colony for Epileptics and Feeble Minded in Virginia, and Carrie Buck had been dismissed as the mother of "an illegitimate feeble minded child." Buck challenged an order of sterilization issued under Virginia's 1924 eugenics law, contending that her forced sterilization violated her substantive due process rights under the Fourteenth Amendment.

Holmes would have none of this. After finding that all the legal procedures prescribed under the Virginia law had been followed, and that procedural due process had been afforded Carrie Buck, Holmes rejected the substantive due process argument. As he put it, "the public welfare may call upon the best citizens for their lives. It would be strange if it could not call upon *those who already sap the strength of the State* for these lesser sacrifices, often not felt to be such by those concerned, *in order to prevent our being swamped with incompetence.* It is better for all the world, if instead of waiting to execute degenerate offspring for crime, or to let them starve for their imbecility, society can prevent those *who are manifestly unfit from continuing their kind.* The principle that sustains compulsory vaccination is broad enough to cover cutting the Fallopian tubes. . . . *Three generations of imbeciles are enough.*"

What Holmes did not know was the following. As Stephen Jay Gould has documented, Carrie Buck had been raped by a relative of her foster parents. Moreover her child, who died in the second grade, had been an average student at the age of eight. Carrie Buck herself lived to the age of eighty-three and proved to be of average intelligence. She read newspapers and did crossword puzzles. As Gould concluded, the real story was that Carrie Buck was "the illegitimate child of an illegitimate woman. *Three generations of bastards are enough.*"

Holmes took great pride in his opinion in *Buck v. Bell.* Within days of that opinion he wrote to his literary pen pals Harold Laski and Lewis Einstein about it. To Laski, he wrote that "I wrote and delivered a decision upholding the constitutionality of a state law for sterilizing imbeciles the other day—and felt that I was getting near the first principle of real reform." He told Einstein that "establishing the constitutionality of the law permitting the sterilization of imbeciles . . . *gave me pleasure.*"

Buck v. Bell is Holmes's dirty little secret. While Holmes is often held up by current United States senators of both parties as the exemplar of the ideal Supreme Court justice, these admirers conspicuously overlook this heartless opinion, which is no less than the *Scott v. Sandford* opinion for the disabled community.

The Rights of Parents and Teachers to Educate Children

Prior to *Buck v. Bell,* the Supreme Court reviewed and invalidated two other pieces of Progressive Era social control legislation that attempted to impose "100% Americanism" on all United States residents. In *Meyer v. Nebraska* (1923), the Court struck down under the Due Process Clause a Nebraska state law that prohibited the teaching of foreign languages to students who had not entered the ninth grade. This legislation was aimed at Germans, who had been the enemy in the recently concluded World War I. A challenge to the law was brought by a teacher who utilized a German language text in a Lutheran religious grade school to teach Bible history.

In a seven-to-two decision, in an opinion written by Justice James Clark McReynolds, the Supreme Court ruled that the Nebraska law deprived both the teacher and the parents of the schoolchildren of the liberty protected by the Fourteenth Amendment. This was the first significant case applying the doctrine of substantive due process to rights that appeared to be social rather than economic. McReynolds did note, however, a quasi-economic basis for the decision, recognizing that the teacher's "right . . . to teach and the right of parents to engage him so to instruct their children, we think, are within the liberty of the amendment."

While acknowledging that the Nebraska legislation stemmed from a "desire . . . to foster a homogeneous people with American ideals prepared readily to understand current discussions of civic matters," McReynolds found that it went too far, depriving both the teacher and parents of a liberty right protected by the Fourteenth Amendment. That liberty right was broad indeed, for it protected "not merely freedom from bodily restraint but also the right of the individual to contract, to engage in any of the common occupations of life, to acquire useful knowledge, to marry, establish a home and bring up children, to worship God according to the dictates of his own conscience, and generally to enjoy those privileges long recognized at common law as essential to the orderly pursuit of happiness by free men."

In an odd pairing of dissenters, Justice Holmes agreed with Justice Sutherland, one of the conservative Four Horsemen, that the Nebraska legislation was valid. In Holmes's view the legislation had the beneficent purpose of assuring that "all the citizens of the United States should speak a common tongue." While Holmes declared that he "appreciate[d] the objection to the law," he found that it presented "a question upon which men reasonably might differ and therefore I am unable to say that the Constitution of the United States prevents the experiment being tried."

This broad view of substantive due process transported by the McReynolds majority opinion in *Meyer* into the social sphere would lead in future cases to protecting reproductive rights, beginning most notably with *Griswold v. Connecticut* (1965), which found a married couple to be protected in buying contraceptives by the same liberty right recognized in *Meyer*, which it (and later *Roe v. Wade*) cited. This development is particularly ironic, given McReynolds's highly conservative background. A lifelong bachelor, and a member of the conservative "Four Horsemen," McReynolds served on the Supreme Court for twenty-six years, between 1914 and 1941. He was a Democrat who had served as Woodrow Wilson's attorney general, and he generally opposed all types of government regulation of both social and economic affairs. He was also a noted anti-Semite, refusing to sit for the official Court photograph in 1924 because Court protocol would have required him to sit next to Wilson's other appointee, Justice Louis Brandeis, the first Jew to sit on the Court.

Shortly after *Meyer*, the Supreme Court had an additional opportunity to apply this expanded view of substantive due process in the social sphere to another educational issue. In *Pierce v. Society of Sisters* (1925), the Supreme Court unanimously invalidated an Oregon state law that required that all normal children between the ages of eight and sixteen who had not yet completed the eighth grade must attend public school. This "Compulsory Education Act" was sponsored by the Ku Klux Klan, which controlled the Oregon legislature in 1922. It was submitted to a statewide referendum and thereafter became law, part of social legislation that the historian Richard White has aptly characterized as "hooded Progressivism."

The Klan feared foreigners and immigrants, particularly Catholics and Jews, and opposed their preference for schooling their children, often in religious schools. The Oregon Act was challenged by the owners of two schools—a Catholic order of nuns who operated a religious school, and the owners of a private, nonreligious military school.

The unanimous opinion of the Court was once again written by Justice McReynolds. Again he noted that the legislation infringed *economic* rights, reciting that it would "seriously impair, perhaps destroy, the profitable features of appellees' business and greatly diminish the value of their property." But he did not limit the protections of substantive due process to these economic rights. Instead, he found additionally that the Oregon law unreasonably interfered with the liberty of parents to direct the education and development of their children, relying upon the decision in *Meyer.* In perhaps the most famous sentences McReynolds ever wrote, he declared that "the fundamental theory of liberty upon which all governments in this Union repose excludes any general power of the state to *standardize its children* by forcing them to accept instruction from public teachers only. *The child is not the mere creature of the state;* those who nurture him and direct his destiny have the right, coupled with a high duty, to recognize and prepare him for additional obligations."

The expansion of the protections of substantive due process to these noneconomic rights in both *Meyer* and *Pierce* would lie about, mostly unused, until the 1960s and 1970s, when substantive due process became reenergized in the context of protecting reproductive rights. As noted above, both *Meyer* and *Pierce* would provide part of the legal underpinning of *Roe v. Wade.*

Free Exercise of Religion: From Mormon Polygamists to Jehovah's Witnesses Who Refused to Salute the Flag

In addition to safeguarding the rights of freedom of speech and freedom of the press, the First Amendment forecloses Congress from passing any law that prohibits the "free exercise" of religion. This part of the First Amendment did not receive any authoritative construction by the Supreme Court until *Reynolds v. United States* (1879), which involved the rights of members of the Church of Jesus Christ of Latter-day Saints, popularly known as Mormons, to practice polygamy.

The Mormon religion was founded by the prophet Joseph Smith in 1830, at the time of the Second Great Awakening in the eastern part of United States. The religion is one of the few authentically American creations, and it has an elaborate set of beliefs, with a centralized hierarchy to guard the religious purity of the doctrines of the Church of Latter-day Saints. The teaching on what the Mormons referred to as "celestial marriage" or simply "the Principle" was revealed to Smith in 1843, but not officially announced as Mormon doctrine until 1852, after Smith's death, by his successor, Brigham Young.

Smith had been killed by Christians in Illinois who had progressively come to fear the inroads made by the Mormons, as well as their insularity, which included separate communities. After Smith's death, Young relocated the Mormon community to what would become the territory of Utah. There he established a government that effectively combined both church and state, incorporating Mormon teachings into the governmental structure, much as Islam does today in some parts of the Middle East. Polygamy was freely practiced and indeed was considered a duty for Mormon men.

These developments caused great concern among the American people and their governmental leaders. Several novels appeared attacking polygamy, and the practice became linked in popular minds to slavery. The platform of the new Republican Party in 1856 described slavery and polygamy as "twin relics of barbarism" and called for the abolition of both slavery and polygamy in the territories of United States. Indeed, at one point in 1857, President James Buchanan sent federal troops into Utah, but they were intercepted by heavy snows and did not reach their destination.

Although Mormons considered their religion to be Christian, the dominant Protestant majority in the United States saw the Church of the Latter-day Saints as attacking the sanctity of marriage, which the Protestant majority viewed as providing the pillar for republican government and a just state. Mormons were linked to the disfavored Roman Catholic religion because of the rigid hierarchical structure of both churches, each of which was seen as un-American. A Thomas Nast cartoon depicted a fierce alligator that was labeled "Roman Church" and a large, snarling turtle that was called "Mormon Church" with the caption "can we allow foreign reptiles to crawl all over US?" The linkage of these two religions was ironic, given the Mormon view of the Roman Catholic Church as the "Mother of Harlots."

The opposition to polygamy led to the enactment of the Morrill Act for the Suppression of Polygamy in 1862. Under this legislation, bigamy was prohibited in the territories, the establishment of the Mormon Church in Utah was annulled, and religious organizations were prohibited from owning real estate valued in excess of fifty thousand dollars. Given the great distance to Utah, and the failure of the Buchanan troop gambit in 1857, the Morrill Act was a dead letter at birth and did nothing to stop polygamy. Indeed the Mormons saw themselves as protected in their practice of polygamy by two pillars of the American legal system. First, they believed that the First Amendment allowed them to establish their church in Utah, since at the time the Supreme Court had held that the Establishment Clause only prevented the federal government from establishing a religion. Moreover the Free Exercise Clause of the First Amendment, in the Mormon view, guaranteed their right to practice polygamy, as a belief of their religion, without federal interference. Second, the Mormons relied upon the same principles of federalism that the Supreme Court had recognized in its civil rights decisions after the Civil War. As such the law of domestic relations was a concern of the state, rather than the federal, government. Since the Mormons controlled the territory of Utah, they were free (in their view) to permit polygamy without federal interference, and the federal government was incompetent to enact legislation prohibiting polygamy.

Despite the Mormon beliefs in the First Amendment and federalism, the federal government stepped up its efforts to stamp out polygamy. In 1874 Congress passed the Poland Act, increasing federal power over the territory of Utah, and began actively to prosecute polygamy in the territorial criminal courts. That led to the *Reynolds* case, after George Reynolds was selected by the Mormon hierarchy to become a test case of the power of the federal government to prosecute polygamy.

When *Reynolds* reached the Supreme Court, the case presented six distinct questions, only one of which involved the First Amendment. That question focused on Reynolds's defense that he was free to practice polygamy because of what was termed "religious belief or duty." In a seven-page portion of his opinion, Chief Justice Waite devoted much of the discussion to a review of the historical precedents relating to religious freedom in the American colonies before the adoption of the First Amendment. Recent sources have suggested that much of this historical research was done for Waite by his friend and neighbor, the famous historian George Bancroft. In the opinion Waite placed particular reliance on a distinction made in the preamble to the Virginia bill on religious freedom, which stated that civil government could interfere with the practice of religion "when principles break out into overt acts against peace and good order." Ironically this distinction between opinions and actions was mirrored later in the free-speech decisions of the Supreme Court in the twentieth century. Waite went on to quote Thomas Jefferson's famous letter to the Danbury Baptist Association, which utilized a metaphor that has become embedded in the Supreme Court's twentieth-century jurisprudence on the First Amendment's religion clauses. That metaphor referred to a "wall of separation between church and state."

Waite concluded that "Congress was deprived of all legislative power over mere *opinion,* but was left free to reach *actions* which were in violation of social duties or subversive of good order." Since polygamy was viewed as "odious," and was linked by Waite to "Asiatic" and "African" people, it was within the power of the federal government to declare polygamy unlawful. Given this conclusion, the only question left in the *Reynolds* case was whether the defendant's religious belief could exempt him from the operation of the law. Waite thought not, declaring that "laws are made for the government of actions, and while they cannot interfere with mere religious belief and opinions, they may with practices." Invoking human sacrifice as an example of actions within religious beliefs of certain pagan tribes that Congress could prohibit, Waite concluded his opinion by asking and answering a question—"Can a man excuse his practices . . . because of his religious belief? To permit this would be to make the professed doctrines of religious belief superior to the law of the land, and in effect to permit every citizen to become a law unto himself. Government could exist only in name under such circumstances."

After *Reynolds*, the Church of Jesus Christ of Latter-day Saints outlawed the practice of polygamy, although some dissidents continue to practice it today. Utah was finally admitted to the Union as a state in 1896 and the Mormon Church today has become one of the strongest defenders of marriage as a pillar of American republican government and the just society.

The next group that caused the Supreme Court to interpret the scope of the Free Exercise Clause was the Jehovah's Witnesses. The Witnesses claimed not to be an organized religion and indeed forcefully attacked the doctrines of most religions, with particular vituperation directed against the Roman Catholic Church. They were millennialists, who saw all of human history as progressing toward the Second Coming of Jesus Christ, eventuating in a final battle between the forces of Jehovah and those of Satan. These beliefs caused the Witnesses to take positions on a wide range of social issues that contradicted popular opinion. The Witnesses proselytized door-to-door, attacking other religions, and refused to fight for the United States in World War II. In 1940 the Supreme Court upheld the right of Jehovah's Witnesses to proselytize door-to-door, handing out pamphlets attacking the Catholic religion in Catholic neighborhoods. In *Cantwell v. Connecticut* (1940), the Court ruled that a complete prohibition of such activities violated the Free Exercise Clause.

But it was another aspect of the beliefs of the Jehovah's Witnesses that brought them to national prominence in the 1940s. This was the Witnesses' refusal to permit their children to salute the flag of the United States in public school classrooms. Salute of the flag was considered to be a violation of the biblical injunction against worshiping "graven images." The excesses of Nazi Germany, with the required stiff-arm Hitler salute of the German flag, energized the Witnesses in Germany to refuse to participate in such activities. Some ten thousand Witnesses were sent to concentration camps because of this very visible expression of dissent.

In the small town of Minersville, Pennsylvania, in the Pennsylvania coal regions, the local school board required all public school children to salute the American flag on a daily basis. Minersville was a majority Catholic community, and two children of a former Catholic parent refused to engage in the compulsory flag salute. Lillian and William Gobitis, ages twelve and ten respectively, were thereupon expelled from school, and sued to gain their readmittance. They were denied relief by the Supreme Court in *Minersville School District v. Gobitis* (1940), even though both lower courts had ruled in their favor.

In an eight-to-one decision, with only future chief justice Harlan Stone dissenting, the Supreme Court upheld the mandatory flag salute policy of the local school board against a challenge under the Free Exercise Clause. The majority opinion was written by Justice Felix Frankfurter. Justice Frankfurter had been born in Vienna, Austria, and came to the United States at the age of twelve with his parents, speaking no English at all at the time. Nevertheless, he went on to graduate first in his class at the Harvard Law School, where he served on the faculty until his appointment to the Supreme Court in 1939. He served on that Court for twenty-three years, retiring in 1962, and died a few years later. Frankfurter had been active in a wide variety of liberal causes, including the defense of the Italian anarchists Sacco and Vanzetti, and was an adviser to President Franklin D. Roosevelt, who made Frankfurter his third appointment to the Supreme Court. Despite his involvement in liberal causes before his appointment to the Supreme Court, Frankfurter became a leading exponent of judicial restraint and what would now be called a "minimalist" approach to deciding questions of constitutional law and federalism, with deference to elected state officials in most circumstances.

In *Gobitis*, Frankfurter saw the question presented as how to "reconcile two rights in order to prevent either from destroying the other." These conflicting rights were those of the state to foster national unity, and those of the Jehovah's Witnesses to freely practice their religion. Relying upon the *Reynolds* decision, Frankfurter's opinion concluded that "the religious liberty which the Constitution protects has never excluded legislation of general scope not directed against doctrinal loyalties of particular sects. Judicial nullification of legislation cannot be justified by attributing to the framers of the Bill of Rights views for which there is no historic warrant. Conscientious scruples have not, in the course of the long struggle for religious toleration, relieved the individual from obedience to a general law not aimed at the promotion or restriction of religious beliefs. The mere possession of religious convictions which contradict the relevant concerns of a political society does not relieve the citizen from the discharge of political responsibilities."

The Austrian immigrant Frankfurter felt that the school board policy was "dealing with an interest inferior to none in the hierarchy of legal values. National unity is the basis of national security." He went on to observe that "'We live by symbols.' The flag is the symbol of our national unity, transcending all internal differences, however large, within the framework of the Constitution." As such this legitimate state interest, applied indiscriminately to all schoolchildren, overrode the limited interests of the Jehovah's Witnesses and was a constitutional exercise of state power.

In dissent Justice Stone felt that a "reasonable accommodation" between the interests of the state and the interests of the Jehovah's Witnesses was called for. In Stone's view "it is the function of courts to determine whether such accommodation is reasonably possible." Viewing the Witnesses as "this small and helpless minority," Stone saw the role of the federal courts as protecting such minorities from excesses of "the popular will." As such the compulsory flag salute was unconstitutional because "I cannot say that the inconveniences which may attend some sensible adjustment of school discipline in order that the religious convictions of these children may be spared, presents a problem so momentous or pressing as to outweigh the freedom from compulsory violation of religious faith which has been thought worthy of constitutional protection."

Following the decision in *Gobitis,* the Jehovah's Witnesses were subjected to harsh treatment across the country. There were hundreds of physical assaults on Witnesses, particularly after the outbreak of hostilities against the United States in World War II. Meeting places of the Witnesses were burnt down in many places, and leaders of the movement were driven out of several towns. There were cases of tar and featherings, and even one case in which a Jehovah's Witness was castrated. School boards across the country, in all forty-eight states, adopted some form of compulsory flag salute based upon the Minersville model upheld in *Gobitis.*

The violence unleashed following *Gobitis* led to calls of moderation. Legal scholars generally criticized the majority opinion in *Gobitis,* with the law reviews at several prominent Catholic law schools coming out in favor of the right of Jehovah's Witnesses to freely exercise their religion. Nevertheless, more than two thousand Jehovah's Witnesses were expelled from public schools across the country. This popular discontent led to the Supreme Court taking another look at the question of compulsory flag salutes just three years after it had decided the *Gobitis* case.

In *West Virginia State Board of Education v. Barnette* (1943), decided on Flag Day of that year, a six-person majority of the Supreme Court overruled *Gobitis.* In an opinion by Justice Robert Jackson, the Court looked at compulsory flag salute as a question of free speech, not merely free exercise of religion. Jackson's opinion pointed out that the West Virginia law had met considerable opposition, including a comment that the flag salute was "too much like Hitler's." He concluded that not saluting the flag is "a form of utterance," and, as speech, could be suppressed only where there was a clear and present danger of some action that the state had a right to prevent. As to Frankfurter's "national unity" approach, Jackson harshly rejected it, pointing out the "ultimate futility of . . . attempts to compel coherence," which he saw as "the lesson of every such effort from the Roman drive to stamp out Christianity as a disturber of its pagan unity, the Inquisition, as a means to religious and dynastic unity, the Siberian exile as a means to Russian unity, down to the fast failing efforts of our present totalitarian enemies. Those who begin coercive elimination of dissent soon find themselves exterminating dissenters. Compulsory unification of opinion achieves only *the unanimity of the graveyard.*"

Jackson concluded by pointing out that "if there is any fixed star in our constitutional constellation, it is that no official, higher or petty, can prescribe what shall be orthodox in politics, nationalism, religion, or other matters of opinion or force citizens to confess by word or act their faith therein."

Three justices dissented. Justices Owen Roberts and Stanley Reed would have followed *Gobitis.* Justice Frankfurter wrote a long individual dissenting opinion. Speaking from the heart, he began that opinion with a reference to his own personal history, in a passage that was controversial then, and continues to be so today. He stated that "one who belongs to the most vilified and persecuted minority in history is not likely to be insensible to the freedoms guaranteed by our Constitution. Were my purely personal attitude relevant I should wholeheartedly associate myself with the general libertarian views in the Court's opinion, representing as they do the thought and action of a lifetime. But as judges we are neither Jew nor Gentile, neither Catholic nor agnostic. We owe equal attachment to the Constitution and are equally bound by our judicial obligations whether we derive our citizenship from the earliest or the latest immigrants to these shores. As a member of this Court I am not justified in writing my private notions of policy into the Constitution, no matter how deeply I may cherish them or how mischievous I may deem their disregard."

Frankfurter made a telling point, which would come back to confront the Court in a large number of cases that we shall discuss in a later chapter. He noted that there were, at the time, more than 250 religions in America and that chaos would result if each of these religions could claim exemption from various state and federal laws because of their religious beliefs. He selected a particular example that would later lead to considerable consternation within the Supreme Court, with a host of contentious viewpoints being expressed. Frankfurter said, "Consider the controversial issue of compulsory Bible-reading in public schools. . . . Is this Court to overthrow . . . variant state educational policies by denying states the right to entertain such convictions in regard to their school systems because of a belief that the King James version is in fact a secretarian text to which parents of the Catholic and Jewish faiths and of some Protestant persuasions may rightly object to having their children exposed?" He went on to identify other issues, questioning, "is this Court to enter the old controversy between science and religion by unduly defining the limits within which a state may experiment with its school curricula? The religious consciences of some parents may be offended by subjecting their children to the Biblical account of creation, while another state may offend parents by prohibiting a teaching of biology that contradicts such

Biblical account." Frankfurter ended by observing that "these questions assume increasing importance in view of the steady growth of parochial schools both in number and in population."

As we shall see, Frankfurter rightly foresaw the controversial issues that the Court would come to confront soon thereafter in the areas of free exercise and establishment of religion. The Supreme Court continues to deal with these issues today, in the midst of swirling, unending, and divisive polemics on both sides.

Part 3

From the Cold War to the Twenty-first Century

Eight

Religion and the Supreme Court

In the sixty years following World War II, the Supreme Court has continuously generated intense controversy through its decisions in the three separate areas of religion, race, and reproductive rights.

Supreme Court decisions in the areas of religion and race have had a great personal impact upon all Americans, particularly as they have affected the public and parochial schools, whose student bodies, activities, finances, and even curricula have been transformed from what they had been prior to World War II. The opinions of the Supreme Court involving reproductive rights have also divided Americans on religious and other lines, creating bitter debate in the public square and spawning continual efforts to overturn the recognition of a constitutional privacy right that permits a woman to terminate a pregnancy and abort a fetus.

In the next three chapters, we deal in turn with the leading Supreme Court opinions in the areas of religion, race, and reproductive rights, exploring their historical contexts and the factors that influenced the Supreme Court in reaching its decisions in each of those areas.

Religion and the First Amendment

The First Amendment deals with religion in two separate clauses. It prohibits Congress both from enacting any "law respecting an establishment of religion" or "prohibiting the free exercise thereof." In this chapter we first examine some of the leading decisions under the Establishment Clause in the areas of aid to parochial schools; prayer in the public schools; teaching of evolution and creation science in the public schools; and limits upon religious expression in public spaces. We then turn to the leading decisions outlining the scope of protection accorded to Americans to practice the "free exercise" of their personal religion.

What is particularly noteworthy in these cases is their inability to reach any long-term consensus or to agree upon any but the broadest of principles in several areas, most notably aid to parochial schools and public displays. This confusion has resulted in ever-shifting majorities, with decisions in the same area often differing one to another on subtle nuances of fact. While there have been two broad groups in the last sixty years favoring either accommodation or complete separation, even the members of those camps have been unable to agree upon the proper mode of analysis of church-state issues. This has led to an unfortunate proliferation of separate opinions, which leaves the controlling standards elusive to grasp. As will be explored below, this jurisprudential confusion is rooted in the very different judicial philosophies, as well as in the personal religious beliefs and prejudices, of the different justices who have served on the Supreme Court since World War II.

The Establishment Clause: Erection of a "Wall of Separation"

The first major case in which the Supreme Court dealt with the Establishment Clause after World War II was *Everson v. Board of Education* (1947). That case dealt with the controversial topic of reimbursing the parents of Catholic school students the costs of their bus transportation to school. The place of the Catholic schools in postwar America was a hot and divisive topic, and those schools provoked a strong voice of opposition in the work of Paul Blanshard. Blanshard wrote several books on what he called the "Catholic problem," beginning with *American Freedom and Catholic Power* in 1949. That book began as a series of articles in the *Nation,* and went through eleven printings, selling one hundred thousand copies, with a place on the *New York Times* best-seller list for seven months. As Blanshard saw it, Catholicism was "antidemocratic," "separatist," and "un-American." He portrayed the religion as a threat to democracy on the same level as Communism, devoting his second book, in 1951, to *Communism, Democracy and Catholic Power.* He argued that Catholics accounted for the majority of white criminals, and identified Catholic schools as "the most important and divisive instrument in the life of American children." His book was praised by a large number of intellectuals and other public figures, including John Dewey, Albert Einstein, Bertrand Russell, and McGeorge Bundy. One of Blanshard's principal points in his attack on Catholicism was the Catholic hierarchy's long-standing and philosophical opposition to the American principle of separation of church and state.

The Catholic school system looked particularly ominous to those who shared Blanshard's views at the time because it was in a great growth mode from the 1940s to 1965, with its attendance doubling during that period. By 1965, 12 percent of American schoolchildren attended Catholic schools; today that attendance has lowered to 5 percent.

Predictably, in this context of public division and debate, the Supreme Court splintered in the *Everson* case. By a five-to-four majority, it upheld the New Jersey school district's reimbursement policy in an opinion by Justice Hugo Black. Black himself was an unlikely candidate to write an opinion upholding aid to the parents of Catholic schoolchildren. He had been, at one time, a member of the Alabama Ku Klux Klan, and Alabama's Grand Dragon had said that "Hugo could make the best anti-Catholic speech you ever heard." Black's own son, a noted lawyer, wrote that Black "suspected the Catholic Church. He used to read all of Paul Blanshard's books exposing power abuse in the Catholic Church. He thought the Pope and bishops had too much power and property. He resented the fact that rental property owned by the church was not taxed; he felt they got most of their revenue from the poor and did not return enough of it." Some historians have suggested that Black's vote in *Everson* was an attempt by him to dampen Catholic criticism, and that Black himself recognized that the general principles his opinion enunciated would be detrimental to the Catholic school system in future cases. Indeed Black later wrote that *Everson* was a Pyrrhic victory for parochial schools.

Black's opinion provided an overview from colonial times of how all religions had suffered where one had been established in any colony, and focused particularly upon the use of tax monies to support religious institutions. As Black saw it, "The 'establishment of religion' clause of the First Amendment means at least this: Neither a state nor the Federal Government can set up a church. Neither can pass laws which aid one religion, aid all religions, or prefer one religion over another. Neither can force nor influence a person to go to or to remain away from church against his will or force him to profess a belief or disbelief in any religion. No person can be punished for entertaining or professing religious beliefs or disbeliefs, for church attendance or non-attendance. No tax in any amount, large or small, can be levied to support any religious activities or institutions, whatever they may be called, or whatever form they may adopt to teach or practice religion. Neither a state nor the Federal Government can, openly or secretly, participate in the affairs of any religious organizations or groups and vice versa. In the words of Jefferson, the clause against establishment of religion by law was intended to erect 'a wall of separation between Church and State.'"

Black wrote that the wall between Church and State "must be kept high and impregnable," but found that the New Jersey reimbursement of the costs of bus transportation for Catholic schoolchildren did not breach that wall. In what has become known as the "child benefit" theory, the majority ruled that it was permissible for New Jersey to extend "general State law benefits to all its citizens without regard to their religious belief." While he admitted that a non-reimbursement policy "would make it far more difficult for the schools to operate," Black wrote that "such is obviously not the purpose of the First Amendment. That Amendment requires the state to be a *neutral* in its relations with groups of religious believers and non-believers; it does not require the state to be their *adversary.* State power is no more to be used so as to handicap religions, than it is to favor them."

To reach a majority to uphold the New Jersey law, Black needed the vote of the Court's lone Catholic, the liberal justice Frank Murphy. Murphy considered recusing himself, but ultimately voted to uphold the law, so as to avoid an equally divided Court on the issue.

The four dissenting justices provided two dissenting opinions, one by Justice Jackson, and the other by Justice Rutledge, in which all four dissenters joined. In a slap against Catholicism, Justice Jackson's opinion commented that "our public school, if not a product of Protestantism, at least is more consistent with it than with the Catholic culture and scheme of values." In arguing against the constitutionality of the reimbursement of the costs of school bus transportation for Catholic school students, Jackson also observed that "Catholic education is the rock on which the whole structure rests."

Justice Wiley Rutledge wrote a long and detailed dissenting opinion on the origins of the Establishment Clause, finding that the New Jersey reimbursement was an impermissible use of tax monies to aid and encourage the Catholic religion. He wrote that *Everson* was "not . . . just a little case over bus fares," but "the first step" to a "complete establishment of religion." Rutledge argued for complete separation and concluded that it was necessary to "keep separate the separate spheres as the First Amendment drew them."

The *Everson* decision evoked strong protest among Protestants, inspiring the organization of Protestants and Other Americans United for the Separation of Church and State in January 1948. That group, today rechristened as *Americans* and Others United, began a campaign against aid to parochial schools. Some religious groups joined this campaign under their own banners, with the Southern Baptists and Seventh-Day Adventists particularly prominent in opposing aid to parochial schools in various cases. They often were joined in such litigation by the American Civil Liberties Union and the American Jewish Congress. Several Catholic groups, and many Catholic law journals, also opposed the *Everson* ruling, recognizing the need for separation of church and state in their writings and Court filings.

The Wall Goes Up and the Wall Goes Down: The Released Time Cases

Within a year of its controversial decision in *Everson,* the Supreme Court revisited the requirements of the Establishment Clause in the first of two cases dealing with the practice of "released time." The "Catholic problem" of Paul Blanshard was missing from this debate, since released time was a concept originated by Protestants, who, lacking the resources of their own school systems on the scale of the Catholic schools, believed that their public school children required more religious instruction than was available to them in their churches on Sunday. Released time permitted religious instruction to be offered to public school children by releasing them from public school instruction during certain periods of the school day. By 1945 some two million public school students were attending religious education classes under released time programs in about forty states. Typically such programs permitted not only Protestant, but also Catholic and Jewish clergy, to teach religious education classes either on school property or at other sites.

In *McCollum v. Board of Education* (1948) the Supreme Court struck down as unconstitutional a released time program under which clergy of various denominations were permitted to come into Illinois public schools during regular hours and teach religious classes to students once a week, for sessions lasting from thirty to forty-five minutes. The released time program had been attacked by an atheist, Vashti McCollum, who was supported in her efforts by the American Civil Liberties Union, and by Baptist, Jewish, and Unitarian groups. In an opinion for eight members of the Court, Justice Black characterized this program as the "use of tax-supported property for religious instruction," noting the "close cooperation between the school authorities and the religious council in promoting religious education." He concluded that "this is beyond all question the utilization of the tax-established and tax-supported public school system to aid religious groups to spread their faith. And it falls squarely under the ban of the First Amendment . . . as we interpreted it in Everson v. Board of Education."

Justice Felix Frankfurter wrote a long concurring opinion for the four justices who had dissented in *Everson.* As we have seen previously in reviewing his opinions in the flag salute cases of the 1940s, Frankfurter, a Jewish agnostic, was a strong supporter of the concept of the public school as a purveyor of American values, freed from sectarian religious influences. He invoked the "basic constitutional principle of *absolute separation*" in voting to strike down the released time concept. He pointed out the great "pressure" placed upon students who chose not to attend the released time religious classes, and how that pressure led to feelings of "separatism," rather than American unity, among public school students.

Justice Jackson also wrote a separate concurring opinion. He warned against taking a constitutional stand that would "isolate and cast out of secular education all that some people may reasonably regard as religious instruction." Jackson noted that "the fact is that, for good or for ill, nearly everything in our culture worth transmitting, everything which gives meaning to life, is saturated with religious influences, derived from paganism, Judaism, Christianity—both Catholic and Protestant—and other faiths accepted by a large part of the world's peoples. One can hardly respect a system of education that would leave the student wholly ignorant of the currents of religious thought that move the world society for a part in which he is being prepared." As such, in Jackson's view, there was a need in the Court's interpretation of the Establishment Clause for "some flexibility to meet local conditions, some chance to progress by trial and error." Jackson's opinion is also notable for warning, at its beginning, of the need to place bounds upon whom may bring challenges to public school practices under the Establishment Clause. Undoubtedly noting the presence of the ACLU and several religious groups in the case, Jackson correctly prophesized "the number of litigations likely to be started as a result of this decision."

The only dissenting opinion was written by Justice Stanley Reed, who pointed out the pervasive presence of religion in American institutions, including the

Congress of the United States, the Armed Forces, and the military academies, all of which had their own religious officials and activities. Given these facts, Reed concluded that "it is clear to me that past practice shows such cooperation between the schools and a non-ecclesiastical body is not forbidden by the First Amendment." He concluded that "devotion to the great principle of religious liberty should not lead us into a rigid interpretation of the constitutional guarantee that conflicts with accepted habits of our people. This is an instance where, for me, the history of past practices is determinative of the meaning of a constitutional clause not a decorous introduction to the study of its text."

The released time issue came back before the Supreme Court four years later in the case of *Zorach v. Clauson* (1952). There, by a vote of six to three, the Supreme Court upheld a version of released time in New York in which students left the public school to attend religious services during the public school day at other locations. As Justice Jackson had foreshadowed in his concurring opinion in *McCollum,* many organizations filed briefs in the case, including eight states supporting the New York practice and the ACLU and the American Jewish Congress opposing it.

The majority opinion was written by Justice William O. Douglas, who began by proclaiming that "there cannot be the slightest doubt that the First Amendment reflects the philosophy that Church and State should be separated," and that such separation must be "complete and unequivocal," as well as "absolute." Nevertheless, Douglas pointed out that "nullification of this law would have wide and profound effects" upon public school students of all religions. Moreover Douglas wrote that "we are a religious people whose institutions presuppose a Supreme Being," and "we sponsor an attitude on the part of the government that shows no partiality to any one group and that lets each flourish according to the zeal of its adherents and the appeal of its dogma." As such there was no need for government to be "hostile" to religion; instead it should be "neutral." Here, the New York public schools had done nothing more than "accommodate their schedules to a program of outside religious instruction."

Justices Black, Frankfurter, and Jackson each wrote separate dissenting opinions, all finding no meaningful difference between the released time program in *Zorach* and that in *McCollum.* As Black wrote, both programs worked to "*channel* children into sectarian classes." In Black's view "New York is manipulating its compulsory education laws to help religious sects get pupils. This is not separation but combination of Church and State." Black also reiterated the concern about divisiveness that Frankfurter had raised in *McCollum.* As Black put it, "State help to religion injects political and party prejudices into a holy field. It too often substitutes force for prayer, hate for love, and persecution for persuasion. Government should not be allowed, under cover of the soft euphemism of 'co-operation,' to steal into the sacred area of religious choice."

Justice Frankfurter's dissenting opinion continued the theme of divisiveness, suggesting that it could be avoided by the simple expedient of dismissing classes in their entirety, and permitting those children who chose to do so to attend religious classes after the school day had been prematurely terminated to accommodate their interests. This concept, known as "dismissed time," was rarely implemented for the simple reason that schoolchildren, left to their own devices, were unlikely to choose to attend religious classes on their free time.

Justice Jackson's dissenting opinion focused upon the element of "coercion," noting that pupils who chose not to attend religious instruction would be pulled "back to the public schoolroom," which would serve as "a temporary jail for a pupil who will not go to Church." He warned that "the day that this country ceases to be free for irreligion it will cease to be free for religion—except for the sect that can win political power." Jackson concluded by referring to "today's passionate dialectics," contending that "the wall which the Court was professing to erect between Church and State has become even more warped and twisted than I expected. Today's judgment will be more interesting to students of psychology and of the judicial processes than to students of constitutional law."

Even though *Zorach* upheld the New York version of released time religious instruction outside the public school building, released time soon expired as a vehicle for religious education, mainly because of other factors, including the demise of the neighborhood school in many large cities. But the released time litigation was significant because it dramatized the deep divisions on the Supreme Court, mirroring those in American society, between those who favored complete separation of church and state and those who wished to accommodate religion. That division has persisted, with the different factions prevailing in some cases and eras, and losing in others, all without agreement upon the controlling principles, even among themselves.

The Wall Goes Back Up and Higher: The School Prayer and Bible-Reading Cases

Ten years after the *Zorach* decision, the Supreme Court had occasion once again to decide an Establishment Clause case arising out of the public schools. *Engel v. Vitale* (1962) dealt with what Justice Brennan would later call a rather "bland" prayer composed by New York state authorities, which was to be said aloud by the class at the start of the school day. The prayer was not compulsory, and any student who wished not to say it would be excused. The prayer read "Almighty God, we acknowledge our dependence upon Thee, and we beg Thy blessings upon us, our parents, our teachers and our Country."

Prayers of this nature were becoming more common as a result of the cold war. As part of the fight against what was then known as "godless communism," federal and state legislation of the 1950s took steps to identify the cause of democracy in the United States with that of the Almighty. In 1954, at the urging of the Knights of Columbus, a Catholic voluntary association, the words "under God" were added to the Pledge of Allegiance. Two years later, "In God we trust," which had appeared on currency since 1865, became the national motto.

Such prayers were opposed by many groups. In *Engel*, briefs opposing the New York State prayer were filed by the American Ethical Union, the American Jewish Committee, and the Synagogue Council of America. The prayer was supported by the attorneys general of twenty-three states.

Once again, Justice Black spoke for the Court in *Engel*. Writing for six members of the Court, he announced that the prayer was unconstitutional because "the constitutional prohibition against laws respecting an establishment of religion must at least mean that in this country it is no part of the business of government to compose official prayers for any group of the American people to recite as a part of a religious program carried on by government." Black pointed out that the Anglican Book of Common Prayer had been mandated as the official form of prayer and religious ceremony in England and in some of the colonies, and that the First Amendment was aimed at prohibiting such an establishment of religion. He also found that the voluntary nature of the prayer did not save it, explaining that "the Establishment Clause, unlike the Free Exercise Clause, does not depend upon a showing of direct governmental compulsion and is violated by the enactment of laws which establish an official religion whether those laws operate directly to coerce non-observing individuals or not." Justice Black concluded his opinion by attributing to the founders "an awareness that governments of the past had shackled men's tongues to make them speak only the religious thoughts that government wanted them to speak and to pray only to the God that government wanted them to pray to. It is neither sacrilegious nor antireligious to say that each separate government in this country should stay out of the business of writing or sanctioning official prayers and leave that purely religious function to the people themselves and to those the people choose to look to for religious guidance."

In a concurring opinion, Justice Douglas pointed to the fact that both the Supreme Court and Congress opened their sessions with prayers, and that the majority opinion dealt with only "an extremely narrow" point. As he saw it, the mere authorization of a prayer might not violate the Establishment Clause, but "once government finances a religious exercise it inserts a *divisive* influence into our communities." Douglas again repeated that the First Amendment mandates that the government be *neutral* in matters of religion. As he saw it, "the First Amendment leaves the government in a position not of hostility to religion but of neutrality. The philosophy is that the atheist or agnostic—the nonbeliever—is entitled to go his own way. The philosophy is that if government interferes in matters spiritual, it will be a divisive force. The First Amendment teaches that a government neutral in the field of religion better serves all religious interests."

Only Justice Potter Stewart dissented, with two justices not participating in the decision. Stewart was an Ohio Republican. He had served in the navy in World War II and was a decorated war veteran. Following that service, he practiced law first in New York, and then in Cincinnati, with private law firms. President Dwight D. Eisenhower named him to the Sixth Circuit federal appeals court in 1954, and then elevated him to the Supreme Court in 1958. A moderate, Stewart often functioned as the swing vote in close cases, a role later played by Justices Sandra Day O'Connor and Anthony Kennedy. He served on the Supreme Court for twenty-two years, retiring in 1981.

Stewart's dissenting opinion in *Engel* explored the tension between the guarantee of "free exercise" and the prohibition against establishment, observing that "I cannot see how an 'official religion' is established by letting those who want to say a prayer say it. On the contrary, I think that to deny the wish of these schoolchildren to join in reciting this prayer is to deny them the opportunity of sharing in the spiritual heritage of our Nation." Stewart found that "the uncritical invocation of metaphors like the 'wall of separation,' a phrase nowhere to be found in the Constitution," was not helpful. Instead, "the history of the religious traditions of our people, reflected in countless practices of the institutions and officials of our government," including the prayers opening Supreme Court and congressional sessions, the revised Pledge of Allegiance, and the use of "In God we trust" on coins since 1865, demonstrated that the New York prayer did not violate the Establishment Clause.

The reaction to the *Engel* decision was fast and fierce. Former presidents Eisenhower and Hoover and former vice president Nixon denounced it. They were joined by a large number of congressmen and religious leaders. Southern Democrats were particularly hostile, linking the *Engel* decision to *Brown v. Board of Education,* with one congressman indicating that the Supreme Court had "put the Negroes in the schools," and "driven God out." Others saw the decision as giving "aid and comfort to Moscow." The Roman Catholic cardinal Francis Spellman of New York and several Protestant leaders also denounced the decision, while other Protestant leaders and most Jewish groups supported it. Legal commentary in law journals was almost evenly split, with a slight tilt against the *Engel* decision.

Notably President John Fitzgerald Kennedy, the first Roman Catholic president, supported the decision, pointing out that the church and the home were the proper places for prayer. In the presidential election campaign of 1960, Kennedy had found great opposition to his candidacy among Protestant ministers, who questioned, along the lines of Paul Blanshard, whether a Catholic could faithfully execute the laws of the United States as president. In his speech to the Greater Houston Ministerial Association during the campaign, Kennedy proclaimed that "I believe in America where the separation of church and state is absolute; where no Catholic prelate would tell the president—should he be Catholic—how to act, and no Protestant minister would tell his parishioners for whom to vote; where no church or church school is granted any public funds or political preference, and where no man is denied public office merely because his religion differs from the President who might appoint him, or the people who might elect him. I believe in an America that is officially neither Catholic, Protestant nor Jewish; where no public official either requests or accepts instructions on public policy from the Pope, the National Council of Churches or any other ecclesiastical source, where no religious body seeks to impose its will directly or indirectly upon the general populace or the public acts of its officials, and where religious liberty is so indivisible that an act against one church is treated as an act against all."

Neither Kennedy's forceful rhetoric, nor his support of *Engel,* stemmed the tide of opposition. For more than twenty years, proposed constitutional amendments were introduced to permit public school prayer. In 1984 a constitutional amendment proposed by President Ronald Reagan received the votes of fifty-six senators, a majority, but short of the two-thirds required for a constitutional amendment to be submitted to the people. That proposal provided that "nothing in this Constitution shall be construed to prohibit individual or group prayers in public schools or other public institutions," while "no person shall be required by the United States or by any state to participate in prayer."

One year after *Engel,* the Supreme Court reentered the controversy by striking down Bible reading in the public schools by a vote of eight to one in *Abington School District v. Schempp* (1963). The *Schempp* opinion was written by Justice Tom Clark, who had been President Harry Truman's attorney general. Clark reviewed the prior cases, concluding that they had determined that the Establishment Clause prohibited more than the preference of one religion over another. He stated that the concept of neutrality that appeared in those cases "stems from a recognition of the teachings of history that powerful sects or groups might bring about a fusion of governmental and religious functions or a concert or dependency of one upon the other to the end that official support of the State or Federal Government would be placed behind the tenets of one or of all orthodoxies." Clark determined that a test had emerged from the prior opinions focusing upon "the purpose and primary effect" of the challenged practice. Under that test, "to withstand the strictures of the Establishment Clause there must be a *secular legislative purpose and a primary effect that neither advances nor inhibits religion.*"

Clark pointed out that the Bible was "an instrument of religion," which could be studied in the public school curriculum only "when presented objectively as part of a secular program of education." He concluded his opinion by observing that "the place of religion in our society is an exalted one, achieved through a long tradition of reliance on the home, the church and the inviolable citadel of the individual heart and mind. We have come to recognize through bitter experience that it is not within the power of government to invade that citadel, whether its purpose or effect be to aid or oppose, to advance or retard. In the relationship between man and religion, the State is firmly committed to a position of neutrality."

Concurring opinions were written by Justice Douglas, and by the Court's lone Catholic, Justice William Brennan, and by the Court's only Jewish member, Justice Arthur Goldberg. The most significant of these was that of Justice Brennan, who wrote a lengthy opinion citing the experience in the United States from colonial times to the present and pointing out how particular religions had been the victims of discrimination. He noted that the early public schools used the King James Protestant Bible as a "textbook of morals," which was offensive to Catholic students who were taught from a different version of the Bible. Based on such experiences, the courts of six states, beginning as early as 1890 in Wisconsin, banned the use of prayers and religious exercises in their public schools under their state constitutions. Brennan also emphasized the importance of the changing composition of the American religious experience. He noted that "our religious composition makes us a vastly more diverse people than were our forefathers. They knew differences chiefly among Protestant sects. Today the nation is far more heterogeneous religiously, including as it does substantial minorities not only of Catholics and Jews but as well of those who worship according to no version of the Bible and those who worship no God at all."

Brennan also included a lengthy exposition of what practices were *not* prohibited by the Establishment Clause, given the guarantees of the Free Exercise Clause. In his enumeration he pointed out the need for accommodation in such areas as the provision of chaplains and churches for the armed forces, the saying of prayers of invocation in legislative and judicial bodies, the nondevotional use of the Bible in social studies or humanities courses, and the granting of tax exemptions for religious institutions.

Once again, only Justice Stewart dissented. He attacked the "sterile metaphor" of the wall of separation and reiterated his objection that "there are areas in which a doctrinaire reading of the Establishment Clause leads to irreconcilable conflict with the Free Exercise Clause." In the case of Bible reading in the public schools, "there is involved . . . a substantial free exercise claim on the part of those who affirmatively desire to have their children's school day open with the reading of passages from the Bible." Stewart noted that the voluntary nature of schoolchildren's participation in the Bible-reading exercise made the state neutral and that a blanket prohibition against Bible reading could be seen as "the establishment of a religion of secularism." Stewart concluded that "in the absence of coercion upon those who do not wish to participate—because they hold less strong beliefs, other beliefs, or no beliefs of all—such provisions cannot, in my view, be held to represent the type of support of religion barred by the Establishment Clause. For the only support which such rules provide for religion is the withholding of state hostility—a simple acknowledgment on the part of secular authorities that the Constitution does not require *extirpation* of all expressions of religious belief."

Evolution, Schoolbooks, and Teachers' Salaries

Five years after its decision in *Schempp*, the Supreme Court was asked to regulate the school curricula under the Establishment Clause in *Epperson v. Arkansas* (1968). At issue was the constitutionality of an Arkansas law that prohibited the teaching of evolution in the public schools. The law dated back to 1928 and was described by the majority opinion of Justice Abe Fortas as "a product of the upsurge of 'fundamentalist' religious fervor of the twenties." Arkansas was one of seven states that adopted such statutes in the wake of the famous Scopes trial in Tennessee. By 1968 only the statutes in Arkansas and Mississippi remained on the books.

In unanimously striking down the law, the Supreme Court ruled that "the overriding fact is that Arkansas' law selects from the body of knowledge a particular segment which it proscribes for the sole reason that it is deemed to conflict with a particular religious doctrine; that is, with a particular interpretation of the Book of Genesis by a particular religious group." Indeed "fundamentalist sectarian conviction was and is the law's reason for existence," and "the law's effort was confined to an attempt to blot out a particular theory because of its supposed conflict with the Biblical account, literally read."

Justice Fortas's opinion recognized, in line with earlier precedent, that the study of the Bible was not totally off-limits in the public school. "While study of religions and of the Bible from a literary and historic viewpoint, presented objectively as part of a secular program of education, need not collide with the First Amendment's prohibition, the state may not adopt programs or practices in its public schools or colleges which 'aid or oppose' any religion. This prohibition is absolute."

In a curious concurring opinion, Justice Black suggested that the Establishment Clause issue was more complex than the Court's opinion recognized. He stated that "unless this Court is prepared simply to write off as pure nonsense the views of those who consider evolution an anti-religious doctrine, then this issue presents problems under the Establishment Clause far more troublesome than are discussed in the Court's opinion." Moreover "certainly the Darwinian theory, precisely like the Genesis story of the creation of man, is not above challenge. In fact the Darwinian theory has not merely been criticized by religionists but by scientists, and perhaps no scientist would be willing to take an oath and swear that everything announced in the Darwinian theory is unquestionably true."

Earlier in 1968, the Supreme Court had revisited the question of which boundaries were appropriate under the Establishment Clause in extending governmental aid to religious schools. In *Board of Education v. Allen* (1968), by a six-to-three vote, the Court upheld a New York State program under which textbooks were lent to children in grades seven through twelve in all schools, including private and religious schools. In New York this aid benefited principally schools operated by Catholic, Jewish, and Lutheran denominations. The New York program was supported in the Supreme Court by the attorneys general of eight states, and by one Lutheran and one Jewish group. It was opposed by the American Jewish Committee and Protestants and Other Americans United.

In an opinion by Justice Byron White, a moderate who had been appointed to the Court by President John Fitzgerald Kennedy, the majority upheld the program under the child-benefit theory of *Everson.* Significantly the majority emphasized that "this Court has long recognized that religious schools pursue two goals, religious instruction and secular education," and that "private education has played and is playing a significant and valuable role in raising national levels of knowledge, competence, and experience."

Three justices dissented, each writing their own opinion. That of Justice Black was one of outrage and apoplexy, characterizing the book-lending program as a "flat, flagrant, open violation of the First and Fourteenth Amendments." In a veiled reference to the Catholics whom he had denounced in his Alabama Klan days, Black wrote that "the same powerful sectarian religious propagandists who have succeeded in securing passage of the present law to help religious schools carry on their sectarian religious purposes can and doubtless will continue their *propaganda,* looking toward complete domination and supremacy of their particular brand of religion." Indicating that he opposed the use of tax dollars, "even to the extent of one penny," to support such sectarian schools, Black explained that "sectarian schools, which, although 'secular,' realistically will in some way inevitably tend to propagate the religious views of the favored sect."

Justice Douglas aimed his dissent even more squarely against the Catholic schools, ignoring the aid that went to Lutheran and Jewish schools under the New York statute. Distinguishing *Everson,* he wryly commented that "there is nothing ideological about a bus." He pointed out that the Catholic schools were permitted to select the particular books to be used in teaching secular classes, and that they would, under the guidance of "priests and nuns," "select the book or books that best promote its sectarian creed." Douglas then went on to quote from various textbooks that promoted Christian views, and cited Catholic authors, including Monsignor John A. Ryan, for the Catholic Church's view that the teaching of religion and secular subjects could not be separated one from the other. He also quoted in full, as an appendix to his opinion, a message from New York's cardinal Spellman, which was read to all parishioners in New York who attended Mass the Sunday before the vote on a proposed state constitution that permitted aid to parochial schools.

The narrow victory of the accommodationists in *Allen* was short-lived. Reacting to a much more controversial approach to aid to religious schools by the states of Pennsylvania and Rhode Island, the Supreme Court enunciated a new standard under the Establishment Clause in the often-attacked, but still-standing decision in *Lemon v. Kurtzman* (1971). While that opinion dealt with several different aspects of aid to private schools, the most significant discussion was devoted to similar attempts by Pennsylvania and Rhode Island to subsidize the salaries of teachers of secular subjects in religious schools. Payments were made either to the teachers or to their schools on the condition that the subsidized teachers could not teach religion and could only use teaching materials then in use in the public schools or approved by the state secretary of education. The states monitored compliance in various ways, including a post-audit program to assure that religion was not taught and written pledges by teachers that they would not teach religion.

Chief Justice Warren Burger's majority opinion found that both teacher reimbursement schemes violated the Establishment Clause. Adding a third test to the criteria previously enunciated in the *Schempp* opinion, *Lemon* erected three obstacles to providing any aid to "sectarian" schools. These were "first, the statute must have a secular legislative purpose; second, its principal or primary effect must be one that neither advances nor inhibits religion . . . finally, the statute must not foster 'an excessive government entanglement with religion.'" Here, the Pennsylvania and Rhode Island statutes flunked the new, third, test by requiring monitoring of teacher compliance. As Burger put it, "These prophylactic contacts will involve excessive and enduring entanglement between state and church." Indeed the statutes presented a "broader base of entanglement of yet a different character," because they necessarily gave rise to "divisive political potential," with different groups warring with each other over state aid.

As has been all too common in religion cases, separate opinions were written by most justices. In *Lemon,* Justice Douglas (joined by Justice Black), Justice Brennan, and Justice White each expressed their separate views. Douglas's opinion once again drew a bead on the Catholic schools. He proclaimed that a proper adjudication of the constitutional questions "must start with the admitted and obvious fact that the raison d'être of parochial schools is the propagation of a religious faith." Again, as in *Allen,* Justice Douglas quoted from many Catholic sources to back up his view. He also focused upon the critical historical fact that "the major force in shaping the pattern of education in this country was the conflict between Protestants and Catholics. The Catholics logically argued the public school was sectarian when it taught the King James version of the Bible. They therefore wanted it removed from the public schools; and in time they tried to get public funds for their own parochial schools." Finally he dismissed, with disgust, the argument that Catholic schools were saving the taxpayers nine billion dollars a year with the comment that "as if that were enough to justify violating the Establishment Clause."

The lone Catholic on the Court, Justice William Brennan, also invoked history in voting to strike down the Pennsylvania and Rhode Island statutes. He documented in detail the bleak history in which subsidies to one religious group or another had led to "bitter controversies" from the beginning of the nation. Such controversies over funding of particular religious schools led to some thirty-five states adopting constitutional prohibitions on the use of public school funds to aid sectarian schools between 1840 and 1900. By 1971 only a handful of states did not have such a constitutional prohibition.

Justice White supported the decision of the Court in the Pennsylvania case, but dissented on the Rhode Island statute. He concluded that the Court was "surely quite wrong in overturning the Pennsylvania and Rhode Island statutes on the ground that they amount to an establishment of religion." Pointing out that there was no evidence that any teacher had actually been involved in inserting religion into his or her teaching of any class, White perceptively noted that the *Lemon* criteria created "an insoluble paradox for the State and parochial schools. The State cannot finance secular instruction if it permits religion to be taught in the same classroom; but if it exacts a promise that religion not be so taught—a promise the school and its teachers are quite willing and on this record able to give—and enforces it, it is then entangled in the 'no entanglement' aspect of the Court's Establishment Clause jurisprudence."

Professor Noah Feldman has characterized *Lemon v. Kurtzman* as "the high point of legal secularism." In the wake of its paradoxical approach, many legislative attempts to provide aid to religious schools failed for the next twenty-plus years. During that time the Supreme Court struck down, among others, state statutes that would have permitted funding for repair and maintenance of buildings, for tuition reimbursement, for tests prepared by teachers, for other testing and guidance counseling services, and for the use of public school teachers in parochial schools. Attempts at accommodation were generally unsuccessful until the 1990s, when new justices and a strong evangelical political movement that united conservative Catholic and Protestant groups tilted the Supreme Court back to an approach that fostered accommodation in some areas.

The Beginnings of Change: New Justices and New Ways of Thinking

The decisions of the Supreme Court banning prayer from the public schools provoked a deep and spirited opposition from evangelical Protestant groups beginning in the 1960s. These groups, which traditionally had been apolitical, entered the public square through several new vehicles, including the Moral Majority, which was founded in 1979. Gradually evangelical Protestants also joined forces with conservative Catholics in speaking out against the Supreme Court's decision in *Roe v. Wade* (1973), which found that states could not absolutely prohibit all abortions. Evangelical Protestants joined this fight most conspicuously through Operation Rescue, founded by Randall Terry in 1987.

The issues of prayer in schools and opposition to abortion united conservative Protestants and Catholics. In the words of Francis Schaeffer, one of the intellectual leaders of this new conservative political opposition, "Sixty years ago could we have imagined that unborn children would be killed by the millions here in our own country? Or that we would have no *freedom of speech* when it comes to speaking of God and biblical truth in our public schools? . . . Sadly we must say that very few Christians have understood the battle that we are in. Very few have taken a strong and courageous stand against the world spirit of this age as it destroys our culture and the Christian ethos that once shaped our country." This coalition of evangelical Protestants with conservative Catholics was unprecedented, and some evangelicals opposed it. Bob Jones Jr., head of a fundamentalist Christian College named after his father, denounced cooperation with Catholics. Indeed, when Pope John Paul II was nearly assassinated in 1981, Jones remarked that "this could be God's way of answering the prayers of his people." Despite such opposition from the lunatic fringe, the new coalition attained some political success and contributed to the election of Ronald Reagan to the presidency in both 1980 and 1984. Reagan, in turn, made four Supreme Court appointments, which, over time, would form the basis for an eventual change to an accommodationist position in the Court's Establishment Clause jurisprudence. Reagan appointed three new justices—Sandra Day O'Connor (the first woman appointed to the Supreme Court) in 1981; Antonin Scalia, in 1986; and Anthony Kennedy, in 1987. Reagan also elevated William Rehnquist to chief justice in 1986. Rehnquist originally had been appointed to the Supreme Court as an associate justice by Richard Nixon in 1971.

The impact of these appointments over time is illustrated through the consideration of three opinions issued by the Supreme Court between 1985 and 1992, a time period over which two of these new justices and two others were seated. In *Wallace v. Jaffree* (1985), the Supreme Court struck down as unconstitutional an Alabama statute that permitted a one-minute period of silence in public schools "for meditation or voluntary prayer." This statute had been supported in the Supreme Court by the United States, by seven state attorneys general, by the Moral Majority, and by the Christian Legal Society. It had been opposed by the ACLU and the American Jewish Committee.

Speaking for a six-person majority, Justice John Paul Stevens, an appointee of President Gerald Ford, found that the statute had "no other purpose" than return of prayer to the public schools. As such the statute was unconstitutional under the first criterion of the *Lemon* test, which required a secular purpose for any legislation. Stevens relied upon the sentiments expressed by the legislative proponent of the statute, who proclaimed that its purpose was to return prayer to the public schools. Moreover, in providing for a moment of silence "for meditation or voluntary prayer," the statute replaced an earlier one permitting the moment of silence "for meditation" only.

Justice O'Connor, in a concurring opinion, noted that she had previously questioned the *Lemon* test, which she felt had "proved problematic." She had proposed instead a focus upon whether a particular statute "actually conveys a message of *endorsement*" of religion by the government. That approach, she concluded, would support the constitutionality of moment of silence statutes in the twenty-five other states that had passed them. O'Connor would become the major pivot in the next twenty years in the Court's Establishment Clause decisions, seeking to create new standards in the area.

While O'Connor agreed that the Alabama statute violated the Establishment Clause, three justices did not. Both Chief Justice Warren Burger and Justice White wrote dissenting opinions. They were accompanied by Justice Rehnquist, who wrote the longest and most reasoned opinion in dissent. Rehnquist was a skilled legal historian, and he went on to write several influential books on the Supreme Court and several of its major decisions in both politics and civil rights. In his opinion Rehnquist referred to "hopelessly divided pluralities" in the previous opinions on the Establishment Clause, which were "neither principled nor unified." He stated that "stare decisis may bind courts as to matters of law, but it cannot bind them as to matters of history." With that premise, Rehnquist went on to criticize the line of decisions starting with the *Everson* case for their "wall of separation" philosophy, which he found reflected "a mistaken understanding of constitutional history." Reviewing the historical record, Justice Rehnquist concluded that the founders saw the First Amendment "as designed to prohibit the establishment of a national religion, and perhaps to prevent discrimination among sects." He pointed out governmental action to support religion, starting with Thomas Jefferson and continuing through the late nineteenth century. Such governmental aid included grants made directly by Congress to Indian tribes for education of tribal members in Catholic schools. He also invoked the writings of Justice Joseph Story and Thomas Cooley, both of whom were noted in the nineteenth century as great constitutional scholars. Based on the historical record, Rehnquist concluded that there was no constitutional basis for a wall of separation between church and state. He also found no basis for a requirement of "government neutrality between religion and irreligion nor did [the Establishment Clause] prohibit the Federal Government from providing nondiscriminatory aid to religion."

Two years after its decision in *Wallace,* the Supreme Court reentered the controversy over evolution in *Edwards v. Aguillard* (1987). There, seven of the nine members of the Court found unconstitutional a Louisiana statute that prohibited the teaching of evolution unless "creation science" was taught at the same time. This statute met formidable opposition, including briefs filed in the Supreme Court by seventy-two Nobel Laureates, the National Academy of Sciences, the

American Association of University Professors, the American Federation of Teachers, the Americans United group, the American Jewish Congress, and People for the American Way. The Christian Legal Society and the Catholic League for Religious and Civil Rights filed briefs in support of the "Creationism Act."

The majority opinion written by Justice William Brennan held that the act failed the first criterion of the *Lemon* test because it had a religious, rather than a secular, purpose. As Justice Brennan saw it, the remarks of the sponsor of the Creationism Act made it clear that the intent of the legislation was "to restructure the science curriculum to conform with a particular religious viewpoint."

Writing on behalf of himself and now chief justice Rehnquist, Justice Scalia dissented. Scalia had joined the Court in the previous year, following a distinguished academic career, which included stints at first the University of Virginia and finally at the University of Chicago law schools. In between, he had worked in the Nixon and Ford administrations in various legal capacities. Scalia was the first academic named to the Court since Felix Frankfurter and shared much in common with him. Frankfurter was an immigrant to the United States, as was Scalia's father, and the two justices shared a fondness for activities that served to awaken the spirit of patriotism among Americans. Scalia writes in a witty and acerbic style and is philosophically allied with those who seek the "original meaning" of provisions of the Constitution.

In *Edwards,* Scalia divided his dissenting opinion into two parts. In the first part, he applied the *Lemon* test, questioning the finding of a religious purpose in the enactment of the Creationism statute. Reviewing the prior cases, he concluded that "our cases in no way imply that the Establishment Clause forbids legislators merely to act upon their religious convictions. We surely would not strike down a law providing money to feed the hungry or shelter the homeless if it could be demonstrated that, but for the religious beliefs of the legislators, the funds would not have been approved. Also, political activism by the religiously motivated is part of our heritage. . . . Today's religious activism may give us the Balanced Treatment Act, but yesterday's resulted in the abolition of slavery, and tomorrow's may bring relief for famine victims." Moreover, based upon a detailed review of the legislative record, Scalia concluded that the statute "did not fly through the Louisiana Legislature on wings of fundamentalist religious fervor—which would be unlikely, in any event, since only a small minority of the state's citizens belong to fundamentalist religious denominations." Indeed "witness after witness urged the legislators to support the act so that students would not be 'indoctrinated' but would instead be free to decide for themselves, based upon a fair presentation of the scientific evidence, about the origin of life." Criticizing the majority for "an intellectual predisposition created by the facts and the legend" of the famous Scopes monkey trial, Scalia observed that "the Court's position is the repressive one. The people of Louisiana, including those who are Christian fundamentalists, are quite entitled, as a secular matter, to have whatever scientific evidence there may be against evolution presented in their schools, just as Mr. Scopes was entitled to present whatever scientific evidence there was for it. . . . Infinitely less can we say (or should we say) that the scientific evidence for evolution is so conclusive that no one could be gullible enough to believe that there is any real scientific evidence to the contrary, so that the legislation's stated purpose must be a lie. Yet that illiberal judgment, that Scopes-in-reverse, is ultimately the basis on which the Court's facile rejection of the Louisiana Legislature's purpose must rest."

In the second part of his dissenting opinion, Justice Scalia criticized the *Lemon* test, citing Justice Rehnquist's dissenting opinion in *Wallace.* He concluded that the secular purpose criterion was not required by the Establishment Clause, and that "a good place to start" in order to get some "clarity and predictability" in the Court's jurisprudence in the area would be to abandon the purpose test of *Lemon v. Kurtzman.*

The Supreme Court returned to the question of prayer in the public schools in *Lee v. Weisman* (1992). By then three new justices had joined the Court—Anthony Kennedy in 1987; David Souter in 1990; and Clarence Thomas in 1991. Kennedy had been President Reagan's last appointment to the Supreme Court, and was Reagan's third nominee for the position. His first choice, Robert Bork, a highly visible conservative hero and scholar, was rejected by the United States Senate in a vote of fifty-eight to forty-two, after an acrimonious and bitter debate. His second nominee, Circuit Justice Douglas Ginsburg, another well-known conservative, withdrew his nomination after it was revealed that he had smoked marijuana as a young man.

Justices Souter and Thomas were appointed by President George Bush, who had been Ronald Reagan's vice president. Souter was thought by liberals to be a "stealth candidate" for the conservative Republicans since he had written little as a judge on either the New Hampshire state courts or the federal Court of Appeals for the First Circuit, and was not well known. He took the place of the liberal Justice William Brennan, and his appointment was thought to endanger the continued viability of *Roe v. Wade,* a decision that he paradoxically turned into a "super precedent" a few years later. Clarence Thomas, a Catholic African American, who had served previously as the chairman of the Equal Employment Opportunity Commission and then briefly on the federal Court of Appeals for the District of Columbia Circuit, received even more venomous treatment than Robert Bork had, because of Thomas's extreme conservative views. He was confirmed by the narrow vote of fifty-two to forty-eight, after unproved charges of sexual harassment had been aired in televised confirmation hearings, an experience that Thomas described as "a high-tech lynching."

Lee v. Weisman dealt with the constitutionality of a nondenominational prayer offered at a Rhode Island public middle-school graduation on public school property. Favoring such prayers in the Supreme Court were the Christian Legal Society; a group of Southern Baptists; the United States Catholic Conference; a Jewish group; and, most significantly, the United States. In a brief by Solicitor General Kenneth Starr, the United States called for reconsideration of *Lemon v. Kurtzman*. Opposing graduation prayers in public schools were the American Jewish Committee and the Americans for Religious Liberty.

By a vote of five to four, the Supreme Court declared the Rhode Island prayer unconstitutional. The majority opinion was written by Justice Anthony Kennedy, one of the Court's three Catholic members at the time. Kennedy had originally voted to uphold the prayer, and circulated a draft opinion doing so. Changing his mind because he felt that his draft opinion was "quite wrong," he changed the result as well.

The prayer at issue in *Lee v. Weisman* had been composed by a Jewish rabbi, who had been supplied by school authorities with "Guidelines" composed by the National Conference of Christians and Jews. Those guidelines called for both "inclusiveness and sensitivity" and the rabbi's prayer was inoffensive to most, if not all, religious believers. Nevertheless, Kennedy found that the prayer was unconstitutional. For the majority the "dominant facts" were that "state officials direct the performance of a formal religious exercise at promotional and graduation ceremonies for secondary schools." This was found to be "pervasive" governmental involvement with religion, and the majority specifically declined the request of the United States to reconsider the *Lemon* decision and its three criteria.

A concurring opinion (originally written as a dissent before Justice Kennedy's change of mind) was written by Justice David Souter, who was joined by Justices O'Connor and Stevens. Souter, in his first year on the Court, demonstrated how he would be a great disappointment to religious conservatives. He wrote an opinion that specifically rejected Chief Justice Rehnquist's view that the Establishment Clause was limited to establishing a religion or favoring one religious sect over another, even though Souter conceded that "a case has been made for this position." He went on also to reject the concept that *coercion* was a necessary element to find a violation of the Establishment Clause; instead, he favored Justice O'Connor's approach that governmental *endorsement* was sufficient. Based on these principles, and the Court's previous "settled" case law, he found the graduation prayer to be "flatly unconstitutional."

Justice Souter's vote was critical, since four justices found the graduation prayer to be permissible. Writing for Chief Justice Rehnquist and Justices White and Thomas, Justice Scalia contended that the majority's reasoning was flawed. First, reviewing many examples of public prayers in governmental settings, Scalia accused the majority of "lay[ing] waste [to] a tradition that is as old as public school graduation ceremonies themselves, and that is a component of an even more long-standing American tradition of nonsectarian prayer to God at public celebrations generally." He accused the majority of using as "its instrument of destruction, the bulldozer of its social engineering," a test of "psychological coercion." This, in his view, was faulty, since an objecting student was free to sit in silence, and the state had not actively involved itself in composing the prayer in question.

Scalia also noted that the majority had not relied upon the *Lemon* test and that "the internment of that case may be the one happy byproduct of the Court's otherwise lamentable decision."

Scalia ended his opinion by pointing out that the Court majority had focused too narrowly on the interests of the objectors to the prayer ceremony and not enough on the interests of the other graduates. He observed: "Church and state would not be such a difficult subject if religion were, as the court apparently thinks it to be, some purely personal avocation that can be indulged entirely in secret, like pornography, in the privacy of one's room. For most believers, it is not that, and has never been." By attempting "to banish" an expression of thanks to God from graduation activities, the majority ignored "the age-old practices of our people." Echoing the views of conservative Protestants and Catholics, Justice Scalia—himself a Catholic—concluded that "the Baptist or Catholic who heard and joined in the simple and inspiring prayers of Rabbi Gutterman on this official and patriotic occasion was inoculated from religious bigotry and prejudice in a manner that cannot be replicated. To deprive our society of that important unifying mechanism in order to spare the non-believer what seems to me the minimal inconvenience of standing, or even sitting in respectful nonparticipation, is as senseless in policy as it is unsupported in law."

By 1992 it had become apparent that the foundations of the Supreme Court's approach to questions raised by the Establishment Clause were being quickly eroded by the addition of the new justices appointed by Presidents Reagan and Bush. The new chief justice William Rehnquist, Reagan appointee Antonin Scalia, and Bush appointee Clarence Thomas were in favor of a bright line position of accommodation. Reagan appointee Sandra Day O'Connor and Bush appointee David Souter supported the prior case law, but called for a new test of endorsement to modify the trinitarian approach of *Lemon v. Kurtzman.* Even Reagan appointee Anthony Kennedy, author of two conflicting *Lee* opinions, would soon come to cast accommodationist votes in some Establishment Clause cases.

The Wall Comes Tumbling Down—A Bit

By the mid-1990s the composition of the Supreme Court had been significantly changed as a result of the election of William Jefferson Clinton as president. Clinton was the only Democrat elected to the presidency in the twenty-eight years between 1980 and 2008. In his first term, he appointed two new justices to the Supreme Court—Ruth Bader Ginsburg in 1993 and Stephen Breyer in 1994.

Ginsburg replaced Justice Byron White, who had tended to vote to accommodate religion in Establishment Clause cases. By contrast Breyer replaced Justice Harry Blackmun, the author of *Roe v. Wade,* who had taken a position of strict separation in controversies involving religion and the public schools.

Both Ginsburg and Breyer had been academics and federal circuit court judges before their elevation to the Supreme Court, and both came from a Jewish religious background. Ginsburg had taught first at Rutgers, and then at Columbia, Law School and had begun the Women's Rights Project of the ACLU, where she served as general counsel from 1973 through 1980. She was appointed by President Jimmy Carter to the federal Court of Appeals for the District of Columbia Circuit in 1980.

Breyer had served in various governmental legal positions and taught at Harvard Law School from 1967 through his 1994 appointment to the Supreme Court. In 1980 he had been appointed by President Carter to the federal Court of Appeals for the First Circuit, where he became chief judge in 1990.

On the Supreme Court, Ginsburg became a strict separationist in Establishment Clause cases; Breyer's approach was more nuanced, which resulted in him usually voting with the separationists, but sometimes voting to uphold aid to religious schools and public displays. The addition of Justices Ginsburg and Breyer led to the emergence of Justices O'Connor and Kennedy as the key swing votes in this area.

Both Justice O'Connor and Justice Kennedy tended to vote to accommodate aid to parochial school students and their parents, but against any type of public school prayer. For example, in *Santa Fe Independent School District v. Doe* (2000), both joined Justice John Paul Stevens's majority opinion in striking down student-led prayers at high school football games, finding that there was a close "entanglement" by the school with the prayers. Because of this entanglement under the third criterion of the *Lemon* test, the majority found that listeners to the prayers would find a message of endorsement by the school and a corresponding marginalization as outsiders of those who did not join in the prayers.

Three cases decided between 1997 and 2002 illustrate the key role played by Justices O'Connor and Kennedy in cases involving aid to religious schools. The most dramatic of these cases was *Agostini v. Felton* (1997). There the Supreme Court dissolved an injunction it had upheld twelve years earlier in *Aguilar v. Felton* (1985) prohibiting the funding of a New York State program that permitted public school teachers to go into private schools to teach remedial education to disadvantaged students. The schoolteachers were assigned on a voluntary basis and were supplied by the state with a "detailed set of written and oral instructions" underlining the secular nature of the services they were to provide.

Writing for herself and for Chief Justice Rehnquist and Justices Scalia, Kennedy, and Thomas, Justice O'Connor found that the *Aguilar* opinion was "not consistent with our subsequent Establishment Clause decisions," in two specific ways. "First, we have abandoned the presumption . . . that the placement of public employees on parochial school grounds inevitably results in the impermissible effect of state sponsored indoctrination or constitutes a symbolic union between government and religion." "Second, we have departed from the rule . . . that all government aid that directly aids the educational function of religious schools is invalid." The majority opinion also folded the entanglement inquiry into the second *Lemon* criterion of secular effect, finding that it was simply "an aspect of the inquiry into a statute's effect." As such, "since we have abandoned the assumption that properly instructed public employees will fail to discharge their duties faithfully, we must also discard the assumption that pervasive monitoring of Title I teachers is required."

Reviewing the state program in question, Justice O'Connor summarized her conclusion that the state program "does not run afoul of any of three primary criteria we currently use to evaluate whether government aid has the effect of advancing religion: it does not result in governmental indoctrination; define recipients by reference to religion; or create an excessive entanglement. We therefore hold that a federally funded program providing supplemental, remedial instruction to disadvantaged children on a neutral basis is not invalid under the Establishment Clause when such instruction is given on the premises of sectarian schools by government employees pursuant to a program containing safeguards such as those present here."

In dissent Justices Souter, Stevens, Ginsburg, and Breyer contended that the New York State program violated what they saw was a "flat ban on subsidization" of sectarian schools, and also constituted an impermissible "religious endorsement" by the state.

Three years later the Supreme Court reviewed a federal program under which "secular, neutral, and non-ideological" educational materials and equipment were lent to public and private schools. This program was challenged in a Louisiana school district where private schools received about 30 percent of the dollars distributed, with the majority of those dollars going to Catholic schools. In *Mitchell v. Helms* (2000), writing for four justices, Justice Clarence Thomas found this federal program permissible under the Establishment Clause, based upon "the principles of neutrality and private choice." In doing so, the plurality of Chief Justice Rehnquist and Justices Scalia, Kennedy, and Thomas rejected contentions that direct aid to a religious school's educational mission was always impermissible, and that aid which was "divertible" to religious use was prohibited.

Justice Thomas's opinion is particularly notable for its attack upon the dissenters' views of the dangers of "pervasively sectarian" schools. As Justice Thomas saw it, "hostility to aid to pervasively sectarian schools has a *shameful pedigree that we do not hesitate to disavow*. . . . Opposition to aid to 'sectarian' schools acquired prominence in the 1870's with Congress's consideration (and near passage) of the Blaine Amendment, which would have amended the Constitution to bar any aid to sectarian institutions. Consideration of the amendment arose at a time of pervasive hostility to the Catholic Church and to Catholics in general, and it was an open secret that 'sectarian' was code for 'Catholic.'" Thomas concluded that "nothing in the Establishment Clause requires the exclusion of pervasively sectarian schools from otherwise permissible aid programs, and other doctrines of this court bar it. *This doctrine, born of bigotry, should be buried now.*"

Justice Thomas's views did not command a majority, and the program was upheld by the votes of Justices O'Connor and Breyer, who joined a concurring opinion written by the former. O'Connor felt that the federal program was permissible because it offered aid on a neutral basis and was secular in content. She went on to note that she still adhered to the endorsement standard, but found that it did not apply where the aid was not directly given to sectarian schools. Here, the program consisted of a lending of materials, with no money distributed directly to the schools.

In dissent, speaking through Justice Souter, Justices Stevens and Ginsburg saw the federal program as violating the fundamental principle that there was to be "no aid to religious mission" under the strictures of the Establishment Clause. Justice Souter also contended that use of the "pervasively sectarian" school model was justified, since there were heightened concerns under the Establishment Clause raised by the "religious indoctrination" practiced by those schools. Responding to Thomas's charges, Souter replied that "the plurality . . . condemns any enquiry into the pervasiveness of doctrinal content as a remnant of anti-Catholic bigotry (as if evangelical Protestant schools and Orthodox Jewish yeshivas were never pervasively sectarian), and it equates a refusal to aid religious schools with hostility to religion (as if aid to religious teaching were not opposed in this very case by at least one religious respondent and numerous religious *amici curiae* in a tradition claiming descent from Roger Williams)." Indeed in his view "the plurality's choice to employ imputations of bigotry and irreligion as terms in the Court's debate makes one point clear: that in rejecting the principle of no aid to a school's religious mission the plurality is attacking the most fundamental assumption underlying the Establishment Clause, that government can in fact operate with neutrality in its relation to religion."

The third—the most controversial—of the cases in which accommodation prevailed was *Zelman v. Simmons-Harris* (2002), which dealt with the political hot-button issue of vouchers given to public school parents for use in paying for private schools for their children. *Zelman* reviewed an Ohio state program that provided aid for the Cleveland public school district, which was then one of the worst in the entire country. Under the program, tuition aid was provided to the parents of public school students in grades one through eight, with greater assistance being provided to the poorer families. Some 96 percent of the participating families chose religious schools, principally those affiliated with the Roman Catholic religion, even though two out of three of the participating families were not Catholic. Part of the attraction of the Catholic schools was their lower cost, which fit within the program's tuition cap.

This voucher program was defended publicly as designed to assist minority schoolchildren, who were being denied an adequate education. This argument resonated with Justice Thomas, the Supreme Court's only African American justice. In a concurring opinion voting to uphold the Ohio program, Justice Thomas began and ended with quotations from the African American Civil War antislavery spokesman Frederick Douglas, who equated education for the emancipated slaves with emancipation itself. Thomas saw the voucher program as affording "greater educational opportunity for underprivileged minority students" and chided "the cognoscenti who oppose vouchers."

The majority opinion of the Court upholding the voucher program was written by Chief Justice Rehnquist, and joined by Justices O'Connor, Scalia, Kennedy, and Thomas. *Zelman* marked the triumph of Chief Justice Rehnquist in remaking the Supreme Court's jurisprudence under the Establishment Clause. Beginning as a lonely dissenter in this area in his first years on the Supreme Court as an associate justice, Rehnquist had reframed the concepts that were to be utilized in deciding these questions. In *Zelman* he characterized the voucher program as one of government neutrality, with the allocation of moneys resulting from "true private choice," a phrase that appears repeatedly in the majority opinion. Since the secular purpose of the Ohio voucher program was stipulated, the only issue before the Court was whether that program had the impermissible effect of advancing religion. Finding that the role of the government in the voucher program "ends with the disbursement of benefits," Chief Justice Rehnquist concluded that aid reached the sectarian schools "only by way of the deliberate choices of numerous individual recipients," whose choices could not be attributed to the government. As such the voucher program was "entirely neutral with respect to religion."

In separate dissenting opinions, Justices Stevens, Souter, and Breyer focused on several factors that, in their respective views, rendered the voucher program unconstitutional under the Establishment Clause. Stevens saw the program as advancing "religious indoctrination at state expense" and as increasing the risk of "religious strife." Souter saw the Establishment Clause as imposing a flat ban on any aid for "religious teaching" and predicted that the decision would lead to a "scramble for money" among "contending sectarians," which in turn would lead to "expectable friction." He explained that "not all taxpaying Protestant citizens, for example, will be content to underwrite the teaching of the Roman Catholic Church condemning the death penalty. Nor will all of America's Muslims acquiesce in paying for the endorsement of the religious Zionism taught in many religious Jewish schools, which combines 'a nationalistic sentiment' in support of Israel with a 'deeply religious' element. Nor will every secular taxpayer be content to support Muslim views on differential treatment of the sexes, or, for that matter, to fund the espousal of a wife's obligation of obedience to her husband, presumably taught in any schools adopting the articles of faith of the Southern Baptist Convention."

Finally, in the most thoughtful dissenting opinion, Justice Breyer raised the specter of "religiously based social conflict." Reviewing the same Protestant versus Catholic conflicts Justice Brennan had previously reviewed in his Establishment Clause opinions in the 1960s, Justice Breyer wrote that those conflicts demonstrated the need for separation, as opposed to what he termed "equal opportunity" for religions to contend one with the other to introduce their brand of religion into the public schools. In his view the existence of some fifty-five religions in the United States in 2002 made such an approach "not workable." Moreover, Breyer saw the voucher program as particularly dangerous because it involved "direct financing of a core function of the church: the teaching of religious truths to young children."

After *Zelman,* as Justice O'Connor pointed out in her concurring opinion, the question of whether the primary effect of a particular program that provided indirect aid to religious schools was or was not religious depended upon consideration of two factors—"first, whether the program administers aid in a neutral fashion, without differentiation based on the religious status of beneficiaries or providers of services; second, and more importantly, whether beneficiaries of indirect aid have a genuine choice among religious and nonreligious organizations when determining the organization to which they will direct that aid. If the answer to either query is 'no,' the program should be struck down under the Establishment Clause."

Policing the Public Square: Reindeer, Menorahs, and Public Displays of Religion

The cases we have reviewed to this point have dealt with government aid to religious schools and religious activities in the public schools, including prayer and Bible reading. An additional area of concern under the Establishment Clause has been the use of religious symbols and texts in displays in the public square. Here, as in other Establishment Clause contexts, the cases have led to sharp divisions, multiple opinions, and lack of clarity regarding any controlling rule of decision.

Four cases decided between 1985 and 2005 illustrate these aspects of the Supreme Court's Establishment Clause jurisprudence during that period in the area of public displays of religious symbols and texts. We began with the seminal opinion in *Lynch v. Donnelly* (1984), where Justice O'Connor contributed a new mode of analysis in her concurring opinion. *Lynch* decided the constitutionality of a Christmas display in the center city shopping district of Pawtucket, Rhode Island. That display included a nativity scene (crèche), accompanied by a panoply of holiday figures including Santa Claus, a Santa Claus house, reindeer pulling Santa's sleigh, a wishing well, candy-striped poles, a Christmas tree, animals, holiday lights, and a large banner reading "seasons greetings." In a five-to-four decision, the Supreme Court decided that this display, which had been sponsored by the city for forty years, was permissible under the Establishment Clause as part of a public celebration of a national holiday and the depiction of its origins. The majority opinion, written by Chief Justice Warren Burger, emphasized that Christmas was a national holiday, and that a public display that celebrated the season and the origins of the holiday served to "engender . . . a friendly community spirit of goodwill," which represented a legitimate secular purpose. In a concurring opinion, Justice O'Connor suggested that the test should be whether a public display such as this sends a message that the government intends to *endorse* religion, or is reasonably perceived to be doing so. As she put it, "What is crucial is that a government practice not have the effect of communicating a message of government endorsement or disapproval of religion. It is only practices having that effect, whether intentionally or unintentionally, that make religion relevant, in reality or public perception, to status in the political community." Since the Pawtucket display did not, in her view, send a message of endorsement, it was constitutionally permissible.

Justices Brennan and Blackmun wrote dissenting opinions. Justice Brennan's opinion found support in the trial record for the conclusion that the public officials included the crèche in the holiday display for the purpose of "keep[ing] Christ in Christmas." Thus "the 'primary effect' of including a Nativity scene in the city's display is, as the District Court found, to place the government's imprimatur of approval on the particular religious beliefs exemplified by the crèche."

Holiday displays continued to be quite controversial after *Lynch,* and were hardly noteworthy for engendering "a friendly community spirit of goodwill," at least in some circles. In *Allegheny County v. ACLU* (1989), the Supreme Court fractured over the constitutionality of two holiday displays in Pittsburgh, Pennsylvania. The first stood alone in the county courthouse and consisted of a crèche scene on the grand staircase of the courthouse, in its most public part. The scene had been donated by a Catholic group and had at its crest an angel bearing a banner proclaiming "Glory to God in the Highest" in Latin.

The second display was placed outside the City-County Building and included an eighteen-foot Chanukah menorah, a forty-five-foot decorated Christmas tree, and a sign below the tree bearing the mayor's name and reference to Pittsburgh's "salute to liberty."

In five separate opinions, the Supreme Court upheld the second display, but rejected the first. Using Justice O'Connor's "endorsement" test, Justice Blackmun wrote an opinion for a majority of five, which declared that the courthouse crèche scene was impermissible under the Establishment Clause. In the majority's view, the angel's banner, with its Latin message, made the crèche's "religious meaning unmistakably clear." Moreover, "unlike in *Lynch*, nothing in the context of the display detracts from the crèche's religious meaning." By contrast the Court found the menorah display permissible because of its context. As Justice O'Connor wrote in her concurring opinion, that context signaled a "message of pluralism," and "not a message that endorses religion over nonreligion."

Justice Kennedy wrote a dissenting opinion on the crèche display for himself, Chief Justice Rehnquist, and Justices White and Scalia. He accused the majority of "unjustified hostility toward religion," and echoed some earlier dissenting opinions in stressing that "government policies of accommodation, acknowledgment, and support for religion are an accepted part of our political and cultural heritage." Rather than the endorsement test, which Kennedy found to be "flawed in its fundamentals and unworkable in practice," he suggested a test of governmental coercion, stating that "noncoercive government action within the realm of flexible accommodation or passive acknowledgment of existing symbols does not violate the Establishment Clause unless it benefits religion in a way more direct and more substantial than practices that are accepted in our national heritage." Justice Kennedy concluded his dissenting opinion by stating that "this Court is ill-equipped to sit as a national theology board," observing that "obsessive, implacable resistance to all but the most carefully scripted and secularized forms of accommodation requires this Court to act as a censor, issuing national decrees as to what is orthodox and what is not. What is orthodox, in this context, means what is secular; the only Christmas the State can acknowledge is one in which references to religion have been held to a minimum. The Court thus lends its assistance to an Orwellian rewriting of history as many understand it. I can conceive of no judicial function more antithetical to the First Amendment."

Public Displays of the Ten Commandments

The controversy over public displays of religious symbols and texts has generated the greatest public reaction in cases involving the Ten Commandments. A particularly noteworthy example that did not reach the Supreme Court involved Chief Justice Roy S. Moore of the Alabama Supreme Court in 2001. Within eight months of his installation as chief justice of that court, Moore had erected in the rotunda of the State Judicial Building a monument that displayed both the Ten Commandments and other historic and religious quotations. After the inevitable litigation was filed, Moore was ordered to remove the monument because it was found to have violated the Establishment Clause. Moore refused to obey the injunction, even after all appeals were exhausted. He told an Alabama Judicial Inquiry Commission trying him for violations of the Canons of Judicial Ethics that "I did what

I did because I upheld my oath. And that's what I did, so I have no apologies for it. I would do it again. I didn't say I would defy the court order. I said I wouldn't move the monument. And I didn't move the monument, which you can take . . . as you will."

Moore was ordered removed from the office of chief justice by the Alabama Court of the Judiciary in a final judgment dated November 13, 2003. Following his removal, Moore ran unsuccessfully for governor of Alabama and wrote a book explaining his beliefs and attacking the courts. This controversy received widespread public attention and media coverage from the erection of the monument on August 1, 2001, through and after Moore's removal in November 2003. Against that background of public controversy, the Supreme Court had occasion to review public displays of the Ten Commandments in Kentucky and Texas in 2005. Again the Court fractured, striking down the Kentucky display in *McCreary County v. ACLU* (2005), but upholding the Texas display in *Van Orden v. Perry* (2005), both by decisions of five to four.

The Kentucky case involved displays of the Ten Commandments in two Kentucky county courthouses. While the Supreme Court only considered the third version of the displays, there had been two previous displays that were accompanied by clear indications of a religious purpose. The original display in 1999 had religious references in its opening ceremony, and the second display had a reference to "Jesus Christ, the Prince of Ethics." The third display was presented in a more neutral presentation called "The Foundations of American Law and Government Display," and contained nine documents of equal size, one of which was the King James Bible version of the Ten Commandments.

Justice David Souter wrote the majority opinion striking down the Kentucky displays of the Ten Commandments, utilizing a neutrality approach, under which the Court examined the purpose behind the display. In doing so, Souter indicated that the Court must find a secular purpose that was "genuine, not a sham, and not merely secondary to a religious objective." This followed, in his view, under the principle of neutrality, because "the government may not favor one religion over another, or religion over irreligion." Finding that "detail is key," Souter's opinion concluded that the history of the displays demonstrated "a predominantly religious purpose" for the third display, emphasizing the fact that the Ten Commandments are "an unmistakably religious statement dealing with religious obligations and with morality subject to religious sanction."

Justice Antonin Scalia wrote a dissenting opinion, which was joined by Chief Justice Rehnquist, Justice Thomas, and (in part) by Justice Kennedy. Scalia criticized the Court for its lack of a "consistently applied principle," stating that "what distinguishes the rule of law from the dictatorship of a shifting Supreme Court majority is the absolutely indispensable requirement that judicial opinions be grounded in consistently applied principle. That is what prevents judges from ruling now this way, now that—thumbs up or thumbs down—as their personal preferences dictate." He saw the majority opinion as having modified the beleaguered *Lemon* test in such a way as to "ratchet up the Court's hostility to religion," particularly in what he saw as the majority's requirement that a secular purpose must predominate, and in its replacement of what had been a "fairly limited inquiry" into purpose with a more probing "rigorous review." In the third display, Justice Scalia found no real evidence of any religious purpose. Moreover he disputed the majority's "demonstrably false principle that the government cannot favor religion over irreligion," and concluded that the majority's other principle that government may not favor one religion over another was "valid . . . where public aid or assistance to religion is concerned . . . or where the free exercise of religion is at issue . . . but it necessarily applies in a more limited sense to public acknowledgment of the Creator."

In the Texas case, decided the same day, the Court issued some five opinions, none of which commanded a majority. Writing for a plurality of four justices, Chief Justice Rehnquist upheld the Texas display. That display consisted of a six-foot-high monolith engraved with the Ten Commandments, with an eagle grasping the American flag at the top. The monument had been donated by a fraternal organization some forty years before and appeared on the Texas State Capitol grounds as one of twenty-eight monuments and historical markers.

Chief Justice Rehnquist's opinion pointed out that the Supreme Court cases, "Januslike, point in two directions in applying the Establishment Clause. One face looks towards the strong role played by religion and religious traditions throughout our Nation's history. . . . The other face looks toward the principle that governmental intervention in religious matters can itself endanger religious freedom." He wrote that the *Lemon* test was "not useful in dealing with the sort of passive monument that Texas has erected on its Capitol grounds." Rehnquist relied heavily upon many specific acknowledgments of religion's role in American life, including public displays of the Ten Commandments in the Supreme Court Courtroom and in multiple places in government buildings in Washington, D.C. He concluded that the Ten Commandments have an "undeniable historical meaning," pointing out that "Moses was a law giver as well as a religious leader." The chief justice concluded that the Texas monument passed muster under the Establishment Clause because its inclusion in the group of monuments and markers "has a dual significance, partaking of both religion and government."

In order to attain a majority to uphold the Texas monument, it was necessary that one of the justices who voted the same day to strike down the Kentucky displays had to change his or her vote. In this case it was Justice Stephen Breyer who did so. In an opinion concurring in the judgment, but not joining the chief justice's opinion, Justice Breyer indicated that the Texas monument presented one of those "difficult borderline cases" that called for the "exercise of legal judgment."

Here, relying upon the context and use of the monument, Breyer concluded that the context demonstrated a secular purpose of promoting civic morality. The monument had been donated by the Fraternal Order of Eagles as part of a campaign to combat juvenile delinquency, a fact that demonstrated a "context of history and moral ideals." He also found it significant that no one had ever complained about the monument in the preceding forty years.

There were three dissenting opinions filed, by Justices Stevens, O'Connor, and Souter, two of which were joined by Justice Ginsburg. Justice Souter's dissenting opinion summarized the nub of the opposition to the Texas monument. Justice Souter stated that "the Ten Commandments constitute a religious statement, . . . their message is inherently religious, and . . . the purpose of singling them out in a display is clearly the same."

Looking at the evolution of these cases over a period of more than twenty years, a clear conflict emerges between those justices who would recognize some role for Judeo-Christian symbols and texts to be displayed in the public square and those who find their religious meaning too obvious and exclusionary toward those of other religions or of no religion at all. Justice Scalia's criticism of the Court for failing to apply consistent principles also seems justified, as the cases show a Court struggling, so far unsuccessfully, to find some principled basis on which to distinguish permissible from impermissible uses of such religious symbols and texts, with no proposal yet accepted by a clear majority.

The Free Exercise Clause: The Primacy of Conscience

While the First Amendment forbids Congress from establishing a religion, it also bars Congress from prohibiting the free exercise of religion. There is, as we have seen, a tension between these two proscriptions of the First Amendment. In the remaining portion of this chapter, we examine some of the leading cases in the post–World War II Supreme Court interpreting the protections afforded individuals and groups in practicing their religion. In the period from the 1960s to the 1990s, the interpretation of the Free Exercise Clause changed to lessen the protections it provided. This, in turn, caused Congress to enact legislation to attempt to restore the broader reading of the clause from the earlier cases, setting up a remarkable confrontation and debate between the Supreme Court and Congress.

The leading early decision on the Free Exercise Clause was *Reynolds v. United States,* the Mormon polygamy case we discussed in chapter 7. There the Supreme Court held that the Free Exercise Clause was not violated where a law of general applicability burdened the practices of one religion—there the practice of polygamy by Mormons, a practice that was generally proscribed as a criminal offense. *Reynolds* drew a distinction between *beliefs,* which could not be the subject of legislation, and *actions,* which the legislature was free to regulate. In the case of *Sherbert v. Verner* (1963), the Supreme Court chose to employ a different approach under the Free Exercise Clause. The question presented was whether a Seventh-Day Adventist could be denied the benefits of unemployment compensation where she refused to work on Saturday, her Sabbath. The plaintiff had worked at a textile mill in an area where all of the employers required their employees to work six days a week, including Saturday. Unable to find any other work that permitted her to worship on her Sabbath, she applied for unemployment compensation benefits, but was denied them on the grounds that she had failed to accept suitable work that was available.

In an opinion for seven members of the Court, Justice William Brennan ruled in favor of the Seventh-Day Adventist, finding that the denial of unemployment compensation constituted a denial of her right to free exercise of her religion. The opinion first held that the denial of benefits imposed a burden on her free exercise of the Seventh-Day Adventist religion, because that denial "forces her to choose between following the precepts of her religion and forfeiting benefits, on the one hand, and abandoning one of the precepts of her religion in order to accept work, on the other hand." The denial of benefits was particularly objectionable because the state law permitted an exception for "the Sunday worshipper." The majority next considered whether there existed any "compelling state interest . . . [that] justifies the substantial infringement of appellant's First Amendment right," and concluded there was not, rejecting perfunctorily as "no more than a possibility," the contention that "the filing of fraudulent claims by unscrupulous claimants feigning religious objections" would result from the ruling.

Both a concurring opinion by Justice Potter Stewart, and a dissenting opinion by Justice John Harlan, joined by Justice Byron White, noted that the Court's ruling conflicted with its then current approach to the Establishment Clause. As Justice Harlan's dissent pointed out, the effect of the majority's ruling was to confer upon the Seventh-Day Adventist "the direct financial assistance to religion" that the Establishment Clause forbade. Emphasizing that "she was denied benefits just as any other claimant would be denied benefits who was not 'available for work' for personal reasons," Justice Harlan concluded that the state was free to choose to create an exception for Sabbatarians, but was not constitutionally required to do so. Relying upon a number of decisions, including *Reynolds,* Justice Harlan pointed out that the plaintiff was not discriminated against because of her religion, but was rather subjected to a "general rule of eligibility" applied to all claimants for unemployment compensation.

Nine years later, the Supreme Court had occasion to reexamine the rights of practitioners of minority religions to the free exercise of their religions in the case of *Wisconsin v. Yoder* (1972). There, Amish and Mennonite parents challenged a Wisconsin state law that required school attendance to the age of sixteen, because their faiths did not permit formal school education beyond the eighth grade. Unchallenged expert testimony supported the position of the parents, pointing out that their faiths were based upon a need to live "in a church community separate and apart from the world and worldly influence," and that compelling continuing education beyond the eighth grade would endanger or even destroy the free exercise of the parents' religious beliefs.

In a six-to-one decision, with two justices not participating, the Supreme Court ruled in favor of the parents. In the majority opinion by Chief Justice Warren Burger, the Court ruled that the state's legitimate interest in requiring universal education was not absolute. Instead, "a State's interest in universal education, however highly we rank it, is not totally free from a balancing process when it impinges on fundamental rights and interests, such as those specifically protected by the Free Exercise Clause of the First Amendment, and the traditional interest of parents with respect to the religious upbringing of their children so long as they, in the words of Pierce [*v. Society of Sisters*], 'prepare [them] for additional obligations.'"

Once again the Court rejected the argument that the state was merely applying a rule of general applicability and not discriminating against the parents' religions. Citing the *Sherbert* opinion, Chief Justice Burger's opinion reasoned that "nor can this case be disposed of on the grounds that Wisconsin's requirement for school attendance to age 16 applies uniformly to all citizens of the State and does not, on its face, discriminate against religions or a particular religion, or that it is motivated by legitimate secular concerns. A regulation neutral on its face may, in its application, nonetheless offend the constitutional requirement for government neutrality if it unduly burdens the free exercise of religion." The majority also ruled that there was no compelling state interest that was sufficient to override the parents' free exercise rights to practice their religions. It held that the "informal vocational education" provided by the parents sufficiently prepared their children for "life in the separated agrarian community that is the keystone of the Amish faith."

Chief Justice Burger summed up the majority's conclusions in the following language: "Aided by a history of three centuries as an identifiable religious sect and a long history as a successful and self-sufficient segment of American society, the Amish in this case have convincingly demonstrated the sincerity of their religious beliefs, the interrelationship of belief with their mode of life, the vital role that belief and daily conduct play in the continued survival of Old Order Amish communities and their religious organization, and the hazards presented by the State's enforcement of a statute generally valid as to others. Beyond this, they have carried the even more difficult burden of demonstrating the adequacy of their alternative mode of continuing informal vocational education in terms of precisely those overall interests that the State advances in support of its program of compulsory high school education."

Only Justice William Douglas dissented. His opinion first focused on the rights of the student children, and the lack of any evidence that they shared the beliefs of their parents. He would have required hearings to be held by the lower court to ascertain their views, because "religion is an individual experience." Justice Douglas made a second point, noting that the majority's approach threatened the continued precedential value of the *Reynolds* opinion, which had ruled that Congress could not legislate over "mere *opinion*," but could constitutionally legislate to prohibit "*actions* which were in violation of social duties or subversive of good order" on a uniform basis in a law of general applicability. As Justice Douglas put it, "Action, which the Court deemed to be antisocial, could be punished even though it was grounded on deeply held and sincere religious convictions. What we do today, at least in this respect, opens the way to give organized religion a broader base than it has ever enjoyed; and it even promises that in time Reynolds will be overruled."

The decisions in both *Sherbert* and *Yoder* may be traced, at least in part, to the temper of the times. They were decided in the 1960s and early 1970s, at a time of social experimentation in which individual self-realization became a more accepted goal, resulting in countercultural social and religious experiments that paradoxically validated the century-old practices of the Seventh-Day Adventists, Amish, and Mennonite religions. *Yoder* marked the high point of constitutional protection for religious activities under the Free Exercise Clause.

The Free Exercise Clause: The Primacy of Law

In 1990, with an influx of new, more conservative justices, the Supreme Court returned to the *Reynolds* approach in the controversial case of *Employment Division v. Smith* (1990). *Smith* involved two Native American workers who were fired from their jobs at a private drug-rehabilitation organization for taking peyote (an illegal drug) as part of a sacramental ritual in a Native American church. When they were denied unemployment compensation benefits because they had been fired for misconduct, the workers attempted to rely upon the *Sherbert* and *Yoder* cases to support their claim that they had been denied their rights under the Free Exercise Clause.

In a six-to-three decision, with the majority opinion written by Justice Antonin Scalia, the Supreme Court held that a "valid and neutral law of general applicability" proscribing criminal conduct did not violate the Free Exercise Clause, and the *Sherbert* compelling-state-interest test did not apply in the context of such a law. *Sherbert* itself was distinguished on the grounds that it did not involve conduct that was illegal and that unemployment compensation cases provided an opportunity for "individualized governmental assessment of the reasons for the relevant conduct." Moreover Justice Scalia's opinion pointed out that "the only decisions in which we have held that the First Amendment bars application of a neutral, generally applicable law to religiously motivated action have involved not the Free Exercise Clause alone, but the Free Exercise Clause in conjunction with other constitutional protections, such as freedom of speech and of the press . . . or the rights of parents . . . to direct the education of their children."

In rejecting the application of the compelling-state-interest test to a neutral law of general applicability, Justice Scalia emphasized that what that test produced in other contexts—"equality of treatment and an unrestricted flow of contending speech—are constitutional norms; what it would produce here—a private right to ignore generally applicable laws—is a constitutional anomaly."

While Justice O'Connor, in a concurring opinion, noted that she agreed with the result reached by the majority, both she and three dissenting justices opposed the abandonment of the compelling-state-interest test. Justice John Paul Stevens, in his dissenting opinion, accused the majority of "effectuat[ing] a wholesale overturning of settled law concerning the Religion Clauses of our Constitution." While Justice Stevens was incorrect in this assessment, since the majority opinion in *Smith* simply returned to the *Reynolds* approach, he was more on point with a second observation, which attributed the result to "overreaction to the serious problems the country's drug crisis has generated." In the decade before the decision in *Smith,* the United States, under the leadership of President Ronald Reagan, had declared a "War on Drugs," targeting *all* illegal drugs, including marijuana and peyote, with Congress enacting strong antidrug criminal legislation, with mandatory minimum sentences and stiff forfeiture laws that permitted the seizing of property used in drug operations. Moreover, in the private sector that formed the context for the *Smith* decision, employer drug testing of employees among Fortune 500 companies rose from 5 percent of those companies in 1982 to 95 percent in 1995. *Smith* provided a particularly graphic context for the application of a stricter approach, in the context of the "War on Drugs," since it involved the use of a controlled substance by workers in a drug-rehabilitation organization.

Congress Confronts the Court: The Religious Freedom Restoration Act

The *Smith* decision unleashed a furious counterattack by religious and libertarian groups, and by liberal academics, all condemning the Court for making what they saw as a fundamental change in the law. Hearings on legislation to overturn the *Smith* decision began within months of the decision and resulted in the 1993 Religious Freedom Restoration Act (RFRA), which passed Congress almost unanimously. The RFRA contained findings that the Supreme Court in *Smith* had "virtually eliminated the requirement that the government justify burdens on religious exercise imposed by laws neutral toward religion," and stated a legislative purpose "to restore the compelling interest test as set forth in" both *Sherbert* and *Yoder.*

The constitutionality of the RFRA came before the Supreme Court in *City of Boerne v. Flores* (1997), which involved the denial of a building permit to a Catholic church located in a historic district that sought permission to increase the size of the church to accommodate its increased membership. By a six-to-three vote, the Supreme Court found that the RFRA was unconstitutional when applied to invalidate *state* laws, because Congress had exceeded its powers to enact "appropriate legislation" under the Fourteenth Amendment "to enforce" its guarantees of due process and equal protection.

In an opinion by Justice Anthony Kennedy, the majority pointed out that Congress was permitted only to "enforce" the provisions of the Fourteenth Amendment. The RFRA, however, was not within congressional power because "legislation which alters the meaning of the Free Exercise Clause cannot be said to be enforcing the Clause. Congress does not enforce a constitutional right by changing what the right is. It has been given the power 'to enforce,' not the power to determine what constitutes a constitutional violation."

Ruling that the power of Congress under the Fourteenth Amendment was "remedial, rather than substantive," the Court went back to its nineteenth-century decisions in the *Civil Rights Cases* and *United States v. Reese,* which we discussed in chapter 4, stating, "Although the specific holdings of these early cases might have been superseded or modified, . . . their treatment of Congress' [section] 5 power as corrective or preventive, not definitional, has not been questioned." While the Court admitted that Congress had the power, in the face of repeated violations of due process or equal protection rights, to enact legislation to deter or remedy a constitutional violation, it could enact such enforcement legislation only if the evil presented warranted it. Contrasting the RFRA with the Voting Rights Act of 1965, the Court found a record of widespread and persisting racial discrimination that justified the voting rights legislation, but no such record to justify the RFRA, the legislative history of which "lacks examples of modern instances of generally applicable laws passed because of religious bigotry."

Justice Kennedy concluded that "our national experience teaches that the Constitution is preserved best when each part of the government respects both the Constitution and the proper actions and determinations of the other branches. When the Court has interpreted the Constitution, it has acted within the province of the Judicial Branch, which embraces the duty to say what the law is. . . . When the political branches of the Government act against the background of a judicial interpretation of the Constitution already issued, it must be understood that in later cases and controversies the Court will treat its precedents with the respect due them under settled principles, including stare decisis, and contrary expectations must be disappointed. RFRA was designed to control cases and controversies, such as the one before us; but as the provisions of the federal statute here invoked are beyond congressional authority, it is this Court's precedent, not RFRA, which must control."

Justices O'Connor, Souter, and Breyer each dissented. In her dissenting opinion, Justice O'Connor urged the Court to revisit its decision in *Smith,* which she contended was "demonstrably wrong," claiming that it was not entitled to respect as a decided precedent because it was too recent and had not induced any reliance upon its decision.

Flores was a remarkable decision, with the Supreme Court overturning as unconstitutional legislation that had passed Congress virtually unanimously. That it was accepted, even given three dissents, demonstrates how much the Court's constitutional authority "to say what the law is" had become both institutionalized and popularly accepted, in stark contrast to its rejection in earlier decisions from the nineteenth century.

Nine years after its decision in *Flores,* the Supreme Court considered the application of the RFRA to actions of the federal government, and upheld the statutory compelling-interest test as applied to the religious activities of the United States branch of a Brazilian church that gave communion in the form of liquid hoasca, a tea brewed from plants containing a controlled substance under federal law. *Gonzales v. O Centro Espirita Beneficente Uniao Do Vegetal* (2006) was the second opinion written by Chief Justice John Roberts, who had been appointed to the Court by President George W. Bush in 2005, and confirmed after lengthy Senate hearings by a vote of seventy-eight to twenty-two. Roberts was then fifty years old, and he had a notable career in both government and the private practice of law. In government he had begun as a law clerk to Justice William Rehnquist and served as an attorney in the Reagan White House and the Department of Justice. He was appointed in 2003 to the United States Court of Appeals for the District of Columbia Circuit. Between these periods of government service, Roberts had been a partner at the Washington, D.C., law firm of Hogan and Hartson, where he chaired the appellate practice group and argued a number of cases in the Supreme Court. Roberts became the fourth Catholic on the Supreme Court in 2005, and would soon be joined by a fifth, Samuel Alito, who was confirmed in a more contentious Senate hearing in 2006, by a vote of fifty-eight to forty-two.

In the *O Centro* case, a unanimous Supreme Court (with new justice Alito not participating) held that the United States had failed to show a compelling interest in barring the American church's sacramental use of hoasca. Finding that the RFRA required an examination of the particular use in question, Chief Justice Roberts could find no congressional intent in the federal drug laws to apply their ban to the sacramental use of the controlled substance hoasca by the church, particularly where the legislation permitted exceptions and had for thirty-five years exempted the use of peyote by the Native American church. As Chief Justice Roberts put it, "If such use is permitted in the face of the congressional findings . . . for hundreds of thousands of Native Americans practicing their faith, it is difficult to see how those same findings alone can preclude any consideration of a similar exception for the 130 or so American members of the UDV who want to practice theirs."

The Supreme Court also found that the federal government could not justify proscribing the sacramental use of the drug on the basis that "if I make an exception for you, I'll have to make one for everybody, so no exceptions." This was because the "RFRA operates by mandating consideration, under the compelling interest test, of exceptions to 'rule[s] of general applicability.'" Moreover Chief Justice Roberts stated that a similar argument had been rejected in *Sherbert,* "dismissing as 'no more than a possibility' the State's speculation 'that the filing of fraudulent claims by unscrupulous claimants feigning religious objections to Saturday work' would drain the unemployment benefits fund."

After *O Centro,* consistent with a dual system of government under principles of federalism, the *Smith* test still applies to state free exercise claims, while the RFRA compelling interest test is applied to federal free exercise claims.

"Play in the Joints": The Interplay between Free Exercise and Establishment

As we have seen in many of the cases discussed in this chapter, actions taken by government to comply with the Establishment Clause may influence an individual's free exercise of his or her religion. By banning school prayer and Bible reading, for example, government action limits the free choice of those public school students who may wish to engage in such religious activities. In *Locke v. Davey* (2004), the Supreme Court expressly dealt with this issue while upholding a Washington State law that excluded students who wished to pursue a theology degree from participating in an otherwise generally available state scholarship program funding a portion of the expense of pursuing college education.

By a seven-to-two vote, in an opinion by Chief Justice Rehnquist, the Supreme Court held that an "exclusion from an otherwise inclusive aid program does not violate the Free Exercise Clause of the First Amendment." Noting that the Establishment and Free Exercise clauses "are frequently in tension," Chief Justice Rehnquist's opinion stated that "'there is room for play in the joints' between them" and that "there are some state actions permitted by the Establishment Clause but not required by the Free Exercise Clause."

Finding that the State of Washington had "merely chosen not to fund a distinct category of instruction," the Supreme Court held that the exclusion of students pursuing theology degrees from the scholarship program was a rational distinction because "the subject of religion is one in which both the United States and state constitutions embody distinct views—in favor of free exercise, but opposed to establishment—that find no counterpart with respect to other callings or professions. That a State would deal differently with religious education for the ministry than with education for other callings is a product of these views, not evidence of hostility toward religion." As such "the State's interest in not funding the pursuit of devotional degrees is substantial and the exclusion of such funding places a relatively minor burden on Promise Scholars. If any room exists between the two Religion Clauses, it must be here."

Only Justices Scalia and Thomas dissented. In his opinion Justice Scalia set up a simple syllogism, stating, "When the State makes a public benefit generally available, that benefit becomes part of the baseline against which burdens on religion are measured; and when the State withholds that benefit from some individuals solely on the basis of religion, it violates the Free Exercise Clause no less than if it had imposed a special tax." He found the Washington statute particularly offensive, as involving "discrimination against a religious minority," stating that "most citizens of this country identify themselves as professing some religious belief, but the State's policy poses no obstacle to practitioners of only a tepid, civic version of faith. Those the statutory exclusion actually affects—those whose belief in their religion is so strong that they dedicate their study and their lives to its ministry—are a far narrower set. One need not delve too far into modern culture to perceive a trendy disdain for deep religious conviction. In an era when the Court is so quick to come to the aid of other disfavored groups, . . . its indifference in this case, which involves a form of discrimination to which the Constitution actually speaks, is exceptional."

Perhaps the most significant factor in the Supreme Court's disposition of the *Locke* case was the recurrent problem of line drawing. At the oral argument, Justice Stephen Breyer underlined the practical problems government would face in funding any general public program if there were no check imposed on the rights to be protected by the Free Exercise Clause. As he put it, in addressing Theodore Olson, the Solicitor General of United States, who was urging the Supreme Court to overturn the Washington statute, "if your side wins, every program, not just educational programs, but nursing programs, hospital programs, social welfare programs, contracting programs throughout the government" could be attacked upon the ground "that they cannot be purely secular, that they must fund all religions who want to do the same thing." Indeed such an outcome would cause contending religions to "get into fights with each other about billions and billions of dollars," fueling the divisiveness that prior Court opinions had found so important to avoid.

Nine

Race and the Supreme Court

From 1948 through 1974, the Supreme Court delivered a series of significant civil rights decisions that ended legal segregation of the races in housing, education, and transportation, and upheld congressional legislation opening public accommodations, and guaranteeing voting rights, to African Americans. In these opinions the Supreme Court effectively overruled some of its own precedent, including *Plessy v. Ferguson* (1896), and found in the Commerce Clause the power to protect racial minorities that it previously had found lacking in the Fourteenth Amendment.

The Supreme Court also examined the thorny issues raised by racial quotas and generalized preferences, both in admission to educational institutions, and in student assignments to particular schools. It delivered three highly splintered decisions in 1978 and 2003, rejecting direct and indirect quotas, but permitting the use of race as a plus factor in college and graduate school admissions. In 2007, in another strongly divided set of opinions, it struck down public school district plans that assigned students to schools based on their race, in order to achieve racial balance.

This chapter reviews these developments, starting with the historic civil rights presidency of Harry Truman, who formulated an ambitious civil rights agenda against strident opposition that splintered his own Democratic Party.

Harry Truman: Civil Rights President

When World War II ended in 1945, the United States had defeated one enemy and was then confronting another. The threats posed first by Germany and then by Russia significantly affected domestic policy in the United States. The attempted racial extermination of European Jews by Nazi Germany caused racial segregation in the United States to be perceived more accurately as the evil that it was. Justice Hugo Black, for example, came to describe segregation as "Hitler's creed." Moreover African Americans who had chosen to fight for their country against the Nazis were no longer tolerant of second-class citizenship in the United States. As one returning African American soldier put it, "I'm hanged if I'm going to let the Alabama version of the Germans kick me around when I get home." The cold war threat posed by Russia also affected racial segregation in the United States. As we saw in chapters 7 and 8, Russia was perceived to be godless and immoral. In fighting such an enemy, it was necessary to eliminate moral stain on our part, and this included ending segregation of the races.

President Harry Truman, who assumed the presidency on Franklin Roosevelt's death in 1945, was a committed cold warrior, and became the first twentieth-century president to advance a vigorous civil rights agenda. In his "Fair Deal," President Truman included a number of specific steps designed to end segregation in the United States. Initially in 1946, he established a Civil Rights Commission, which delivered a report, "To Secure These Rights," on October 29, 1947. Truman followed by giving the first presidential address to Congress on Civil Rights, delivering a special message on February 2, 1948, which called for implementation of the recommendations of the Civil Rights Commission. Those recommendations called for a number of specific steps, including the establishment of both a Permanent Commission on Civil Rights and a Fair Employment Practices Commission; congressional enactment of an antilynching law and legislation to protect African American voting rights; and an end to racial discrimination in interstate transportation.

A Gallup poll taken that same year reported that some 82 percent of the American people opposed President Truman's plan. At the Democratic Convention held in July 1948, the adoption of a strong civil rights plank led to a walkout by southern Democratic "Dixiecrats," who formed their own third party with Strom Thurmond of South Carolina as their presidential candidate. Thurmond and Henry Wallace, the left-wing candidate of the Progressive Party, each polled about 2.5 percent of the popular vote, with Thurmond receiving thirty-nine electoral votes in five southern states. Much to the surprise of the political pundits who had loudly predicted a Truman loss, President Truman was elected in his own right as president in 1948, defeating Governor Thomas E. Dewey of New York.

On July 26, 1948, less than two weeks after the close of the convention that nominated him, President Truman signed Executive Orders 9980 and 9981, ordering integration of both the armed forces and the federal workplace. He did so, in the case of the armed forces, over the objections of General Dwight D. Eisenhower and General Omar Bradley, both heroes of World War II. Indeed Eisenhower would succeed Truman as president in 1953.

After his election, Truman proposed a strong civil rights program in 1949, which again failed to garner significant congressional support. While Truman was unable to obtain the passage of civil rights legislation, he accomplished some of his objectives through the courts. During his years as president, he was able to appoint four justices to the Supreme Court, and their votes contributed to unanimous decisions that prohibited the enforcement of racial covenants in real-estate transactions, ended segregation in interstate transportation, and used the "separate but equal" doctrine to require both the admission to, and the equal treatment of African American students in, graduate schools.

Three of Truman's appointments to the Supreme Court served with him either in the House of Representatives or the United States Senate. Harold Burton of Ohio, a Republican, was his first appointment in 1945. He and Sherman Minton, Truman's fourth appointment (in 1949) had both served in the Senate with Truman. Fred Vinson, a Democrat from Kentucky, was appointed chief justice by President Truman in 1946. He had served with Truman in the House of Representatives. Truman's third appointment, Tom Clark, a Democrat from Texas who took his seat in 1949, had previously served as Truman's attorney general.

The Vinson Court and Civil Rights

Chief Justice Fred Vinson has not found favor with most legal scholars, especially in light of the accomplishments of his successor, Chief Justice Earl Warren. Nevertheless, a fair reading of the Vinson Court's decisions on civil rights between 1948 and Vinson's death in 1953 demonstrates the significant beginnings of a pro-civil-rights orientation that would be extended in the Warren Court's more famous rulings.

This trend began with Vinson's unanimous opinion for a six-member Court in *Shelley v. Kramer* (1948), which was decided two months before the beginning of the Democratic Convention that called for the enactment of strong civil rights legislation. The issue in *Shelley* was whether judicial enforcement of restrictive covenants that limited the use or occupancy of real estate to members of the white race constituted impermissible state action under the Equal Protection Clause of the Fourteenth Amendment. The Court held that it did, with the help of friend of the court briefs filed by Truman's solicitor general and by some fifteen different groups. These groups included the NAACP and Native American, labor, fraternal, and religious organizations, some of which pointed out that these types of restrictive covenants affected not only African Americans, but also Jews, Indians, Chinese, Japanese, Mexicans, Hawaiians, Puerto Ricans, and Filipinos.

Vinson's opinion noted that "it cannot be doubted that among the civil rights intended to be protected from discriminatory state action by the Fourteenth Amendment are the rights to acquire, enjoy, own and dispose of property. Equality in the enjoyment of property rights was regarded by the framers of that Amendment as an essential precondition to the realization of other basic civil rights and liberties which the Amendment was intended to guarantee." The key question, however, was whether the *private* discrimination between and among the signers of such restrictive covenants could constitutionally be attributed to the state, since the Court's nineteenth-century precedents established that the prohibitions of the Fourteenth Amendment applied solely to the states. Since such restrictive covenants only were effective if they were backed by judicial enforcement, the Court concluded that this enforcement turned otherwise private action into state action. As Vinson put it, "It is clear that but for the active intervention of the state courts, supported by the full panoply of state power, petitioners would have been free to occupy the properties in question without restraint."

The pervasiveness of racially restrictive covenants in the United States before the decision in *Shelley v. Kramer* is perhaps most graphically illustrated by the recusal in that case of Justices Reed, Jackson, and Rutledge, all of whom reportedly had properties subject to such covenants.

June 5, 1950: The Vinson Court Expands Civil Rights

At the end of its session in 1950, the Vinson Supreme Court released three opinions on June 5, 1950, which outlawed segregation and differential treatment of African Americans in higher education and interstate transportation. In three unanimous opinions, the Supreme Court carefully limited the issues it was addressing and declined to overrule *Plessy v. Ferguson* in reaching its decisions.

In *Sweatt v. Painter* (1950), for the first time in its history, the Supreme Court ordered the admission of an African American to a previously all-white school. The petitioner had been denied admission to the University of Texas Law School at a time when there was no law school for blacks in Texas. After he challenged the rejection of his application in court, the State of Texas was permitted time by the trial court to open a law school for African Americans, and a hearing was held to determine whether the new school's educational facilities were "equal" to those available to whites. When the case reached the Supreme Court, Chief Justice Vinson's opinion compared the University of Texas Law School, with a faculty of nineteen professors, a student body of 850, and a library with more than 65,000 volumes, with the law school for African Americans, which would have no independent faculty, but would be taught by four members of the University of Texas faculty, would not be accredited, and would have fewer than 10,000 volumes in its library. The Court went on to note that, after the trial, another law school opened at Texas State University for African Americans with a faculty of five, a student body of 23, and a library of 16,500 volumes.

In finding that there was a denial of "substantial equality in the educational opportunities offered white and Negro law students by the State," the Court went beyond the statistics listed above to state that "what is more important, the University of Texas Law School possesses to a far greater degree those qualities which are *incapable of objective measurement* but which make for greatness in a law school. Such qualities, to name but a few, include reputation of the faculty, experience of the administration, position and influence of the alumni, standing in the community, traditions and prestige. It is difficult to believe that one who had a free choice between these law schools would consider the question close." The Court also pointed out that the law school for African Americans "excludes from its student body members of the racial groups which number 85% of the population of the State and include most of the lawyers, witnesses, jurors, judges and other officials with whom petitioner will inevitably be dealing when he becomes a member of the Texas Bar. With such a substantial and significant segment of society excluded, we cannot conclude that the education offered petitioner is substantially equal to that which he would receive if admitted to the University of Texas Law School."

While ruling for the African American student, the Supreme Court declined to reach the "contention that Plessy v. Ferguson should be re-examined in the light of contemporary knowledge respecting the purposes of the Fourteenth Amendment and the effects of racial segregation." The Court had been urged to do so by the NAACP. Others, including the United States, the American Federation of Teachers, the American Jewish Committee, and the American Veterans Committee, also filed *amicus* briefs in support of the petitioner. On the other side, friend of the court briefs were filed supporting the position of the University of Texas Law School in denying admission to African American students by the attorneys general of eleven southern states.

In a companion case decided the same day, the Court dealt with the separate question of what protections were available to an African American student who *had* been admitted to a previously all-white school. In *McLaurin v. Oklahoma State Regents* (1950), again in an opinion by Chief Justice Vinson, the Court noted that it was deciding "only [the] issue" of whether the state might, after admitting an African American to graduate school, "afford him different treatment from other students solely because of his race." Friend of the Court briefs were filed in support of McLaurin by the United States, the American Federation of Teachers, the American Veterans Committee, the Congress of Industrial Organizations (CIO) (represented by future Supreme Court justice Arthur J. Goldberg), the Japanese American Citizens League, and the ACLU.

McLaurin was admitted to the University of Oklahoma to pursue a Doctorate in Education. After admission, he initially "was required to sit apart at a designated desk in an anteroom adjoining the classroom; to sit at a designated desk on the mezzanine floor of the library, but not to use the desks in the regular reading room; and to sit at a designated table and to eat at a different time from the other students in the school cafeteria." After the hearing in the trial court, McLaurin's conditions somewhat improved. He was then "assigned to a seat in the classroom in a row specified for colored students; he is assigned to a table in the library on the main floor; and he is permitted to be at the same time in the cafeteria as other students, although here again he is assigned to a special table."

In unanimously ruling that "the Fourteenth Amendment precludes differences in treatment by the state based upon race," the Court emphasized that the differential treatment accorded to McLaurin signified "that the State, in administering the facilities it affords for professional and graduate study, sets McLaurin apart from the other students. The result is that appellant is handicapped in his pursuit of effective graduate instruction. Such restrictions impair and inhibit his ability to study, to engage in discussions and exchange views with other students, and, in general, to learn his profession." The Court therefore ordered the University of Oklahoma to extend "the same treatment" to McLaurin as was extended to "students of other races."

In the final case decided on June 5, 1950, the Supreme Court ruled that segregated facilities in dining cars on interstate railroad routes violated the prohibition of the Interstate Commerce Act against "subject[ing] any particular person . . . to any undue or unreasonable prejudice or disadvantage in any respect whatsoever." Once again, a number of friend of the court briefs were filed. The United States, attempting to implement one of President Truman's civil rights initiatives, called for an end to segregation in interstate transportation and was supported by most of the same groups that had filed briefs in *Sweatt* and *McLaurin.* On the other side, supporting continued segregation in railroad transportation, was "The Honorable Sam Hobbs, a member of the Committee on the Judiciary of the House of Representatives," who argued the case in the Supreme Court.

In an opinion by Justice Harold Burton, President Truman's first appointee to the Supreme Court, the Court unanimously ruled in *Henderson v. United States* (1950) that "the curtains, partitions and signs [separating white and black diners in the same dining car] emphasize the artificiality of a difference in treatment which serves only to call attention to a racial classification of passengers holding identical tickets and using the same public dining facility." Because it found a violation of the Interstate Commerce Act, the Court was careful to note that "we do not reach the constitutional or other issues suggested."

Each of the three decisions delivered on June 5, 1950, by the Vinson Court was narrowly drawn to avoid deciding broader constitutional issues, including the continued viability of *Plessy v. Ferguson* and the scope of Fourteenth Amendment protections afforded African Americans and others against racial discrimination. Nevertheless these decisions, along with *Shelley v. Kramer,* established a foundation from which the Warren Court would later deliver its broader rulings ending segregation throughout the United States.

Brown v. Board of Education

The opinions in *Sweatt* and *McLaurin* dealt only with graduate education and held only that the education provided to specific African Americans in specific schools was not equal to that provided to whites in those schools. Those opinions left unresolved the broader questions relating to the constitutionality of segregated schooling where the educational facilities were equal. This was the major concern of the NAACP, the leading civil rights organization in the United States in the twentieth century. Founded in 1909 by W. E. B. DuBois and others, the National Association for the Advancement of Colored People began its long campaign to challenge the constitutionality of school segregation in the 1930s, when it hired its first full-time lawyer, Nathan Margold, a white Harvard Law School graduate who would later take a position with Franklin Delano Roosevelt's New Deal. With the assistance of a grant for one hundred thousand dollars from the Garland Fund in 1930 (a grant that was never fully funded), Margold did in-depth research on ways to challenge public school segregation. In May 1931 he delivered a 218-page report that suggested that a campaign of litigation challenge the equality of the educational facilities afforded to African Americans as compared to those afforded to whites, using the Equal Protection Clause as it had been interpreted by the Supreme Court in the *Yick Wo v. Hopkins* opinion discussed in chapter 4. The hoped-for outcome of such a campaign of litigation would be either to force equal funding for white and African American educational facilities, or, more optimistically, to convince white legislators to adopt voluntary integration to avoid the staggering costs of equalizing the separate educational systems.

When Margold went to the New Deal in 1933, he was replaced by Charles Hamilton Houston as lead counsel for the NAACP. Houston was an African American Phi Beta Kappa graduate of Amherst who went on to become the first African American member of the Harvard Law Review. Ultimately he would become Dean of Howard Law School in Washington, DC. Houston decided to put the focus in the NAACP litigation campaign upon graduate education. Joined by Thurgood Marshall, who would later become the first African American justice of the Supreme Court, they began a campaign of litigation that led to an initial victory in *Missouri ex rel Gaines v. Canada* (1938). That case found a denial of equal protection when the State of Missouri, which had not established a law school for African Americans, denied admission to an African American applicant who had applied to the white law school. Since the Court did not order the admission of the African American applicant, this initial victory was hollow.

After the victories in *Sweatt* and *McLaurin* in 1950, which were decided shortly after the death of Houston, Thurgood Marshall turned from the equalization strategy in graduate education to one of integration at the grade-school level. He launched a series of legal challenges in South Carolina, Virginia, Delaware, Kansas, and the District of Columbia, the first four of which came before the Supreme Court in consolidated cases we know as *Brown v. Board of Education* (1954).

At the time Marshall began these cases, seventeen southern and border states required school segregation, while four others—Arizona, Kansas, New Mexico, and Wyoming—permitted local school districts to impose a system of segregated schooling in their districts. Some 11.5 million African American children attended segregated schools in 11,173 school districts across the nation. In total 39 percent of American schoolchildren at the time attended segregated schools.

The inequality of the education supplied to white and African American children in the segregated schools was stark. In the South Carolina *Briggs* case, which was part of *Brown v. Board of Education,* the African American schools had no electricity, no desks, no indoor plumbing, and no bus transportation for the students. This inequality was so profound that South Carolina did not even attempt to defend it, promising instead to equalize the schools, a promise that led the lower court to give South Carolina six months to report back on its attempts to equalize them.

The South Carolina case also introduced a new, psychological approach to attacking school segregation. An African American social psychologist named Kenneth Clark presented several studies of the impact of segregation on African American children. In one study white and black children aged three to seven were given a white doll and a black doll and were asked to pick the doll they would like to play with; the doll that was the "nice" doll; the doll that "looks bad"; and the doll that was a "nice color." Most of the children of both races picked the white doll as the one they would like to play with and the one that was nice; and even most of the black children picked the black doll as the one that looked bad.

Of the four cases that came before the Supreme Court in *Brown,* only the Delaware case had resulted in a lower court order to admit the black children to the white school. That case came before Vice Chancellor Collins Seitz, then a thirty-five-year-old trial-court judge in Delaware's Chancery Court. In 1952 Vice Chancellor Seitz ordered integration, after finding that the school facilities were unequal, and called for the Supreme Court to reject the separate but equal doctrine of *Plessy v. Ferguson.*

While not ordering integration, the Kansas case made factual findings that became important in the Supreme Court *Brown* opinion. The Kansas court found that segregation had a "detrimental effect" on black children, leading to a "sense of inferiority" that affected "the motivation of a child to learn."

The United States entered *Brown v. Board of Education* with a friend of the court brief supporting Marshall and the NAACP. In that brief the solicitor general attached a letter from Secretary of State Dean Acheson, advancing the cold war issues discussed above. That letter stated that segregation in the District of Columbia often affected black foreign diplomats, was a source of embarrassment to the United States government, and was viewed by foreign governments as "a measure of our attitude toward minorities generally."

Brown v. Board of Education was argued three times in the Supreme Court, twice on the issue of the constitutionality of school segregation, and the third time on the appropriate remedy. After the first argument on December 9, 1952, the Court appeared split, with four potential votes to uphold segregated schools. The firmest of these votes was that of Justice Stanley Reed, a Roosevelt appointee from Kentucky, who lived at the Mayflower Hotel in Washington. According to notes from the initial conference, Reed indicated that an order of integration would permit a black man to go into the Mayflower restaurant and "sit next to Mrs. Reed." Chief Justice Vinson, along with Justices Jackson and Clark, were unsure on their votes, with Chief Justice Vinson apparently leaning to uphold the constitutionality of segregation. Moreover most of the justices were concerned about what remedy would be appropriate if segregation were struck down and about how much time should be permitted to achieve integrated schools.

Reargument of the *Brown* cases was ordered for June 1953, with a new chief justice, Earl Warren, presiding, after the death of Chief Justice Vinson. Justice Felix Frankfurter had drafted five questions, with subparts, for the parties to address at the reargument, focusing on the intent of the Fourteenth Amendment Congress with respect to public school segregation and on the appropriate remedy to be imposed if segregation were now outlawed.

Chief Justice Earl Warren, a skilled politician who had been governor of California (where he had supported Japanese internment during World War II) wanted to order integration in a unanimous opinion written in plain language that could be read by all Americans. Warren became chief justice because of his support of the candidacy of World War II general Dwight Eisenhower in the Republican presidential convention of 1952. Eisenhower promised to give Warren the first Supreme Court vacancy, but hesitated when that vacancy was for chief justice. Eisenhower would later say that his appointments of Warren and William Brennan were the worst mistakes he had made in his two terms as president.

Warren convinced all of the justices to join his opinion in *Brown,* with Justice Reed the last holdout. The unanimous opinion began by indicating that the legislative history of the Fourteenth Amendment was "inconclusive." It next noted that the education in the four states before the Court was either equalized or in the process of being equalized with respect to all "tangible" factors. As such the Court was required to "look . . . to the effect of segregation itself on public education." In doing so, Warren stated that "in approaching this problem, we cannot turn the clock back to 1868 when the [Fourteenth] Amendment was adopted, or even to 1896 when Plessy v. Ferguson was written. We must consider public education in the light of its full development and its present place in American life throughout the nation."

Having set the stage, Chief Justice Warren then wrote, "We come then to the question presented: Does segregation of children in public schools solely on the basis of race, even though the physical facilities and other 'tangible' factors may be equal, deprive the children of the minority group of equal educational opportunities? We believe that it does." In reaching this conclusion, the Court relied upon its previous decisions in *Sweatt* and *McLaurin* as well as on the findings of the Kansas court, all of which rested upon "intangible considerations." The Supreme Court quoted the findings of the Kansas court, as well as citing a similar finding from the Delaware case, that segregation had a detrimental effect upon African American children and was interpreted as "denoting the inferiority of the negro group." Based upon these findings, the Court rejected the contrary view it had expressed in *Plessy,* holding that "whatever may have been the extent of psychological knowledge at the time of Plessy v. Ferguson, this finding is amply supported by modern authority." A footnote to that statement referenced a number of psychological studies, including an article by Kenneth Clark.

Against this factual backdrop, Chief Justice Warren's opinion of the Court then announced that "we conclude that in the field of public education the doctrine of 'separate but equal' has no place. Separate educational facilities are inherently unequal." The opinion concluded by ordering argument on the question of appropriate relief "because of the wide applicability of this decision, and because of the great variety of local conditions."

After hearing the third argument in the cases in April 1955, the Supreme Court resolved the issue of remedy in *Brown v. Board of Education II* (1955). All eleven former Confederate states had been invited to brief and/or argue the remedy issue, and oral arguments were presented by the Offices of Attorney General of the States of Arkansas, Florida, Maryland, North Carolina, Oklahoma, and Texas.

Chief Justice Warren's unanimous opinion began by pointing to the progress that had been made in desegregation of the schools before the *Brown* Court in Kansas and Delaware, as well as in the District of Columbia. The District had been the subject of the separate case of *Bolling v. Sharpe* (1954), which had ordered desegregation under the Due Process Clause. The remedial opinion in *Brown* stated that "full implementation of these constitutional principles may require solution of varied local school problems. School authorities have the primary responsibility for elucidating, assessing, and solving these problems; courts will have to consider whether the action of school authorities constitutes good faith implementation of the governing constitutional principles. Because of their proximity to local conditions and the possible need for further hearings, the courts which originally heard these cases can best perform this judicial appraisal. Accordingly, we believe it appropriate to remand the cases to those courts." On remand, the courts were permitted to consider "problems related to administration, arising from the physical condition of the school plant, the school transportation system, personnel, revision of school districts and attendance areas into compact units to achieve a system of determining admission to the public schools on nonracial basis, and revision of local laws and regulations which may be necessary in solving the foregoing problems." All this was to be done while making sure that defendants "make a prompt and reasonable start toward full compliance with our May 17, 1954, ruling." Remand was then ordered directing the lower courts to enter appropriate decrees "to admit to public schools on a racially nondiscriminatory basis *with all deliberate speed* the parties to these cases."

The South Defies the Court

The *Brown* decisions were widely attacked in the South. Mississippi senator James Eastland, for example, dismissed *Brown* as having been "based on the writings and teaching of pro-communist agitators and other enemies of the American form of government." In March 1956 ninety-six southern congressmen issued a "Southern Declaration on Integration," which characterized *Brown v. Board of Education* as an "unwarranted exercise of power by the court, contrary to the Constitution," and pledged the signers "to use all lawful means to bring about a reversal of this decision which is contrary to the Constitution and to prevent the use of force in its implementation." Nineteen of the twenty-two southern senators, including liberal luminaries such as J. William Fulbright of Arkansas, signed this manifesto. The three who did not—Senators Lyndon Johnson of Texas, and Albert Gore Sr. and Estes Kefauver, both of Tennessee—had presidential aspirations that would have been endangered by signing a pro-segregation document.

This opposition to the Supreme Court's actions led to many dramatic confrontations resisting public school integration in southern states. The most notorious of these took place in Little Rock, Arkansas, in 1957. While the Little Rock School Board was formulating a plan to desegregate its schools, Governor Orval Faubus and the Arkansas legislature enacted a series of laws to block public school integration in that state. Faubus then sent in the Arkansas National Guard on September 2, 1957, to bar the admission of black students to Little Rock's public schools. When a federal court issued an injunction against this action, and Faubus refused to obey, President Eisenhower dispatched over one thousand federal troops to Little Rock on September 25, 1957. They remained there until November 27, 1957, when they were replaced by a federalized National Guard.

Against this backdrop, the Little Rock School Board petitioned the federal Court for a delay in implementing school desegregation. The Supreme Court explained that the school board had argued that "because of extreme public hostility, which they stated had been engendered largely by the official attitudes and actions of the Governor and Legislature, the maintenance of a sound educational program at Central High School, with the Negroes in attendance, would be impossible. The Board therefore proposed that the Negro students already admitted to the school be withdrawn and sent to segregated schools, and all further steps to carry out the Board's desegregation program be postponed for a period later suggested by the Board to be two and one-half years."

In *Cooper v. Aaron* (1958), in a special summer session, the Supreme Court unanimously rejected the school board's request and ordered immediate implementation of the lower court's desegregation order. The Court did so in an opinion signed by each of the nine justices, the only time in the history of the Supreme Court on which this was done.

The Court's opinion began by stating that "as this case reaches us it raises questions of the highest importance to the maintenance of our federal system of government. It necessarily involves a claim by the Governor and Legislature of a State that there is no duty on state officials to obey federal court orders resting on this Court's considered interpretation of the United States Constitution. Specifically it involves actions by the Governor and Legislature of Arkansas upon the premise that they are not bound by our holding in Brown v. Board of Education."

In rejecting the state's position, the Court noted that "the constitutional rights of respondents are not to be sacrificed or yielded to the violence and disorder which have followed upon the actions of the Governor and Legislature." It explained that in order to "answer the premise of the actions of the Governor and Legislature that they are not bound by our holding in the Brown case [it] is necessary only to recall some basic constitutional propositions which are settled doctrine. Article VI of the Constitution makes the Constitution the 'supreme Law of the Land.' In 1803 Chief Justice Marshall, speaking for a unanimous Court, referring to the Constitution as 'the fundamental and paramount law of the nation,' declared in the notable case of Marbury v. Madison . . . that 'It is emphatically the province and duty of the judicial department to say what the law is.' This decision declared the basic principle that the federal judiciary is supreme in the exposition of the law of the Constitution, and that principle has ever since been respected by this Court and the Country as a permanent and indispensable feature of our constitutional system. It follows that the interpretation of the Fourteenth Amendment enunciated by this Court in the Brown case is the supreme law of the land, and [Article] VI of the Constitution makes it of binding effect on the States 'any Thing in the Constitution or Laws of any State to the Contrary notwithstanding.'" As such "no state legislator or executive or judicial officer can war against the Constitution without violating his undertaking to support it."

Despite the Supreme Court's forceful opinion in *Cooper v. Aaron,* Arkansas officials still resisted its mandate, closing the public schools for one year. Only later did a newly elected school board accept integration.

Southern resistance did not end with the integration of the Little Rock schools. For twenty years after the original *Brown* opinion, the Supreme Court reviewed, and invalidated, a number of schemes to evade public school integration. In *Griffin v. County School Board* (1964), the Supreme Court held that public school officials could not close all schools to block desegregation, and noted in Justice Black's opinion that "the time for mere 'deliberate speed' has run out." Attempts to implement a "freedom of choice" plan were struck down in *Green v. County School Board* (1968), where the Court found that there was an "affirmative duty . . . to convert to a unitary system in which racial discrimination would be eliminated root and branch." In *Alexander v. Holmes County Board of Education* (1969), the Court ordered the dismantling "at once" of all dual school systems, finding that the doctrine of "all deliberate speed" was "no longer constitutionally permissible" where "many thousands of schoolchildren . . . are presently attending Mississippi schools under segregated conditions contrary to the applicable decisions of this Court." The Supreme Court went further in *Swann v. Charlotte-Mecklenburg County Board* (1971), ruling that mandatory busing could be ordered to facilitate desegregation.

These and other actions by the Supreme Court had a profound effect on public school integration in the South. While 78 percent of black students in 1968 attended southern schools that were at least 90 percent black, by 1972 this figure had been reduced to 25 percent, resulting in more integration of the races than was present in northern schools at the time.

The unparalleled success of the NAACP and other civil rights organizations over this twenty-year period following *Brown v. Board of Education* ended with the Supreme Court's decision in *Milliken v. Bradley* (1974). There the Supreme Court refused to order integration of the Detroit public schools on a regional basis with suburban schools because only the Detroit schools had been segregated as a matter of law. As such, since the suburban school districts had not been guilty of imposing segregation, they could not be ordered to combine their schools with those of Detroit. In dissent Justice Thurgood Marshall referred to "a perceived public mood that we have gone far enough in enforcing the Constitution's guarantee of equal justice."

Justice Marshall's comment correctly read the tenor of the times. In both 1968 and 1972, Governor George Wallace of Alabama had run as a third-party presidential candidate, tapping northern opposition to mandatory school busing in cities such as Boston and opposition across the country to protests against the Vietnam War. In 1968 Wallace received nearly ten million votes, accounting for 13.5 percent of the total, and forty-six electoral votes in five southern states. Wallace demonstrated his continuing appeal in 1972, when he won Democratic primaries in Maryland and Michigan, as well as in the South, before his candidacy ended in an attempted assassination, which left him paralyzed and forced his withdrawal from the presidential campaign.

The Sit-in Movement and the Desegregation of Public Accommodations

Segregation in the United States in the 1950s went well beyond the public school system. As we saw in chapter 4, after the Supreme Court's decision in the *Civil Rights Cases* (1883), which struck down the Civil Rights Act of 1875 as beyond the authority of Congress under the Fourteenth Amendment, a pervasive system of mandated segregation of the races emerged over time in the southern states. This system reached its apogee in the early 1950s, by which time segregation extended not only to public accommodations such as restaurants, movies and transportation facilities, but also to hospitals, waiting rooms, public toilets, and even public water fountains.

Opposition to this pervasive system of segregation was persistent, but unsuccessful until the 1950s. Public transportation became the first focus of African

American efforts at desegregation, beginning with the successful boycott of the Baton Rouge, Louisiana, streetcars in 1953. That was followed by the more famous bus boycott in Montgomery, Alabama, which began on December 1, 1955, when Rosa Parks refused to give up a seat in the white section of a Montgomery bus to a white person and was jailed for her refusal to do so. That boycott lasted for a full year, but also ended in success. It was led by the then twenty-six-year-old Baptist minister Martin Luther King Jr., who implemented the boycott based upon his principles of nonviolence.

Public accommodations were the next target of those opposing legal segregation of the races. A "sit-in" movement began on February 1, 1960, when four black college students in Greensboro, North Carolina, sat at Woolworth's lunch counter in that city and refused to leave. Woolworth's was a leading department store in that city. While it permitted African Americans to shop there, its lunch counter was segregated. Indeed Martin Luther King once observed that "all Africa will be free before black Americans will be served a Coke in Woolworth's." On the second day of the sit-in, twenty-four students participated, and the movement grew exponentially. One week later, there were sit-ins in fifteen cities in nine states, and eventually seventy thousand protesters participated in demonstrations across the country, including in some northern states. These sit-ins called for desegregation of restaurants, parks, museums, libraries, swimming pools, and other public facilities.

During the presidential election campaign of 1960 Martin Luther King Jr. was jailed in Atlanta, Georgia, on October 19, 1960, for sitting at a segregated lunch counter in that city. He was sentenced to four months of hard labor to be served in a state prison in rural Georgia. Even though three southern senators had told John Kennedy that they would support the Republican candidate, Richard Nixon, if Kennedy tried to help King, John Kennedy called Mrs. King and interceded with the governor of Georgia on King's behalf, after which Robert Kennedy called the judge who had refused to permit bail for King. As a result of these efforts, King was released. John Kennedy capitalized on this success by passing out campaign literature in African American areas proclaiming that "Jack Kennedy called Mrs. King—Richard Nixon did not." In the end Martin Luther King Sr., who was also a Baptist minister, switched his considerable political support from Nixon to Kennedy, assisting Kennedy to win the election in the next month.

By 1961 public accommodations associated with interstate bus transportation became the next focus of protests by "Freedom Riders," who boarded buses and tried to desegregate bus terminals along the routes the buses traveled. They relied upon the Supreme Court's decision in *Boynton v. Virginia* (1960), in which the Court held that the Interstate Commerce Act prohibited segregation in a restaurant located in the bus terminal building, even though the restaurant was not owned or controlled by the bus company. The Court ruled that interstate passengers had an essential need to be able to get food and that the restaurant was an integral part of the bus transportation service for interstate passengers. After some protesters were beaten in a widely publicized incident in Birmingham, Alabama, the Interstate Commerce Commission entered an order in September 1961 prohibiting segregation by interstate bus and railroad companies.

The continuing successes of the civil rights movement in the 1950s and early 1960s, both in court and in sit-ins and other protests, culminated in the enactment of the Civil Rights Act of 1964. That legislation came about, much as the Reconstruction legislation in the 1860s had, because of a combination of public protests and a presidential assassination. In May 1963 millions on television watched as some one thousand protesters were confronted by the police in Birmingham, Alabama, under the leadership of "Bull" Connor, and assailed with high-pressure water hoses, dogs, and cattle prods for engaging in a continued demonstration against segregation in that city. With the intervention of the Kennedy administration, Birmingham businesses eventually agreed to desegregate their stores and lunch counters. Prodded by these public protests, Kennedy gave a speech in June calling civil rights "a moral issue," and proposed a civil rights act on July 1, 1963. That draft legislation was aimed mainly at public accommodations and voting rights.

In the following month, more than 250,000 people (some 60,000 of whom were white) engaged in a "March on Washington for Jobs and Freedom." Their agenda was broad-based, calling for passage of Kennedy's civil rights legislation without a filibuster, immediate elimination of all racial segregation in public schools, a public works program for the unemployed, a national minimum wage of two dollars an hour, withholding of federal funds from programs that discriminated, enforcement of the Fourteenth Amendment to reduce congressional representation in states that discriminated against African Americans, a broadening of federal labor legislation, and enactment of legislation to permit the attorney general to sue for injunctions to stop violations of civil rights. In a festive but peaceful atmosphere, the demonstrators presented their program around the Washington Monument. They were witnessed on television by millions, culminating with the famous "I have a dream" speech of Martin Luther King Jr.

While Kennedy's civil rights bill languished, his assassination reinvigorated efforts to pass it under his successor, Lyndon Johnson of Texas. Johnson was personally committed to passing the bill, and he kept a daily scorecard of the position of each senator. Passage in the House of Representatives was assured, and the House easily passed what became the Civil Rights Act of 1964. Passage in the Senate was highly questionable, given the efforts of southern senators to filibuster the legislation until it died. In the end there was a three-month period of filibuster, which Johnson broke with persistent efforts, including intense personal lobbying of the Republican Senate leader, Everett Dirksen of Illinois.

As enacted, the Civil Rights Act of 1964 was the most significant piece of civil rights legislation in American history. It contained three key "titles," respectively providing for open access to public accommodations, tracing the path first laid by the Civil Rights Act of 1875; barring discrimination on the basis of race, color, or national origin "under any program or activity receiving Federal financial assistance"; and barring discrimination in employment on the grounds of race, color, sex, religion, or national origin. This last provision, in Title VII, established an Equal Employment Opportunity Commission to decide administrative complaints and review individual complaints prior to their court filing.

Title II of the 1964 act provided that "all persons shall be entitled to the full and equal enjoyment of the goods, services, facilities, privileges, advantages, and accommodations of any place of public accommodation . . . without discrimination or segregation on the ground of race, color, religion, or national origin." "Places of public accommodation" were defined to include, among others, inns, hotels, motels, and other lodging establishments, as well as restaurants, cafeterias, motion picture houses, and any establishments physically located within such establishments.

The Supreme Court reviewed the constitutionality of Title II in the year of its enactment, in two separate cases. In *Heart of Atlanta Motel, Inc. v. United States* (1964), a unanimous Supreme Court upheld Title II as applied to a motel in Atlanta, Georgia, which had refused to admit African Americans for lodging. The motel had 216 rooms and was readily accessible to interstate highways, obtaining approximately 75 percent of its registered guests from other states.

Justice Tom Clark's opinion for six members of the Court noted that "the sole question posed is . . . the constitutionality of the Civil Rights Act of 1964 as applied to these facts." Clark first had to deal with the binding precedent of the *Civil Rights Cases* (1883), which had ruled that similar prohibitions were beyond the power of Congress under the Fourteenth Amendment. He did so in a brief section of the opinion, holding that "we think that decision inapposite, and without precedential value in determining the constitutionality of the present Act. Unlike Title II of the present legislation, the 1875 act broadly proscribed discrimination in 'inns, public conveyances on land or water, theaters, and other places of public amusement,' without limiting the categories of affected businesses to those impinging upon interstate commerce. In contrast the applicability of Title II is carefully limited to enterprises having a direct and substantial relation to the interstate flow of goods and people, except where state action is involved."

The Court relied on the Commerce Clause to uphold the legislation, citing Chief Justice John Marshall's opinion in *Gibbons v. Ogden* (1824) on two occasions for its pronouncements regarding the breadth of congressional power under that clause. Clark's opinion then cited a host of prior decisions upholding congressional power under the Commerce Clause, including the New Deal Court's decisions in cases such as *Wickard v. Filburn* (1942). The argument that the motel's operation was "of a purely local character" was rejected because "the power of Congress to promote interstate commerce also includes the power to regulate the local incidents thereof, including local activities in both the States of origin and destination, which might have a substantial and harmful effect upon that commerce. One need only examine the evidence which we have discussed above to see that Congress may—as it has—prohibit racial discrimination by motels serving travelers, however 'local' their operations may appear."

In its second decision on Title II, announced the same day, the Supreme Court dealt with a local restaurant in the case of *Katzenbach v. McClung* (1964). Ollie's Barbecue was a family-owned restaurant in Birmingham, Alabama, with a seating capacity of 220 customers. It was located on a state highway situated within eleven blocks of an interstate highway. In the year before Title II was passed, the restaurant made local purchases of food, nearly 50 percent of which was meat purchased from a local provider who had procured it from outside the state. The trial court "expressly found that a substantial portion of the food served in the restaurant had moved in interstate commerce."

Justice Clark again wrote for a unanimous Court, indicating that "there is no claim that interstate travelers frequented the restaurant. The sole question, therefore, narrows down to whether Title II, as applied to a restaurant annually receiving about $70,000 worth of food that has moved in commerce, is a valid exercise of the power of Congress." The Court found that it was, and that the congressional testimony in hearings on the Act "afforded ample basis for the conclusion that established restaurants in such areas sold less interstate goods because of the discrimination, that interstate travel was obstructed directly by it, that business in general suffered and that many new businesses refrained from establishing there as a result of it." Quoting *Wickard v. Filburn* (1942), Clark's opinion stated that "much is said about a restaurant business being local but 'even if appellee's activity be local and though it may not be regarded as commerce, it may still, whatever its nature, be reached by Congress if it exerts a substantial economic effect on interstate commerce.'"

Clark's opinion ended with the following statements: "The power of Congress in this field is broad and sweeping; where it keeps within its sphere and violates no express constitutional limitation it has been the rule of this Court, going back almost to the founding days of the Republic, not to interfere. The Civil Rights Act of 1964, as here applied, we find to be plainly appropriate in the resolution of what the Congress found to be a national commercial problem of the first magnitude. We find it in no violation of any express limitations of the Constitution and we therefore declare it valid."

The Struggle to Secure the Right to Vote

Beyond pervasive segregation, African Americans also experienced an exclusion from the ballot from the end of the nineteenth century to the mid-1960s. The battle for voting rights began in earnest in the 1960s, starting with the Twenty-fourth

Amendment, which was proposed in 1962, and ratified in January 1964. That amendment, which was binding on both federal and state governments, prohibited denying the right to vote in any federal election "by reason of failure to pay any poll tax or other tax." Poll taxes were still used to exclude African American voters in five states—Alabama, Arkansas, Mississippi, Texas, and Virginia. Their exclusionary purpose was freely admitted in Virginia in 1902, where (as the Supreme Court pointed out in *Harman v. Forssenius* [1965]), the sponsor of the poll tax expressly linked it to "Discrimination! . . . with a view to the elimination of every negro voter who can be gotten rid of, legally, without materially impairing the numerical strength of white electorate."

The elimination of the poll tax was only a partial palliative measure. As we saw in chapter 4, a large variety of means and methods was employed to disenfranchise African American voters in southern states, beginning in the nineteenth century. Indeed by the mid-1960s as many as 90 percent of eligible African American voters were not registered to vote in the Deep South. To combat the varied tactics employed to exclude them, thousands of volunteers, both white and black, declared a "Freedom Summer" in 1964, during which a drive took place in the South to secure voting rights for African Americans. Early that summer, however, three volunteers—Andrew Goodman, Michael Schwerner, and James Chaney, only one of whom was African American—were murdered by local law enforcement officials in Mississippi.

Freedom Summer was followed in early 1965 by a drive for voting rights focused on Selma, Alabama. That city of twenty-nine thousand was more than 50 percent African American, but fewer than four hundred African Americans were registered to vote. Early efforts in January and February of that year were met with violence and three thousand arrests. In March 1965, under the leadership of Martin Luther King Jr., a fifty-six-mile march was planned from Selma to the state capital in Montgomery. While a liberal federal judge, Frank Johnson, enjoined the march, the more militant African American protesters attempted to carry it out. They were met on "Bloody Sunday," March 7, 1965, by police officials who stopped them at a bridge and beat many protesters, in a chaotic stream of violence witnessed on national television. In a serendipitous bit of irony, ABC Television interrupted its showing of "Judgment at Nuremberg" to cover the violence. That movie dealt with the faithlessness of the German judiciary under the Nazi regime of Aryan racial superiority. Martin Luther King Jr. and fifteen hundred demonstrators restarted the march two days later, with an understanding reached with local officials that King would turn around after crossing the same bridge.

The violence in Selma galvanized President Lyndon Johnson to push harder for a new federal voting-rights law. On March 15, 1965, he gave a speech in favor of a new law, ending it with the civil-rights anthem, "we shall overcome." In the following week, the four-day march to Montgomery from Selma finally took place with twenty-five thousand whites and blacks marching together. The march was marred by the murder of a white northern civil-rights demonstrator, Viola Liuzzo of Detroit, Michigan.

Within five months, the Voting Rights Act of 1965 became law. While it easily passed the House of Representatives by almost a four-to-one margin, there were twenty-five days of Senate debate, which ended only when a cloture vote was successful. Ultimately the Senate voted seventy-seven to nineteen in favor of the act. There were three key provisions at the heart of the act. The first prohibited the use of literacy tests and other similar voting qualifications for five years in those voting districts where fewer than half of those of voting age had voted in 1964. A second provision provided for the suspension of new voting regulations in such districts pending screening by federal authorities. The third key provision permitted the use of federal examiners or registrars to list those applicants who were qualified to vote.

The Supreme Court soon had occasion to review the constitutionality of the Voting Rights Act of 1965. In *South Carolina v. Katzenbach* (1966), it upheld all three key provisions as within the powers of Congress as authorized under Section 2 of the Fifteenth Amendment, which provides that "Congress shall have power to enforce this article by appropriate legislation." The case challenging the act was filed directly in the Supreme Court by South Carolina, and the Supreme Court invited all fifty states to submit briefs on the constitutionality of the act. A majority of states participated, with seven actually making oral arguments before the Court.

Chief Justice Warren's opinion for eight members of the Court emphasized the pervasive and long-standing history of voting discrimination in the southern states affected by the Voting Rights Act. He stated, "The Voting Rights Act was designed by Congress to banish the blight of racial discrimination in voting, which has infected the electoral process in parts of our country for nearly a century." Warren's opinion labeled the tactics used as "an insidious and pervasive evil which has been perpetuated in certain parts of our country through unremitting and ingenious defiance of the Constitution." Those tactics included "grandfather clauses, property qualifications, 'good character' tests, and the requirement that registrants 'understand' or 'interpret' certain matter."

The Court also found that previous legislation and litigation had been ineffective to address this pervasive discrimination. Using Selma, Alabama, as an example, Chief Justice Warren's opinion pointed out that after four years of litigation African American registration had been increased only from 156 to 383 in the county in which Selma was located.

South Carolina contended that the Court precedents only permitted the striking down of state statutes and procedures, and did not countenance the far-ranging remedial provisions enacted by Congress. In response Chief Justice Warren's opinion avoided the Court's nineteenth-century jurisprudence under the Fourteenth Amendment, focusing instead upon Chief Justice John Marshall's "classic formulation" in *McCulloch v. Maryland* (1819) that "let the end be legitimate, let it be within the scope of the constitution, and all means which are appropriate, which are plainly adapted to that end, which are not prohibited, but consist with the letter and spirit of the Constitution, are constitutional." In addition, the Court found that the Voting Rights Act was an appropriate congressional response "after enduring nearly a century of systematic resistance to the Fifteenth Amendment," and justified "shift[ing] the advantage of time and inertia from the perpetrators of the evil to its victims."

The Voting Rights Act of 1965 was phenomenally successful in increasing African American voter registration in the Deep South. In Mississippi, for example, the number of black registered voters increased from 22,000 in 1960 to 175,000 by the end of 1965, while the registration of black voters in six southern states increased from 30 percent to 46 percent in the first year after the act was passed. By 1967 the number of registered black voters in those states exceeded 50 percent of those eligible.

The key provisions of the Voting Rights Act of 1965 have been extended repeatedly and are still in effect.

Affirmative Action: Remediation or Fostering Diversity?

First used in an Executive Order issued by President John Kennedy in 1961, the concept of "affirmative action" has been controversial since its beginning. The phrase refers generally to attempts by both state and private colleges and graduate schools and by government and private employers to remediate the effects of past segregation. In endorsing affirmative action, President Lyndon Johnson explained that "you do not take a person who, for years, has been hobbled by chains and liberate him, bring him up to the starting line of a race and then say 'you are free to compete with all the others' and still justly believe that you have been completely fair."

In education, schools promoting affirmative action sought to admit minority applicants under special admissions programs. Where such programs were utilized by state universities, their actions raised questions of equal protection under the Fourteenth Amendment when white applicants were passed over in favor of minority applicants who appeared less qualified based on test results and scholastic performance.

The use of affirmative-action programs in both employment and education led to significant white backlash, beginning in the mid-1960s, contributing to the electoral successes of Richard Nixon in 1968 and 1972, and the strong presidential candidacies of George Wallace of Alabama at the same time. Indeed opposition to these programs was typically phrased in the same language utilized one hundred years earlier in the debate over the Civil Rights Act of 1875. As we discussed in chapter 4, the Yale professor William Graham Sumner then introduced the concept of "the forgotten man," who paid for government "paternal" assistance to "the less fortunate classes." Singling out a particular group for "special treatment" was seen in those days as violating the fundamental principle of "equal rights for all, but special privileges to none." It also was seen as inconsistent with the prevalent Free Labor philosophy, which distinguished *political* rights from *social* rights. While the former were legally assured to all, the latter had to be "earned." Echoing this philosophy, the Supreme Court in the nineteenth century refused to permit use of the Fourteenth Amendment to justify enactment of the Civil Rights Act of 1875, which mandated equal access to public accommodations to members of all races.

The Supreme Court took up the equal-protection issues raised by the use of affirmative action in education in a number of cases. The most significant case was *Regents of University of California v. Bakke* (1978), where the Court fractured, issuing six separate opinions, over the legality of a special admissions program at the University of California—Davis Medical School. That program selected the entering class of one hundred by setting up two separate admissions pools. The regular admissions pool admitted eighty-six candidates based upon interviews, grade point averages, scores on the MCAT admissions test, grades in science courses, letters of recommendation, and extracurricular activities. Any applicant with a grade point average below 2.5 was automatically rejected. A special admissions pool admitted fourteen candidates. To be eligible for consideration in this pool, an applicant had to be minority or disadvantaged economically or educationally. Minorities were considered to include African Americans, Hispanics, Asians, and Native Americans. An applicant considered in the special admissions pool was eligible even if his or her grade-point average was below 2.5. In the previous four years, no white candidates were admitted in the special admissions pool, although many applied as economically or educationally disadvantaged. Of the minority candidates who applied to the medical school in the previous four years, sixty-three were admitted under the special admissions program, and forty-four were admitted under the regular admissions program.

Some fifty-seven amicus briefs were filed in the *Bakke* case in the Supreme Court. Allan Bakke, a rejected white candidate, sued the university, claiming violation of his equal-protection rights. He was supported, among others, by the American Federation of Teachers, the American Jewish Congress, the Anti-Defamation League of B'nai B'rith, the United States Chamber of Commerce, the Fraternal Order of Police, and the Order of Sons of Italy in America. The position of the medical school was supported by another large number of groups, including the ACLU, the NAACP, the Asian American Bar Association, the Puerto Rican Legal Defense and Education Fund, the Association of American Law Schools, and the National Council of Churches of Christ.

When the six separate opinions were analyzed, the Court held, by vote of five to four, that the special admissions program was unconstitutional, but that it was permissible for the medical school to take race into account as a factor in future admissions. In reaching this decision, two groups of four justices split evenly. The first group, consisting of Chief Justice Burger and Justices Stevens, Stewart, and Rehnquist, considered only the legality of the special admissions program under Title VI of the Civil Rights Act of 1964. As mentioned above, that portion of the act prohibited discrimination "on the ground of race, color, or national origin" under any program or activity receiving federal financial assistance. Given the broad mandate of section 601 of Title VI, Justice Stevens's opinion for these justices concluded that "the University, through its special admissions policy, excluded Bakke from participation in its program of medical education because of his race. The University also acknowledges that it was, and still it is, receiving federal financial assistance. The plain language of the statute therefore requires affirmance of the judgment below [ordering the admission of Bakke]. A different result cannot be justified unless that language misstates the actual intent of the Congress that enacted the statute or the statute is not enforceable in a private action. Neither conclusion is warranted."

Justices Brennan, White, Marshall, and Blackmun each wrote separate opinions, concluding that the special admissions program was constitutional under the Equal Protection Clause and therefore valid as well under Title VI. Each of these justices joined the opinion written by Justice Brennan. That opinion viewed racial classifications as "not per se invalid under the Fourteenth Amendment," concluding that "in our view, Title VI prohibits only those uses of racial criteria that would violate the Fourteenth Amendment if employed by a State or its agencies; it does not bar the preferential treatment of racial minorities as a means of remedying past social discrimination to the extent that such action is consistent with the Fourteenth Amendment." After a lengthy review of the Court's precedents, Justice Brennan's opinion concluded: "Properly construed, therefore, our prior cases unequivocally show that a state government may adopt race-conscious programs if the purpose of such programs is to remove the disparate racial impact its actions might otherwise have and if there is reason to believe that the disparate impact is itself the product of past discrimination, whether its own or that of society at large. There is no question that Davis' program is valid under this test."

Justice Marshall, the Court's only African American member, wrote a powerful separate opinion with a detailed historical review of the discrimination directed at African Americans in the United States, and the Supreme Court's role in perpetuating that discrimination by narrow interpretations of the Fourteenth and Fifteenth amendments in the nineteenth-century cases discussed in chapter 4. He then stated that "in the light of the sorry history of discrimination and its devastating impact on the lives of Negroes, bringing the Negro into the mainstream of American life should be a state interest of the highest order. To fail to do so is to ensure that America will forever remain a divided society." Justice Marshall singled out the 1866 Freedmen's Bureau Act, which was passed over presidential vetoes by Andrew Johnson because of his view that it extended special benefits to African Americans, concluding that "since the Congress that considered and rejected the objections to the 1866 Freedmen's Bureau Act concerning special relief to Negroes also proposed the Fourteenth Amendment, it is inconceivable that the Fourteenth Amendment was intended to prohibit all race-conscious relief measures." Justice Marshall then concluded that "it is unnecessary in 20th-century America to have individual Negroes demonstrate that they have been victims of racial discrimination; the racism of our society has been so pervasive that none, regardless of wealth or position, has managed to escape its impact. The experience of Negroes in America has been different in kind, not just in degree, from that of other ethnic groups. It is not merely the history of slavery alone but also that a whole people were marked as inferior by the law. And that mark has endured. The dream of America as the great melting pot has not been realized for the Negro; because of his skin color he never even made it into the pot."

Since the two groups of four justices differed on the legality of the special admissions program, the decisive vote was cast by Justice Lewis Powell. Justice Powell was the epitome of the white Anglo-Saxon establishment in the United States. He was a descendent of settlers of the Jamestown colony in Virginia in 1607 and had held many prestigious positions, including president of the American Bar Association. A decorated World War II U.S. Air Force intelligence officer, Powell became head of a prominent Richmond law firm. He was a centrist on the Supreme Court and cast the decisive vote in several close cases, including a number involving abortion.

Justice Powell's opinion in *Bakke* saw the equal-protection guarantee of the Fourteenth Amendment as meaning what it said. "The guarantee of equal protection cannot mean one thing when applied to one individual and something else when applied to a person of another color. If both are not accorded the same protection, then it is not equal." It followed that "if [the university's] purpose is to assure within its student body some specified percentage of a particular group merely because of its race or ethnic origin, such a preferential purpose must be rejected not as insubstantial but as facially invalid. Preferring members of any one group for no reason other than race or ethnic origin is discrimination for its own sake. This the Constitution forbids." Moreover "the purpose of helping certain groups whom the faculty of the Davis Medical School perceived as victims of 'societal discrimination' does not justify a classification that imposes disadvantages upon persons like respondent, who bear no responsibility for whatever harm the beneficiaries of the special admissions program are thought to have suffered. To hold otherwise would be to convert a remedy heretofore reserved for violations of legal rights into a privilege that all institutions throughout the Nation could grant at their pleasure to whatever groups are perceived as victims of societal discrimination. This is a step we have never approved."

Justice Powell then turned to what types of programs were permissible in considering race in the admissions process. Looking at a program at Harvard University, he pointed out that "in such admissions program, race or ethnic background may be deemed a 'plus' in a particular applicant's file, yet it does not insulate the individual from comparison with all other candidates for the available seats. The file of a particular black applicant may be examined for his potential contribution to diversity without the factor of race being decisive when compared, for example, with that of an applicant identified as an Italian-American if the latter is thought to exhibit qualities more likely to promote beneficial educational pluralism. . . . This kind of program *treats each applicant as an individual* in the admissions process. The applicant who loses out on the last available seat to another candidate receiving a 'plus' on the basis of ethnic background will not have been foreclosed from all consideration for that seat simply because he was not the right color or had the wrong surname. It would mean only that his combined qualifications, which may have included similar nonobjective factors, did not outweigh those of the other applicant. His qualifications would have been weighed fairly and competitively, and he would have no basis to complain of unequal treatment under the Fourteenth Amendment."

At the end of his opinion, Justice Powell summarized that "it is evident that the Davis special admissions program involves the use of an explicit racial classification never before countenanced by this Court. It tells applicants who are not Negro, Asian, or Chicano that they are *totally excluded* from a specific percentage of the seats in an entering class. No matter how strong their qualifications, quantitative and extracurricular, including their own potential for contribution to educational diversity, they are never afforded the *chance to compete* with applicants from the preferred groups for the special admission seats. At the same time, the preferred applicants have the opportunity to compete for every seat in the class."

Bakke Revisited: Disguised Quotas and the Multiple Goals of Diversity

The six splintered opinions in *Bakke* reflected the same debate that went on in American society both at that time and in the nineteenth century at the time of the Civil Rights Act of 1875. That debate has continued, and the Supreme Court revisited the issue in two 2003 cases involving the admissions processes of the University of Michigan and its law school.

In *Grutter v. Bollinger* (2003), the Court upheld the admissions process followed by the University of Michigan Law School by a vote of five to four. The law school considered traditional factors such as grade-point average, scores on the Law School Admissions Test, and letters of recommendation in its admission process. It also took "soft variables" into account. Those included evaluation of a personal essay, the quality of the college attended, the enthusiasm of the recommenders, and the quality of the undergraduate courses taken. Most significantly the admissions policy sought to achieve diversity for the purpose of enriching the education of all who attended the law school. Diversity itself was not restricted to any particular group, but did expressly include African Americans, Hispanics, and Native Americans. Indeed the law school sought to admit a "critical mass" of such minority students. Testimony by the law school's expert in the trial court indicated that 35 percent of minority applicants had been admitted in 2000, but that only 10 percent of those applicants would have been admitted had race not been considered. In that case only 4 percent of the entering class would have been underrepresented minority students. In fact some 14.5 percent of that class consisted of such minority students.

In an opinion by Justice Sandra Day O'Connor, the five-member majority "endorse[d] Justice Powell's view that student body diversity is a compelling state interest that can justify the use of race in university admissions." The majority opinion further stated that racial classifications must be analyzed by applying a standard of strict scrutiny, but "not every decision influenced by race is equally objectionable and strict scrutiny is designed to provide a framework for carefully examining the importance and the sincerity of the reasons advanced by the governmental decisionmaker for the use of race in that particular context."

In a departure from the reasoning of the dissenters in the *Bakke* case, Justice O'Connor's opinion relied upon the benefits of diversity, as opposed to the remediation of past discrimination, to uphold the consideration of race in the law school's admission process. In doing so, the majority pointed to amicus briefs filed by American businesses and retired military officers, "who point to the educational benefits that flow from student body diversity." Justice O'Connor further observed that "effective participation by members of all racial and ethnic groups in the civic life of our Nation is essential if the dream of one Nation, indivisible, is to be realized. . . . In order to cultivate a set of leaders with legitimacy in the eyes of the citizenry, it is necessary that the path to leadership be visibly open to talented and qualified individuals of every race and ethnicity."

Repeating Justice Powell's condemnation of quotas, and reaffirming that "a university may consider race or ethnicity only as a 'plus in a particular applicant's file,' without 'insulat[ing] the individual from comparison with all other candidates for the available seats,'" the majority concluded that the law school's admissions process constituted a "narrowly tailored use of race in admissions decisions to further a compelling interest in obtaining the educational benefits that flow from a diverse student body."

Justice O'Connor cautioned, however, that "race-conscious admissions policies must be limited in time," and noted that "we expect that 25 years from now, the use of racial preferences will no longer be necessary to further the interest approved today."

In a dissenting opinion written by Chief Justice Rehnquist, four members of the Court found that the law school admissions process was really a disguised quota that was inconsistent with the Equal Protection Clause and the *Bakke* decision. These justices pointed out that "the correlation between the percentage of the Law School's pool of applicants who are members of the three minority groups and the percentage of the admitted applicants who are members of the same groups is far too precise to be dismissed as merely the result of the school paying 'some attention to [the] numbers.'" Indeed, "in 1995, when 9.7% of the applicant pool was African American, 9.4% of the admitted class was African American. By 2000, only 7.5% of the applicant pool was African American, and 7.3% of the admitted class was African American. This correlation is striking." Based on this "correlation," Chief Justice Rehnquist stated that "I do not believe that the Constitution gives the Law School such free rein in the use of race. The law school has offered no explanation for its actual admissions practices and, unexplained, we are bound to conclude that the law school has managed its admission program, not to achieve a 'critical mass,' but to extend offers of admission to members of selected minority groups in proportion to their statistical representation in the applicant pool. But this is precisely the type of racial balancing that the Court itself calls 'patently unconstitutional.'"

In a separate dissenting opinion, Justice Kennedy criticized the majority for purporting to follow Justice Powell's approach in *Bakke,* but failing to apply his version of strict scrutiny in the evaluation of racial classifications. Justice Kennedy stated that "it is unfortunate . . . that the Court takes the first part of Justice Powell's rule but abandons the second. Having approved the use of race as a factor in the admissions process, the majority proceeds to nullify the essential safeguard Justice Powell insisted upon as the precondition of the approval. The safeguard was rigorous judicial review, with strict scrutiny as the controlling standard."

Justice Kennedy went on to point out that without "meaningful strict scrutiny," admissions officials could game the admissions process to define racial groups in such a way as to grant preference to those whom they preferred to admit. Testimony by the former director of the law school's admissions office, for example, noted that the faculty had debated whether to classify Cubans as Hispanics for purposes of the consideration of race, and that "one professor objected on the grounds that Cubans were Republicans."

On the same day it upheld the law school's admissions process in *Grutter,* the Supreme Court struck down the University of Michigan's undergraduate admissions process in *Gratz v. Bollinger* (2003). That process utilized a "selection index" under which a score of one hundred points or more resulted in admission. Applicants were entitled to twenty points "based upon his or her membership in an underrepresented racial or ethnic minority group."

In an opinion by Chief Justice Rehnquist on behalf of five members of the Court, the majority found that "the University's policy, which automatically distributes 20 points, or one-fifth of the points needed to guarantee admission, to every single 'underrepresented minority' applicant solely because of race, is not narrowly tailored to achieve the interest in educational diversity that respondents claim justifies their program." Moreover "Justice Powell's opinion in *Bakke* emphasized the importance of considering each particular applicant as an individual, assessing all the qualities that individual possesses, and in turn, evaluating that individual's ability to contribute to the unique setting of higher education. . . . The current [admissions] policy does not provide such individualized consideration. The . . . policy automatically distributes 20 points to every single applicant from an 'underrepresented minority' group, as defined by the University. The only consideration that accompanies this distribution of points is a factual review of an application to determine whether an individual is a member of one of these minority groups."

Six members of the Court voted to strike down this undergraduate admissions process, including Justices O'Connor and Breyer, both of whom had voted to uphold the law school's admissions process in *Grutter.* Three dissenting opinions were issued in *Gratz,* by Justices Stevens, Souter, and Ginsburg. Justice Stevens's opinion was directed to a technical standing issue.

Justice Souter pointed out that the undergraduate admissions process "lets all applicants compete for all places and values an applicant's offering for any place not only on grounds of race, but on grades, test scores, strength of high school, quality of course of study, residence, alumni relationships, leadership, personal character, socioeconomic disadvantage, athletic ability, and quality of the personal essay. . . . A nonminority applicant who scores highly in these other categories can readily garner a selection index exceeding that of a minority applicant who gets the 20-point bonus."

Justice Ginsburg's dissent was notable because of her reliance upon historic discrimination practiced against minority groups. While this had been the principal justification advanced to support special admissions programs in Justice Brennan's opinion for four members of the Court in *Bakke,* only Justice Ginsburg relied upon this factor in *Gratz.* Justice Ginsburg stated that "the racial and ethnic groups to which the College accord special consideration (African Americans, Hispanics, and Native Americans) have been relegated to inferior status by law and social practice; their members continue to experience class-based discrimination to this day. . . . The stain of generations of racial oppression is still visible in our society, . . . and the determination to hasten its removal remains vital."

In the twenty-five-year period between *Bakke* and *Grutter* and *Gratz,* the Supreme Court came to view the consideration of race as a plus factor as a legitimate state interest in a different way. The concept of remediation for past wrongs was replaced by a societal recognition that diversity plays an important role in a democracy. Justice Stephen Breyer attempted to explain this in his book *Active Liberty: Interpreting Our Democratic Constitution* (2006), where he wrote that special admissions programs considering race as a plus factor "would facilitate the functioning of democracy," because "some form of affirmative action [is] necessary to maintain a well-functioning participatory democracy." He, as Justice O'Connor had done in her majority opinion in *Grutter*, pointed to the amicus briefs filed by American business and military interests in that case, supporting the use of affirmative-action programs in college and graduate-school admissions.

The use of such affirmative-action admissions programs has continued to be controversial despite these perceived benefits, and comparatively few institutions of higher learning utilize such programs. A 2006 estimate suggested that only about 20 percent of four-year colleges and universities in the United States employed such programs, although those that did were among the most prestigious in the nation.

The Roberts Court Examines School Assignment

Do the benefits of diversity identified by the Supreme Court in the University of Michigan cases support assigning public school children to particular schools based on their race, in order to foster racial balancing in those schools? Or does such an approach violate the underlying principles of *Brown v. Board of Education?* In 2007 consolidated cases that generated five separate opinions, the Supreme Court struck down public school district student assignment plans from Seattle, Washington, and Louisville, Kentucky. A majority of the Court in *Parents Involved in Community Schools v. Seattle School District No. 1* (2007) found that those plans violated the Equal Protection Clause of the Fourteenth Amendment. In an opinion by Chief Justice John Roberts, these plans were characterized as "rel[ying] upon an individual student's race in assigning that student to a particular school, so that the racial balance at the school falls within a predetermined range based on the racial composition of the school district as a whole."

As in the *Bakke* case, the Court split into two groups of four, with Justice Anthony Kennedy casting the decisive vote. Recognizing the importance of his vote, and defying Court conventions, Justice Kennedy read his concurring opinion aloud on June 28, 2007, at the closing session of the Supreme Court's October 2006 term. Kennedy had been the decisive vote in many opinions during the term and voted with the majority in all twenty-four cases decided by a five-vote margin. His opinion left open the possibility that the goal of attaining diversity would constitute a compelling state interest sufficient in some cases to justify a student assignment plan that looked at race.

Chief Justice Roberts's plurality opinion for himself and Justices Scalia, Thomas, and Alito emphasized that when government makes decisions based on race, those decisions are reviewed under the standard of strict scrutiny. Under that standard, the use of race must be "'narrowly tailored' to achieve a 'compelling' state interest." Chief Justice Roberts explained that the Court had recognized such an interest to exist in two specific areas. First, decisions may be based upon race where they are necessary for "remedying the effects of past intentional discrimination." Second, the Supreme Court recognized as compelling "the interest in diversity in higher education upheld in *Grutter.*"

The plurality found that the first interest was not present here, because there had never been a judicial finding of de jure segregation in the Seattle School District, and a desegregation decree covering the Louisville School District had been dissolved in 2000, when the district court found that the effects of past segregation had been eliminated in that district. Nor was the second interest involved in these cases, since the *Grutter* Court had spoken of a diversity that embraced "all factors that may contribute to student body diversity," whereas here, the school districts had looked at race alone.

Chief Justice Roberts's opinion emphasized that school assignment programs must focus on "each applicant as an individual." Here, by contrast, race was not simply one factor but "for some students, is determinative standing alone." Moreover these cases were not controlled by *Grutter,* because that opinion specifically relied upon "the unique context of higher education," and identified a broader diversity than that resting upon race alone.

The plurality next considered whether "racial diversity" itself could constitute a third compelling interest sufficient to survive a strict-scrutiny review. The opinion found that it could not in the context of these cases since "the racial classifications employed by the districts are not narrowly tailored to the goal of achieving the educational and social benefits asserted to flow from racial diversity. In design and operation, the plans are directed only to racial balance, pure and simple, an objective this Court has repeatedly condemned as illegitimate. The plans are tied to each district's specific racial demographics, rather than to any pedagogic concept of the level of diversity needed to obtain the asserted educational benefits." To recognize such "racial balancing as a compelling end in itself would 'effectively assur[e] that race will always be relevant in American life, and that the 'ultimate goal' of 'eliminating entirely from governmental decision-making such irrelevant factors as a human being's race' will never be achieved."

The plurality opinion also pointed out that both school districts had rejected, with little or no consideration, other potential methods for achieving the desired diversity, including alternative assignment plans that were not expressly based on racial classifications. Responding to the charge in Justice Breyer's dissenting opinion that the plurality's approach would strike down such other means for attaining diversity, Chief Justice Roberts responded that "these other means—e.g., where to construct new schools, how to allocate resources among schools, and which academic offerings to provide to attract students to certain schools—implicate different considerations than the explicit racial classifications at issue in these cases, and we express no opinion on their validity—not even in dicta."

Finally Chief Justice Roberts's opinion invoked both the arguments made, and the principles underlying the decision, in *Brown v. Board of Education.* He pointed out that the counsel who argued that case for the African American students explicitly contended that race could not be used as a factor in affording educational opportunities to schoolchildren. Moreover, "before *Brown,* schoolchildren were told where they could and could not go to school based on the color of their skin. . . . *The way to stop discrimination on the basis of race is to stop discriminating on the basis of race.*"

There were two concurring opinions. Justice Clarence Thomas, who had replaced Thurgood Marshall as the Court's only African American, wrote a thirty-six-page opinion. Justice Thomas emphasized that "*racial imbalance is not segregation,*" and that there had been no demonstrated danger in either school district of "resegregation." In his view racial balancing could only be utilized to remedy past de jure segregation.

Most of Justice Thomas's concurring opinion was devoted to rebutting points made in Justice Breyer's dissenting opinion. Justice Thomas pointed out that the approach taken by the dissent attempted to distinguish the approach of the two school districts in these cases from that of the segregationists in the *Brown* cases because the current plans were not "aimed at oppressing blacks." He found that the controlling principles of a "color-blind Constitution" did not permit such a distinction. In Justice Thomas's view, the approach of the Breyer dissent was analytically similar to that of the majority in *Plessy v. Ferguson* and the segregationists in the *Brown* case. All of them, in one way or another, relied upon "current societal practice and expectations, deference to local officials, likely practical consequences, and reliance on previous statements from this and other courts." All of these must be rejected because "what was wrong in 1954 cannot be right today."

Citing *Scott v. Sandford,* Justice Thomas concluded that "if our history has taught us anything, it has taught us to beware of elites bearing racial theories." In a footnote to that sentence, he observed that "Justice Breyer's good intentions, which I do not doubt, have the shelf life of Justice Breyer's tenure."

Concurring in the judgment but only in parts of the plurality opinion, Justice Kennedy cast the deciding vote to invalidate the Seattle and Louisville plans. He agreed with the plurality on several points. To begin with, there was a difference between de jure and de facto segregation that affected the permissible scope of considering race in pupil assignment, making it impermissible in the absence of de jure segregation unless there was a compelling state interest involved. Second, he agreed that the use of racial classifications to differentiate the treatment of individuals was presumptively invalid.

Justice Kennedy disagreed with the plurality opinion, as well as the separate opinion of Justice Thomas, in other ways. He rejected use of the color-blind Constitution model as controlling, reasoning that "in the real world, it is regrettable to say, it cannot be a universal constitutional principle." Moreover, in contrast to the plurality and Justice Thomas, he believed that diversity could be "a compelling educational goal a school district may pursue." Indeed he expressly noted that "to the extent the plurality opinion suggests the Constitution mandates that state and local school authorities must accept the status quo of racial isolation in schools, it is, in my view, profoundly mistaken."

Justice Kennedy summarized his opinion by stating that "this Nation has a moral and ethical obligation to fulfill its historic commitment to creating an integrated society that ensures equal opportunity for all of its children. A compelling interest exists in avoiding racial isolation, an interest that a school district, in its discretion and expertise, may choose to pursue. Likewise, a district may consider it a compelling interest to achieve a diverse student population. Race may be one component of that diversity, but other demographic factors, plus special talents and needs, should also be considered. What the government is not permitted to do, absent a showing of necessity not made here, is to classify every student on the basis of race and to assign each of them to schools based on that classification. Crude measures of this sort threaten to reduce children to racial chits valued and traded according to one school's supply and another's demand."

In the cases before the Court, Justice Kennedy found that the strict-scrutiny standard of review required the two school districts to explore alternatives to pure racial classifications. Such racial classifications, in his view, could only be used as "a last resort to achieve a compelling interest." Some alternatives suggested by Justice Kennedy were "strategic site selection of new schools; drawing attendance zones with general recognition of the demographics of neighborhoods; allocating resources for special programs; recruiting students and faculty in a targeted fashion; and tracking enrollments, performance, and other statistics by race." These alternatives could be considered because they are "race conscious but do not lead to different treatment based on a classification that tells each student he or she is to be defined by race."

There were two dissenting opinions. Justice John Paul Stevens, the senior member of the Court, wrote a short opinion, finding a "cruel irony" in the plurality's reliance on *Brown v. Board of Education.* Indeed Justice Stevens accused the Court of having "changed significantly" since 1968. He opined: "It was then more faithful to *Brown* and more respectful of our precedent than it is today. It is my firm conviction that no Member of the Court that I joined in 1975 would have agreed with today's decision."

The principal dissenting opinion was written by Justice Stephen Breyer and joined by Justices Stevens, Souter, and Ginsburg. Breyer's dissent was seventy-seven pages long, the longest opinion he ever wrote to that time, and he read portions of it aloud in open court. To the opinion's printed text he added the oral observation that "it is not often in the law that so few have so quickly undone so much."

Justice Breyer saw the plurality's opinion as inconsistent with the Court's landmark ruling in *Brown v. Board of Education* (1954). He concluded his dissenting opinion with the observation that "the last half-century has witnessed great strides toward racial equality, but we have not yet realized the promise of *Brown.* To invalidate the plans under review is to threaten the promise of *Brown.* The plurality's position, I fear, would break that promise. This is a decision that the Court and the Nation will come to regret."

In Justice Breyer's view, there were four basic considerations that justified the student assignment plans before the Court. First, there had been a prior history of either segregation or litigation about segregation in both Louisville and Seattle, leading both school districts to undertake remedial measures themselves to address the racial imbalance in their school systems. Second, the dissenters believed that the Court's desegregation precedent fully supported the use of "compulsory race-conscious measures to combat segregated schools." Quoting from *Swann v. Charlotte-Mecklenburg Board of Education* (1971), Justice Breyer noted that that opinion specifically stated that "school authorities . . . might well conclude, for example, that in order to prepare students to live in a pluralistic society each school should have a prescribed ratio of Negro to white students reflecting the proportion for the district as a whole. *To do this as an educational policy is within the broad discretionary powers of school authorities.*"

Justice Breyer admitted that the passage he quoted from *Swann* was "not a technical holding," but he nevertheless considered it to represent "a basic principle of constitutional law." Moreover, in his view, "law is not an exercise in mathematical logic. And statements of a legal rule set forth in a judicial opinion do not always divide neatly into 'holdings' and 'dicta.'" In addition the Court's prior decisions established that the strict-scrutiny standard of review did not require all racial classifications to be treated the same. Thus there is an important constitutional difference between "state action that excludes and thereby subordinates racial minorities and state action that seeks to bring together people of all races."

The third consideration relied upon by Justice Breyer was that the plans at issue were narrowly tailored to accomplish goals that represented compelling state interests—here "diversity in public primary and secondary schools." This diversity interest had several elements. One was an "educational" element, representing "an interest in overcoming the adverse educational effects produced by and associated with highly segregated schools." Another element was "democratic," representing "an interest in producing an educational environment that reflects the 'pluralistic society' in which our children will live." In summary, "the compelling interest at issue here . . . includes an effort to eradicate the remnants, not of general 'societal discrimination,' . . . but of primary and secondary school segregation . . . ; it includes an effort to create school environments that provide better educational opportunities for all children; it includes an effort to help create citizens better prepared to know, to understand, and to work with people of all races and backgrounds, thereby furthering the kind of democratic government our Constitution foresees. If an educational interest that combines these three elements is not 'compelling,' what is?"

Justice Breyer's fourth consideration was that "the plurality's approach risks serious harm to the law and for the Nation." He defined that risk to include the "risk of a return to school systems that are in fact (though not in law) resegregated." In so contending, Justice Breyer cited statistics, further supported by charts included as appendices at the back of his opinion, indicating that more than 5 percent of all public school students attended schools with a white population of less than 1 percent, and that over one in six black students attended a school that was at least 99 percent minority.

The reaction to the opinions in *Parents Involved* was predictably divided between liberal and conservative commentators. The *New York Times* titled its editorial on the cases "Resegregation Now," and warned that "there should be no mistaking just how radical this decision is." It concluded that "it was a sad day for the court and for the idea of racial equality." By contrast the *Wall Street Journal* editorialized that liberals were bringing out "sackcloth and outrage," despite the fact that "the decision curbed the excesses of the racial-classification policy that has been promoted by too many courts in recent decades."

The sharp divisions in the Supreme Court and among the editorial commentators continued the debate over the appropriate breadth of the Fourteenth Amendment that has played out among the American people for over 140 years. From the nineteenth-century Free Labor Republicans and the "Forgotten Man" of William Graham Sumner, George Wallace, and Richard Nixon, to twenty-first-century neoconservatives, there have been continuing disagreements as to the use of race in any governmental decision making. Indeed an August 2007 poll reported that 71 percent of the American public agreed with the Supreme Court's decision that "public schools may not consider an individual's race when deciding which students are assigned to specific schools," while 24 percent disagreed. The opinions in *Parents Involved* did not resolve the ongoing debate, but instead promised to sharpen it. For example the views expressed by Justice Kennedy and by the four dissenters indicate that fostering diversity and pluralism will qualify as a compelling state interest for a majority of the 2007 Supreme Court. Indeed even the plurality opinion recognized that possibility. As such the practical impact of the contending opinions in *Parents Involved* may well be that school districts will be forced more carefully to examine what the benefits of the diversity and pluralism they seek actually are, and then to select appropriate methods to realize those specific benefits. Most significantly the methods selected will need to be more nuanced than what Justice Kennedy termed the "crude" approach of racial balancing.

Ten

The Supreme Court and Abortion

The Supreme Court's abortion decisions have been at least as controversial as its decisions on race and religion. Indeed the decision in *Roe v. Wade* is at or near the top of the list of the Court's most-vilified opinions from the twentieth century. In this chapter we review six of the Supreme Court's major decisions on abortion, beginning with *Roe v. Wade* and ending with the April 2007 opinion on the constitutionality of the federal legislation banning the partial-birth abortion procedure.

Regulation of Abortion in the United States

Legal regulation of abortion in the United States arose from a complex interaction of legislative concerns for women's safety, medical science, the power of organized medicine, religious beliefs, and nativism. In the 1820s and 1830s, state laws were enacted that were essentially poison control measures, regulating the sale of drugs taken to induce abortions, in order to protect the woman's life and health. This approach changed in midcentury with organized efforts by the American Medical Association to make all abortions illegal. In 1857 and 1871 the AMA Committee on Criminal Abortion described abortion as the "unwarrantable destruction of human life" and attributed the frequency of abortion to "a wide-spread popular ignorance of the true character of the crime—a belief, even among mothers themselves, that the foetus is not alive till after the period of quickening." The AMA action was also motivated by a desire to control medical practice and restrict homeopaths and midwives from competing with medical doctors.

The banning of abortions was also supported by American nativists, with an eye toward preserving Anglo-Saxon dominance against the newly emerging Catholic immigrant population, as well as African Americans. Religious concerns also played a part in criminalizing abortion, with the Catholic Church officially condemning abortion in 1869 and extending that ban to therapeutic abortions in 1895. Finally early feminists were consistent voices against abortion. Susan B. Anthony characterized abortion as "child-murder," and Alice Paul stated that "abortion is the ultimate exploitation of women."

These forces worked in tandem to catalyze enactment of abortion legislation, and, by 1880, every state had enacted a criminal abortion law. The campaign to criminalize abortion gained new force in the 1890s, led by the medical community. Doctors took renewed aim at what became known as the "midwife problem," since abortions continued to be performed outside the organized medical profession, despite the legislative banning of the procedure except to save the woman's life. These efforts continued to the 1920s, with most abortions remaining illegal throughout the country.

Popular attitudes toward abortion changed with the Great Depression of the 1930s. From 1929 to 1939, against the background of economic stress and a shrinking job market, it is estimated that at least six hundred thousand abortions occurred annually. A vocal minority within the medical profession split off from the official view at that time, with two medical doctors writing books in the 1930s calling for the repeal of strict abortion laws. This remained a minority view, however, and the crackdown on abortion in fact accelerated during the 1940s and 1950s. Abortion clinics were closed, and hospitals became the only approved venue for abortions. Hospitals in turn imposed strict rules to restrict access to abortion, including acting as gatekeepers through specialized abortion committees populated by medical doctors. Abortions outside hospitals were totally banned, resulting in a reduction in abortions by the early 1960s to less than half of that of the average twenty years earlier in large cities such as New York. There was also a corresponding dramatic decline in the number of abortions nationally between 1945 and 1962.

With legal access to abortion dramatically decreased, back-alley abortions became more common, resulting in an increasing death rate, including a tripling of the death rate from abortion between the 1920s and the 1960s in New York City. This led to the targeting of illegal abortions by law enforcement, with raids on abortion clinics and arrests of abortion providers becoming front-page news, particularly in large cities such as Chicago.

These measures effectively foreclosed abortion as an option for most pregnant women and led to a backlash from a combination of legal reformers and law professors, medical doctors, an emerging feminist movement, and social movement lawyers. A Planned Parenthood conference on abortion in 1955 released a statement that called for liberalizing abortion laws for "psychiatric, humanitarian and eugenic indications." In 1959 the prestigious American Law Institute released its Model Penal Code, which would permit abortions to preserve a woman's physical and mental health and also permitted abortions in the cases of rape and incest or where the fetus was likely to suffer grave physical or mental birth defects. Versions of this legislation were adopted by twelve states by 1970.

Two episodes of severe birth defects in the 1960s accelerated the movement toward liberalizing abortion laws. In 1962 a Phoenix, Arizona, media personality named Sherri Finkbine traveled to Sweden to obtain a legal abortion after she had taken thalidomide, a legal drug that caused severe birth defects, including missing or flipper-like appendages in children. Three years later, there was an epidemic of German measles in the United States, where a woman faced up to a 50 percent chance that her child would be born with birth defects.

In 1969 the California Supreme Court struck down its criminal abortion laws as unconstitutionally vague, and New York, Alaska, and Hawaii followed the next year by repealing their criminal abortion laws. Despite these early successes in this incremental state-by-state action to change abortion laws, a split began to emerge among abortion reformers. A newly emerging feminist movement opposed the American Law Institute approach in the Model Penal Code, since that approach continued the use of hospital committees to decide whether a woman was entitled to an abortion.

Women had become much more active politically in the 1960s, starting with economic issues, and then addressing social ones. In 1963, for example, the Equal Pay Act was passed as federal legislation, while the 1964 Civil Rights Act contained a Title VII, banning discrimination on the basis of gender. The abortion issue split the women's movement, with one group seeing abortion as a woman's right, analogizing their efforts to obtain legal abortions to the civil rights movement for African Americans. To this group of feminists, it was necessary to reject male medical authority over the abortion decision. These feminists were joined by many medical school deans and faculty across the country in litigation commenced in Illinois federal court in 1970 to establish a woman's right to choose to terminate her pregnancy through abortion. It was within this context, and against this background, that the Supreme Court decided *Roe v. Wade* and *Doe v. Bolton* in 1973.

Roe v. Wade and *Doe v. Bolton*

The Supreme Court considered the constitutionality of two very different abortion statutes in *Roe v. Wade* (1973) and *Doe v. Bolton* (1973), which were decided on the same day. The Texas statute at issue in *Roe* only permitted an abortion where it was necessary to preserve a woman's life. By contrast the Georgia statute in *Doe* was derived from the Model Penal Code, permitting abortions where they were necessary to save the life or health of the mother, or where the pregnancy resulted from rape, or the fetus was likely to be born with a serious defect.

The cases were argued twice. After the first argument, the *Roe* opinion was assigned to Justice Harry Blackmun, who prepared a draft opinion striking down the Texas statute as impermissibly vague, in its use of the undefined term "life." Blackmun also prepared a broader opinion in the *Doe* case, finding that the Ninth and Fourteenth amendments protected a woman's interest regarding whether "to bear an unwanted child." This draft opinion went on to state that eventually "another being becomes involved and the privacy the woman possessed has become dual rather than sole" and therefore "must be balanced against the state's interest." Blackmun left open in this draft at which point the state's interest became paramount.

Because Blackmun's draft opinions were unsatisfactory to the more liberal justices then on the Court, and because there were two vacancies, the cases were reargued after the confirmations of Justices Lewis Powell and William Rehnquist. Following reargument, both cases were decided by identical seven-to-two votes, invalidating both the Texas and Georgia statutes as unconstitutional. Justice Blackmun wrote both of the majority opinions, with Justices Rehnquist and Byron White dissenting.

Justice Blackmun's opinion for the Court in *Roe* contains an elaborate historical discussion regarding the history of abortion from ancient times, examining the opinions of philosophers and the medical profession, as well as the evolution of English and American law, including American legislation on the topic. Justice Blackmun's papers reveal that this part of the opinion can be traced to research he conducted at the Mayo Clinic in Minnesota, for which he had been counsel before he joined the Court. Blackmun had requested his former client to gather materials on abortion for his review, even though one of the Mayo Clinic's department chairs joined a brief arguing for the invalidity of the Texas statute at issue in *Roe.* One of the articles Blackmun copied to take back with him to Washington was a June 1972 Gallup poll that reported more liberal attitudes toward abortion, including a response that 64 percent of the individuals polled believed that the decision on abortion should be left to the woman and her doctor.

Blackmun's opinion was rooted in the right of privacy, which he believed was "founded in the Fourteenth Amendment's concept of personal liberty and restrictions upon state action." This concept was "broad enough to encompass a woman's decision whether or not to terminate her pregnancy," because denial of an abortion by the state would involve imposing a "detriment . . . upon the pregnant woman." This was because giving birth to a child "may force upon the woman a distressful life and future. Psychological harm may be imminent. Mental and physical health may be taxed by child care. There is also the distress, for all concerned, associated with the unwanted child, and there is the problem of bringing a child into a family already unable, psychologically and otherwise, to care for it."

Having found that "the right of personal privacy includes the abortion decision," Blackmun went on to state that "this right is not unqualified and must be considered against important state interests in regulation." Because the right involved was "fundamental," the state would need to show a compelling state interest in order to limit abortion. Such an interest was not shown by the argument that the fetus is a "person" within the meaning of the Fourteenth Amendment, since "there has always been strong support for the view that life does not begin until live birth," and it was not necessary to "resolve the difficult question of when life begins."

Blackmun's majority opinion concluded that a trimester approach was appropriate in determining what limitations, if any, a state may place on a woman's right to have an abortion. During the first trimester, "the abortion decision and its effectuation must be left to the medical judgment of the pregnant woman's attending physician." After the first trimester, the state could regulate the abortion procedure only "in ways that are reasonably related to maternal health." Finally "subsequent to viability, the State in promoting its interest in the potentiality of human life may, if it chooses, regulate, and even proscribe, abortion except where it is necessary, in appropriate medical judgment, for the preservation of the life or health of the mother." Blackmun saw this approach as one that "vindicates the right of the physician to administer medical treatment according to his professional judgment up to the points where important state interests provide compelling justifications for intervention."

In distributing his draft opinion to the other justices for review and approval, Blackmun admitted that his trimester approach was "arbitrary, but perhaps any other selected point, such as quickening or viability, is equally arbitrary."

In dissenting, the new justice William Rehnquist first took issue with the contention that the right to an abortion could only be abridged by the state if it showed a compelling state interest for doing so. Rehnquist pointed out that the Fourteenth Amendment protects liberty only against deprivation without due process of law, and that the Court had traditionally utilized a test of whether a state law had "a rational relation to a valid state objective." He also pointed out that at the time the Fourteenth Amendment was adopted at least thirty-six state or territorial laws limited abortion.

Rehnquist went on to make a second point, criticizing the imposition of a rigid trimester system to determine whether the state could deny an abortion. He argued that "the decision here to break pregnancy into three distinct terms and to outline the permissible restrictions the State may impose in each one . . . partakes more of judicial legislation that it does of a determination of the intent of the drafters of the Fourteenth Amendment."

In *Doe v. Bolton,* Blackmun's opinion of the Court applied the right of privacy recognized in *Roe* to invalidate three requirements of the Georgia law. These requirements were that the abortion (1) must be performed in an accredited hospital; (2) must be approved by a hospital abortion committee; and (3) the performing physician's judgment must be confirmed by independent examinations by two other licensed physicians. With respect to the hospital abortion committee, Blackmun concluded that "the woman's right to receive medical care in accordance with her licensed physician's best judgment and the physician's right to administer it are substantially limited by this statutorily imposed overview." Similarly the required concurrence by two other doctors was unconstitutional because it had "no rational connection with a patient's needs and unduly infringes on the physician's right to practice."

In a dissent that also applied to *Roe,* Justice White observed that "the Court apparently values the convenience of the pregnant mother more than the continued existence and development of the life or potential life that she carries." In Justice White's view, the issue of abortion "should be left with the people and to the political processes the people have devised to govern their affairs." Instead, the majority opinion was one that "simply fashions and announces a new constitutional right for pregnant mothers and, with scarcely any reason or authority for its action, invests that right with sufficient substance to override most existing state abortion statutes. The upshot is that the people and the legislatures of the 50 States are constitutionally disentitled to weigh the relative importance of the continued existence and development of the fetus, on the one hand, against a spectrum of possible impacts on the mother, on the other hand. As an exercise of raw judicial power, the Court perhaps has authority to do what it does today; but in my view its judgment is an improvident and extravagant exercise of the power of judicial review that the Constitution extends to this Court."

Reactions to *Roe*

Since the decisions in *Roe* and *Doe,* more than forty million legal abortions have been performed in the United States. From 1973 to the present, Americans have been divided on the wisdom of this result of *Roe.* The General Social Survey, for example, has reported in each year during this period on the public views on abortions, finding a remarkable consistency over the years. Approximately 60 percent of respondents have opposed abortions on demand, or for the reason that the woman was not married, while about 40 percent would permit an abortion for any reason. By contrast about 90 percent believe that abortions should be permitted to protect a woman's health, and about 75–80 percent would permit abortions in cases of rape or birth defect. These latter results mirror the approach taken years earlier by the American Law Institute in its Model Penal Code.

Despite the facts that the opinion of the Court in *Roe v. Wade* was joined by seven of the Court's nine members, and that the two dissents were quite short, the reaction to the opinion by academics was overwhelmingly critical on the legal reasoning (or lack thereof). The comments at the time by two leading law professors, one at Harvard and the other at Yale Law School, both of whom who were supporters of abortion rights, are particularly noteworthy. Harvard Law professor Laurence Tribe, in his Forward to the Harvard Law Review's annual review of the preceding Supreme Court term, saw the opinion in *Roe v. Wade* as casting a "verbal smokescreen," behind which "the substantive judgment on which it rests is nowhere to be found." In an extensive critique of the opinion, Yale law professor

John Hart Ely wrote an article in the *Yale Law Journal* that has become the third most cited of any article from that publication. Ely saw multiple deficiencies in Justice Blackmun's work product.

Ely calls *Roe v. Wade* "a very bad decision" because it is "bad constitutional law" that fails to identify the source of the privacy right it relies upon to justify its holding. Moreover, in his view, the liberty interest utilized by Justice Blackmun is afforded more protection from state interference than is customary under due process analysis, which typically seeks only to discover a reasonable relationship between a legitimate state interest and the provisions of the legislation in issue. Indeed Ely compares *Roe* unfavorably to the *Lochner* substantive due process opinion discussed in chapter 5, since *Roe* required a compelling state interest to justify abortion-restricting legislation, while *Lochner* only looked for a rational relationship between the limitation of bakers' work hours imposed by the New York legislation and the protection of bakers' health. Finally Ely criticized the manner in which the *Roe* opinion minimized the interest of the state in protecting the fetus. Observing that "a fetus may not be a 'person in the whole sense,' but it is certainly not nothing," Ely concludes that the state has a legitimate interest in protecting the fetus, because "dogs are not 'persons in the whole sense' nor have they constitutional rights, but that does not mean the state cannot prohibit killing them." Here, "abortion ends (or if that makes a difference, prevents) the life of a human being other than the one making the choice."

Beyond the perceived inadequacies in the legal reasoning utilized by Justice Blackmun, other commentators (both at the time of the *Roe* and *Doe* decisions and thereafter) have raised an even more fundamental separation of powers argument against the approach taken in *Roe.* A year before she was appointed to the Supreme Court of the United States, future justice Ruth Bader Ginsburg pointed out in a law review article that *Roe* "halted a political process that was moving in a reform direction," and generated "prolonged divisiveness." As we examined in chapter 8, the opinion in *Roe v. Wade* was a catalyzing force in impelling the entry of evangelical Protestants and conservative Catholics into politics, in order to overturn the recognition of a general right to abortion. This new political force contributed to the elections of Presidents Ronald Reagan and George H. W. Bush, permitting them to appoint five new justices, as well as a new chief justice, in their twelve years in office. As we will see in the discussion that follows, these new justices turned the seven-to-two *Roe* and *Doe* rulings into narrow five-to-four decisions that chipped away at the base of the constitutional right recognized in *Roe.*

Roe v. Wade also contributed to a realignment of the two major political parties in the United States, with Democrats generally supporting the pro-choice position, while Republicans mainly adopted a pro-life position. In many ways this was a significant reversal in their prior positions, since most abortion reform legislation in the 1960s and 1970s took place under Republican governors. By contrast some of the strongest voices in favor of limiting abortion before *Roe* came from prominent Democrats, including presidential candidates such as Senators Edward Kennedy and Edmund Muskie and Speaker of the House Thomas ("Tip") O'Neill.

Roe under Attack: Legal Assaults on the Citadel of Privacy

During the presidencies of Ronald Reagan and George H. W. Bush, briefs filed by the solicitor general of the United States called for the Supreme Court to overrule *Roe v. Wade* on six different occasions in ten years. The first major test for the viability of *Roe* during those years came in *Webster v. Reproductive Health Services* (1989), where amicus briefs were filed by sixty-seven religious groups, multiple states attorneys general, and legal, historical, and other interest groups. *Webster* was argued after Justice Anthony Kennedy joined the Court. Kennedy had been confirmed in 1988, in the place of Judge Robert Bork, whose nomination was rejected by the Senate, at least partially because of his critical stance against the *Roe* opinion.

Kennedy joined Reagan appointees Sandra Day O'Connor and Antonin Scalia on the Court, and the predicted pairing of O'Connor, Scalia, and Kennedy with the *Roe* dissenters, Justice William Rehnquist (now elevated to chief justice) and Justice Byron White, was seen as the death knell for *Roe* by many commentators and Court watchers. Justice O'Connor had recently dissented in *Thornburgh v. American College of Obstetricians & Gynecologists* (1986), a five-to-four decision that invalidated a number of Pennsylvania restrictions on abortion. In her first important abortion opinion, moreover, she had dissented in *Akron v. Akron Center for Reproductive Health, Inc.* (1983), writing a separate opinion that was critical of *Roe*'s trimester approach.

Webster involved an attack on four provisions of a Missouri law restricting abortions. Initially the Preamble to the legislation was attacked, because it proclaimed that life began "at conception" and provided that "unborn children have protectable interests in life, health and well-being." Second, the law prohibited use of public employees or facilities, including hospitals, to perform or assist abortions except where they were necessary to save the woman's life. The third provision that was attacked in *Webster* required a doctor to perform appropriate medical examinations or tests to ascertain if the fetus was viable where the woman was believed to be twenty or more weeks pregnant. Finally the legislation prohibited the use of public funds, employees, or facilities to encourage or counsel an abortion not necessary to save a woman's life. The opinion in *Webster* ultimately reached only the second and third issues, finding that the Preamble did not regulate abortions and had no independent legal effect and that the challenge to the encouraging and counseling provision had become moot.

The remaining two provisions were upheld by five-to-four votes, in three separate opinions. In an opinion of the Court, Chief Justice Rehnquist was joined by Justices White, O'Connor, Scalia, and Kennedy in upholding the ban on use of public employees or facilities to perform abortions. This provision was found constitutional because the Due Process Clause does not confer any "affirmative right to governmental aid." Moreover this ban was constitutional under the reasoning of the Court's earlier five-to-four decision in *Harris v. McRae* (1980), which upheld the Hyde amendment ban on federal funding of abortions under Medicaid, except where they were necessary to save the woman's life.

The viability testing provision was more controversial, even among the five justices who voted to uphold it. Here, Chief Justice Rehnquist's opinion was only for a plurality of three justices, including himself, Justice White, and Justice Kennedy. Their opinion interpreted the Missouri statute to permit the physician to determine whether medical tests or examinations were necessary in the physician's reasonable medical judgment, and they found this provision to be constitutional even though twenty weeks fell within the second trimester, where *Roe* would not permit state regulation of abortion except to protect the woman's health. This set up squarely the question of whether to overrule *Roe.* Indeed, when Justice Kennedy first saw Chief Justice Rehnquist's draft opinion, he wrote a note to Rehnquist stating that he "would have used the occasion to overrule [*Roe*] and return this difficult issue to the political systems of the states." Justice Scalia was also firmly in favor of overruling *Roe,* and said so in his concurring opinion in *Webster.* Since Justice White had previously called for *Roe* to be overruled in his dissenting opinion in *Thornburgh,* there were three justices prepared to overrule *Roe* in *Webster.* Chief Justice Rehnquist, although he had joined Justices White's 1986 dissenting opinion in *Thornburgh,* concluded that it was not necessary to reach the question of overruling *Roe* since the Texas statute in *Roe* was quite different, banning all abortions except to save the life of the woman.

In his final opinion Chief Justice Rehnquist called the "rigid trimester analysis" of *Roe* "a virtual Procrustean bed" that was "unsound in principle and unworkable in practice." He explained that "the rigid *Roe* framework is hardly consistent with the notion of a Constitution cast in general terms, as ours is, and usually speaking in general principles, as ours does. The key elements of the *Roe* framework—trimesters and viability—are not found in the text of the Constitution or any place else one would expect to find a constitutional principle. Since the bounds of the inquiry are essentially indeterminate, the result has been a web of legal rules that have become increasingly intricate, resembling a code of regulations rather than a body of constitutional doctrine."

More significantly Chief Justice Rehnquist's opinion concluded that "we do not see why the State's interest in protecting potential human life should come into existence only at the point of viability, and that there should therefore be a rigid line allowing state regulation after viability but prohibiting it before viability." As such "we are satisfied that the requirement of these tests permissibly furthers the State's interest in protecting potential human life, and we therefore believe [the statute] to be constitutional."

Finally Chief Justice Rehnquist's opinion rejected a request by the United States solicitor general and multiple friends of the Court to overrule *Roe,* given the differences between the Texas statute involved in that case and the Missouri statute. The Rehnquist opinion concluded that it left *Roe* "undisturbed," but that "to the extent indicated in our opinion, we would modify and narrow *Roe* and succeeding cases."

In a separate concurring opinion, Justice Scalia stated that he would "more explicitly" overrule *Roe.* He explained that a "broad holding" repudiating Roe was necessary because "our retaining control, through *Roe,* of what I believe to be, and many of our citizens recognize to be, a political issue, continuously distorts the public perception of the role of this Court." Viewing Chief Justice Rehnquist's approach as too piecemeal, Justice Scalia observed that "it thus appears that the mansion of constitutional abortion law, constructed overnight in *Roe v. Wade,* must be disassembled doorjamb by doorjamb, and never entirely brought down, no matter how wrong it may be."

As would so often happen in abortion and other controversial cases, Justice O'Connor became the deciding vote. When she had seen Chief Justice Rehnquist's draft opinion, she viewed it as effectively overruling *Roe* and would not join it. Instead, she reverted to her view that a ban on abortions was permissible so long as the nature of the ban did not place an "undue burden" on the woman. In her *Webster* opinion, Justice O'Connor indicated that she still continued to view the trimester framework of *Roe* "problematic" but said *Webster* did not properly present the issue of "the constitutional validity of *Roe v. Wade.*" On the viability testing procedures, Justice O'Connor concluded that "requiring the performance of examinations and tests useful to determining whether a fetus is viable, when viability is possible, and when it would not be medically imprudent to do so, does not impose an undue burden on the woman's abortion decision."

There were two dissenting opinions in *Webster.* Justice Blackmun's dissent was joined by Justices Brennan and Marshall, while Justice Stevens wrote an individual dissent. Justice Blackmun's dissent was angry and almost apocalyptic in its language. He began by stating, "Today, *Roe v. Wade* . . . and the fundamental constitutional right of women to decide whether to terminate a pregnancy, survive but are not secure." He went on in the opening paragraphs of the opinion to state that "I fear for the future. I fear for the liberty and equality of the millions of women who have lived and come of age in the 16 years since *Roe* was decided. I fear for the integrity of, and public esteem for, this Court. I dissent." Justice Blackmun concluded his dissent by observing that "for today, at least, the law of abortion stands undisturbed. For today, the women of this Nation still retain the liberty to control their destinies. But the signs are evident and very ominous, and a chill wind blows."

In Justice Blackmun's view, "the plurality repudiates every principle for which *Roe* stands; in good conscience, it cannot possibly believe that *Roe* lies 'undisturbed' merely because this case does not call upon the Court to reconsider the Texas statute, or one like it. If the Constitution permits a State to enact any statute that reasonably furthers its interest in potential life, and if that interest arises as of conception, why would the Texas statute fail to pass muster?"

Planned Parenthood v. Casey

Three years after *Webster* was decided, another frontal assault was launched on *Roe v. Wade,* with the United States once again requesting the Supreme Court to overrule the *Roe* decision. As noted in the very first paragraph of the major opinion written in the case of *Planned Parenthood v. Casey* (1992), this was the sixth time in ten years that the Solicitor General of the United States had called for the reversal of *Roe v. Wade.*

In the three years after *Webster,* the composition of the Supreme Court had changed dramatically. The liberal justices William Brennan and Thurgood Marshall retired and were replaced by two nominees of President George H. W. Bush. Those nominees, David Souter in 1990 and Clarence Thomas in 1991, were generally thought at the time to be certain votes in favor of overruling *Roe.* The relatively unknown Souter, who had been a New Hampshire state court appellate judge, and then briefly a federal circuit judge on the Court of Appeals for the First Circuit, was considered by pro-choice women's groups as a "stealth candidate" because of his sparse written record of judicial decisions. Judge Thomas, then on the Court of Appeals for the District of Columbia Circuit, was a known conservative, although he had never expressed an opinion on *Roe v. Wade.* Since each of the four opponents of *Roe v. Wade* was still on the Court, it was expected that Justices Souter and Thomas would join Chief Justice Rehnquist, and Justices Scalia, Kennedy, and White, to form a six-person majority overruling, or severely cutting back, *Roe v. Wade.* This expected scenario left only Justices Blackmun, Stevens and possibly O'Connor to defend even the weakened "undue burden" version of *Roe.*

Planned Parenthood v. Casey involved a challenge to several provisions of the Pennsylvania Abortion Control Act of 1982. That law provided, among other restrictions, for a twenty-four-hour waiting period before a woman could have an abortion, during which time she would be provided information to permit her to give informed consent to the procedure. This information included the nature of the abortion procedure, the health risks of birth and abortion, the probable fetal age, and the availability of adoption and child support if the fetus were not aborted. Other provisions of the act in issue provided that one parent of a minor must give informed consent to an abortion for the minor, subject to a judicial bypass procedure and that a married woman must provide a written statement that she had notified her husband about the abortion.

As had been the case in *Webster*, once again there was a torrent of friend of the court filings, which included briefs by numerous states attorneys general; medical and religious groups; legislators and historians. When the dust settled, *Roe* was not overruled, but it was significantly diluted.

Justices O'Connor, Kennedy, and Souter wrote a joint opinion for five members of the Court, holding that the legal principle of stare decisis ("let it stand") prevented the overruling of *Roe v. Wade.* While all but the husband notification provision of the challenged parts of the Pennsylvania abortion law were upheld, there was no consensus on exactly what rights a woman had to choose an abortion or what standard governed the constitutionality of abortion restrictions. Justices O'Connor, Kennedy, and Souter felt that "the line should be drawn at viability, so that before that time the woman has a right to choose to terminate her pregnancy." Those three justices rejected the "rigid" trimester approach of *Roe,* choosing instead to apply the "undue burden" standard Justice O'Connor suggested in *Webster* to assess the validity of laws that attempted to regulate the abortion process before viability. Their view did not command a majority of the Court. Chief Justice Rehnquist, along with Justices White, Scalia, and Thomas, expressly rejected it, advocating instead the *Webster* standard that "States may regulate abortion procedures in ways rationally related to a legitimate state interest." Under this standard, these four justices considered each of the Pennsylvania abortion restrictions at issue to be constitutional. Justice Blackmun, by contrast, was in favor of retaining his *Roe* trimester and strict-scrutiny approaches and would have invalidated all of the challenged provisions of the Pennsylvania law.

The joint opinion of Justices O'Connor, Kennedy, and Souter began by noting that groups were still questioning a woman's right to "terminate her pregnancy in its early stages" some nineteen years after the *Roe* decision. Proclaiming that "Liberty finds no refuge in a jurisprudence of doubt," the opinion announced that "the essential holding of Roe v. Wade should be retained and once again reaffirmed." This result is rooted in "principles of institutional integrity and the rule of stare decisis," and is reached by the three justices despite "the reservations any of us may have in reaffirming the central holding of Roe," because those reservations "are outweighed by the explication of individual liberty we have given, combined with the force of stare decisis." The "individual liberty" protected by the Fourteenth Amendment included "personal decisions relating to marriage, procreation, contraception, family relationships, child rearing, and education." In the words of the joint opinion, "These matters, involving the most intimate and personal choices a person may make in a lifetime, choices central to personal dignity and autonomy, are central to the liberty protected by the Fourteenth Amendment. At the heart of liberty is the right to define one's own concept of existence, of meaning, of the universe, and of the mystery of human life."

In an elaborate and prolonged explication of the doctrine of stare decisis written by Justice Souter, and joined by Justices O'Connor, Kennedy, Blackmun, and Stevens, a majority of the Court concluded that nothing had happened since the decision in *Roe* to change its factual assumptions or to contest "Roe's central holding, that viability marks the earliest point at which the State's interest in fetal life is constitutionally adequate to justify a legislative ban on non-therapeutic abortions." *Roe* was distinguished from the discredited, and ultimately overruled, decisions in *Plessy v. Ferguson,* with its separate-but-equal doctrine, and *Lochner v. New York,* which invalidated limitations on workers' hours. In the majority's view, those cases were decided upon false factual assumptions relating respectively to the impact of racial segregation on African Americans and the operations of the free market.

Based upon this analysis, the majority called for the acceptance of the Supreme Court's resolution of the abortion rights dispute, stating that it was an example of "the Court's interpretation of the Constitution [calling] the contending sides of a national controversy to end their national division by accepting a common mandate rooted in the Constitution." Analogizing the abortion controversy in *Roe* to the school segregation issue resolved in *Brown v. Board of Education,* the majority concluded that when the Court reaches a decision in such controversial cases, "its decision requires an equally rare precedential force to counter the inevitable efforts to overturn it and to thwart its implementation."

While Justice Blackmun joined this part of the joint opinion, he again resorted to the apocalyptic rhetoric he had employed in *Webster,* beginning his opinion with the observations that "all that remained between the promise of Roe and the darkness of the plurality [in *Webster*] was a single, flickering flame," but that "now, just when so many expected the darkness to fall, the flame has grown bright." Nevertheless, in his view, "I fear for the darkness as four Justices anxiously await the single vote necessary to extinguish the light."

Blackmun did not join the other portions of the joint opinion, contending instead that it was proper to continue to employ a strict-scrutiny review of most abortion regulations, which, in his view, would invalidate all of the challenged portions of the Pennsylvania Abortion Control Law. He ended his opinion, as he had started, recording his fears for the future, stating, "I am 83 years old. I cannot remain on this Court forever, and when I do step down, the confirmation process for my successor may well focus on the issue before us today. That, I regret, may be exactly where the choice between the two worlds will be made."

Two separate opinions, one by Chief Justice Rehnquist and the other by Justice Scalia, both called for the overruling of *Roe v. Wade.* Four justices (Rehnquist, White, Scalia, and Thomas) joined both opinions. Chief Justice Rehnquist's opinion began by stating that "We believe that Roe was wrongly decided, and that it can and should be overruled consistently with our traditional approach to stare decisis in constitutional cases." In the view of these four justices, the undue-burden standard favored by Justices O'Connor, Kennedy, and Souter represented "an unjustified constitutional compromise, one which leaves the Court in a position to closely scrutinize all types of abortion regulations despite the fact that it lacks the power to do so under the Constitution."

The Rehnquist opinion went on to conclude that in characterizing a woman's right to terminate her pregnancy as a fundamental one, "the Court in Roe read the earlier opinions upon which it based its decision much too broadly. Unlike marriage, procreation, and contraception, abortion 'involves the purposeful termination of a potential life.'" As such application of a strict-scrutiny standard to evaluate restrictions upon abortion was improper. Instead, these four justices would rule that "a woman's interest in having an abortion is a form of liberty protected by the Due Process Clause, but States may regulate abortion procedures in ways rationally related to a legitimate state interest."

Justice Scalia began his opinion with his conclusion that "the States may, if they wish, permit abortion on demand, but the Constitution does not require them to do so. The permissibility of abortion, and the limitations upon it, are to be resolved like most important questions in our democracy: by citizens trying to persuade one another and then voting." Concluding that "the power of a woman to abort her unborn child" is not a liberty protected by the Constitution, Justice Scalia explained that he reached this conclusion "because of two simple facts: (1) the Constitution says absolutely nothing about it, and (2) the long-standing traditions of American society have permitted it to be legally proscribed."

In a direct and passionate assault upon the recognition of abortion rights, Justice Scalia wrote that "the emptiness of the 'reasoned judgment' that produced Roe is displayed in plain view by the fact that, after more than 19 years of effort by some of the brightest (and most determined) legal minds in the country, after more than 10 cases upholding abortion rights in this Court, and after dozens upon dozens of amicus briefs submitted in this and other cases, the best the Court can do to explain how it is that the word 'liberty' must be thought to include the right to destroy human fetuses is to rattle off a collection of adjectives that simply decorate a value judgment and conceal a political choice." Justice Scalia went on to reject the approach that called for acceptance of the Court's resolution of a divisive issue. Concluding that "the Imperial Judiciary lives," he stated that "to portray Roe as the statesmanlike 'settlement' of a divisive issue, a jurisprudential Peace of Westphalia that is worth preserving, is nothing less than Orwellian. Roe fanned into life an issue that has inflamed our national politics in general, and has obscured with its smoke the selection of Justices to this Court, in particular, ever since. And by keeping us in the abortion-umpiring business, it is the perpetuation of that disruption, rather than of any Pax Roeana that the Court's new majority decrees."

Justice Scalia also rejected the majority's appeal to honor its resolution of the divisive abortion issue by noting that the decision in *Scott v. Sandford* was thought by Chief Justice Taney to have resolved the controversy over slavery. He concluded his opinion by stating, "We should get out of this area, where we have no right to be, and where we do neither ourselves nor the country any good by remaining."

Partial-Birth Abortion 1: *Stenberg v. Carhart*

The Supreme Court did in fact "get out of [the abortion] area" for eight years after its decision in *Planned Parenthood v. Casey.* But, in 2000, it reentered the area to determine the constitutionality of a Nebraska statute that banned the partial-birth abortion procedure. In *Stenberg v. Carhart* (2000), a highly fractured Supreme Court invalidated that statute by a five-to-four vote, with eight of the nine justices writing their own separate opinions.

The procedure at issue in *Stenberg* was described by Justice Scalia as "horrible" and "visibly brutal." Justice Thomas referred to it as "a procedure that approaches infanticide," and a 1997 American Medical Association publication characterized partial-birth abortion as "ethically wrong." Justice Kennedy's dissenting opinion described the partial-birth abortion procedure, or dilation and extraction (D & X), in detail: "The fetus' arms and legs are delivered outside the uterus while the fetus is alive; witnesses to the procedure report seeing the body of the fetus moving outside the woman's body. . . . At this point, the abortion procedure has the appearance of a live birth. . . . With only the head of the fetus remaining in utero, the abortionist tears open the skull. . . . Witnesses report observing the portion of the fetus outside the woman react to the skull penetration. . . . The abortionist then inserts a suction tube and vacuums out the developing brain and other matter found within the skull."

Writing for a majority of five, Justice Breyer explained that the Nebraska statute was unconstitutional for two reasons. First, it failed to provide an exception where the partial-birth abortion procedure was necessary to preserve the woman's health. In the view of the majority, "The word 'necessary' in *Casey's* phrase 'necessary, in appropriate medical judgment, for the preservation of the life or health of the mother,' . . . cannot refer to an absolute necessity or to absolute proof." Instead, that standard was met "where substantial medical authority supports the proposition that banning a particular abortion procedure could endanger women's health." Second, as written, the majority believed that the statute was overbroad and could be interpreted to cover other abortion procedures, including the most common form, known as dilation and evacuation (D & E), utilized during the second trimester. As such the statute imposed an undue burden on a woman's ability to choose that form of abortion.

In a separate concurring opinion, Justice O'Connor joined the majority in striking down the Nebraska statute but provided guidelines under which the partial-birth abortion procedure could constitutionally be banned. She stated that "a ban on partial birth abortion that only proscribed the D & X method of abortion and that included an exception to preserve the life and health of the mother would be constitutional in my view."

Four justices wrote separate dissenting opinions. Justice Scalia was especially vehement, beginning his opinion with the following statement: "I am optimistic enough to believe that, one day, *Stenberg v. Carhart* will be assigned its rightful place in the history of this Court's jurisprudence beside *Korematsu* and *Dred Scott*. The method of killing a human child—one cannot even accurately say an entirely unborn human child—proscribed by this statute is so horrible that the most clinical description of it evokes a shudder of revulsion." As to the undue-burden standard utilized by the majority, Justice Scalia characterized this as "a value judgment, dependent upon how much one respects (or believes society ought to respect) the life of a partially delivered fetus, and how much one respects (or believes society ought to respect) the freedom of the woman who gave it life to kill it."

Justice Kennedy's dissenting opinion demonstrated his belief that the standards set forth in his joint opinion with Justices O'Connor and Souter in *Planned Parenthood v. Casey* had been grievously misapplied. In his view "*Casey* is premised on the States having an important constitutional role in defining their interests in the abortion debate. It is only with this principle in mind that Nebraska's interests can be given proper weight. The State's brief describes its interests as including concern for the life of the unborn and 'for the partially-born,' in preserving the integrity of the medical profession, and in 'erecting a barrier to infanticide.'" Justice Kennedy concluded that "States also have an interest in forbidding medical procedures that, in the State's reasonable determination, might cause the medical profession or society as a whole to become insensitive, even disdainful, to life, including life in the human fetus." Finally Justice Kennedy contended that the Nebraska statute should reasonably be construed only to apply to the partial-birth abortion, or D & X, procedure, eliminating any question of statutory overbreadth.

Justice Thomas's dissenting opinion began by contending that *Roe v. Wade* "was grievously wrong." He also contended that "the *Casey* joint opinion was constructed by its authors out of whole cloth. The standard set forth in the *Casey* plurality has no historical or doctrinal pedigree. The standard is a product of its authors' own philosophical views about abortion, and it should go without saying that it has no origins in or relationship to the Constitution and is, consequently, as illegitimate as the standard it purported to replace." Based on the decision reached by the majority, Justice Thomas argued that *Stenberg v. Carhart* represented "a reinstitution of the pre-*Webster* abortion-on-demand era in which the mere invocation of 'abortion rights' trumps any contrary societal interest."

Justice Thomas also wrote an extended analysis of the Nebraska statute and rules of statutory construction, concluding, consistently with Justice Kennedy, that only the partial-birth abortion procedure fell within the statute.

Finally Justice Thomas concluded that "States may, without a doubt, express this profound respect [for the life of the unborn] by prohibiting a procedure that approaches infanticide, and thereby dehumanizes the fetus and trivializes human life."

Chief Justice Rehnquist wrote a short dissenting opinion, reiterating his belief that *Planned Parenthood v. Casey* was "wrongly decided." He also joined the dissenting opinions of both Justice Kennedy and Justice Thomas.

Partial-Birth Abortion 2: A Reversal in Course

The Supreme Court revisited the issue of partial-birth abortion in *Gonzales v. Carhart* (2007), this time to determine the constitutionality of a federal statute that banned the use of the procedure except where it was necessary to save the woman's life. No health exception was provided, since Congress found that the partial-birth abortion procedure was never necessary to preserve the health of the woman and that other abortion options were available to her.

The composition of the Court had changed significantly in the seven years since the decision in *Stenberg v. Carhart.* President George W. Bush, a conservative Republican, was able to appoint a new chief justice and a new associate justice in his second term. They replaced Sandra Day O'Connor, who retired because of the declining health of her husband, and Chief Justice William Rehnquist, who died of thyroid cancer. In their place President Bush nominated John Roberts to be chief justice, and Samuel Alito to be associate justice. Alito's nomination followed the withdrawal of the previous nomination of Harriet Miers, who had been President Bush's White House Counsel. Her nomination had been opposed by conservative Republican leaders.

Both Roberts and Alito were well-known and highly respected federal circuit court judges. Roberts had served in the Reagan White House and had been a leading appellate advocate, having argued dozens of cases in the Supreme Court and served as chair of the appellate practice of a well-known Washington, D.C., law firm. Immediately before his nomination to the Supreme Court, he had served slightly more than two years as a circuit judge on the District of Columbia Circuit. He was sworn in as the seventeenth chief justice of the United States on September 29, 2005, after being confirmed by the Senate by a vote of seventy-eight to twenty-two.

Samuel Alito had served as an assistant to the solicitor general and as deputy assistant to the attorney general in the Reagan administration. Between 1990 and 2006, he served as a circuit judge on the Third Circuit Court of Appeals. He was confirmed by the Senate by a vote of fifty-eight to forty-two and sworn in as an associate justice on January 31, 2006.

The question of the precedential status of *Roe v. Wade* was a major topic in the confirmation hearings of both John Roberts and Samuel Alito. Roberts stated that he considered *Roe v. Wade* to be settled law and that there was nothing in his personal views that would prevent him from following it or *Planned Parenthood v. Casey.* Alito testified that he had an open mind on *Roe v. Wade.*

In *Gonzales v. Carhart,* the Court ruled by a five-to-four margin that the federal statute banning use of the partial-birth abortion procedure was constitutional. Chief Justice Roberts and Justice Alito joined the majority opinion of Justice Anthony Kennedy upholding the statute. Justices Thomas and Scalia joined that opinion, but also concurred in a separate opinion by Justice Thomas where he "reiterate[d] my view that the Court's abortion jurisprudence, including *Casey* and *Roe v. Wade* . . . has no basis in the Constitution."

Justice Kennedy's majority opinion found the statute banning use of the partial-birth abortion procedure overcame both of the constitutional infirmities found in the Nebraska statute in the *Stenberg* case. First the congressional statute was not unconstitutionally vague, because it utilized specific "anatomical landmarks" to differentiate what the opinion characterized as the "intact D&E" procedure from the more common second-trimester abortion procedures. These anatomical landmarks included the requirement that either the entire fetal head, or any part of the trunk past the navel, were drawn outside the woman's body during the procedure.

Second Justice Kennedy saw the principal issues as being "whether the Act furthers the legitimate interests of the Government in protecting the life of the fetus that may become a child," and "whether the Act, measured by its text in this facial attack, imposes a substantial obstacle to late-term, but previability, abortions."

Justice Kennedy concluded that "where it has a rational basis to act, and it does not impose an undue burden, the State may use its regulatory power to bar certain procedures and substitute others, all in furtherance of its legitimate interests in regulating the medical profession in order to promote respect for life, including life of the unborn." He went on to explain, echoing his dissenting opinion in *Stenberg v. Carhart,* that "D&E is a procedure itself laden with the power to devalue human life. Congress could nonetheless conclude that the type of abortion proscribed by the Act requires specific regulation because it implicates additional ethical and moral concerns that justify a special prohibition. Congress determined that the abortion methods it proscribed had a 'disturbing similarity to the killing of a newborn infant.'"

As to whether an exception was required where the procedure was necessary to preserve the woman's health, Justice Kennedy's majority opinion rejected the *Stenberg* approach that required such an exception where substantial medical authority supported the proposition that banning a procedure could endanger the woman's health. Justice Kennedy explained: "A zero tolerance policy would strike down legitimate abortion regulations, like the present one, if some part of the medical community were disinclined to follow the proscription. This is too exacting a standard to impose on the legislative power, exercised in this instance under the Commerce Clause, to regulate the medical profession." Here, while the Court did not give deference to the congressional findings that the partial-birth abortion procedure was never necessary to preserve a woman's health, the majority concluded that "the Act is not invalid on its face where there is uncertainty over whether the barred procedure is ever necessary to preserve a woman's health, given the availability of other abortion procedures that are considered to be safe alternatives."

Where a particular woman had true medical necessity requiring use of the partial-birth abortion procedure to preserve her health, she would have standing to make a challenge to the statute on an "as-applied" basis. Thus, while the statute was constitutional on its face, it could be challenged in its application to specific cases.

Justice Ginsburg delivered a forceful dissent on the behalf of four justices, including Justices Stevens, Souter, and Breyer. She took the unusual step of reading a summary of her opinion in open court, beginning with the statement that the four justices "strongly" dissent, a word absent from her written opinion.

Justice Ginsburg characterized the opinion of the Court as "alarming," explaining that "it refuses to take *Casey* and *Stenberg* seriously. It tolerates, indeed applauds, federal intervention to ban nationwide a procedure found necessary and proper in certain cases by the American College of Obstetricians and Gynecologists. . . . It blurs the line, firmly drawn in *Casey,* between previability and postviability abortions. And, for the first time since *Roe,* the Court blesses a prohibition with no exception safeguarding a woman's health."

The dissenters also shifted the privacy basis for the majority decision in *Roe v. Wade,* explaining that "legal challenges to undue restrictions on abortion procedures do not seek to vindicate some generalized notion of privacy; rather, they center on a woman's autonomy to determine her life's course, and thus to enjoy equal citizenship stature."

Justice Ginsburg's dissenting opinion went on, at great length, to discuss the factual findings of the trial courts in the separate cases at issue, especially in their conclusions that Congress was wrong in its statutory findings that the partial-birth abortion procedure was never necessary to preserve a woman's health and that it was not safer than other procedures available for late-term abortions.

More significantly the dissenters criticized the majority for invoking "moral concerns," and for invoking "an antiabortion shibboleth for which it concededly has no reliable evidence: Women who have abortions come to regret their choices, and consequently suffer from 'severe depression and loss of esteem.'" Justice Ginsburg's dissenting opinion saw the majoritiy's "way of thinking" as reflecting "ancient notions about women's place in the family and under the Constitution—ideas that have long since been discredited."

Justice Ginsburg's dissent also criticized the majority for blurring the line between pre- and post-viability restrictions upon abortion. She saw the references to the fetus as an "unborn child" and as a "baby" as evidencing an unconcealed "hostility to the right *Roe* and *Casey* secured." And she concluded that "one wonders how long a line that saves no fetus from destruction will hold in face of the Court's 'moral concerns.'"

At the end of her dissenting opinion, Justice Ginsburg referred to the addition of the new justices to the Court, observing that "though today's opinion does not go so far as to discard *Roe* or *Casey*, the Court, *differentially composed than it was when we last considered a restrictive abortion regulation*, is hardly faithful to our earlier invocations of 'the rule of law' and the 'principles of *stare decisis*.'" She went on to implicitly call for an overruling of the majority opinion, stating that "a decision so at odds with our jurisprudence should not have staying power." Justice Ginsburg concluded that "in sum, the notion that the Partial-Birth Abortion Ban Act furthers any legitimate governmental interest is, quite simply, irrational. . . . In candor, the Act, and the Court's defense of it, cannot be understood as anything other than an effort to chip away at a right declared again and again by this Court—and with increasing comprehension of its centrality to women's lives."

What Hath *Gonzales v. Carhart* Wrought?

Gonzales v. Carhart was the subject of immediate and extreme comment by both conservative and liberal observers of the Court. Liberal media commentators immediately attacked the decision. The *New York Times,* for example, accused the majority of "fundamental dishonesty," and saw the decision as coming "at a real cost to the Court's credibility, its integrity and the rule of law," while the *Los Angeles Times* saw the Court as having "executed an unconscionable U-turn on abortion." By contrast the *Boston Herald* saw the decision as "a decision all but the most pro-choice zealots can live with," particularly since the partial-birth abortion procedure "represents a direct affront to human decency," while the *Washington Times* saw it as a "victory for commonsense morality and for constitutional jurisprudence."

The *Gonzales v. Carhart* decision is notable for its potential impact on the Supreme Court's abortion jurisprudence in several ways. First, the majority opinion gave increased emphasis to legitimacy of legislative action to protect the life of the fetus, an emphasis also contained in the prior joint opinion in *Planned Parenthood v. Casey.* Second, by rebuffing a facial challenge to the Partial-Birth Abortion Act, the Supreme Court erected a significant obstacle to striking down future abortion regulations, although it left open the critical question of whether an across-the-board challenge to abortion legislation required a demonstration that there was no set of circumstances under which the legislation would be valid or the lesser standard of whether the legislation created an undue burden on a woman's right to terminate her pregnancy in a large fraction of the cases involving application of the statute. Third, by not mandating a health exemption to the application of an abortion statute, the Court changed prior case law, although only in a specific context where it explicitly found that safe alternatives were available to preserve the woman's health. Fourth, the opinion of the Court continued to lessen the distinction between the legislative power to legislate abortion regulations pre- and post-viability, a blurring that began in the joint opinion coauthored by Justice Kennedy in *Planned Parenthood v. Casey.* Fifth, and finally, *Gonzales v. Carhart* conclusively discarded the strict-scrutiny standard of review for abortion regulations from *Roe v. Wade,* replacing it with a rational-basis test.

Eleven

Judicial Power and a New Federalism

The Most Dangerous Branch?

In the introduction to this book, we quoted Alexander Hamilton's famous description of the Supreme Court in Federalist 78 as being "the least dangerous branch." Hamilton explained that the Court "has no influence over either the sword or the purse" and that it "may truly be said to have neither FORCE nor WILL, but merely judgment; and must ultimately depend upon the need of the executive arm even for the efficacy of its judgments."

Hamilton's description seems antiquated today, when the Supreme Court has changed the course of American society in so many different ways, as documented in the previous chapters. Indeed, in the views of those on both the left and the right, when the Court decides an issue against their preferred positions, the Supreme Court has become the *most* dangerous branch. In this final chapter, we review how the Court's power was expanded in the last half of the twentieth century and the first decade of the twenty-first in three discrete areas. First we examine how the Supreme Court was able to utilize the federal executive and state government to enforce its opinions in the areas of school desegregation and abortion rights, as well as the Court's extraordinary opinion in *Bush v. Gore,* which resolved the contested 2000 presidential election. Second we analyze two examples of how the Court created new constitutional rights, protecting both gay people from sodomy prosecutions and teenage criminals threatened with capital punishment. Finally we see how the Court took some initial steps to limit congressional power to enact legislation under the Commerce Clause, but then retreated.

The decisions discussed in this chapter were mainly decided by the Supreme Court while William H. Rehnquist served as chief justice. That Court, which served together without any new justices from 1994 until late 2005, finally changed with the addition of Chief Justice John Roberts in 2005 and Justice Samuel Alito in 2006.

Enforcing School Desegregation

As we saw in chapter 9, the reaction to the Supreme Court's decision in *Brown v. Board of Education* (1954) was massive resistance in the southern states. As such the Supreme Court was faced with the same problem that it faced before with Georgia, in the Cherokee cases (1831–32), and with Wisconsin, in *Ableman v. Booth* (1859). How would the Supreme Court's mandate for desegregation with all deliberate speed be enforced?

Unlike its previous experience in the nineteenth century with recalcitrant state governments that opposed its mandates, the Supreme Court found support for its desegregation mandate in the executive branch under President Dwight D. Eisenhower. This was somewhat surprising, since Eisenhower personally believed that the decision in *Brown v. Board of Education* was "wrong." Eisenhower had felt that the Supreme Court should only have ordered "equal opportunity" to African American children in public education. Nevertheless, when Arkansas used its National Guard to block access to the Little Rock public schools to defeat Court-ordered desegregation, President Eisenhower sent eleven hundred federal troops to Little Rock in September 1957. They remained there for more than two months and then were replaced by a federalized National Guard. This show of force enabled the Supreme Court to reject Arkansas's request for a delay of implementation of the desegregation order in Little Rock. Instead, the Court ordered immediate desegregation in the famous case of *Cooper v. Aaron* (1958), where all nine justices signed the opinion of the Court.

Eisenhower explained that he felt constitutionally bound, by his oath of office, to enforce orders of the Supreme Court, and that "I will obey." By the 1950s the Supreme Court had become a powerful and equal branch of government, supported by the public by a large margin, and able to secure support to enforce its orders because of this public attitude at that time. This was a sea change from the nineteenth century, when the Court's decisions in cases such as the Cherokee cases and *Scott* were disregarded by the political powers of that time.

Enforcing Abortion Rights

Roe v. Wade (1972) and the subsequent Supreme Court abortion decisions generated even lengthier and wider spread public opposition than the Court's desegregation cases. In the case of abortion, state opposition to recognition of a woman's right to choose to abort a fetus tested that right at the margins, enacting legislation that sought to put various limits on that choice. Justice Harry Blackmun, the author of *Roe v. Wade,* saw this resistance as paralleling the southern resistance to school desegregation, going so far as to cite *Cooper v. Aaron* in his majority opinion striking down a Pennsylvania abortion statute in *Thornburgh v. American College of Obstetricians & Gynecologists* (1986).

Before the decision in *Planned Parenthood v. Casey* (1992), the Supreme Court regularly struck down all types of abortion regulations at the state level, with few exceptions. In addition the Court upheld state statutes that limited abortion protesters in picketing abortion clinics and verbally signifying their opposition to abortion in front of those clinics. The most significant case in this area is *Hill v. Colorado* (2000), decided on the same day as *Stenberg v. Carhart,* which struck down the Nebraska legislation banning partial-birth abortions. By a six-to-three margin, *Hill* upheld the constitutionality of a Colorado law that made it a criminal offense to "knowingly approach another person within eight feet of such person, unless such other person consents, for the purpose of passing a leaflet or handbill to, displaying a sign to, or engaging in oral protest, education, or counseling with such other person in the public way or sidewalk area within a radius of one hundred feet from any entrance door to a health care facility."

Justice John Paul Stevens's majority opinion rejected a number of separate constitutional attacks on this statute based upon the First Amendment. He found that the statute did not regulate speech, but only the place in which some speech might occur. In addition he found that anti-abortion speech had not been singled out, because the statute applied to all demonstrators, no matter what their message or cause. Moreover he found that the state regulation was not related to the content of the speech. Finally Justice Stevens considered the eight-foot restriction as insufficient to preclude communication of a message through verbal or visual speech, since voices could be heard from that distance and signs and pictures could be seen.

Dissenting opinions by Justice Scalia and Justice Kennedy vigorously challenged the Court's conclusion. Justice Scalia, joined by Justice Thomas, felt that "what is before us, after all, is a speech regulation directed against the opponents of abortion, and it therefore enjoys the benefit of the 'ad hoc nullification machine' that the Court has set in motion to push aside whatever doctrines of constitutional law stand in the way of that highly favored practice." He also stated that "I have no doubt that this regulation would be deemed content based *in an instant* if the case before us involved antiwar protesters, or union members seeking to 'educate' the public about the reasons for their strike. . . . But the jurisprudence of this Court has a way of changing when abortion is involved."

The dissenting opinions of both Justice Scalia and Justice Kennedy went on at length to review prior opinions of the Court involving interpretation of the First Amendment, challenging the majority opinion's conclusions that the Colorado statute was constitutional. Justice Scalia concluded that the "deck" was "stacked" against abortion opponents in the Supreme Court, and that "today's decision is not an isolated distortion of our traditional constitutional principles, but is one of many aggressively proabortion novelties announced by the Court in recent years." He made the critical point that "for those who share an abiding moral or religious conviction (or, for that matter, simply a biological appreciation) that abortion is the taking of a human life, there is no option but to persuade women, one by one, not to make that choice. And as a general matter, the most effective place, if not the only place, where that persuasion can occur is outside the entrances to abortion facilities. By upholding these restrictions on speech in this place the Court ratifies the State's attempt to make even that task an impossible one."

Justice Kennedy's dissenting opinion also reviewed the First Amendment precedents of the Court in detail, but went on to add that, in his view, the decision conflicted with the underlying principles set forth in his joint opinion with Justices Souter and O'Connor in *Planned Parenthood v. Casey* (1992) because "the vital principle of the opinion was that in defined instances the woman's decision whether to abort her child was in its essence a moral one, a choice the State could not dictate." Barring protests at abortion clinics in the way specified by the Colorado law "tears away from the protesters the guarantees of the First Amendment when they most need it. So committed is the Court to its course that it denies these protesters, in the face of what they consider to be one of life's gravest moral crises, even the opportunity to try to offer a fellow citizen a little pamphlet, a handheld paper seeking to reach a higher law."

Deciding the Presidency: *Bush v. Gore*

The presidential election of 2000 came down to the votes of a single state—Florida. Without Florida, the Democratic candidate, Vice President Al Gore, was three votes short of a majority in the electoral college. The Republican candidate, Governor George W. Bush of Texas, could thus prevail only if he took Florida's twenty-five electoral votes.

On the day after the election, the Florida Division of Elections reported a 1,784-vote majority (out of more than 5.8 million votes cast) for Governor Bush. Vice President Gore then demanded a recount in four counties of so-called undervotes, and the American public was introduced to the concept of a "chad," which was a rectangular perforated area on a punch-card ballot, which the voters punched through next to the names of the candidates for whom they intended to vote. "Chadology" had its own mysterious lexicon, involving "hanging," "dangling," "dimpled," and "pregnant" chads, terminology that referred to the various degrees to which the chad had been dislodged or perforated.

Vice President Gore contended that actual votes had not been counted, because the machinery that read the punch cards had failed to record votes cast by individuals who failed to completely dislodge the chad from their punch-card ballot. The Florida Supreme Court ordered a recount. No standards were specified as to how those who were counting the ballots were to identify the intent of the voter from ballots in various states of chad detachment. In his book on the 2000 election, Judge Richard Posner of the Seventh Circuit Court of Appeals identified seven "alternative criteria for recovering a vote from an undervoted punchcard ballot by hand recount." The most conservative alternative was to count only chads that were hanging or swinging, while the most liberal alternative was to count "dangling chads plus all dimpled chads plus chads that are near an indentation or other mark (maybe made in pen or pencil rather than with the stylus that the voter is given to vote with) in the ballot, provided the counter feels able to discern the voter's intent from the character or location of the indentation or relation to other marks on the ballot."

In an unsigned opinion for five members of the Court, the Supreme Court observed in *Bush v. Gore* (2000) that "we are presented with a situation where a state court with the power to assure uniformity has ordered a statewide recount with minimal procedural safeguards. When a court orders a statewide remedy, there must be at least some assurance that the rudimentary requirements of equal treatment and fundamental fairness are satisfied." Seven members of the Court found a violation of the Equal Protection Clause in this standardless recount, but disagreed as to the appropriate remedy for this violation. Chief Justice Rehnquist, joined by Justices O'Connor, Scalia, Kennedy, and Thomas, found that a proper recount conducted under appropriate standards could not be completed in the six days remaining to assure that Florida's electoral votes would be counted under the so-called safe-harbor provision of federal law. That provision, contained in 3 U.S.C. § 5, made conclusive the state's selection of electors to vote in the electoral college, provided only that those electors were chosen under laws in place before Election Day, and the selection process was completed six days before the electoral college met.

Since the Supreme Court had previously ordered that the recount be stopped pending the Supreme Court's decision, the decision in *Bush v. Gore* assured the election of Governor Bush as president. The five-member majority implicitly recognized this, stating that "none are more conscious of the vital limits on judicial authority than are the Members of this Court, and none stand more in admiration of the Constitution's design to leave the selection of the President to the people, through their legislatures, and to the political sphere. When contending parties invoke the process of the courts, however, it becomes our unsought responsibility to resolve the federal and constitutional issues the judicial system has been forced to confront."

A concurring opinion by Chief Justice Rehnquist, joined by Justices Scalia and Thomas, found the Florida recount violated the safe-harbor provision of federal law both by departing from the Florida statutory framework in counting votes and by ordering the recount to continue in an open-ended fashion that could not have been completed in the six days remaining under that provision. Chief Justice Rehnquist's opinion emphasized that "we deal here not with an ordinary election, but with an election for the President of the United States." Quoting an earlier opinion from the New Deal era, he noted that "the importance of his election and the vital character of its relationship to and effect upon the welfare and safety of the whole people cannot be too strongly stated."

There were four dissenting opinions in *Bush v. Gore*. The senior dissenting justice, John Paul Stevens, criticized the majority for its "unstated lack of confidence in the impartiality and capacity of the state judges who would make the critical decisions if the vote count were to proceed." He concluded his opinion by stating that "time will one day heal the wound to that confidence [in the judicial system] that will be inflicted by today's decision. One thing, however, is certain. Although we may never know with complete certainty the identity of the winner of this year's Presidential election, the identity of the loser is perfectly clear. It is the Nation's confidence in the judge as an impartial guardian of the rule of law."

Justice Stephen Breyer, in his dissenting opinion, conceded the presidential election was of "fundamental national importance," but felt that importance was "political, not legal. And this Court should resist the temptation unnecessarily to resolve tangential legal disputes, where doing so *threatens to determine the outcome of the election.*" He concluded his opinion by noting that "we run no risk of returning to the days when a President (responding to this Court's efforts to protect the Cherokee Indians) might have said, 'John Marshall has made his decision; now let him enforce it!' . . . But we do risk a self-inflicted wound—a wound that may harm not just the Court, but the Nation. I fear that in order to bring this agonizingly long election process to a definitive conclusion, we have not adequately attended to that necessary 'check upon our own exercise of power,' 'our own sense of self restraint.' . . . What it does today, the Court should have left undone. I would repair the damage done as best we now can, by permitting the Florida recount to continue under uniform standards."

Justices Breyer and Souter would have permitted the recount to continue, but only under uniform standards to be established by the Florida courts for counting undervotes. Justices Ginsburg and Stevens would have left the election to the Florida courts, without any restriction. In her dissenting opinion, Justice Ginsburg noted that "the extraordinary setting of this case has obscured the ordinary principle that dictates its proper resolution: Federal courts defer to a state high court's interpretations of the State's own law. This principle reflects the core of federalism, on which all agree." Criticizing the conservative majority for retreating from its historic deference to federalism, she noted that "were the other Members of this Court as mindful as they generally are of our system of dual sovereignty, they would affirm the judgment of the Florida Supreme Court."

The unsigned majority opinion in *Bush v. Gore* received the same type of widespread criticism previously aimed at *Roe v. Wade.* Both liberal and conservative commentators found the opinion, which admittedly was rendered under an unusually brief and compressed schedule, legally insufficient. Six hundred twenty-five law professors signed a letter criticizing the decision and most law review commentary was unfavorable. Professor Randall Kennedy characterized the decision as a "scandal" initiated by a "Gang of Five," while Professor Cass Sunstein saw it as "illegitimate, undemocratic, and unprincipled." Professor Michael Klarman concluded that the "result can be explained only in terms of the conservative majority's partisan political preferences."

Only a few commentators, principally on the conservative side, approved the majority opinion. Viewing the decision from his usual pragmatic viewpoint, Judge Richard Posner saw *Bush v. Gore* as "a pragmatically defensible series of responses to a looming political and constitutional crisis" that resolved an important national problem. Despite Judge Posner's view, contemporary polls reported that some 53 percent felt that the opinion stopping the recount was based mainly on politics, while other polls showed that 37–65 percent believed that the justices were influenced by their personal political preferences. As predicted (and perhaps influenced) by the dissenting justices' opinions, public confidence in the Supreme Court began to erode. During the late 1990s, approximately 70 percent of the American people had a favorable view of the Supreme Court. Right after *Bush v. Gore,* polls recorded a slight dip to 68 percent, and that figure continued to decline, with attacks on the Court from both the right and the left, to a low of 57 percent in June 2005.

An even more intriguing statistical analysis of the voting of the justices after *Bush v. Gore* found that the five-person conservative majority in that case was less cohesive thereafter. While they had voted together nearly 48 percent of the time in decisions rendered by a five-to-four vote before that opinion, in the next four Supreme Court terms that agreement dipped to approximately 39 percent in such cases. David Cole, the Georgetown law professor who performed the analysis, saw this shift as demonstrating a "checking" function or power of public opinion upon the Court, with Justices Kennedy and O'Connor being particularly affected in their somewhat more liberal votes after *Bush v. Gore.* The accuracy of that analysis is borne out by the discussion in the next section of the decisions in *Lawrence v. Texas* and *Roper v. Simmons,* to which we now turn.

Creating Constitutional Rights 1: *Lawrence v. Texas* and Gay Sex

While *Bush v. Gore* demonstrated the Supreme Court's power to determine the outcome of a presidential election, *Lawrence v. Texas* and *Roper v. Simmons* show how the Court has created constitutional rights that are not apparent in the text of the Constitution itself. Both cases are particularly noteworthy because they overruled or abrogated earlier decisions and because they relied upon foreign law, two factors that subjected the Court to considerable criticism.

Lawrence v. Texas (2003) presented the question whether a Texas statute criminalizing homosexual sodomy (anal sex in that case) was constitutional. In *Bowers v. Hardwick* (1986), decided seventeen years earlier, the Court had refused to recognize any constitutional right to engage in such sexual activity, based upon what the five-member majority found to be long-settled prohibitions of such conduct.

Employing a Fourteenth Amendment due process analysis rooted in *Roe v. Wade,* as refined by *Planned Parenthood v. Casey,* five members of the Court in *Lawrence* expressly found that homosexuals had a protected liberty right to express their sexuality. Justice Kennedy's majority opinion explained that "when sexuality finds overt expression in intimate conduct with another person, the conduct can be but one element in a personal bond that is more enduring. The liberty protected by the Constitution allows homosexual persons the right to make this choice." The opinion expressly overruled *Bowers,* finding that it was based upon both bad history and bad law.

Relying upon a brief filed by historians, the Court explained that sodomy laws had been rooted in a more general prohibition of "non-procreative sexual activity" and that criminal prosecutions had typically been pursued only for nonconsensual and predatory behavior against minors or victims of assault. The same historical analysis indicated that criminal laws targeting same-sex couples had only developed in the last third of the twentieth century. Nine states had enacted such laws in the 1970s, but only four states continued to criminalize same-sex sodomy by 2003.

Justice Kennedy's majority opinion found a more basic objection to laws criminalizing same-sex sodomy. Finding that "for centuries there have been powerful voices to condemn homosexual conduct as immoral," he questioned "whether the majority may use the power of the State to enforce these views on the whole society through operation of the criminal law." Ruling that it could not, he found that the *Bowers* result could not stand in light of the reasoning of the joint opinion in *Planned Parenthood v. Casey.* The majority opinion also found support to overrule *Bowers* in academic criticism of that opinion, as well as in the decisions of several states to decriminalize homosexual sodomy, and a ruling by the European Court of Human Rights invalidating an Irish law prohibiting consensual homosexual sodomy.

Given the strong statements in favor of *stare decisis* in *Planned Parenthood v. Casey,* Justice Kennedy explained that it was nevertheless appropriate to overrule *Bowers* because that decision "had not induced detrimental reliance comparable to some instances where recognized individual rights are involved."

Concurring in the judgment, but not joining the majority opinion by Justice Kennedy, Justice O'Connor found the Texas statute unconstitutional as a violation of the Equal Protection Clause. She explained that it criminalized sodomy only between same-sex partners, and therefore was unconstitutional on that basis alone.

Justice Scalia filed a vigorous dissenting opinion, which was joined by Chief Justice Rehnquist and Justice Thomas. He began with a direct swipe at Justice Kennedy, by quoting the famous opening line from the joint opinion in *Planned Parenthood v. Casey* that "liberty finds no refuge in a jurisprudence of doubt." He then pointed out that the *Casey* opinion had applied *stare decisis* to save the twenty-year-old opinion in *Roe v. Wade,* but that *Lawrence* ignored the same doctrine in the case of a precedent that was only seventeen years old. From this arithmetic he concluded that "*Casey*'s extraordinary deference to precedent" was a "result-oriented expedient."

Justice Scalia then launched a frontal attack on the theory that the Due Process Clause somehow created a right to "liberty." Instead, he reasoned, the Fourteenth Amendment expressly provides that a state *may* deprive a person of liberty if due process of law is provided. Here, since the majority did not consider the right to engage in homosexual sodomy to be a fundamental right, that right could be abridged if there was a legitimate state interest in prohibiting that conduct. Justice Scalia found such a legitimate state interest in the underlying basis for laws prohibiting such conduct as bigamy, adultery, and beastiality, laws whose constitutionality could be endangered by the majority's reasoning.

Justice Scalia's dissenting opinion criticized the use of foreign law, pointing out that many foreign countries continued to criminally proscribe same-sex sodomy. He concluded that "today's opinion is the product of a Court, which is the product of a law-profession culture, that has largely signed on to the so-called homosexual agenda, by which I mean the agenda promoted by some homosexual activists directed at eliminating the moral opprobrium that has traditionally attached to homosexual conduct." He warned that the majority opinion "dismantles the structure of constitutional law that has permitted a distinction to be made between heterosexual and homosexual unions, insofar as formal recognition in marriage is concerned."

Justice Thomas also issued a short dissenting opinion, characterizing the Texas law as "uncommonly silly," but concluding that there was no basis for any general right of privacy or liberty set forth in the Constitution.

Attacks on *Lawrence v. Texas* and the Specter of Gay Marriage

Popular opposition to the *Lawrence* opinion soon emerged. Between May and July of 2003, Gallup polls found that public support for legalizing gay sexual relations dropped from 60 percent to 48 percent after the June opinion in *Lawrence.* Even more significantly, the specter raised by Justice Scalia's dissenting opinion that the majority opinion in *Lawrence* portended a legalization of gay marriage turned out to be prophetic. In November 2003, citing the majority opinion in *Lawrence,* the highest court of Massachusetts ruled that the Massachusetts legislature must provide for legal marriages for same-sex couples. This provoked an intense firestorm of controversy that affected the presidential election one year later, in November 2004, between the Republican, President George W. Bush, and his Democratic challenger, Senator John F. Kerry of Massachusetts. On the same day as the presidential election, the voters in eleven separate states voted in favor of state constitutional bans on same-sex marriages. The turnout of conservative voters in the states of Arkansas, Georgia, Kentucky, Michigan, Montana, Mississippi, Ohio, North Dakota, Oklahoma, Oregon, and Utah help reelect President Bush, who defeated Senator Kerry by more than three million popular votes.

Beginning in 2003, other state courts rejected constitutional attacks on prohibitions of same-sex marriages. The highest courts of Arizona, Indiana, Georgia, New York, New Jersey, Oregon, and Washington rejected the existence of any constitutional right under state or federal constitutions that would require state recognition of same-sex marriage. Various types of activists also attempted to extend the reasoning of *Lawrence* to legitimatize other sexual practices. Since Justice Kennedy's opinion had cautioned that the *Lawrence* case did not extend beyond private homosexual behavior, these attacks were largely unsuccessful. One notable example was the 2006 decision of the Utah Supreme Court, over the dissent of its chief justice, upholding the criminal prosecution for bigamy of a Mormon polygamist.

Creating Constitutional Rights 2: *Roper v. Simmons* and Cruel and Unusual Punishment

The Supreme Court's power to make new law has been manifested most dramatically in the interpretation of the Eighth Amendment's prohibition against "cruel and unusual punishments." In *Roper v. Simmons* (2005), once again in an opinion for a majority of five written by Justice Kennedy, the Court struck down as unconstitutional under this provision laws permitting the execution of a murderer who committed the crime prior to his eighteenth birthday. In reaching this conclusion, the Court "abrogated" its prior opinion in *Stanford v. Kentucky* (1989), which had been decided only sixteen years earlier.

The majority opinion in *Roper* explained the approach taken by the Court in making determinations under the "cruel-and-unusual-punishments" provision of the Eighth Amendment. The standard it followed was to determine whether a punishment was consistent with "the evolving standards of decency that mark the progress of a maturing society." In making this determination, "the Constitution contemplates that in the end *our own judgment* will be brought to bear on the question of the acceptability of the death penalty under the Eighth Amendment." Before exercising this independent judgment, however, the Court will first review "objective indicia of consensus, as expressed in particular by the enactments of legislatures that have addressed the question."

With respect to the objective criteria relevant to the question presented in *Roper,* Justice Kennedy's majority opinion focused on three specific developments. First, including those states that totally banned the imposition of capital punishment, some thirty states prohibited executions of individuals under the age of eighteen at the time of the *Roper* decision. Moreover the penalty was infrequently imposed even by those states that permitted it. Second, psychological studies indicated that teenagers under the age of eighteen were less mature, were more susceptible to negative influences, and had characters that were less well formed than those of adults. As such there was a weaker case for imposing capital punishment on a theory of retribution than there would be with an adult, and, in the majority's view, it was not clear whether executing such a teenager would have a deterrent effect on others of the same age. Third, five states that had permitted imposition of the death penalty for teenagers under eighteen at the time of the *Stanford* decision had since abandoned capital punishment for such teenagers.

Justice Kennedy's opinion found additional support for its conclusion in the "stark reality that the United States is the only country in the world that continues to give official sanction to the juvenile death penalty." Citing the United Nation's Convention on the Rights of the Child, the majority opinion pointed out that only seven countries other than the United States had executed juvenile offenders since 1990 and that all those countries had either abolished or disavowed the intent to impose such capital punishment in the future. As such "it is fair to say that the United States now stands alone in a world that has turned its face against the juvenile death penalty."

Four justices dissented, in two separate opinions. The principal dissenting opinion was that of Justice Scalia, writing for himself, Chief Justice Rehnquist, and Justice Thomas. Justice Scalia began his opinion by citing Alexander Hamilton's observation in Federalist 78 with which we began both this book and this chapter. He concluded that "what a mockery today's opinion makes of Hamilton's expectation, announcing the Court's conclusion that the meaning of our Constitution has changed over the past 15 years—not, mind you, that this Court's decision 15 years ago was *wrong*, but that the Constitution *has changed*. . . . The Court thus proclaims itself sole arbiter of our Nation's moral standards—and in the course of discharging that awesome responsibility purports to take guidance from the views of foreign courts and legislatures."

Justice Scalia then proceeded to question the application of some of the factors the majority had considered in reaching its conclusion that the death penalty should not be imposed upon so-called juvenile offenders. He noted that fewer than half of those states that impose capital punishment banned its imposition on such offenders, and that the psychological evidence relied upon by the majority was dubious, since leading authorities in the area had previously told the Supreme Court that such juveniles were capable of making mature decisions regarding whether to obtain an abortion without parental consent.

Justice Scalia's dissent also starkly criticized the Court for employing foreign authorities in support of its decision. He pointed out that the Court did not follow foreign law in areas such as establishment of religion and abortion and that the law of the United States was radically different from that of foreign countries in those areas. In the end, however, the positions of the three dissenting justices joining in Justice Scalia's opinion was that "more fundamentally, however, the basic premise of the Court's argument—that American law should conform to the laws of the rest of the world—ought to be rejected out of hand." While Justice O'Connor, in her separate dissent, disagreed with the majority on other issues, she pointedly noted that she did not agree with this portion of the dissenting opinion by Justice Scalia.

Interpreting Constitutional Rights: The Right of the People to Keep and Bear Arms

In *District of Columbia v. Heller* (2008), the Supreme Court was called upon to interpret the reach of the right to "keep and bear Arms" protected by the Second Amendment. That amendment provides that "a well regulated Militia, being necessary to the security of a free State, the right of the people to keep and bear Arms, shall not be infringed." By a vote of five to four, in a majority opinion written by Justice Antonin Scalia, the Court held that the amendment "guarantee[d] the *individual* right to possess and carry weapons in case of confrontation," which right was not limited by the prefatory clause. That clause was read "not [to] limit the latter [clause] grammatically, but rather announces a purpose." As such the majority held unconstitutional District of Columbia laws that completely banned the private possession of handguns in the home, and also mandated that any firearms permitted to be kept at an individual's home must be unloaded and disassembled or rendered inoperative by a trigger lock or other device. There were two dissenting opinions, the first by Justice John Paul Stevens and the second by Justice Stephen Breyer. Both dissenting opinions were joined by Justices Stevens, Breyer, Souter, and Ginsburg, who found that the Second Amendment (in the words of Justice Breyer's dissenting opinion) only "protects *militia-related,* not self-defense related, interests."

The dissenting opinions relied heavily on the Supreme Court's prior opinion in *United States v. Miller* (1939), which upheld against a Second Amendment challenge a federal conviction for transporting a short-barreled shotgun in interstate commerce. *Miller* concluded that "in the absence of any evidence tending to show that possession or use of a 'shotgun having a barrel of less than eighteen inches in length' at this time has some reasonable relationship to the preservation or efficiency of a well regulated militia, we cannot say that the Second Amendment guarantees the right to keep and bear such an instrument." Justice Scalia dismissed the ruling in *Miller,* arguing that the inapplicability of the Second Amendment there stemmed from the fact that "the *type of weapon at issue* was not eligible for Second Amendment protection."

All of the opinions in *Heller* recognized that the right protected by the Second Amendment (whatever its scope) was subject to limitations. Justice Scalia, for example, noted that the right "is not unlimited," and that the majority opinion should not be taken "to cast doubt on longstanding prohibitions on the possession of firearms by felons and the mentally ill, or laws forbidding the carrying of firearms in sensitive places such as schools and government buildings, or laws imposing conditions and qualifications on the commercial sale of arms," a list he noted was not "exhaustive."

In reaching their respective conclusions regarding the proper scope of the Second Amendment right to keep and bear arms, both Justice Scalia's majority opinion and Justice Stevens's dissenting opinion followed an analysis far different than that utilized in the Court's Eighth Amendment approach to discerning the meaning of "cruel and unusual punishments." Rather than consulting "evolving standards of decency" or "our own judgment," as Justice Kennedy did in *Roper v. Simmons,* both opinions consulted the historical record. Indeed the majority opinion manifests Justice Scalia's "textualism" approach, which he explained in his 1997 book, *A Matter of Interpretation: Federal Courts and the Law.* As applied to constitutional provisions, this approach focuses upon the *original* meaning of the constitutional text, not its *current* meaning. Indeed Justice Scalia's majority opinion begins its analysis with the text of the Second Amendment, relies upon "other leading documents of the founding era," and cites an amicus brief by professors of Linguistics and English to support its reading of the text. By contrast, in discussing what standard of review should be used to determine if a firearms regulation passed constitutional muster, Justice Breyer's dissenting opinion calls for "an interest-balancing inquiry," contending that "a court, not a legislature, must make the ultimate constitutional conclusion, exercising its '*independent judicial judgment*' in light of the whole record to determine whether a law exceeds constitutional boundaries." In response Justice Scalia called such an approach "judge-empowering" and observed that "a constitutional guarantee subject to future judges' assessments of its usefulness is no constitutional guarantee at all. Constitutional rights are enshrined with the scope they were understood to have when the people adopted them, whether or not future legislatures or (yes) even future judges think that scope is too broad."

This tension between Justice Scalia's majority opinion and Justice Breyer's dissenting opinion demonstrates that the proper method of discerning the existence or scope of a constitutional right still closely divides the Supreme Court and that neither the textualists nor the exponents of a "living constitution" have ended their debate on this issue at the Supreme Court.

Limiting Congressional Power: A New Federalism

Midway in the last decade of the twentieth century, there was a renewed and successful effort by conservative members of the Supreme Court to restore a balance between the power of state and federal governments to legislate on certain domestic matters. Popularly known as the "Federalist Revolution," this effort resulted in two highly controversial five-to-four opinions striking down congressional legislation in 1995 and 2000. Moreover, as noted in an article by Senator Charles E. Schumer of New York, between 1994 and 2004 the Supreme Court struck down some thirty-one federal statutes as unconstitutional, questioning the breadth of the power of Congress to enact legislation under both the Commerce Clause and the Fourteenth Amendment. This raised serious concerns in Congress because, as Senator Schumer pointed out, the Commerce Clause was "the source of a significant bulk of congressional legislation," representing the constitutional basis for some seven hundred statutes contained in the United States Code.

These decisions were particularly noteworthy since it had been nearly sixty years since the Supreme Court had previously found a federal statute unconstitutional where it had been based on the Commerce Clause power. In the interim, however, scholars of federalism had consistently criticized the New Deal cases we reviewed in chapter 6 as having departed from settled constitutional law. They began a "Constitution in Exile" movement that denounced the "Revolution of 1937" and called for a restoration of the prior limits imposed on the congressional power to legislate under the Commerce Clause. *Wickard v. Filburn* (1942) became the great white whale these scholars set out to kill, since, to them, it was the symbol of overarching federal power exercised under the Commerce Clause. As the former New Jersey state court judge Andrew Napolitano put it in his popular book, *The Constitution in Exile*, "*Wickard* must die. It is a precedent that allows the heavy hand of government to do whatever it wants."

Guns, Schools, and the Commerce Clause: *United States v. Lopez*

In *United States v. Lopez* (1995), the Supreme Court invalidated the Gun-Free School Zones Act of 1990, which prohibited the knowing possession of a firearm in a school zone. *Lopez* involved a twelfth-grade student who was arrested for carrying a concealed .38-caliber handgun and five bullets. In a majority opinion on behalf of five members of the Court, Chief Justice Rehnquist found that the statute exceeded the powers of Congress to legislate under the Commerce Clause.

Lopez generated six separate opinions, including three dissents. Chief Justice Rehnquist's opinion of the Court "start[ed] with first principles. The Constitution creates a Federal Government of enumerated powers." Recognizing that the New Deal Court had expanded the traditional reach of the power of the Commerce Clause, he noted that "even these modern-era precedents which have expanded congressional power under the Commerce Clause confirm that this power is subject to outer limits."

The question presented by *Lopez* was "whether the regulated activity 'substantially affects' interstate commerce." Chief Justice Rehnquist concluded that the legislation was defective because it failed to limit its reach by imposing any jurisdictional element tied to interstate commerce and also because it was not supported by any congressional findings that the activity at issue substantially affected interstate commerce. Most important, the legislation was attempting to regulate *noncommercial activity,* unlike the Court's New Deal jurisprudence.

Rejecting the argument that Congress had the power to regulate the possession of firearms within school zones based on a "cost-of-crimes" approach, Chief Justice Rehnquist stated that, if such an approach were adopted, "it is difficult to perceive any limitation on federal power, even in areas such as criminal law enforcement or education where States historically have been sovereign. Thus, if we were to accept the Government's arguments, we are hard pressed to posit any activity by an individual that Congress is without power to regulate." Moreover, "if Congress can, pursuant to its Commerce Clause power, regulate activities that adversely affect the learning environment, then, *a fortiori,* it can also regulate the educational process itself. Congress could determine that a school's curriculum has a 'significant' effect on the extent of classroom learning. As a result Congress could mandate a federal curriculum for local elementary and secondary schools because what is taught in local schools has a significant 'effect on classroom learning,' and that, in turn, has a substantial effect on interstate commerce."

In a concurring opinion for himself and Justice O'Connor, Justice Anthony Kennedy admitted that he had "some pause about today's decision," but joined the majority opinion with some additional "observations on what I conceive to be its necessary though limited holding." Justice Kennedy also urged that the doctrine of *stare decisis* be followed because "the Court as an institution and the legal system as a whole have an immense stake in the stability of our Commerce Clause jurisprudence as it has evolved to this point. *Stare decisis* operates with great force in counseling us not to call into question the essential principles now in place respecting the congressional power to regulate transactions of a commercial nature." Relying on the fact that the educational process was an area of traditional state concern, Justice Kennedy concluded that "the statute now before us forecloses the States from experimenting and exercising their own judgment in an area to which States lay claim by right of history and expertise, and it does so by regulating an activity beyond the realm of commerce in the ordinary and usual sense of the term."

In a separate and lengthy concurring opinion, Justice Clarence Thomas signaled his willingness in future cases to reexamine past Commerce Clause decisions from the New Deal era because he considered the "substantial-effects" test to confer a limitless police power upon Congress.

While three dissenting opinions were filed, the principal opinion was that of Justice Breyer, who was joined by three other justices in his dissent. He articulated three "basic principles of Commerce Clause interpretation." These were that Congress may regulate even local activities where they significantly affect interstate commerce; that Congress must consider "not the effect of an individual act (a single instance of gun possession), but rather the cumulative effect of all similar instances (that is, the effect of all guns possessed in or near schools); and that the Supreme Court must defer to Congress by giving it a degree of leeway in determining the existence of a significant factual connection between the regulated activity and interstate commerce." This required leeway was to be measured by the standard of whether or not Congress had a rational basis for its conclusion.

Violence against Women and the Commerce Clause: *United States v. Morrison*

Five years after *Lopez,* the Supreme Court decided the second major case in the so-called Federalist Revolution. In *United States v. Morrison* (2000), again in a five-to-four opinion, the Court struck down as unconstitutional the Violence Against Women Act of 1994. Unlike *Lopez*'s Gun-Free School Zones Act of 1990, this congressional legislation was enacted only after four years of hearings, ending with extensive findings, including the necessity for a federal civil remedy to address gender-motivated violence. *Morrison* presented the application of this statute to the case of a woman college student who was raped and suffered such severe depression that she was forced to withdraw from school.

Chief Justice Rehnquist's opinion of the Court noted the limited reach of the majority opinion in *Lopez.* He observed that "a fair reading of *Lopez* shows that the noneconomic, criminal nature of the conduct at issue was central to our decision in that case." Nevertheless, as in the prior case, the activity at issue in *Morrison* was also noneconomic. Moreover, while there were extensive congressional findings in *Morrison,* those findings were not binding upon the Supreme Court. Chief Justice Rehnquist explained that "the reasoning that petitioners advance seeks to follow the but-for causal chain from the initial occurrence of violent crime (the suppression of which has always been the prime object of the States' police power) to every attenuated effect upon interstate commerce. If accepted, petitioners' reasoning would allow Congress to regulate any crime as long as the nationwide, aggregated impact of that crime has substantial effects on employment, production, transit, or consumption. Indeed, if Congress may regulate gender-motivated violence, it would be able to regulate murder or any other type of violence since gender-motivated violence, as a subset of all violent crime, is certain to have lesser economic impacts than the larger class of which it is a part."

Chief Justice Rehnquist concluded that "we accordingly reject the argument that Congress may regulate noneconomic, violent criminal conduct based solely on that conduct's aggregate effect on interstate commerce. The Constitution requires a distinction between what is truly national and what is truly local."

The majority opinion in *Morrison* went on to conclude that Congress also lacked the power to pass the Violence Against Women Act under the Fourteenth Amendment. Chief Justice Rehnquist's opinion followed the nineteenth-century precedents we reviewed in chapter 4, including the *Civil Rights Cases* (1883), in concluding that congressional power under the Fourteenth Amendment was limited to enacting legislation to *correct* illegal *state* action, and could not be employed to legislate against wrongs committed by one individual against another individual.

There were two dissenting opinions, each of which was joined, in whole or in part, by four justices. Justice Souter's dissenting opinion accused the majority of attempting to devise a "new animating theory" that would be "useful in serving a conception of federalism." In his opinion, while the majority did not overrule the Court's New Deal Commerce Clause precedents, its "thinking betokens" a return to a more formalistic approach reminiscent of the jurisprudence that preceded the so-called Revolution of 1937. Justice Souter concluded that "the facts that cannot be ignored today are the facts of integrated national commerce and a political relationship between States and Nation much affected by their respective treasuries and constitutional modifications adopted by the people. The federalism of some earlier time is no more adequate to account for those facts today than the theory of laissez-faire was able to govern the national economy 70 years ago."

Justice Breyer's dissenting opinion addressed not only the Commerce Clause, but also congressional power under the Fourteenth Amendment. In his view that latter power was broad enough to support the legislation at issue, because it sought to correct failures by the states to provide an adequate remedy to women who were victimized by gender-motivated violence.

Federalism in Retreat: How Marijuana Saved the New Deal

Conservatives had hoped that the majority opinions in *Lopez* and *Morrison* would signal the beginnings of a widespread Federalist Revolution that would overturn the Revolution of 1937 and harpoon once and for all the dreaded decision in *Wickard v. Filburn.* Those hopes were dealt a shattering blow in *Gonzales v. Raich* (2005), where six members of the Court held that the federal Controlled Substances Act was a valid enactment under the Commerce Clause and could be used to prohibit the use of home-grown marijuana for personal medical purposes even where such use was permitted by California state law.

In an opinion for five members of the Court, Justice John Paul Stevens posed the question presented in the case in the following terms: "whether Congress' power to regulate interstate markets for medicinal substances encompasses the portions of those markets that are supplied with drugs produced and consumed locally." Having thus posed the question, Stevens's opinion immediately answered that "well-settled law controls our answer. The [Controlled Substances Act] is a valid exercise of federal power, even as applied to the troubling facts of this case." Stevens explained that "our case law firmly establishes Congress' power to regulate purely local activities that are part of an economic 'class of activities' that have a substantial effect on interstate commerce."

Stevens's majority opinion relied heavily upon *Wickard v. Filburn,* which he found "of particular relevance." Justice Stevens explained that "*Wickard* . . . establishes that Congress can regulate purely intrastate activity that is not itself 'commercial,' in that it is not produced for sale, if it concludes that failure to regulate that class of activity would undercut the regulation of the interstate market in that commodity. The similarities between this case and *Wickard* are striking."

Attempts to distinguish *Wickard* as having involved economic activity, and thus to bring the case within the ambit of *Lopez* and *Morrison,* were rejected. The majority opinion explained that "unlike those at issue in *Lopez* and *Morrison,* the activities regulated by the CSA are quintessentially economic. 'Economics' refers to 'the production, distribution, and consumption of commodities.'" Since Congress had a rational basis upon which to reach its conclusion that strict federal regulation was required, the Controlled Substances Act was a constitutional exercise of congressional power under the Commerce Clause.

Two of the justices who had joined the majority opinions in *Lopez* and *Morrison* joined in the conclusion that the Controlled Substances Act was constitutional. Justice Anthony Kennedy joined Justice Stevens's opinion of the Court, while Justice Antonin Scalia filed a separate concurring opinion. In his concurrence Justice Scalia relied upon the opinion in *Wickard,* finding no contradiction between that opinion, on the one hand, and those in *Lopez* and *Morrison,* on the other hand. He explained: "As we implicitly acknowledged in *Lopez,* . . . Congress's authority to enact laws necessary and proper for the regulation of interstate commerce is not limited to laws directed against economic activities that have a substantial effect on interstate commerce. Though the conduct in *Lopez* was not economic, the Court nevertheless recognized that it could be regulated as 'an essential part of a larger regulation of economic activity, in which the regulatory scheme could be undercut unless the intrastate activity were regulated.'"

Three justices dissented, in two opinions. Justice Sandra Day O'Connor, joined in full by Chief Justice William Rehnquist and in part by Justice Clarence Thomas, saw the federal preemption of the California law permitting the use of homegrown marijuana for medicinal purposes as inconsistent with the federalist view that states could function, in the words of Justice Brandeis, as "laboratories" to try "novel social and economic experiments without risk to the rest of the country." In addition Justice O'Connor saw the majority opinion as creating both a rule and a result that were "irreconcilable" with the decisions in *Lopez* and *Morrison.*

In the final part of her lengthy dissenting opinion, a part not joined by Justice Thomas, Justice O'Connor stated that "if I were a California citizen, I would not have voted for the medical marijuana ballot initiative; if I were California legislator I would not have supported the Compassionate Use Act. But whatever the wisdom of California's experiment with medical marijuana, the federalism principles that have driven our Commerce Clause cases require that room for experiment be protected in this case."

In a solitary but lengthy dissent, Justice Thomas began by stating that "if Congress can regulate this under the Commerce Clause, then it can regulate virtually anything—and the Federal Government is no longer one of limited and enumerated powers." In his view, the use of the Controlled Substances Act to override the California medical marijuana law was an encroachment by Congress on the "States' traditional police powers to define the criminal law and to protect the health, safety, and welfare of their citizens." Moreover, quoting the majority opinion in *Morrison,* Justice Thomas pointed out that "this Court has never held that Congress can regulate noneconomic activity that substantially affects interstate commerce."

Appealing to basic principles of federalism, Justice Thomas complained that "one searches the Court's opinion in vain for any hint of what aspect of American life is reserved to the States." He concluded that "our federalist system, properly understood, allows California and a growing number of other States to decide for themselves how to safeguard the health and welfare of their citizens."

With the decision in *Gonzales v. Raich,* the Federalist Revolution seen to have had its beginnings in *Lopez* and *Morrison* ended, or at least stalled pending new appointments to the Supreme Court by future presidents. Congressional power broadly to legislate under the Commerce Clause was strengthened, and the New Deal was saved. At the beginning of the twenty-first century, the Commerce Clause was safely reestablished by the Supreme Court of the United States as the great *fons et origo* of congressional power to regulate all forms of economic activity. The process begun by John Marshall enabling the federal government to shape American society thus continued unabated. The Supreme Court was at the zenith of its power.

Conclusion

> You cannot step into the same river twice,
> for new waters constantly flow in.
>
> *Heraclitus*

To understand the outcomes of Supreme Court decisions at any point in its history requires an assessment of three factors—the presence of strong-willed justices who helped to shape the Court's jurisprudence, the influence of the dominant political culture of the times, and the existence of deeply held public attitudes on specific controversial issues. The Supreme Court lives in this history and has not escaped it. Since these factors have both changed and interacted differently throughout the Court's history, the quotation from the pre-Socratic philosopher Heraclitus that heads this chapter nicely captures the flux that characterizes the Court's development over time.

The Supreme Court and the Currents of History

In this chapter we will first review examples of how each of these three factors illuminates the work of the Supreme Court in its 220-year history. Then we will examine how the interaction of these factors helps to explain those cases in which the Court has successfully resolved an issue of constitutional law, and those in which it has not.

The Influence of Specific Justices

The power granted by Article II, Section 2, of the Constitution to nominate and appoint (with the advice and consent of the Senate) justices to the Supreme Court is among the most significant granted to the president. As we discussed in the introduction, the appointments by Presidents John Adams and Andrew Jackson of Chief Justices John Marshall and Roger Taney dramatically shaped the Supreme Court in its early years, while the appointments of Justices Antonin Scalia and Clarence Thomas more recently by Presidents Ronald Reagan and George H. W. Bush steered the Court to a more conservative position in several areas of constitutional law. In this section we review chronologically the influence of other key justices on the Court's jurisprudence, starting with several associate justices whose dissenting opinions planted seeds for future changes in constitutional law.

The Dissenters

From the time of Roger Taney's death in 1864 until the appointment of William H. Taft in 1921, there were four chief justices who did little to change the Supreme Court. These were Salmon P. Chase (1864–73), Morrison R. Waite (1874–88), Melville W. Fuller (1888–1910), and Edward D. White (1910–21). In this fifty-seven-year period, one of the most dominant justices was Stephen J. Field, an associate justice who served between 1863 and 1897—for one month longer than Chief Justice Marshall's tenure on the Court. Field was born and educated in Massachusetts, and he graduated from Williams College. He moved to California in 1849 and served in legislative and judicial posts in that state, including on the California Supreme Court. A pro-union Democrat, Field was appointed to the Supreme Court of the United States by President Abraham Lincoln. He wrote more than six hundred opinions during his lengthy service on the Court.

Field's focus was on protecting property rights. Rooted in natural-law fundamental-rights theories, his jurisprudence found freedom of labor and contract protected against government regulation by the Due Process Clause of the Fourteenth Amendment. His dissenting opinions in the *Slaughterhouse Cases* in 1873 and *Munn v. Illinois* in 1877 formed the basis for the Supreme Court's later adoption of the theory of substantive due process to protect the freedom of parties freely to contract without interference by state or federal government regulation. That theory reached the apex of its influence in the economic area in cases such as the often-reviled *Lochner v. New York* in 1905, as well as in several decisions of the Taft Court in the 1920s.

As shown by Justice Field's career on the Supreme Court, dissenting opinions often form the basis for later changes in constitutional doctrine, laying the groundwork for reconsideration and refinement of such doctrines. In this respect the career of Justice John Marshall Harlan in the late nineteenth and early twentieth centuries is a powerful example. Appointed to the Court in 1877 by President Rutherford B. Hayes, Harlan served on the Court for thirty-four years, until his death in 1911. Harlan's vocal dissenting opinions protesting the invalidation of federal civil rights legislation in the *Civil Rights Cases* in 1883 and the upholding of Jim Crow segregation in *Plessy v. Ferguson* in 1896 were vindicated in the twentieth and twenty-first centuries. His invocation of a "color-blind Constitution" was embraced in later cases, including the 2007 majority opinions in *Parents Involved in Community Schools v. Seattle School District No. 1,* particularly in Justice Thomas's concurring opinion.

In the first third of the twentieth century, Oliver Wendell Holmes Jr. was the most effective dissenter in the long run. A well-known legal scholar and author, Holmes served on the Massachusetts Supreme Judicial Court for twenty years, ending as its chief justice. At the age of sixty-one, he was appointed to the Supreme Court of the United States in 1902 by President Theodore Roosevelt and served until his retirement in 1932 at the age of ninety, becoming the oldest justice ever to serve on the Court. During his nearly thirty-year tenure, he wrote more than 850 opinions for the Court, but he is best remembered for dissenting opinions that would later change constitutional law. Like Justice Antonin Scalia today, Holmes's opinions were often lyrical, sometimes trenchant, and typically clear.

Two of his dissenting opinions demonstrate these qualities well. Writing in *Abrams v. United States* in 1919 regarding the scope of the protections secured by the First Amendment for political dissenters, he wrote that speech could only be punished where it posed an imminent threat of an immediate interference with the purposes supporting a law because "the best test of truth is the power of the thought to get itself accepted in the competition of the market. . . . That at any rate is the theory of our Constitution. It is an experiment, as all life is an experiment." Similarly, in dissenting in *Lochner v. New York* in 1905, he noted that he would have upheld the New York statute setting maximum hours for bakers because "this case is decided upon an economic theory which a large part of the country does not entertain. . . . The Fourteenth Amendment does not enact Mr. Herbert Spencer's [a noted Social Darwinist] *Social Statics.*"

In both these areas, Holmes's dissents ultimately became law. In other areas, however, his majority opinions, particularly on questions of race and eugenics, failed to stand the test of time because of their reactionary nature.

The Chief Justices

In the period following World War II, two chief justices had significant impacts upon the Supreme Court's decisions under their leadership. The first of these was Earl Warren, who was appointed to the Court in 1953 by President Dwight D. Eisenhower. Warren served for fifteen years, until his retirement in 1969.

Now best remembered for his Court's decisions in the area of criminal procedure—most notably the rights warnings originating in the 1966 opinion in *Miranda v. Arizona*—Warren was also instrumental in bringing about political reapportionments based upon the principle of one person, one vote. His greatest accomplishment, however, was ending de jure racial segregation and overruling the separate-but-equal doctrine rooted in *Plessy v. Ferguson.* When he came to the Supreme Court in 1953, the first major oral argument Warren presided over was that held in *Brown v. Board of Education,* which was being reargued after the death of the prior chief justice, Fred Vinson. The Court had been divided under Vinson, and Warren carefully over the next months following the oral argument, brought each of the justices around so that a unanimous opinion written by him could be announced. To attain unanimity and lessen the southern backlash, he also decided to defer a ruling on remedy until later. Following *Brown,* Warren obtained another unanimous Court in the 1958 decision in *Cooper v. Aaron* to stop the State of Arkansas from blocking the desegregation of the Little Rock public schools.

From the 1958 decision in *Cooper v. Aaron* to Warren's retirement in 1969, the Warren Court struck down every effort to impede integration that it reviewed. These overturned efforts included closing the public schools, "freedom of choice" plans, and dual school systems.

The second post–World War II chief justice whose influence on the Court was both significant and measurable was William H. Rehnquist. Appointed as an associate justice by President Richard M. Nixon in 1972, he was elevated to chief justice by President Ronald Reagan in 1986. He served on the Court until his death in 2005, and his tenure as chief justice was surpassed only by John Marshall, Roger Taney, and Melville Fuller.

Rehnquist began his service as an associate justice as an isolated dissenter. That isolation was so profound that his law clerks presented him with a Lone Ranger doll, which he kept displayed in his chambers. But, over time, his lonely dissents did change the law in several areas, after other conservative justices joined the Court. Two areas of change in constitutional law are particularly noteworthy. First, as we traced in chapter 8, Rehnquist's 1985 dissent in *Wallace v. Jaffree,* where the majority struck down a state law permitting a one-minute period of silence for public school students to meditate or pray silently, carefully reviewed the history of the Establishment Clause, and called for a more narrow interpretation of its prohibition against establishing a religion. While his specific views were never embraced by a majority on the Court, the concepts used in deciding Establishment Clause cases were reframed, particularly in the area of aid to religious schools. This more lenient approach can be seen in cases such as *Agostini v. Felton* in 1997, which overturned an earlier precedent banning such aid, and in Rehnquist's own 2002 majority opinion upholding a state voucher program in *Zelman v. Simmons-Harris.* That program permitted parents to spend their vouchers to educate their children in religious schools.

A second area of important change under the Rehnquist Court was in the key field of federalism. As we saw in chapter 11, Chief Justice Rehnquist wrote the majority opinions in both *United States v. Lopez* (1995) and *United States v. Morrison* (2000). Those decisions struck down federal legislation seeking respectively to outlaw the possession of guns in school zones and to redress violence against women, by making both federal violations. Rehnquist's majority opinions invalidated both statutes as beyond congressional power under the Commerce Clause, limiting that power for the first time since the days of Franklin Roosevelt's New Deal. This was part of Rehnquist's overall view of the need to rebalance the federal-state relationship to afford more power to the states.

The Influence of the Dominant Political Culture

The dominant political culture of the time serves to explain many decisions of the Supreme Court throughout its history. This factor clearly interacts with the others.

For example appointments to the Court, as we have seen in the preceding discussion in this chapter, themselves often reflect the dominant political culture, since they are made initially by the president of the prevailing political party, but only with the concurrence of the United States Senate. The debates in recent years over prospective appointees, particularly in the context of divided government, become windows into what is thought to be the accepted majority views on constitutional issues.

This section will examine two examples of the influence of the dominant political culture on Supreme Court decisions. First, the discussion in chapter 5 of the evolution of the limits placed upon government regulation of business in the post–Civil War period through the early 1930s reflects the ascendancy of generally accepted principles supporting the domestic growth of industrial capitalism. Reflected in the inaugural addresses of the Republican presidents up to the turn of the twentieth century, these principles called for fostering American business through such efforts as protective tariffs, internal improvements in transportation to open up new markets and facilitate commercial intercourse on an interstate basis, and a stable, "sound" currency. Notably many of these probusiness views were shared by Grover Cleveland, the only Democratic president to serve between the Civil War and 1913.

The Supreme Court also contributed to the effort to assist the growth of American business by limiting the permissible scope of governmental regulation of business throughout the 1800s and into the 1930s. Early populist calls for strict regulation of monopoly powers were heeded initially by the Court in the Granger cases of 1877 but, with the guidance of Justice Field, the Court slowly cabined such regulation, ultimately adopting the concepts of substantive due process and freedom of contract to protect corporate property rights from strict governmental regulation. This same view of the need to protect business is revealed in the construction of the antitrust laws in the famous *Standard Oil* decision of 1911, where the majority opinion of Chief Justice White interpreted the biblical prohibitions of the Sherman Act against *any* restraint of trade only to forbid *unreasonable* restraints. The opposition to regulation continued, with some detours, into the 1930s, fostered by President Warren Harding's appointments of George Sutherland and Pierce Butler, who would join James McReynolds and Willis Van Devanter to become the "Four Horsemen," championing freedom of contract.

A second example of the importance of the dominant political culture in Supreme Court decisions was examined in chapter 6, which covered the Supreme Court and the New Deal. An economic upheaval in the form of the Great Depression caused great suffering and called for new approaches and remedies, including a vast expansion of regulation of business at the federal level. While resisted by the Four Horsemen and others on the Court at the time Franklin D. Roosevelt was first elected in 1932, their favored concepts of freedom of contract, limited federal power under the Commerce Clause, and retained states' rights were swept overboard in the economic storms of the time. Again, this sea change in doctrine was accelerated by vast public support for the "Roosevelt Revolution," and Roosevelt's resulting appointment power, which in turn was strengthened by a strong Senate majority held by his Democratic Party. By the end of his presidency, he was able to replace six of the nine justices who sat when he was first inaugurated, and who had invalidated many of his early legislative victories. Significantly four of his new justices had served in some capacity in the Roosevelt New Deal administrations and one (Hugo Black) had been a pro–New Deal senator. These new justices had readily embraced the New Deal mindset that regulation was necessary to restore economic prosperity. As such they readily expanded the powers of the federal government under the Commerce Clause beyond any limits discernable at the time, while simultaneously restricting the powers reserved to the states. In the New Deal era, the dominant political culture overturned the precedent of several decades in a few years.

The Influence of Public Attitudes

A third factor that helps explain some decisions of the Supreme Court is issue specific, relating to strong public attitudes on particular topics. As we noted in the introduction, the 2008 decision in *District of Columbia v. Heller,* discussed in chapter 11, is a good example, since it reflected a strong public sentiment in favor of an individual's right to own a handgun for self-defense. Two other examples further illustrate the influence on the Supreme Court of strong public sentiment on specific issues. First, the 1883 decision in the *Civil Rights Cases,* which invalidated federal legislation mandating the opening of public accommodations such as hotels and theaters to freed African Americans, reflected strong public views at the time, both in the dominant political culture and in the specific public attitude on the issue of forced integration. The latter was felt to be an unwarranted intrusion into a private, social realm beyond the proper reach of government. As the discussion in chapter 4 noted, there was a distinction drawn between *legal* and *social* equality.

Voters from both major political parties overwhelmingly shared this view, and strongly opposed mandatory social integration. The *Hartford Weekly Times,* a Democratic newspaper, compared the preferred treatment accorded the freedmen to the contemporary refusal by the resort hotel at Saratoga to admit Jews as lodgers. It stated that "no one questioned [the] right" of the resort owner to implement such exclusions, and that "no person, black or white, male or female, has a right to force himself or herself upon the premises and the bed and board of the owner of a hotel or saloon." Even the radical Republican *Chicago Tribune* opposed the Civil Rights Act on the following reasoning: "Is it not time for the colored race to stop playing baby? The whites of America have done nobly in outgrowing the old prejudices against them. They cannot hurry this process by law. Let them obtain social equality as every other man, woman, and child in this world obtain it,—by showing themselves in their lives the social equals of those with whom they wish to consort. If they do this, year by year the prejudices will die away." Thus most adherents of both major political parties opposed what they perceived to be "special privileges" afforded only to African Americans.

Another example of the influence on the Court of strong public attitudes on specific issues may be found in the initial treatment of Communists by the Supreme Court in the 1951 cold war decision in *Dennis v. United States.* That case upheld the convictions under the Smith Act of eleven high officials of the United States Communist Party. As we saw in chapter 7, the case was decided at the height of the cold war with Russia, and South Korea was invaded by North Korea while the case was on appeal.

Many of the opinions in the *Dennis* case refer, both directly and indirectly, to the anticommunist tenor of public opinion at the time. Thus Chief Justice Fred Vinson's plurality opinion for four members of the Court narrowed First Amendment protections, commenting on "the inflammable nature of world conditions." Justice Frankfurter's concurring opinion more directly noted the "impregnating atmosphere of the times," while, in dissent, Justice Hugo Black noted that "public opinion being what it now is, few will protest the conviction of these Communist petitioners." Black referred to hopes that "in calmer times, when present pressures, passions and fears subside, this or some later Court will restore the First Amendment liberties to the high preferred place where they belong in a free society."

Triumphs and Tragedies

The interaction of the three factors we have discussed in this chapter helps to explain why some decisions of the Supreme Court on controversial questions of constitutional law gained general acceptance while others did not. The history of the Supreme Court suggests that it has been most successful when its judgments reached the same outcomes as those suggested by both the dominant political culture and the strongest public attitudes on the issues presented.

One example illustrating a successful resolution of an important constitutional issue is that of the 1964 decisions in the *Heart of Atlanta Motel* and *McClung* cases, which found constitutional those provisions of the Civil Rights Act of 1964 that mandated full and equal access by all to places of public accommodation. The Supreme Court faced formidable precedential barriers to upholding this legislation, since the 1883 decision in the *Civil Rights Cases* had so narrowly interpreted the Fourteenth Amendment that it could not be used to validate the 1964 act without overruling those cases. Given this problem, the Court instead turned to the Commerce Clause to support the power of Congress to ban discrimination in public accommodations, since the scope of that clause had been vastly expanded during the New Deal years of the Court.

As we saw in chapter 9, the decisions in the 1964 cases reflected the emerging political power of the civil rights movement and its acceptance by Presidents John F. Kennedy and Lyndon B. Johnson. While many (but not all) in the South opposed the Civil Rights Act of 1964, the successes of the sit-in strategy, coupled with the violence directed against peaceful protesters in such venues as Birmingham, Alabama, in 1963, galvanized both public-opinion leaders and a shocked public itself, which had witnessed the violence on national television, to support the integration of public facilities. Both the dominant political culture and public attitudes had shifted greatly since the days of the *Civil Rights Cases* and *Plessy v. Ferguson,* leading to a different result in the 1964 public accommodations decisions.

By contrast the Supreme Court has been largely unsuccessful when it has attempted to resolve an issue of constitutional law where both the dominant political culture and public attitudes were strongly divided on the proper outcome. For example the 1857 *Scott v. Sandford* decision attempted to resolve the question of whether or not Congress had the power to ban slavery in the territories. This divisive issue had literally reshaped the political party system, destroying one major party and creating another, while realigning the remaining party on sectional lines. No public consensus had emerged when the Court attempted to resolve the constitutional issue once and for all time. Thus, whatever the outcome on the question, any decision on the power of Congress to ban slavery in the territories was likely to provoke great opposition. That inherent difficulty was further exacerbated by Chief Justice Taney's inflammatory rhetoric directed against African Americans.

The 1973 decision in *Roe v. Wade* provides another example of an unsuccessful resolution of a controversial issue of constitutional law. As we saw in chapters 9 and 10, *Roe v. Wade* galvanized a political revolution of conservative religious opposition, which contributed to returning the Republican Party to ascendancy for much of the last quarter of the twentieth century. By announcing a broad constitutional right of a woman to choose to abort a fetus, and by setting out in minute detail precise parameters for that right, the Supreme Court entered an area of deep public division over fundamental religious and moral issues, where, as in *Scott v. Sanford,* no consensus had emerged, either in the dominant political culture or in the attitudes of the public.

These examples are not advanced to justify an argument that the Supreme Court should follow the election returns. What they and other examples set forth in this book do suggest, however, is that the Supreme Court's continued authority and acceptance by the public will generally require the avoidance of broad pronouncements where the country is deeply divided on an issue and the political process has not yet come to a consensus or an acceptable political compromise. Premature attempts at a Court-imposed solution are often unsuccessful, particularly where, as in *Scott v. Sandford* and *Roe v. Wade,* the political process is actively addressing the issue.

One way out when the Court is obliged to confront such an issue is to proceed in small steps over time and to leave a final resolution to a later date while the issue receives additional attention in the political process or until public passion has been dissipated. Here, three examples from cases we have previously discussed may be instructive. In *Scott* itself, as we discussed in chapter 2, the Supreme Court could have avoided deciding the issue of congressional power to ban slavery in the territories in several ways. One approach would have been to end the discussion of other issues after deciding that the Court lacked jurisdiction. Indeed Justice Nelson's original draft opinion did avoid the larger questions but was rejected because of the felt need by politicians for the Court to resolve the broader issues.

The World War II Japanese internment cases discussed in chapter 7 demonstrate an attempt to avoid going too far too fast where public attitudes are inflamed during a period of war, and the Court consequently could be pressured to reach a popular result that would narrow the proper scope of civil liberties. Whatever the merits of what *was* decided in cases such as *Korematsu v. United States,* it bears emphasis that the Court did not reach or resolve the legality of the relocation orders issued to Japanese citizens and residents of the west coast. Instead, Korematsu's conviction was upheld in 1944 only on the charge that he had illegally remained in a military area. The broader question of the legality of the relocation orders was left unresolved.

Another way of avoiding the decision of broader questions during times of war or of inflammatory public passion is demonstrated by the 1957 decision in *Yates v. United States.* There the second Justice John Marshall Harlan avoided the question of whether banning Communist advocacy of overthrowing the government was constitutional by interpreting the Smith Act to require an advocacy of *action,* not simply of *belief.* That result was reached six years after the Supreme Court had decided the *Dennis* case, upholding the convictions of the leadership of the Communist Party of the United States under the same legislation. *Dennis* led to the prosecutions of more than one hundred Communists, with a conviction rate approaching 90 percent. Following *Yates,* these Communist prosecutions ended. Significantly the Korean War had ended by then, and the Communist dictator Joseph Stalin and the anticommunist senator Joseph McCarthy had both died. Moreover four new justices had been appointed to the Court between the decisions in *Dennis* and *Yates.* Harlan's approach avoided the potential for creating a narrow interpretation of the protections of the First Amendment during the climate of the cold war, which continued the crusade against Communism in the United States.

There will, of course, be cases in which the Supreme Court must act at once to resolve an issue even when the dominant political culture and/or strong public attitudes will not welcome its judgment. Cases such as *Brown v. Board of Education,* the school-prayer cases, and *Bush v. Gore* must either be avoided completely or decided when presented, even in the absence of public support for their outcome. In deciding how to proceed when such an issue is presented, the Supreme Court must ask whether and why a particular issue must be decided now, or whether and why the further passage of time will assist the Court in reaching a judgment that will receive greater public tolerance, if not acceptance. In performing this calculus, however, the Court must not abandon a class of litigants to illegal discrimination or unfair treatment. The appropriate assessment of these factors is the challenge the Supreme Court faces today, as it has done throughout its history. In selecting justices to serve on this Court of last resort, the need for uncommon wisdom is paramount. "Where there is no vision," we are reminded by the Book of Proverbs, "the people perish."

Notes

General Sources

Kermit L. Hall, William M. Wiecek, and Paul Finkelman, *American Legal History: Cases and Materials,* 2d ed. New York, Oxford University Press, 1995.

Kermit L. Hall, ed., *The Oxford Companion to the Supreme Court of the United States,* 1st ed. New York, Oxford University Press, 1992. 2d ed. 2005.

John W. Johnson, ed., *Historic U.S. Court Cases: An Encyclopedia,* 2d ed. 2 vols. New York, Routledge, 2001.

Stephen B. Presser and Jamil S. Zainaldin, *Law and Jurisprudence in American History: Cases and Materials,* 2d ed. St. Paul, West Publishing, 1989.

Introduction

The Stages of Supreme Court Development

For the quote from Federalist 78, see *The Federalist* 504. New York, Modern Library.

For the Jay quotation, see *Oxford Companion* 447. For the history of circuit riding, see *Oxford Companion* 145, 475–476.

The Influences That Shaped the Supreme Court's Role in American Society

For Professor Calabresi's views, see Steven G. Calabresi, "'A Shining City on a Hill': American Exceptionalism and the Supreme Court's Practice of Relying on Foreign Law," 86 Boston Univ. L. Rev. 1335, 1338 (2006).

Chapter 1. Building Federal Power

For an outstanding overview of the intellectual underpinnings of the American system of dual sovereignty, see Forrest McDonald, *States' Rights and the Union: Imperium in Imperio, 1776–1876.* Lawrence, University Press of Kansas, 2000.

For the "United States" as a plural noun, and the impact of Lincoln in the Gettysburg Address, see Garry Wills, *Lincoln at Gettysburg: The Words That Remade America* 145. New York, Simon & Schuster Touchstone, 1992 (paperback ed.).

For the Marshall and Jefferson quotations, see R. Kent Newmyer, *John Marshall and the Heroic Age of the Supreme Court* 322. Baton Rouge, Louisiana State University Press, 2001.

Treason and the Tax Collector

For an account of the trials of Vigol and Mitchell, see Mary K. Bonsteel Tachau, "Treason and the Whiskey 'Insurrection,'" I *Historic Cases* 34. On Fries Rebellion, see Burton Alva Konkle, *Joseph Hopkinson* 85–94. Philadelphia, University of Pennsylvania Press, 1931.

For accounts of the impeachment of Justice Chase, see Richard E. Ellis, "Can Intemperate Behavior Be a 'High Crime or Misdemeanor,'" in I *Historic Cases* 275; Presser and Zainaldin, *Law and Jurisprudence* 223–247.

Following the early treason trials summarized in this chapter, no significant Supreme Court opinions were delivered on treason until World War II, and those cases focused on the meaning of "Aid and Comfort" in Article III, Section 3, rather than on "levying War." See, for example, *Cramer v. United States,* 325 U.S. 1 (1945); *Haupt v. United States,* 330 U.S. 631 (1947); *United States v. Tomoya Kawakita,* 343 U.S. 717 (1952).

Judging Sovereign States

For accounts of the background of and the reaction to the *Chisholm* opinion, see Robert S. Lambert, "A Rebuke to the Court," I *Historic Cases* 205; For the quotes from Federalist 81, see *The Federalist* 529–530.

For recent invocations of the concept of inherent state immunity, see, for example, *Federal Maritime Commission v. South Carolina State Ports Authority,* 535 U.S. 743, 751–754 (2002).

Invalidating State Legislation

For the quotes from Federalist 78, see *The Federalist* 505, 507. For the Marshall quote, see Kermit L. Hall, *The Magic Mirror: Law in American History* 83. New York, Oxford University Press, 1989.

For discussions of *Marbury v. Madison* and its place in history, see William H. Rehnquist, *The Supreme Court: How It Was, How It Is* 99–114. New York, William Morrow and Company, 1987; Mark Tushnet, "*Marbury v. Madison* and the Theory of Judicial Supremacy," in *Great Cases in Constitutional Law* 17–54. Princeton, Princeton University Press, 2000.

For a discussion of John Marshall's involvement as the losing lawyer before the Supreme Court in *Ware v. Hylton,* see Newmyer, *John Marshall and the Heroic Age of the Supreme Court* 98–101.

For a discussion of the background to *Fletcher v. Peck* and the Yazoo land deal, see Newmyer, *John Marshall and the Heroic Age of the Supreme Court* 222–235.

For the history of Indian removal efforts and the role of Andrew Jackson, see Robert V. Remini's excellent discussion in his *Andrew Jackson and His Indian Wars* 226–281. New York, Viking Penguin, 2001.

For a discussion of the *Cherokee Nation* and *Worcester* cases, see John R. Wunder, "The Cherokee Cases," in II *Historic Cases* 685–694.

Declaring Federal Judicial Supremacy

For a discussion of *Martin v. Hunter's Lessee,* see Richard E. Ellis, "Judicial Review of State Court Decisions," in I *Historic Cases* 183–186.

Expanding the Reach of Federal Government

Hamilton's views on the need for a national bank, and Madison's congressional opposition to the creation of such, are summarized in Richard Brookhiser, *Alexander Hamilton: American* 89–92. New York, Free Press, 1999.

For a discussion of *McCulloch v. Maryland,* see Newmyer, *John Marshall and the Heroic Age of the Supreme Court* 291–302; for Marshall's newspaper defense against Spencer Roane and others, see id. at 335–353.

Jackson's 1829 Inaugural Address is reprinted in Library of Freedom, *The Inaugural Addresses of the Presidents* 87–90. New York, Gramercy Books, 1995. Portions of Jackson's 1832 Veto Message on the Recharter of the Bank of the United States are reprinted in *Problems in American History* 204–206 (Richard W. Leopold and Arthur S. Link, eds.). Englewood Cliffs, N.J., Prentice-Hall, 2d ed. 1957, and in *American Legal History* at 132–134.

Chapter 2: The Supreme Court and the Slave Power

The 1790 census data are taken from Joseph J. Ellis, *Founding Brothers* 102. New York, Vintage Books, 2002 (paperback ed.). The percentages of slaves living within their borders in 1790 was approximately 43 in South Carolina, 39 in Virginia, 35 in Georgia, 32 in Maryland, and 25 in North Carolina. Virginia had the most total slaves—292,627—over 42 percent of the nation's total in 1790.

For a masterful account of Polk's slaveholdings and political posturing, see William Dusinberre, *Slavemaster President: The Double Career of James Polk.* New York, Oxford University Press, 2003.

The figures on slave percentages, and the geography of slavery and its southern movement, are taken from William W. Freehling, *The Reintegration of American History: Slavery and the Civil War.* New York, Oxford University Press, 1994. The figures on slave movement and sales in the 1850s are taken from Dusinberre, *Slavemaster President* at 56 and 215 n. 3.

Slavery and the Constitution

The 30 percent figure for the additional representation of the slave states in the House of Representatives is taken from Don E. Fehrenbacher, *The Dred Scott Case: Its Significance in American Law and Politics* 20. New York, Oxford University Press, 2001 (paperback ed.). The Stevens speech is from the *Congressional Globe* of December 18, 1865, at 72–75, and is reprinted in Irwin Unger and Robert R. Tomes, II *American Issues: A Primary Source Reader in United States History* (3d ed.) 7–10. Upper Saddle River, N.J., Prentice-Hall, 2002.

Jefferson's presidential victory over John Adams in 1800 is examined by Garry Wills in his *"Negro President": Jefferson and the Slave Power* 2–5, 234. Boston/New York, Houghton Mifflin, 2003. Wills records that Jefferson's eight-electoral-vote victory was aided by between twelve and sixteen extra southern votes tied to the Three-fifths Clause, without which Jefferson would have been defeated. Wills also examines the origin and importance of the Three-fifths Clause with copious quotations from the debates in the Constitutional Convention on that issue. Id. at 50–61.

Abolitionism and the Second Great Awakening

For a detailed discussion of the antislavery petitions of 1790, see Joseph J. Ellis, *Founding Brothers* 81–119.

For a detailed discussion of John Quincy Adams's role in the antislavery petitions of the 1830s and 1840s, see Garry Wills, *"Negro President": Jefferson and the Slave Power* 214–222. The 693 petition figure is found at page 203 of Wills's book.

The Supreme Court and the Fugitive Slave in the 1840s

For a discussion of the background and facts of *Prigg v. Pennsylvania,* see Paul Finkelman, "Upholding the Fugitive Slave Act of 1793," in II *Historic Cases* 591, and Fehrenbacher, *The Dred Scott Case* 43–47. The provisions of the federal Fugitive Slave Act of 1793 are summarized in Fehrenbacher, *The Dred Scott Case* 40–41.

Things Fall Apart: From Prigg *to* Scott

For discussions of the Compromise of 1850, the new Fugitive Slave Law that was part of it, the Kansas-Nebraska Act of 1854, and the various fugitive slave incidents mentioned in the text, see James M. McPherson, *Battle Cry of Freedom: The Civil War Era* 70–85, 119–129, 145–153. New York, Oxford University Press, 1998, and Forrest McDonald, *States' Rights and the Union: Imperium in Imperio, 1776–1876* 136, 151–161. Lawrence, University Press of Kansas, 2000.

Justice Grier's opinion in the Christiana, Pennsylvania, treason trial is reported as *United States v. Hanway*, 26 Fed. Cases 105 (C.C.E.D.Pa. 1851).

Chief Justice Roger Taney and the Dred Scott Case

The *magnum opus* on the *Scott* decision is Don E. Fehrenbacher, *The Dred Scott Case.*

Chief Justice Hughes said of Taney and *Scott* that "it is apparent that there was a fundamental error in the supposition that the imperious question which underlay the [slavery] controversy could be put at rest by a judicial pronouncement." Hughes's remarks are found in his article "Roger Brooke Taney: A Great Chief Justice," 17 ABA Journal 785 (Dec. 1931), reprinted in *The Supreme Court and Its Justices* 53, 57–58. Chicago, American Bar Association, 1987.

Different portions of the Catron-Buchanan-Grier correspondence are reprinted in *The Dred Scott Case* 312; Kenneth Stampp, *America in 1857: A Nation on the Brink* 90–92. New York, Oxford University Press, 1990; *Great Cases in Constitutional Law* 73 (Robert P. George, ed.). Princeton, Princeton University Press, 2000 (paperback ed.); and in the opinion in *United States v. International Union*, 352 U.S. 567, 591 n. 5 (1957).

Lincoln's "House Divided" Speech of June 16, 1858, is reprinted in *Abraham Lincoln, Speeches and Writings 1832–1858* at 426. New York, Library of America, 1989. The quotations in the text are found at 431.

On the actual rulings in the *Scott* case, the opinions reveal the following. First, on the citizenship issue, Taney's opinion expressly holds that the descendants of slaves cannot be citizens. His opinion, in turn, is expressly adopted by Wayne "entirely" with his "unqualified assent," 60 U.S. at 456, and by Grier on both the citizenship point and the validity of the Missouri Compromise, id. at 469. Campbell's opinion states that Scott is not a citizen, id. at 517–518, as does Daniel's. Id. at 481–482, 492. On the validity of the Missouri Compromise, Taney's opinion is joined by both Wayne and Grier, as noted above, with Grier expressly stating that the Compromise is "unconstitutional and void." Id. at 469. Wayne's opinion claims that six justices agreed on this ruling. Two other opinions either expressly (Catron, id. at 529, states that the Missouri Compromise is "void") or in dictum (Campbell, id. at 517, states that Congress has "no power" to "dissolve the relationship of the master and the slave" anywhere, but his opinion also states that the judgment should be reversed on the jurisdictional point that Scott was not a citizen, id. at 517–518) state that the Missouri Compromise is an invalid exercise of congressional power. Daniel's opinion states that dismissal of the case should be ordered on the jurisdictional issue, id. at 492, but has a lengthy discussion on the constitutionality issue, id. at 483–492, the thrust of which is that Congress lacked the power to interfere with a slaveholder's property right in his slaves.

The quotations in the text from Taney's opinion appear at 60 U.S. 404–405, 407, 409, 410, 451, and 452.

Wisconsin Defies the Supreme Court: Ableman v. Booth

The reactions to the *Scott* decision on multiple levels are documented in Fehrenbacher, *The Dred Scott Case,* 417–448.

The quotations in the text from Taney's opinion appear at 62 U.S. 514, 522–523, 525, and 526.

The factual background of the *Ableman* cases is covered in Thomas D. Morris, "Slavery, Freedom, and Federal Judicial Power," II *Historic Cases* 604–607. Chief Justice Hughes's comment is found in his article "Roger Brooke Taney: A Great Chief Justice," 62.

The quotations from the Wisconsin Legislature are found in Morris, "Slavery, Freedom, and Federal Judicial Power," at 607, and in the *Oxford Companion* at 2.

Chapter 3: Making the Nation Safe for Commerce

Two Nations Divisible: The United States in 1860

The percentages of industrial and agricultural populations in North and South are found in James M. McPherson, *Battle Cry of Freedom: The Civil War Era* 91, 95. New York, Oxford University Press, 1998; James M. McPherson, *Drawn with the Sword* 13. New York, Oxford University Press, 1996 (paperback ed.).

The Texas senator's remarks are found in *Drawn with the Sword* 8.

For a discussion of the Nullification Controversy over protective tariffs, see Forrest McDonald, *States' Rights and the Union: Imperium in Imperio, 1776–1876* 103–110. Lawrence, University Press of Kansas, 2000.

On Polk's four "great measures," and the Walker Tariff of 1846, see John Seigenthaler, *James K. Polk* 102–103, 113–116. New York, Times Books, 2003.

On the antitariff provision of the Confederate Constitution, see William C. Davis, *Look Away!: A History of the Confederate States of America* 62. New York, Free Press, 2002.

Law Follows Economics: The Evolution of Tort and Contract Theories in the Nineteenth Century

For general discussions of the changes in contract and tort theories in this period, see *American Legal History* 156–159, 179–186, and Kermit L. Hall, *The Magic Mirror: Law in American History* 119–126, 134–136. New York, Oxford University Press, 1989. The quotations from the *McFarland, Woods, Farwell,* and *Ryan* cases are taken from the excerpts from those opinions reproduced in *American Legal History* at 173 (both *Woods* and *McFarland*), 157–158, and 185–186, respectively.

For discussions of the *Farwell* opinion of Chief Justice Shaw, see John W. Johnson, "Fellow Servants Beware," I *Historic Cases* 507–511, and Leonard W. Levy, *The Law of the Commonwealth and Chief Justice Shaw,* chapter 10, 166–182. New York, Harper & Row, 1967 (paperback ed.). The industrial accident and death estimates as of 1900 come from Johnson at 510. The legal commentator who made the felicitous analogy comparing the fellow servant rule to the protective tariff in 1883 was one John M. Shirley, whose remarks are quoted in Levy at 179.

The Marshall Court and the Protection of Emerging Mercantile and Corporate Interests

The quotations in the text from *Fletcher v. Peck* appear at 10 U.S. 133–134 and 139.

The quotations from *Laidlaw v. Organ* appear at 15 U.S. 195.

For a discussion of the legal issues concerning disclosure involved in *Laidlaw,* see Randy E. Barnett, "Rational Bargaining Theory and Contract: Default Rules, Hypothetical Consent, the Duty to Disclose, and Fraud," 15 Harv. J. of Law & Pub. Policy 783 (1992).

The quotations in the text from the *Dartmouth College* case appear at 17 U.S. 645, 652–653, 667, 681, and 684.

For a discussion of *Trustees of Dartmouth College v. Woodward,* including Story's involvement in setting up the case, see Francis N. Stites, "Balancing Private Good and Public Good," I *Historic Cases* 331–339.

The figures on the number of business corporations in the text are taken from R. Kent Newmyer, *John Marshall and the Heroic Age of the Supreme Court* 247. Baton Rouge, Louisiana State University Press, 2001.

For a discussion of the background of *Gibbons v. Ogden,* see Newmyer, *John Marshall and the Heroic Age of the Supreme Court,* 302–315, and Francis N. Stites, "A More Perfect Union: The Steamboat Case," I *Historic Cases* 357–364.

The quotations in the text from *Gibbons v. Ogden* appear at 22 U.S. 189–190, 194, 195, 196, 209, and 210.

The Taney Court Attacks Monopoly

For a discussion of the Jefferson-Madison debate on monopolies, see Deboarah A. Garza, "Editor's Note," *Antitrust* (Summer 2002) at 6.

For a discussion of the background of the *Charles River Bridge* case, see Elizabeth B. Monroe, "Abridging Vested Interests: The Battle of the Massachusetts Bridges," I *Historic Cases* 343–351.

The quotations in the text from the *Charles River Bridge* opinions of Taney and Story appear at 36 U.S. 544, 547, 548, 552–553, 608, and 615.

The quotations in the text from the *Briscoe* opinions of McLean and Story appear at 36 U.S. 317, 319, 328, 331, 339, 340, 348, and 350.

The Triumph of Commerce

For a discussion of the background of the *Bank of Augusta* case, see Eric Monkkonen, "Corporate Growth v. States' Rights," I *Historic Cases* 430–435.

The quotations in the text from Taney's *Bank of Augusta* opinion appear at 38 U.S. 588, 590–591, and 597. Those from McKinley's dissent appear at 38 U.S. 598 and 606.

The quotations from Story's letters to Sumner and Taney appear in Monkkonen, "Corporate Growth vs. States' Rights," 431 and 434, respectively.

For a discussion of the background of *Swift v. Tyson,* see F. Thornton Miller, "Federal Common Law?" I *Historic Cases* 221–224.

The quotations in the text from Justice Story's opinion for a unanimous Court in *Swift v. Tyson* appear at 41 U.S. 15 and 20.

The quotations in the text from *Cooley v. Board of Wardens* appear at 53 U.S. 319.

Chapter 4: From Emancipation to "Separate but Equal"

For the quotation from Lincoln's second inaugural address, see Ronald C. White Jr., *Lincoln's Greatest Speech,* 18, 97. New York, Simon & Schuster, 2002.

The Thirteenth Amendment

On the Corwin Amendment, see A. Christopher Bryant, "Stopping Time: The Pro-Slavery and 'Irrevocable' Thirteenth Amendment," 26 Harv. J. of Law & Pub. Policy 501 (2003).

For the current texts of the 1866 and 1867 acts, see 42 U.S.C. sections 1982, 1994. The Peonage Act was upheld in *Clyatt v. United States,* 197 U.S. 207, 215–218 (1905).

For examples of "black codes" from Mississippi, see *American Legal History* 231–233.

The quotations in the text from the majority opinion in the *Civil Rights Cases* appear at 109 U.S. 22 and 25. Those from Justice Harlan's dissent appear at 109 U.S. 43.

The quotation in the text from the majority opinion in *Jones v. Alfred H. Mayer Co.* appears at 392 U.S. 440. The majority opinion went on to observe: "Just as the Black Codes, enacted after the Civil War to restrict the free exercise of those rights, were substitutes for the slave system, so the exclusion of Negroes from white communities became a substitute for the Black Codes. And when racial discrimination herds men into ghettos and makes their ability to buy property turn on the color of their skin, then it too is a relic of slavery." Id. at 441–443.

An attempt to use the Thirteenth Amendment to attack the military draft was summarily rejected in the last paragraph of the unanimous Supreme Court opinion in the *Selective Draft Law Cases [Arver v. United States],* 245 U.S. 366 (1918).

The Fourteenth Amendment

On the incorporation doctrine, see *Oxford Companion 2* at 491–492.

For the quotations characterizing Thaddeus Stevens, see James McPherson, "Reconstruction Reconsidered," *Atlantic* 261, April 1988, at 75–77, and II Morison and Commager, *The Growth of the American Republic* 37. New York, Oxford University Press, 1950. For Stevens's "perpetual ascendancy" quotation, see id. at 33.

The restrictions of Section 3 of the Fourteenth Amendment were generally overturned by the Amnesty Act of 1872, which lifted the disability imposed on Confederate traitors for all but approximately 500 key leaders.

The ability of Congress to refuse to seat elected representatives was later limited by the Supreme Court in the case of the noted Harlem African American politician Adam Clayton Powell, *Powell v. McCormack,* 395 U.S. 486 (1969), with the Court holding that Congress could not refuse to seat an elected official who met the constitutional qualifications prescribed in Article I, Section 2.

The *Slaughterhouse Cases*

For descriptions of the background of the *Slaughterhouse Cases,* I have relied heavily upon the excellent biography of Justice Miller by Michael A. Ross, *Justice of Shattered Dreams: Samuel Freeman Miller and the Supreme Court during the Civil War Era* 189–210. Baton Rouge, Louisiana State University Press, 2003, as well as upon Donald G. Nieman, "The Fourteenth Amendment Receives Its First Judicial Construction," I *Historic Cases* 469–477.

For short biographies of Justices Campbell and Field, see *Oxford Companion 2* at 137–138 and 336–338, respectively.

The quotations in the text from Justice Miller's majority opinion in the *Slaughterhouse Cases* appear at 83 U.S. 62, 76, 78, 81, and 82. Those from Justice Field's dissent appear at 83 U.S. 87, 93, 97, 101, and 110.

For the evolution of the free labor philosophy from before the Civil War to the end of the nineteenth century, see the introduction added to the paperback edition of Eric Foner, *Free Soil, Free Labor, Free Men: The Ideology of the Republican Party before the Civil War* ix–xxxix. New York, Oxford University Press, 1995. The quotation from Abraham Lincoln appears at 30, and the impact of Justice Field's dissenting opinion in the *Slaughterhouse Cases* is discussed at xxxvii.

In 1999, the Supreme Court revisited the privileges and immunities clause in *Saenz v. Roe.* Over a strong dissent by Justice Thomas, the Court found that a California statute limiting welfare recipients first receiving benefits to the level given in their prior state of residence violated their right to travel protected by the privileges and immunities clause.

The *Civil Rights Cases*

For the background of the *Civil Rights Cases,* see Jonathan Lurie, "Civil Rights or Last Rites," II *Historic Cases* 618–623.

For the dichotomy between political/civil and social rights, see Heather Cox Richardson, *The Death of Reconstruction: Race, Labor, and Politics in the Post–Civil War North* 184. Cambridge, Harvard University Press, 2001, and Linda Przybyszewski, *The Republic according to John Marshall Harlan* 81–85. Chapel Hill, University of North Carolina Press, 1999.

The quotations in the text from Justice Bradley's majority opinion in the *Civil Rights Cases* appear at 109 U.S. 11, 13, 22, and 25. Those from Justice Harlan's dissent appear at 109 U.S. 53, 58, 61, and 62.

The newspaper articles commenting on the decision in the *Civil Rights Cases* are discussed in Richardson, *The Death of Reconstruction* 152

The quotations from Justices Bradley and Harlan on social rights are found respectively in Lurie, *Civil Rights or Last Rights* 620—621, and Przybyszewski, *The Republic according to John Marshall Harlan* 83, 87.

Plessy v. Ferguson

The quotation from George M. Frederickson is found in his *Racism: A Short History* 99. Princeton, Princeton University Press, 2002.

For the background of *Plessy v. Ferguson,* see Robert P. Green Jr., "'Separate but Equal' Approved," II *Historic Cases* 624–628, and Michael J. Klarman, *From Jim Crow to Civil Rights* 8–23. New York, Oxford University Press, 2004.

The quotations in the text from Justice Brown's opinion in *Plessy v. Ferguson* appear at 163 U.S. 544, 550, and 551–552. Those from Justice Harlan's dissent appear at 163 U.S. 555, 559, 560, and 563.

For a short biography of Justice Brown, see *Oxford Companion 2* at 110–111.

For a discussion of Justice Harlan's views on race, see Przybyszewski, *The Republic according to John Marshall Harlan,* 10–11, 14–43, and 81–117.

Yick Wo v. Hopkins: A Beacon for the Oppressed

For the statistics cited in the text on the Chinese in California, see Alexander Saxton, *The Indispensable Enemy: Labor and the Anti-Chinese Movement in California* xi n. 9, 4–5, and 19–20. On the Asian black codes, see John R. Wunder, "Chinese Laundries and the Fourteenth Amendment," II *Historic Cases* 717–718.

On the California Workingmen's Party and the California Constitutional Convention of 1878, see Saxton, *The Indispensable Enemy* 113–156.

For the background of the *Yick Wo v. Hopkins* case, see Wunder, "Chinese Laundries and the Fourteenth Amendment" 717–721.

The quotations in the text from Justice Matthews's opinion in *Yick Wo v. Hopkins* appear at 118 U.S. 369–370 and 373–374. The actual facts differ slightly from those cited in the opinion. There were actually 201 Chinese applicants, one of whom obtained consent. That one, however, had an Irish-sounding surname. See Wunder, "Chinese Laundries and the Fourteenth Amendment" 719.

The Fifteenth Amendment

For the background of the *Reese* and *Cruikshank* cases, see Robert M. Goldman, "No 'Right' to Vote: The Reconstruction Election Cases," II *Historic Cases* 613–617.

The quotations in the text from the *Reese* opinion appear at 92 U.S. 217 and 219. The quotation in the text from the *Cruikshank* opinion appears at 92 U.S. 556. The quotations in the text from the *Williams* opinion appear at 170 U.S. 221 and 225. For a short biography of Justice McKenna, see *Oxford Companion 2* at 625–627.

The quotation from W. E. B. DuBois is found in his *Black Reconstruction in America* 30. New York, Oxford University Press, 1935.

Chapter 5: The Supreme Court and Government Regulation of Business before the New Deal

For an excellent overview of the rise of industrial capitalism in the last half of the nineteenth century in the United States, see Walter Licht, *Industrializing America: The Nineteenth Century* 102–196. Baltimore, Johns Hopkins University Press, 1995.

The quotations in the text from the inaugural addresses of Presidents Grant and Harrison are reprinted in *The Inaugural Addresses of the Presidents* 213, 254–255.

The Granger Movement Reaches the Supreme Court

For background on *Munn v. Illinois,* state regulation of railroads, and the Granger movement, see James W. Ely Jr., *Railroads and American Law* 71–90. Lawrence, University Press of Kansas, 2001; Richard R. Broadie, "The Court Enters the Age of Reform," I *Historic Cases* 478–481; and Charles N. Lord, "*Munn v. Illinois,* the Grangers, and a 'Republican' Court," unpublished paper prepared for the author's United States Legal History Seminar, University of Pennsylvania, 2002.

The quotations in the text from Chief Justice Waite's majority opinion in *Munn v. Illinois* appear at 94 U.S. 126, 130, 133, and 134. Those from Justice Field's dissent appear at 94 U.S. 136, 138, and 140.

The Grangers Get Derailed

On the 1877 Railroad strike, see Walter Licht, *Industrializing America,* 166–168.

On the 1886 Haymarket Riot, see Licht, *Industrializing America* 169–170.

On the 1892 Homestead strike, see Licht, *Industrializing America* 170–171; H. W. Brands, *The Reckless Decade: America in the 1890s* 128–144. Chicago, University of Chicago Press, 2002 (paperback ed.); and Les Standiford, *Meet You in Hell: Andrew Carnegie, Henry Clay*

Frick, and the Bitter Partnership That Transformed America 146–226. New York, Crown Publishers, 2005.

On the 1894 Pullman Strike, see Licht, *Industrializing America* 171–172, and Brands, *The Reckless Decade* 144–160.

The quotation in the text from Justice Brewer's opinion of the Court in *In re Debs* appears at 158 U.S. 599.

The quotations in the text from Mary Elizabeth Lease appear in Brands, *The Reckless Decade* 186–187.

The quotation in the text from Justice Fields's separate opinion in *Pollock v. Farmers' Loan & Trust Co.* appears at 157 U.S. 607.

The best books on the Populist Party and the Farmers' Alliances are Robert C. McMath Jr., *American Populism: A Social History 1877–1898.* New York, Hill & Wang, 1993; Lawrence Goodwyn, *The Populist Moment: A Short History of the Agrarian Revolt in America.* New York, Oxford University Press, 1978; and Norman Pollack, *The Populist Response to Industrial America: Midwestern Populist Thought.* Cambridge, Harvard University Press, 1962.

The quotations in the text from Justice Samuel Miller's University of Iowa speech are found in Michael A. Ross, *Justice of Shattered Dreams* 242–243.

The quotation in the text from *County of Santa Clara v. Southern Pacific R.R. Co.* appears at 118 U.S. 396.

The quotations in the text from Justice Miller's majority opinion in the *Wabash* case appear at 118 U.S. 567, 568, 572–573, and 575. Those from Justice Bradley's dissent appear at 118 U.S. 580 and 588.

The quotation in the text from Justice Miller's *Lectures on the Constitution* (1889) appears in Przybyszewski, *The Republic according to John Marshall Harlan* 153.

The quotation in the text from Justice Blatchford's majority opinion in the *Chicago, Milwaukee* case appears at 134 U.S. 456–457. Those from Justice Bradley's dissent appear at 134 U.S. 461, 462, and 466.

For a short biography of Justice Bradley, see *Oxford Companion 2* at 96–97.

The quotations in the text from *Smyth v. Ames* appear at 169 U.S. 526, 527–528, and 546.

On Bryan's career, and the Vachel Lindsay poem "Bryan, Bryan, Bryan, Bryan," see II Morison and Commager, *The Growth of the American Republic* 256–265.

The Emergence of Substantive Due Process

The reference to 184 state laws being invalidated by the Supreme Court is found in Robert G. McCloskey, *The American Supreme Court* 101. Chicago, University of Chicago Press, 2000 (3d ed. Sanford Levinson revision).

For a short biography of Justice Peckham, see *Oxford Companion 2* at 725–726. The communistic tendencies quotation is found in Fred D. Ragan, "'Mere Meddlesome Interferences': The Apogee of Substantive Due Process," I *Historic Cases* 485, 490.

The quotation in the text from the *Allgeyer* opinion appears at 165 U.S. 509.

For the background of *Lochner v. New York,* see Fred D. Ragan, "'Mere Meddlesome Interferences,'" and Hadley Arkes, "*Lochner v. New York* and the Cast of Our Laws," *Great Cases in Constitutional Law* 94–129. Princeton, Princeton University Press, 2000.

The quotations in the text from the *Lochner* majority opinion appear at 198 U.S. 52, 53, 56, 57, 58, and 59. That from Justice Harlan's dissent appears at 198 U.S. 72. Those from Justice Holmes's dissent appear at 198 U.S. 75–76.

Lochner *in Retreat*

The quotations in the text from *Muller v. Oregon* appear at 208 U.S. 421 and 422.

The Four Horsemen Rescue Lochner

For a discussion of the "Four Horsemen," see "The Four Horsemen," in *The United States Supreme Court: The Pursuit of Justice* 246–248. Boston and New York, Houghton Mifflin, 2005 (Christopher Tomlins, ed.).

The quotations in the text from Justice Sutherland's majority opinion in *Adkins v. Children's Hospital* appear at 261 U.S. 542–543, 546, 547, 554, 558, and 561. Those from Chief Justice Taft's dissent appear at 261 U.S. 562 and 567. Those from Justice Holmes's dissent appear at 261 U.S. 568, and 569–570.

The Iceman Cometh: Preaching a New Federalism with Laboratories of Democracy

The quotations in the text from Justice Sutherland's majority opinion in *New State Ice Co. v. Liebmann* appear at 285 U.S. 278 and 279. Those from Justice Brandeis's dissent appear at 285 U.S. 303, 307, 308, and 311.

The Supreme Court Confronts the Sherman Antitrust Act

For the background and legislative history of the Sherman Act, see William Letwin, *Law and Economic Policy in America: The Evolution of the Sherman Antitrust Act* 53–99. Chicago, University of Chicago Press, 1965 (paperback ed. 1981), and Presser and Zainaldin, *Law and Jurisprudence* 641–655.

The Olney quotation appears in Letwin, *Law and Economic Policy* 122.

For the background on the *Knight* case, see Robert Stanley, "When Monopoly Mattered," I *Historic Cases* 368–372.

For an account of the career of John G. Johnson, see Robert R. Bell, *The Philadelphia Lawyer: A History, 1735–1945* at 177–193. Selinsgrove, Susquehanna University Press, 1992. The newspaper account of Johnson's oral argument in the *Northern Securities* case is quoted at 187.

The quotations in the text from Chief Justice Fuller's majority opinion in *Knight* appear at 156 U.S. 11, 12, 13, and 16. Those from Justice Harlan's dissent appear at 156 U.S. 32 and 42.

T. R., Holmes, Morgan, and Hill

For the background of the *Trans-Missouri* case, see Letwin, *Law and Economic Policy* 167–172, and Robert A. Waller, "Regulation in the Public Interest," I *Historic Cases* 373–375.

For the background of the *Northern Securities* case, see Letwin, *Law and Economic Policy* 182–237; Edmund Morris, *Theodore Rex* 59–65, 87–94, 219, 303–305, and 313–316. New York, Random House, 2001; and David Walker, "Busting Trusts with More Backbone Than a Banana," I *Historic Cases* 379–382.

Theodore Roosevelt's letter to Jacob Schiff is quoted in James Chace, *1912: Wilson, Roosevelt, Taft & Debs—The Election That Changed the Country* 18. New York, Simon & Schuster, 2004.

The quotations in the text from Justice Harlan's majority opinion in the *Northern Securities* case appear at 193 U.S. 346, 351, and 354. Those from Justice Brewer's concurring opinion appear at 193 U.S. 361 and 364. That from Justice White's dissenting opinion appears at 193 U.S. 380–381. Those from Justice Holmes's dissenting opinion appear at 193 U.S. 400, 405–406, 407, and 411.

Justice Holmes's view of the Sherman Act is quoted in Letwin, *Law and Economic Policy* 235.

The quotation from Theodore Roosevelt on the most powerful men in the country appears in Letwin, *Law and Economic Policy* 237. The quotation from Theodore Roosevelt on Justice Holmes appears in full in Edmund Morris, *Theodore Rex* 316.

The Rule of Reason Finally Prevails

For a short biography of Chief Justice White, see *Oxford Companion 2* at 1086–1087.

The muckrakers' attack on Standard Oil included two books—Ida Tarbell's *The History of the Standard Oil Company* (1904), and William Demarest Lloyd's *Wealth and Commonwealth* (1894). Lloyd was then a Chicago Populist. Tarbell's father had been driven out of business by John D. Rockefeller.

The quotations in the text from Chief Justice White's majority opinion in *Standard Oil* appear at 221 U.S. 50, 59, 60, 63, 64, and 75–76. Those from Justice Harlan's concurring and dissenting opinion appear at 221 U.S. 83, 102, and 103.

For a detailed account of the election of 1912 and the candidates' respective platforms and views, see Chace, *1912: Wilson, Roosevelt, Taft & Debs.*

The quotation in the text on the current methodology under the rule of reason appears in *State Oil Company v. Khan,* 522 U.S. 3, 10 (1997).

The influence of Justice Powell on the adoption of modern antitrust economic theory by the Supreme Court is traced in Andrew I. Gavil, "A First Look at the Powell Papers: *Sylvania* and the Process of Change in the Supreme Court," *Antitrust,* Fall 2002, at 8–13 (American Bar Association).

Chapter 6: The Supreme Court and the New Deal

The Coming of the New Deal

For general, well-written surveys of the various New Deals and President Franklin D. Roosevelt, see David M. Kennedy, *Freedom from Fear: The American People in Depression and War 1929–1945*. New York, Oxford University Press, 1999, and Page Smith, *Redeeming the Time: A People's History of the 1920s and the New Deal.* New York, McGraw-Hill, 1987.

The Supreme Court Strikes Back

For an account of the facts surrounding the *Schechter* case, see Amity Shlaes, *The Forgotten Man: A New History of the Great Depression* 214–245. New York, HarperCollins, 2007. The quotations in the text from Chief Justice Hughes's majority opinion in the *Schechter* case appear at 295 U.S. 528, 537, 538, 541, 542, 546, and 547. That from Justice Cardozo's concurring opinion appears at 295 U.S. 553.

The quotations in the text from Justice Brandeis's majority opinion in the *Radford* case appear at 295 U.S. 598 and 602.

The quotations in the text from Justice Roberts's majority opinion in *United States v. Butler* appear at 297 U.S. 63, 68, 75, and 76. Those from Justice Stone's dissenting opinion appear at 297 U.S. 85 and 88.

Pressure from the Left

On Dr. Townsend, Father Coughlin, and Huey Long, see David M. Kennedy, *Freedom from Fear;* Page Smith, *Redeeming the Time;* Michael Kazin, *The Populist Persuasion: An American History* 109–133. Ithaca, N.Y., Cornell University Press, 1998 (rev. paperback ed.); and T. Harry Williams, *Huey Long.* New York, Alfred A. Knopf, 1969.

Chief Justice Taft's view of Huey Long is quoted in Page Smith, *Redeeming the Time* 653. For the "Morgan and Rockefeller, Mellon and Baruch" quotation, see Ken Burns's Public Television American Experience Program on Huey Long (1985, 1996).

Roosevelt Strikes Back: The "Court-Packing" Plan

Portions of the text of President Roosevelt's "Fireside Chat" of March 9, 1937, are reprinted in *American Legal History* at 483–486.

Twelve period cartoons attacking the "Court-Packing" Plan are reproduced in Jeff Phillips, "Roosevelt's Misguided Failure to Persuade," 12 *Penn History Review* 1 (May 2005): 8 at 19–21.

The "Switch in Time Saves Nine"

The quotations from Chief Justice Hughes's majority opinion in *West Coast Hotel Co. v. Parrish* appear at 300 U.S. 390, 391–392, 397, 399, and 400. Those from Justice Sutherland's dissenting opinion appear at 300 U.S. 402 and 404.

A New Court Reviews the Second New Deal

The quotations in the text from Chief Justice Hughes's majority opinion in *Jones & Laughlin* appear at 301 U.S. 31, 37, and 41. Those from Justice McReynolds's dissenting opinion appear at 301 U.S. 76 and 99.

The quotations in the text from Justice Cardozo's majority opinion in the *Steward Machinery* case appear at 301 U.S. 578, 586–587, and 593. Those from his majority opinion in the *Helvering* case appear at 301 U.S. 640–641 and 644.

The quotation in the text from Justice Stone's majority opinion in *United States v. Carolene Products Co.* appears at 304 U.S. 152.

The quotation in the text from Justice Roberts's majority opinion in *Mulford v. Smith* appears at 307 U.S. 47.

The quotations in the text from Justice Stone's opinion in *United States v. Darby* appear at 312 U.S. 116–117 and 119.

No Limits: Wickard v. Filburn *and the Triumph of Federal Power*

The quotations in the text from Justice Jackson's opinion in *Wickard v. Filburn* appear at 317 U.S. 114, 118, 119, 124–125, and 128.

The quotations in the text from Justice White's dissenting opinion in *Northern Securities Co. v. United States* appear at 193 U.S. 397.

The Roosevelt Revolution: A Postscript

For a good overview of the debate among historians over the effect of the court-packing plan and the election of 1936 on the decisions of the Supreme Court in and after 1937, see the American Historical Review Forum on the Debate over the Constitutional Revolution of 1937, in *American Historical Review* 110 (Oct. 2005), beginning at page 1046, especially Laura Kalman, "The Constitution, the Supreme Court, and the New Deal," id. at 1052.

Chapter 7: The Supreme Court and Civil Liberties

Freedom of Speech in Wartime: The Civil War Experience

For the background of *Ex Parte Vallandigham,* see Geoffrey R. Stone, *Perilous Times: Free Speech in Wartime* 82–112. New York, W. W. Norton & Co, 2004, and William H. Rehnquist,

All the Laws but One: Civil Liberties in Wartime 63–74. New York, Vintage Press, 2000 (paperback ed.).

The quotation from Abraham Lincoln on the "simple-minded soldier boy" appears in Rehnquist, *All the Laws but One* 73.

The excerpts from General Order No. 38 and Vallandigham's speech appear in the Supreme Court Reports at 68 U.S. 244 and 245. The excerpts from Vallandigham's defenses appear at 68 U.S. 246–247.

The Writ of Habeas Corpus *and the Use of Military Tribunals in Wartime: The Civil War Experience*

For the background of *Ex Parte Merryman,* see Rehnquist, *All the Laws but One* 18–45, and Stone, *Perilous Times* 84–87, 120–124. See also Daniel Farber, *Lincoln's Constitution* 157–165. Chicago, University of Chicago Press, 2003.

The excerpts from Chief Justice Taney's opinion in *Ex Parte Merryman* and from President Lincoln's "all the laws, but one" message to Congress appear in Rehnquist, *All the Laws but One* 38.

For the background of *Milligan,* including the lawyers who argued the case and the justices who wrote the opinions, see Rehnquist, *All the Laws but One* 75–137 and Charles Fairman, *Reconstruction and Reunion 1864–88, Part 1* 185–237. New York, Macmillan, 1971.

The quotations in the text from the majority opinion in *Milligan* appear at 71 U.S. 109, 119, 120–121, 122, 125, 127, and 130. Those from Chief Justice Chase's concurring opinion appear at 71 U.S. 140 and 142.

For a discussion of the reaction of the press to *Milligan,* see Fairman, *Reconstruction and Reunion* 214–222.

For two differing opinions on the majority opinion in *Milligan,* see that of the late chief justice in Rehnquist, *All the Laws but One* 134–137, and that of the former governor of New York in Mario M. Cuomo, *Why Lincoln Matters* 80–86, 153. Orlando, Harcourt, 2004.

For a comprehensive discussion "with minute care" of the background and decision in *Ex Parte McCardle,* see Fairman, *Reconstruction and Reunion* 413–433, 437–497.

Freedom of Speech in Wartime: The World War I Experience

For the background of the *Schenck, Debs,* and *Abrams* opinions and the Espionage and Sedition Acts, see Stone, *Perilous Times* 135–233; G. Edward White, *Justice Oliver Wendell Holmes: Law and the Inner Self* 415–436. New York, Oxford University Press, 1993; Louis Menand, *The Metaphysical Club: A Story of Ideas in America* 420–433. New York, Farrar, Straus and Giroux, 2001; and Rehnquist, *All the Laws but One* 170–183.

Excerpts from two "poison of disloyalty" speeches of Woodrow Wilson appear in Patrick J. Buchanan, *A Republic, Not an Empire: Reclaiming America's Destiny* 188. Washington, D.C., Regnery Publishing, 1999; and Rehnquist, *All the Laws but One* at 173.

The quotations in the text from Justice Holmes's opinion in *Schenck v. United States* appear at 249 U.S. 50, 51, and 52.

The quotations in the text from Justice Holmes's opinion in *Debs v. United States* appear at 249 U.S. 214.

The quotations in the text from Justice Clarke's majority opinion in *Abrams v. United States* appear at 250 U.S. 617, 620, 621, and 622. Those from Justice Holmes's dissent appear at 250 U.S. 627, 628, and 630.

Freedom of Speech in Wartime: The World War II Experience

For the background of the *Quirin* opinion, see Jonathan Turley, "'Quirin' Revisited: The Dark History of a Military Tribunal," National Law Journal, Oct. 28, 2002, A17; Rehnquist, *All the Laws but One* 136–137, 221. The quotations in the text from the *Quirin* opinion appear at 317 U.S. 29, 31, 45, 46, and 47.

The Japanese Internment Cases

For the background of the *Hirabayashi, Korematsu,* and *Endo* cases, see David M. Kennedy, *Freedom from Fear* 746–760; Paul Finkelman, "The Japanese Internment Cases," II *Historic Cases* 722–731; Rehnquist, *All the Laws but One* 184–211.

For Justice Black's view of the cases, see Roger K. Newman, *Hugo Black: A Biography* 312–319. New York, Pantheon Press, 1994.

For short biographies of Justices Black, Jackson, and Murphy, see *Oxford Companion 2* at 84–87, 512–514, and 659–660, respectively. Justice Jackson's friendship with President Franklin D. Roosevelt is documented in a manuscript prepared by Jackson that was published only years after Jackson's death. It is entitled *That Man: An Insider's Portrait of Franklin D. Roosevelt.* New York, Oxford University Press, 2003.

The quotations in the text from Chief Justice Stone's majority opinion in *Hirabayashi v. United States* appear at 320 U.S. 90, 91, 93, 96, 97, and 101. Those from Justice Douglas's concurring opinion appear at 320 U.S. 107. Those from Justice Murphy's concurring opinion appear at 320 U.S. 110, 111, and 113.

The quotations in the text from Justice Black's majority opinion in *Korematsu v. United States* appear at 323 U.S. 216, 219, 222, and 232. Those from Justice Robert's dissenting opinion appear at 323 U.S. 226 and 230. Those from Justice Murphy's dissenting opinion appear at 323 U.S. 233, 235, and 237. Those from Justice Jackson's dissenting opinion appear at 323 U.S. 245 and 246.

The Cold War and the Crusade against Communism

For the background of the *Dennis* and *Yates* cases, see Michael R. Belknap, "Cold War, Communism and Free Speech," II *Historic Cases* 858–866; Jerold L. Simmons and Karen Bruner, "The Smith Act Narrowed," II *Historic Cases* 867–870; and Stone, *Perilous Times* 395–416.

The quotations in the text from Chief Justice Vinson's opinion in *Dennis v. United States* appear at 341 U.S. 504, 510 and 511. Those from Justice Black's dissenting opinion appear at 341 U.S. 579 and 581. That from Justice Douglas's dissenting opinion appears at 341 U.S. 590. Those from Justice Frankfurter's concurring opinion appear at 341 U.S. 528 and 547. Those from Justice Jackson's concurring opinion appear at 341 U.S. 562, 563, 567, and 568.

Justice Black's handwritten comments on Chief Justice Vinson's opinion are reported in Newman, *Hugo Black* 402–403.

The quotations in the text from Justice Harlan's opinion in *Yates v. United States* appear at 354 U.S. 316, 320, 324 and 325. Those from Justice Black's concurring and dissenting opinion appear at 354 U.S. 340 and 344. That from Justice Clark's dissenting opinion appears at 354 U.S. 345.

The quotation in the text from Senator Jenner appears in Simmons and Bruner, "The Smith Act Narrowed" 870.

September 11, 2001, and the War against Terror

The quotations in the text from Justice Kennedy's majority opinion in *Boumediene v. Bush* appear in the slip opinion at 36–37, 41, 49, 66 and 70. Those from Justice Scalia's dissenting opinion appear in the slip opinion at 2, 23, and 25.

Eugenics in the Supreme Court: "A Different Kind of Men and Women"

Two excellent accounts of the social legislation of the Progressive Era are James A. Morone, *Hellfire Nation: The Politics of Sin in American History* 257–344. New Haven, Conn., Yale University Press, 2003, and Michael McGerr, *A Fierce Discontent: The Rise and Fall of the Progressive Movement in America 1870–1920*, 77–117, 182–218, 245–278. New York, Free Press, 2003.

On the support of the eugenics movement by mainline Protestant churchmen, see Christine Rosen, *Preaching Eugenics: Religious Leaders and the American Eugenics Movement.* New York, Oxford University Press, 2004. On Catholic opposition, see John T. McGreevy, *Catholicism and American Freedom: A History* 223–225. New York, W. W. Norton, 2003.

The quotation in the text from Justice Holmes's opinion in *Buck v. Bell* appears at 274 U.S. 207.

The actual facts about Carrie Buck are eloquently recounted in Stephen Jay Gould, "Carrie Buck's Daughter," *Natural History* 12–17 (July/August 2002).

Holmes's letters to Harold Laski and Lewis Einstein on *Buck v. Bell* are quoted in Albert W. Alschuler's brilliant reassessment of Holmes, *Law without Values: The Life, Work, and Legacy of Justice Holmes* 67. Chicago, University of Chicago Press, 2000 (paperback ed.).

The Rights of Parents and Teachers to Educate Children

For a brief biography of Justice McReynolds, see *Oxford Companion 2* at 629–630. For additional insight into Justice McReynolds, see the memoir of his law clerk for the 1936–37 term, *The Forgotten Memoir of John Knox.* Chicago, University of Chicago Press, 2002 (Dennis J. Hutchinson and David J. Garrow, eds.). The editors' foreword at xix records the refusal of McReynolds to appear for the Court photograph in 1924.

The quotations in the text from Justice McReynolds's opinion in *Meyer v. Nebraska* appear at 262 U.S. 399, 400, and 402. That from Justice Holmes dissent in a related case appears at 262 U.S. 412.

The Klan background of the Oregon Compulsory Education Act is mentioned in Richard White, *"It's Your Misfortune and None of My Own": A History of the American West* 384. Norman, University of Oklahoma Press, 1991.

The quotations in the text from *Pierce v. Society of Sisters* appear at 268 U.S. 531 and 535.

Free Exercise of Religion: From Mormon Polygamists to Jehovah's Witnesses Who Refused to Salute the Flag

For the background of *Reynolds v. United States* and the Mormon teachings on polygamy, see Sarah Barringer Gordon, *The Mormon Question: Polygamy and Constitutional Conflict in Nineteenth-Century America.* Chapel Hill, University of North Carolina Press, 2002 (paperback ed.).

The quotations in the text from Chief Justice Waite's opinion in *Reynolds v. United States* appear at 98 U.S. 161, 163, 164, 166, and 167.

For the background of the Flag Salute cases and the beliefs of the Jehovah's Witnesses, see Edwin Gaustad and Leigh Schmidt, *The Religious History of America* 226–228, 332, 350–353. New York, HarperSanFrancisco, 2002 (rev. paperback ed.), and Paul Finkelman, "The Flag Salute Cases," II *Historic Cases* 947–956.

The quotations in the text from Justice Frankfurter's majority opinion in *Gobitis* appear at 310 U.S. 594, 595, and 596. Those from Justice Stone's dissenting opinion appear at 310 U.S. 603, 606, and 607.

The quotations in the text from Justice Jackson's majority opinion in *Barnette* appear at 319 U.S. 627, 632, 641, and 642. Those from Justice Frankfurter's dissenting opinion appear at 319 U.S. 646–647, 659, and 660.

For a brief biography of Justice Frankfurter, see *Oxford Companion 2* at 364–367.

Chapter 8: Religion and the Supreme Court

The Establishment Clause: Erection of a "Wall of Separation"

For the background of the *Everson* case, see Philip Hamburger, *Separation of Church and State* 454–472. Cambridge, Harvard University Press, 2002, and Roger K. Newman, *Hugo Black* 361–364.

On Paul Blanshard and his works, see John T. McGreevy, *Catholicism and American Freedom: A History* 166–169. New York, W. W. Norton, 2003, and Mark S. Massa, *Anti-Catholicism in America: The Last Acceptable Prejudice* 59–76. New York, Crossroad Publishing Co., 2003.

On Justice Black's Klan career and views on Catholics and Blanshard, see Hamburger, *Separation of Church and State* 422–434.

The quotations in the text from Justice Black's majority opinion in *Everson* appear at 330 U.S. 15, 16, and 18. Those from Justice Jackson's dissenting opinion appear at 330 U.S. 23 and 24. Those from Justice Rutledge's dissenting opinion appear at 330 U.S. 57 and 62.

The Wall Goes Up and the Wall Goes Down: The Released Time Cases

For the background of the *McCollum* and *Zorach* cases and the released time concept, see Hamburger, *Separation of Church and State* 472–478, and Frank J. Sorauf, "Religion in the Public School Day: The Released Time Cases," in II *Historic Cases* 957–964.

The quotations in the text from Justice Black's majority opinion in *McCollum* appear at 333 U.S. 209 and 210. Those from Justice Frankfurter's concurring opinion appear at 333 U.S. 329. Those from Justice Jackson's concurring opinion appear at 333 U.S. 232, 235, 236, and 237. Those from Justice Reed's dissenting opinion appear at 333 U.S. 255 and 256.

The quotations in the text from Justice Douglas's majority opinion in *Zorach* appear at 343 U.S. 312, 313, 314, and 315. Those from Justice Black's dissenting opinion appear at 343 U.S. 317, 318, and 320. Those from Justice Jackson's dissenting opinion appear at 343 U.S. 323, 324, and 325.

The Wall Goes Back Up and Higher: The School Prayer and Bible-Reading Cases

For the background of *Engel v. Vitale,* see Paul L. Murphy, "To Pray or Not to Pray: The Supreme Court Says No to Prayer in the Public Schools," II *Historic Cases* 965–971.

The quotations in the text from Justice Black's majority opinion in *Engel v. Vitale* appear at 370 U.S. 422, 425, 430, and 435. Those from Justice Douglas's concurring opinion appear at 370 U.S. 440, 442, and 443. Those from Justice Stewart's dissenting opinion appear at 370 U.S. 445 and 446.

For a short biography of Justice Potter Stewart, see *Oxford Companion 2* at 978–979.

John F. Kennedy's September 12, 1960, speech to the Greater Houston Ministerial Association may be found in full text at AmericanRhetoric.com under the heading "Top 100 Speeches."

The text of the proposed Reagan constitutional amendment on school prayer is quoted in Edwin Gaustad and Leigh Schmidt, *The Religious History of America* 360.

The quotations in the text from Justice Clark's majority opinion in *Abington School District v. Schempp* appear at 374 U.S. 223, 224, and 225. Those from Justice Brennan's concurring opinion appear at 374 U.S. 240, 267, and 270. Those from Justice Stewart's dissenting opinion appear at 374 U.S. 309, 312, 313, and 316.

Evolution, Schoolbooks, and Teachers' Salaries

The quotations in the text from Justice Fortas's majority opinion in *Epperson v. Arkansas* appear at 393 U.S. 98, 103, 106, and 108. Those from Justice Black's concurring opinion appear at 393 U.S. 113 and 114.

The quotations in the text from Justice White's majority opinion in *Board of Education v. Allen* appear at 392 U.S. 245 and 247. Those from Justice Black's dissenting opinion appear at 392 U.S. 250, 252, and 254. Those from Justice Douglas's dissenting opinion appear at 392 U.S. 256.

The quotations in the text from Chief Justice Burger's majority opinion in *Lemon v. Kurtzman* appear at 403 U.S. 612–613, 619, and 622. Those from Justice Douglas's concurring opinion appear at 403 U.S. 628, 629, and 630. That from Justice Brennan's concurring opinion appears at 403 U.S. 645. Those from Justice White's separate opinion appear at 403 U.S. 662 and 668.

For the view that *Lemon v. Kutzman* was "the high point of legal secularism," see Noah Feldman, *Divided by God: America's Church-State Problem—And What We Should Do about It* 223. New York, Farrar, Straus and Giroux, 2005.

For a review of the many cases striking down aid to parochial schools from *Lemon* through the 1980s, see James Hitchcock, *The Supreme Court and Religion in American Life: Volume I—The Odyssey of the Religion Clauses* 128–139. Princeton, Princeton University Press, 2004.

The Beginnings of Change: New Justices and New Ways of Thinking

On the emergence of the conservative religious coalition of evangelical Protestants and conservative Catholics, see Patrick Allitt, *Religion in America since 1945: A History* 150–169, 180–196. New York, Columbia University Press, 2003, and James T. Patterson, *Restless Giant: The United States from Watergate to Bush v. Gore* 133–145. New York, Oxford University Press, 2005.

For a statistics-laden discussion of the evangelical impact on presidential elections, see Kevin Phillips, *American Theocracy* 179–204. New York, Viking, 2006.

The quotations in the text from Francis Schaeffer and Bob Jones Jr. appear in Patrick Allitt, *Religion in America since 1945* 153 (Jones) and 156 (Schaeffer).

The quotation in the text from Justice Stevens's majority opinion in *Wallace v. Jaffree* appears at 472 U.S. 43. Those from Justice O'Connor's concurring opinion appear at 472

U.S. 68 and 69. Those from Justice Rehnquist's dissenting opinion appear at 472 U.S. 92, 98, 99, 106, and 107.

The quotation in the text from Justice Brennan's majority opinion in *Edwards v. Aguillard* appears at 482 U.S. 593. Those from Justice Scalia's dissenting opinion appear at 482 U.S. 615, 619, 631, 634, and 640.

Justice Scalia explains his view of proper constitutional interpretation in Antonin Scalia, *A Matter of Interpretation: Federal Courts and the Law* 37–47. Princeton, Princeton University Press, 1997.

The quotations in the text from Justice Kennedy's majority opinion in *Lee v. Weisman* appear at 505 U.S. 586 and 587. Those from Justice Souter's concurring opinion appear at 505 U.S. 612 and 631. Those from Justice Scalia's dissenting opinion appear at 505 U.S. 631–632, 633, 643, 644, 645, and 646.

The "quite wrong" quotation comes from a March 30, 1992, note from Justice Kennedy to Justice Blackmun quoted in Tinsley E. Yarbrough, *David Hackett Souter: Traditional Republican on the Rehnquist Court* 171. New York, Oxford University Press, 2005.

The Wall Comes Tumbling Down—A Bit

The quotations in the text from Justice O'Connor's majority opinion in *Agostini v. Felton* appear at 521 U.S. 209, 223, 225, 233, and 234–235. Those from Justice Souter's dissenting opinion appear at 521 U.S. 242 and 243.

The quotations in the text from Justice Thomas's plurality opinion in *Mitchell v. Helms* appear at 530 U.S. 802, 810, and 828–829. Those from Justice Souter's dissenting opinion appear at 530 U.S. 877 and 912–913.

The quotations in the text from Chief Justice Rehnquist's majority opinion in *Zelman v. Simmons-Harris* appear at 536 U.S. 650, 652, and 662. That from Justice O'Connor's concurring opinion appears at 536 U.S. 536. Those from Justice Thomas's concurring opinion appear at 536 U.S. 677 and 682. Those from Justice Stevens's dissenting opinion appear at 536 U.S. 684 and 686. Those from Justice Souter's dissenting opinion appear at 536 U.S. 715 and 716. Those from Justice Breyer's dissenting opinion appear at 536 U.S. 717, 721–722, and 736.

Policing the Public Square: Reindeer, Menorahs, and Public Displays of Religion

The quotation in the text from Chief Justice Burger's majority opinion in *Lynch v. Donnelly* appears at 465 U.S. 685. That from Justice O'Connor's concurring opinion appears at 465 U.S. 692. That from Justice Brennan's dissenting opinion appears at 465 U.S. 701.

The quotation in the text from Justice Blackmun's majority opinion in *Allegheny County v. ACLU* appears at 492 U.S. 598. That from Justice O'Connor's concurring opinion appears at 492 U.S. 635. Those from Justice Kennedy's dissenting opinion appear at 492 U.S. 655, 657, 662–663, 669, and 677–678.

The history of Chief Justice Roy S. Moore and the dispute over the Alabama Ten Commandments Monument is summarized in the Final Judgment of the Alabama Court of the Judiciary in *In the Matter of: Roy S. Moore, Chief Justice of the Supreme Court of Alabama*, Case No. 33 (November 13, 2003). The quotation from Moore which appears in the text is found on page 5 of that Judgment.

The quotations in the text from Justice Souter's majority opinion in *McCreary County v. ACLU* appear at 125 S. Ct. 2729, 2735, 2738, 2739, 2742, and 2745. Those from Justice Scalia's dissenting opinion appear at 125 S. Ct. 2751, 2752, 2753, 2757, and 2758.

The quotations in the text from Chief Justice Rehnquist's plurality opinion in *Van Orden v. Perry* appear at 125 S. Ct. 2859, 2861, 2863, and 2864. Those from Justice Breyer's concurring opinion appear at 125 S. Ct. 2869 and 2870. That from Justice Souter's dissenting opinion appears at 125 S. Ct. 2892.

The Free Exercise Clause: The Primacy of Conscience

The quotations in the text from Justice Brennan's majority opinion in *Sherbert v. Verner* appear at 374 U.S. 404, 406, and 407. Those from Justice Harlan's dissenting opinion appear at 374 U.S. 419–420 and 423.

For the background of *Wisconsin v. Yoder,* see Steven D. Reschly, "Expanded Exercise: The Amish, Compulsory Education, and Religious Freedom," II *Historic Cases* 978–982.

The quotations in the text from Chief Justice Burger's majority opinion in *Wisconsin v. Yoder* appear at 406 U.S. 210, 214, 220, 222, and 235. Those from Justice Douglas's dissenting opinion appear at 406 U.S. 243 and 247.

The Free Exercise Clause: The Primacy of Law

For the background of *Employment Division v. Smith,* see Tinsley E. Yarbrough, "Religious Practices and the First Amendment," II *Historic Cases* 986–989.

The quotations in the text from Justice Scalia's majority opinion in *Employment Division v. Smith* appear at 494 U.S. 878, 879, 881, 884, and 886. Those from Justice Stevens's dissenting opinion appear at 494 U.S. 908.

For a brief background on the "War on Drugs" in the 1980s, see Philip Jenkins, *Decade of Nightmares: The End of the Sixties and the Making of Eighties America* 125–129, 247–255. New York, Oxford University Press, 2006.

Congress Confronts the Court: The Religious Freedom Restoration Act

For the background of *City of Boerne v. Flores* by the lawyer who represented the City, as well as a thoughtful overview of the cases from *Sherbert* to *Flores,* see Marci A. Hamilton, *God vs. the Gavel: Religion and the Rule of Law* 203–237. New York, Cambridge University Press, 2005.

The quotations in the text from Justice Kennedy's majority opinion in *City of Boerne v. Flores* appear at 521 U.S. 516, 519, 520, 525, 530, and 535–536. That from Justice O'Connor's dissenting opinion appears at 521 U.S. 548.

The quotations in the text from Chief Justice Roberts's opinion for the Court in *Gonzales v. O Centro Espirita Beneficente Uniao Do Vegetal* appear at 126 S. Ct. 1221–1222 and 1223.

"Play in the Joints": The Interplay between Free Exercise and Establishment

The quotations in the text from Chief Justice Rehnquist's majority opinion in *Locke v. Davey* appear at 124 S. Ct. 1309, 1311, 1313, and 1315. Those from Justice Scalia's dissenting opinion appear at 124 S. Ct. 1316 and 1320.

The quotations from Justice Breyer from the oral argument in *Locke v. Davey* appear in Linda Greenhouse, "Justices Resist Religious Study Using Subsidies," *New York Times,* December 3, 2003, available online at www.nytimes.com.

Chapter 9: Race and the Supreme Court

Harry Truman: Civil Rights President

For an excellent treatment of the Truman civil rights record, see Michael R. Gardner, *Harry Truman and Civil Rights: Moral Courage and Political Risks.* Carbondale, Southern Illinois University Press, 2002.

The quotations in the text from Justice Black and the unnamed African American veteran of World War II are reported in James T. Patterson, *Brown v. Board of Education: A Civil Rights Milestone and Its Troubled Legacy* 1, 54. New York, Oxford University Press, 2001.

The Vinson Court and Civil Rights

The quotations in the text from Chief Justice Vinson's opinion for the Court in *Shelley v. Kramer* appear at 334 U.S. 10 and 19.

June 5, 1950: The Vinson Court Expands Civil Rights

The quotations in the text from Chief Justice Vinson's opinion for the Court in *Sweatt v. Painter* appear at 339 U.S. 633, 634, and 636.

The quotations in the text from Chief Justice Vinson's opinion for the Court in *McLaurin v. Oklahoma State Regents* appear at 339 U.S. 640, 641, and 642.A remarkable picture of McLaurin, seated just outside the segregated classroom at the University of Oklahoma, appears in Michael Gardner, *Harry Truman and Civil Rights,* on the fifth page of photographs appearing between pages 146 and 147. Notably, Mr. McLaurin is the only student dressed in a suit and tie.

The quotations in the text from Justice Burton's opinion for the Court in *Henderson v. United States* appear at 339 U.S. 825 and 826.

Brown v. Board of Education

For the background of *Brown v. Board of Education,* see James T. Patterson, *Brown v. Board of Education;* Robert J. Cottrol, Raymond T. Diamond, and Leland B. Ware, *Brown v. Board of Education: Caste, Culture, and the Constitution.* Lawrence, University Press of Kansas, 2003; and Robert P. Green Jr., "Separate Education Is Not Equal Education," II *Historic Cases* 645–656.

The quotations in the text from Chief Justice Warren's opinion of the Court in *Brown v. Board of Education* appear at 347 U.S. 489, 492, 493, 494, and 495.

The quotations in the text from Chief Justice Warren's opinion of the Court in *Brown v. Board of Education II* appear at 349 U.S. 299 and 300–301.

The South Defies the Court

The remarks of Senator Eastland are quoted in James T. Patterson, *Brown v. Board of Education* 88.

The text of the March 12, 1956, "Southern Declaration on Integration" is reproduced in *American Legal History* at 513–515.

The quotations in the text from the opinion in *Cooper v. Aaron* appear at 358 U.S. 4, 16, 17–18, and 19.

The quotation in the text from Justice Black's opinion in *Griffin v. County School Board* appears at 377 U.S. 234.

The quotation in the text from the opinion in *Green v. County School Board* appears at 391 U.S. 437–438.

The quotations in the text from the opinion in *Alexander v. Holmes County Board of Education* appear at 396 U.S. 20.

The quotation in the text from the dissenting opinion of Justice Thurgood Marshall in *Milliken v. Bradley* appears at 418 U.S. 814.

The Sit-in Movement and the Desegregation of Public Accommodations

The statistics in the text on the sit-in movement appear in James T. Patterson, *Grand Expectations: The United States, 1945–1974* 430–433. New York, Oxford University Press, 1996.

For an account of the assistance to Martin Luther King Jr. by John and Robert Kennedy in the Atlanta jailing incident of November 1960, see Evan Thomas, *Robert Kennedy: His Life* 100–104. New York, Simon & Schuster, 2000.

The quotations in the text from Justice Clark's opinion in *Heart of Atlanta Motel, Inc. v. United States* appear at 379 U.S. 249, 250, 251, and 258.

The quotations in the text from Justice Clark's opinion in *Katzenbach v. McClung* appear at 379 U.S. 296–297, 298, 300, 302, and 305.

The Struggle to Secure the Right to Vote

For the background of the Twenty-fourth Amendment and its subsequent interpretation by the Supreme Court, see Akhil Reed Amar, *America's Constitution: A Biography* 442–445. New York, Random House, 2005.

The quotation in the text from the 1902 Virginia poll-tax legislative debates appears in *Harman v. Forssenius,* 380 U.S. at 543.

The statistics in the text on voting registration in the South appear in James T. Patterson, *Grand Expectations* 579–587.

For good, brief accounts of the 1965 March from Selma to Montgomery, Alabama, see id. and Garry Wills, "An American Iliad" (Book Review of Taylor Branch, *At Canaan's Edge: America in the King Years, 1965–68*), *New York Review,* April 6, 2006, at 20, 22–24.

The quotations in the text from Chief Justice Warren's opinion in *South Carolina v. Katzenbach* appear at 383 U.S. 308, 309, 311, 326, and 328.

Affirmative Action: Remediation or Fostering Diversity?

The quotations in the text from President Lyndon Johnson come from a speech he gave to Howard University in 1965, and are quoted in Howard Schweber, "Affirmative Action," *Oxford Companion to American Law* 10. New York: Oxford University Press, 2002 (Kermit L. Hall, ed.).

The quotations in the text from Justice Stevens's opinion in the *Bakke* case appear at 438 U.S. 412–413. Those from Justice Brennan's opinion appear at 438 U.S. 328, 356, and 369. Those from Justice Marshall's opinion appear at 438 U.S. 396, 398, and 400–401. Those from Justice Powell's opinion appear at 438 U.S. 289–290, 307, 310, 317, 318, and 319–320.

For a short biography of Justice Powell, see *Oxford Companion 2* at 766–767.

Bakke *Revisited: Disguised Quotas and the Multiple Goals of Diversity*

The quotations in the text from Justice O'Connor's majority opinion in *Grutter v. Bollinger* appear at 539 U.S. 325, 327, 330, 332, 334, 342, and 343. Those from Chief Justice Rehnquist's dissenting opinion appear at 539 U.S. 383, 385, and 386. Those from Justice Kennedy's dissenting opinion appear at 539 U.S. 387, 388, and 393.

The quotations in the text from Chief Justice Rehnquist's majority opinion in *Gratz v. Bollinger* appear at 539 U.S. 270 and 271–272. That from Justice Souter's dissenting opinion appears at 539 U.S. 293–294. Those from Justice Ginsburg's dissenting opinion appear at 539 U.S. 303 and 304.

For Justice Breyer's observations on *Grutter,* see Stephen Breyer, *Active Liberty: Interpreting Our Democratic Constitution* 82, 83. New York, Alfred A. Knopf, 2005.

The statistics on the use of affirmative action programs in four-year colleges and universities are referenced in "Affirmative Action: Anyone for a Bit of Legal Fudge?," *Economist* 27, 28 (June 28, 2003).

The Roberts Court Examines School Assignment

The quotations in the text from Chief Justice Roberts's plurality opinion in *Parents Involved in Community Schools v. Seattle School District No. 1* appear at 127 S. Ct. 2746, 2752, 2753, 2754, 2755, 2758, 2766, and 2768. Those from Justice Thomas's concurring opinion appear at 127 S. Ct. 2768, 2783, 2786, and 2787. Those from Justice Kennedy's concurring opinion appear at 127 S. Ct. 2791, 2792, and 2797. Those from Justice Stevens's dissenting opinion appear at 127 S. Ct. 2797 and 2800. Those from Justice Breyer's dissenting opinion appear at 127 S. Ct. 2811, 2812, 2816, 2820, 2821, 2823, 2834, 2835, and 2837.

The oral remarks by Justice Breyer in open court are contained in a bench statement attached to a posting by Lyle Denniston on www.scotusblog.com entitled "Breyer statement on school decisions," July 2, 2007. The quotation in the text appears at page 10 of the bench statement.

The quotations in the text from the *New York Times* appear on that newspaper's website for June 29, 2007, under the editorial titled "Resegregation Now." Those from the *Wall Street Journal* appear in the June 29, 2007, edition of that newspaper under the editorial titled "Race and the Roberts Court," at page A14.

The August 2007 poll referenced in the text appears in an August 16, 2007, press release from Quinnipiac University, a copy of which is posted as an attachment to the "Round-Up" section on www.scotusblog.com for August 20, 2007.

Chapter 10: The Supreme Court and Abortion

Regulation of Abortion in the United States

On the history of abortion in the United States, I have relied heavily on Leslie J. Reagan, *When Abortion Was a Crime: Women, Medicine, and Law in the United States, 1867–1973.* Berkeley and Los Angeles, University of California Press, 1997 (paperback ed. 1998).

The quotations from the AMA Committee on Criminal Abortion are cited in Justice Blackmun's opinion of the Court in *Roe v. Wade,* 410 U.S. 113, 141–142 (1973).

The quotations from Susan B. Anthony and Alice Paul appear in Claire Voight, "The Feminist Perspective on Abortion from a Pro-life Stance: A Study of the Social History Surrounding *Roe v. Wade,*" unpublished paper prepared for the author's course on American History after 1865, University of Pennsylvania, 2004.

The estimate of 600,000 abortions annually during the Great Depression is found in Peter Charles Hoffer and N. E. H. Hull, "Abortion and Reproductive Decisions," *Oxford Companion to American Law,* 1.

The quotation from the Planned Parenthood 1955 conference on abortion appears in Reagan, *When Abortion Was a Crime* 220.

Roe v. Wade *and* Doe v. Bolton

For the background of *Roe v. Wade* and *Doe v. Bolton* based on Justice Blackmun's private Supreme Court papers, see Linda Greenhouse, *Becoming Justice Blackmun: Harry Blackmun's Supreme Court Journey* 78–101. New York, Times Books, 2005. The quotations from Blackmun's draft opinion in the *Doe* case appear at page 89, while the involvement of the Mayo Clinic is discussed at pages 82–83, 90–92, and 101.

The quotations in the text from Justice Blackmun's majority opinion in *Roe v. Wade* appear at 410 U.S. 153, 154, 159, 160, 164–165, and 165–166. Those from Justice Rehnquist's dissenting opinion appear at 410 U.S. 173 and 174.

The quotation in the text from Justice Blackmun's cover memorandum distributing his draft opinion in *Roe v. Wade* appears in Greenhouse, *Becoming Justice Blackmun* 95.

The quotations in the text from Justice Blackmun's majority opinion in *Doe v. Bolton* appear at 410 U.S. 197 and 199. Those from Justice White's dissenting opinion appear at 410 U.S. 221 and 222.

Reactions to Roe

For a graph summarizing the public views on abortion reported in the General Social Survey since 1972, see Ben Schott, "Who Do You Think We Are," *New York Times,* Week in Review 15, February 25, 2007.

The quotations in the text from Laurence Tribe come from his article, "The Supreme Court, 1972 Term—Forward: Toward a Model of Roles in the Due Process of Life and Law," 87 Harvard Law Review 1, 7 (1973). Those from John Hart Ely come from his article, "The Wages of Crying Wolf: A Comment on *Roe v. Wade,*" 82 Yale Law Journal 920 (1973).

The quotations in the text from Ruth Bader Ginsburg come from her article, "Speaking in a Judicial Voice," 67 New York University Law Review 1185, 1208 (1992). The criticism of *Roe* and *Doe* as having disrupted the political process and generated political divisiveness has gained increased support over the years in academic circles. For example, in *What Roe v. Wade Should Have Said: The Nation's Top Legal Experts Rewrite America's Most Controversial Decision* 53–54, 170–171, and 185–186. New York, New York University Press, 2005 (Jack M. Balkin, ed.), law professors Jack M. Balkin and Jeffrey Rosen composed "opinions" in *Roe* and *Doe* which make or attempt to address these points.

On the realignment of the Democratic and Republican parties over the abortion issue, and the pro life views of pre *Roe* Democrats, see John T. Mc Greevy, *Catholicism and American Freedom* 278–281. New York, W. W. Norton, 2003.

Roe *under Attack: Legal Assaults on the Citadel of Privacy*

For an insider's view of *Webster v. Reproductive Health Services,* see Edward Lazarus, *Closed Chambers: The Rise, Fall, and Future of the Modern Supreme Court* 373–429. New York, Penguin Books, 1999 (updated paperback ed.). Lazarus had been one of Justice Blackmun's law clerks during the October 1988 Term. For additional background on *Webster,* see Joan Biskupic, *Sandra Day O'Connor: How the First Woman on the Supreme Court Became Its Most Influential Justice* 216–233. New York, Ecco Press, 2005.

The quotations in the text from Chief Justice Rehnquist's opinion in *Webster v. Reproductive Health Services* appear at 492 U.S. 507, 517, 518, 519–520, and 521. Those from Justice Scalia's concurring opinion appear at 492 U.S. 532, 535, and 537. Those from Justice O'Connor's concurring opinion appear at 492 U.S. 526 and 530. Those from Justice Blackmun's dissenting opinion appear at 492 U.S. 537, 538, 556, and 560.

The quotation in the text from Justice Kennedy's note to Chief Justice Rehnquist appears in Lazarus, *Closed Chambers* 406–407. Justice O'Connor's view that the Rehnquist draft opinion effectively overruled *Roe* appears in the same source at 405.

Planned Parenthood v. Casey

For the background of *Planned Parenthood v. Casey,* see Joan Biskupic, *Sandra Day O'Connor* 265–274; Jan Crawford Greenburg, *Supreme Conflict: The Inside Story of the Struggle for Control of the United States Supreme Court* 150–163. New York, Penguin Press, 2007; and Tinsley E. Yarbrough, *David Hackett Souter: Traditional Republican on the Rehnquist Court* 175–178, 189, 196–198, 221–222. New York, Oxford University Press, 2005.

The quotations in the text from the joint opinion of Justices O'Connor, Kennedy, and Souter in *Planned Parenthood v. Casey* appear at 505 U.S. 844, 845–846, 851, 853, 859, 867, and 870. Those from Justice Blackmun's concurring and dissenting opinion appear at 505 U.S. 922, 923, and 943. Those from Chief Justice Rehnquist's concurring and dissenting opinion appear at 505 U.S. 944, 945, 951–952, and 966. Those from Justice Scalia's concurring and dissenting opinion appear at 505 U.S. 979, 980, 983, 995–996, and 1002.

Partial-Birth Abortion 1: Stenberg v. Carhart

The quotations in the text from Justice Breyer's majority opinion in *Stenberg v. Carhart* appear at 530 U.S. 937 and 938. The quotation from Justice O'Connor's concurring opinion appears at 530 U.S. 951. The quotation from Chief Justice Rehnquist's dissenting opinion appears at 530 U.S. 952. The quotations from Justice Scalia's dissenting opinion appear at 530 U.S. 953 and 954–955. Those from Justice Kennedy's dissenting opinion appear at 530 U.S. 959–960, 961, and 963. Those from Justice Thomas's dissenting opinion appear at 530 U.S. 980, 982, 983, and 1006.

Partial-Birth Abortion 2: A Reversal in Course

For background on the nominations and confirmations of Chief Justice John Roberts and Justice Samuel Alito, see Jan Crawford Greenburg, *Supreme Conflict* 185–313.

The quotations in the text from Justice Kennedy's majority opinion in *Gonzales v. Carhart* appear at 127 S. Ct. 1626, 1632, 1633, and 1638. That from Justice Thomas's concurring opinion appears at 127 S. Ct. 1639. Those from Justice Ginsburg's dissenting opinion appear at 127 S. Ct. 1641, 1647, 1648, 1649, 1650, 1652, and 1653.

Justice Ginsburg's oral summary of her dissenting opinion in *Gonzales v. Carhart* is reported in the Legal Times Online (www.legaltimes.com) for April 18, 2007, under the title "Justice Ruth Bader Ginsburg Offers Summary of Dissent."

For the editorial comments on *Gonzales v. Carhart,* see the editorial pages of the April 19, 2007, editions of the *New York Times,* the *Los Angeles Times,* the *Boston Herald,* and the *Washington Times,* all of which are available on their online editions.

Chapter 11: Judicial Power and the New Federalism: The Most Dangerous Branch?

Enforcing School Desegregation

For President Eisenhower's views on *Brown v. Board of Education* and his duties as president to enforce the Supreme Court's mandates, see Tom Wicker, *Dwight D. Eisenhower* 46–47. New York, Times Books, 2002.

Enforcing Abortion Rights

For Justice Blackmun's view that opposition to abortion was similar to southern opposition to desegregation and for his reference to *Cooper v. Aaron,* I am indebted to Edward Lazarus, *Closed Chambers* 380–381. The reference to *Cooper* appears in *Thornburgh v. American College of Obstetricians & Gynecologists,* 476 U.S. 747, 771 (1986).

The quotations in the text from Justice Scalia's dissenting opinion in *Hill v. Colorado* appear at 530 U.S. 741, 742, 763, and 764. Those from Justice Kennedy's dissenting opinion appear at 530 U.S. 791 and 792.

Deciding the Presidency: Bush v. Gore

For the background of *Bush v. Gore,* see Richard A. Posner, *Breaking the Deadlock: The 2000 Election, the Constitution, and the Courts.* Princeton, Princeton University Press, 2001. Judge Posner's alternative criteria for counting undervotes appear at page 56.

The quotations in the text from the majority opinion in *Bush v. Gore* appear at 531 U.S. 109 and 111. Those from Chief Justice Rehnquist's concurring opinion appear at 531 U.S. 112. Those from Justice Stevens's dissenting opinion appear at 531 U.S. 128 and 129. Those from Justice Breyer's dissenting opinion appear at 531 U.S. 153 and 158. Those from Justice Ginsburg's dissenting opinion appear at 531 U.S. 142 and 143.

The quotations in the text from Professor Randall Kennedy appear in "Contempt of Court," reprinted in *Bush v. Gore: The Court Cases and the Commentary* 336, 337. Washington, D.C., The Brookings Institution, 2001 (E. J. Dionne Jr. and William Kristol, eds.). The quotation from Cass Sunstein appears in "What We'll Remember in 2050," id. at 340. The quotation from Michael Klarman appears in Richard Posner, *Breaking the Deadlock* 201 n. 70.

The quotation in the text from Judge Posner on *Bush v. Gore* appears in his *Breaking the Deadlock* ix.

The contemporary polls on *Bush v. Gore* referred to in the text are referenced in David Cole, "The Liberal Legacy of *Bush v. Gore,*" 94 Georgetown Law Review 1427, 1430 (2006). The references to the "checking" power of public opinion appear in the same article at 1427 and 1428, and the statistics on the voting of the majority in *Bush v. Gore* before and after that decision appear at page 1442.

Creating Constitutional Rights 1: Lawrence v. Texas *and Gay Sex*

The quotations in the text from Justice Kennedy's majority opinion in *Lawrence v. Texas* appear at 539 U.S. 567, 568, 571, and 577. Those from Justice Scalia's dissenting opinion appear at 539 U.S. 586, 592, 602, and 604. That from Justice Thomas's dissenting opinion appears at 539 U.S. 605.

The May and July 2003 polling figures in the text appear in "The Meaning of Marriage," *Economist,* August 9, 2003, at 24.

The Massachusetts Supreme Judicial Court opinion referred to in the text is *Goodridge v. Department of Public Health,* 798 N.E. 2d 941 (2003).

The Utah Supreme Court opinion referred to in the text is *State of Utah v. Holm,* 2006 UT 31 (2006).

Creating Constitutional Rights 2: Roper v. Simmons *and Cruel and Unusual Punishment*

The quotations in the text from Justice Kennedy's majority opinion in *Roper v. Simmons* appear at 125 S. Ct. 1190, 1191, 1192, 1198, and 1199. Those from Justice Scalia's dissenting opinion appear at 125 S. Ct. 1217 and 1226.

Interpreting Constitutional Rights: The Right of the People to Keep and Bear Arms

The quotations from Justice Scalia's majority opinion in *District of Columbia v. Heller* appear in the slip opinion at 3, 19, 49, 54–55, 62, and 63. Those in Justice Breyer's dissenting opinion appear in the slip opinion at 1, 10, and 11. For Justice Scalia's own discussion of his views on textualism and originalism in constitutional interpretation, see Antonin Scalia, *A Matter of Interpretation: Federal Courts and the Law* 23–25 and 37–47. Princeton, Princeton University Press, 1997 (paperback ed.).

Limiting Congressional Power: A New Federalism

Senator Schumer's observations are contained in Charles E. Schumer, "Under Attack: Congressional Power in the Twenty-first Century," 1 Harvard Law and Policy Review 25, 26, 28 (2007).

Two popular books written by lawyers who are also conservative media commentators, both of which attack the modern Supreme Court's construction of the Commerce Clause, are Andrew P. Napolitano, *The Constitution in Exile: How the Federal Government Has Seized Power by Rewriting the Supreme Law of the Land* 149–167. Nashville, Nelson Current, 2006; and Mark R. Levin, *Men in Black: How the Supreme Court Is Destroying America* 131–141. Washington, Regnery Publishing, 2006 (paperback ed.). Judge Napolitano's "*Wickard* must die" quotation appears at page 166 of *The Constitution in Exile.*

Guns, Schools, and the Commerce Clause: United States v. Lopez

The quotations in the text from Chief Justice Rehnquist's majority opinion in *United States v. Lopez* appear at 514 U.S. 552, 556–557, 564, and 565. Those from Justice Kennedy's concurring opinion appear at 514 U.S. 568, 574, and 583. Those from Justice Breyer's dissenting opinion appear at 514 U.S. 615 and 616.

Violence against Women and the Commerce Clause: United States v. Morrison

The quotations in the text from Chief Justice Rehnquist's majority opinion in *United States v. Morrison* appear at 529 U.S. 610, 615, and 617–618. Those from Justice Souter's dissenting opinion appear at 529 U.S. 644, 654, and 655.

Federalism in Retreat: How Marijuana Saved the New Deal

The quotations in the text from Justice Stevens's majority opinion in *Gonzales v. Raich* appear at 125 S. Ct. 2201, 2205, 2206, and 2211. That from Justice Scalia's concurring opinion appears at 125 S. Ct. 2217. Those from Justice O'Connor's dissenting opinion appear at 125

S. Ct. 2220, 2221, and 2229. Those from Justice Thomas's dissenting opinion appear at 125 S. Ct. 2229, 2234, 2235, 2237, and 2239.

Conclusion

The Influence of Public Attitudes

The quotations in the text from the *Chicago Tribune* and the *Hartford Weekly Times* may be found in Heather Cox Richardson, *The Death of Reconstruction* 137 and 152, respectively.

Index

About the Author

EDWARD F. MANNINO is a graduate of the University of Pennsylvania and its law school. A trial lawyer concentrating on business litigation, he has been named one of the nation's top litigators by the *National Law Journal.* Mannino has taught at Temple University Law School and the University of Pennsylvania and is the author of three books on legal topics. He lives in Gwynedd Valley, Pennsylvania.